THE ORIGINS OF CONFLICT IN AFGHANISTAN

THE ORIGINS OF CONFLICT IN AFGHANISTAN

JEFFERY J. ROBERTS

PRAEGER

Westport, Connecticut
London

Library of Congress Cataloging-in-Publication Data

Roberts, Jeffery J.
    The origins of conflict in Afghanistan / Jeffery J. Roberts.
      p. cm.
    Includes bibliographical references and index.
    ISBN 0–275–97878–8 (alk. paper)
    1. Afghanistan—History—19th century. 2. Afghanistan—History—20th
century. 3. Afghanistan—Foreign relations—19th century. 4. Afghanistan—
Foreign relations—20th century. I. Title.
DS361.R56 2003
958.1—dc21   2002075519

British Library Cataloguing in Publication Data is available.

Library of Congress Catalog Card Number: 2002075519
ISBN: 0–275–97878–8

First published in 2003

Praeger Publishers, 88 Post Road West, Westport, CT 06881
An imprint of Greenwood Publishing Group, Inc.
www.praeger.com

Printed in the United States of America

The paper used in this book complies with the
Permanent Paper Standard issued by the National
Information Standards Organization (Z39.48–1984).

10 9 8 7 6 5 4 3 2 1

CONTENTS

PREFACE

Those searching for the origins of the Soviet war in Afghanistan would do well to begin in December 1955. That month, Afghan Prime Minister Mohammed Daoud signed an economic aid agreement with the U.S.S.R. valued at over 100 million dollars. A subsequent agreement signed the following August promised a wholesale renovation of the Afghan military establishment. The loans enabled Daoud to implement many economic programs, while modernization of the armed forces provided him with the means to enforce a variety of social reforms, notably the abolition of traditional *purdah* (the seclusion of women) and *chadhri* (the wearing of a veil in public). Military assistance, however, also provided the conduit through which the Soviet Union would attempt to impose its will upon Afghanistan. Over time, Soviet training converted several hundred Afghan officers to radical ideologies. These officers played critical roles in both the 1973 coup that overthrew the monarchy and the 1978 revolt that brought the Communist "People's Democratic Party of Afghanistan" (PDPA) to power. Thereafter, several ill-advised reform programs, implemented amidst severe government repression, alienated the majority of the Afghan population and prompted civil war. With the government on the verge of collapse, the Soviet Union sent in troops in December 1979, which remained in Afghanistan for nearly a decade.

Afghanistan suffered tremendously during the war. Casualty estimates generally place the Afghan dead at between 1 and 2 million. The majority of the population became, at one time or another, refugees. Sadly, the Soviet withdrawal in 1989 did not bring peace to the Afghan people. Attempts to form coalition governments from the various *mujahidin* groups failed, and the country degenerated into multifactioned civil war, with rival warlords jostling for power, disrupting the economy, and terrorizing the population. The Taliban rose amidst the chaos. Initially this militia of religious students attracted support from many Afghans and even some international observers through promises to end the violence, crime, and corruption. This support began to dwindle once their reactionary vision for Afghanistan became evident. In time, their intolerance toward women, dissenting religious views, national minorities, and even such innocuous pastimes as kite flying and bird keeping attracted increased international indignation. Ultimately, their harboring of Al Qaeda terrorists brought down the wrath of an international coalition upon them. Afghans today face a most difficult task in attempting to rebuild amidst the carnage of a quarter century of warfare.

Though the news media often ignored the Soviet-Afghan war, the scholarly community produced several publications, most of which discuss the immediate origins of war, the fighting itself, and the potential consequences. It would be no exaggeration, however, to claim that more Western scholarship on Afghanistan has appeared in the 20-odd years since the outbreak of war than in the 200 years preceding it.

Afghanistan, one of the world's most underdeveloped nations, has attracted relatively few specialized studies. Sitting astride the junction of Central Asia, South Asia, and the Middle East, Afghanistan has often been omitted from all three geographic groupings and excluded from area surveys. When included, the nation often has been poorly described, differing as it does from its neighbors in topography, language, economics, cultural traditions, and government.

Great Britain's encounters with Afghanistan are an exception, having always received considerable, if predictably biased, coverage. The only other exception occurred during the twenty-five years immediately prior to the Soviet invasion. General surveys such as Donald Wilber's *Afghanistan* (1962) and Louis Dupree's extensive, identically titled effort (1963) helped introduce Afghan society, history, and culture to the scholarly community. Several specialized studies also appeared. Such works as Varton Gregorian's *Emergence of Modern Afghanistan: Politics of Reform and Modernization* (1969), Richard Newell's *The Politics of Afghanistan* (1972), and Ludwig W. Adamec's *Afghanistan's Foreign Affairs to the Mid-Twentieth Century* (1974), to name a few, added considerable depth to the existing scholarship.

During the time in which these works appeared, Afghanistan pursued an official policy of "*bi-tarafi*" (literally "without sides," i.e., nonalignment or neutralism). The extent of Soviet economic and military involvement within the country led some scholars and most popular journalists to consign Afghanistan to the Soviet sphere of influence. While other scholars stressed that the nation was neither communist nor controlled by the U.S.S.R., given the similarities of Afghan policy and that pursued in the nineteenth century, even they remained content to reassert a neutralist heritage.

Most general and specialized studies, however, halted their in-depth analysis with the overthrow of the modernist king Amanullah (1919–1929). His failed reform programs, fascinating in their goals, implementation, and ultimate failure and readily comparable with more successful efforts in other Islamic states, attracted a disproportionate amount of attention. Few scholars undertook extensive discussion of Amanullah's immediate successors (perhaps for want of sources). Most dismissed the domestic policies of Nadir Shah (king from 1929 to 1933) and Hashim Khan (prime minister from 1933 to 1946) as a return to gradualism and their foreign policy as traditional neutralism. Afghanistan's posture during the final years of British rule in India received virtually no attention, and Afghanistan's role in the postwar world likewise suffered only cursory examination.

This study attempts to rectify these deficiencies in part by examining Afghan relations with the West during the second and third quarters of the twentieth century. In so doing, it offers new insights on the long-term origins of Afghanistan's recent tragedies. The evidence presented herein demonstrates that twentieth-century Afghanistan was neither historically opposed to alliances nor philosophically obsessed with neutralism. It demonstrates that following Amanullah's ouster, the Afghans pursued policies far more complex, and considerably more pro-Western, than previous authors have surmised. Despite the outwardly Islamophile and neutralist rhetoric of his regime, Nadir Shah, no longer fearful of British invasion yet aware of Soviet threats to Afghan independence, championed increased cooperation with British India. Nadir's successors continued his initiative. During the 1930s and early 1940s, in fact, Afghanistan moved closer to the West than ever before. By the end of the Second World War, Afghanistan showed little hesitation in requesting Western economic and military assistance. Despite nineteenth-century setbacks, Britain and Afghanistan seemed headed toward an extensive partnership, with Britain assuming a dominant influence in training and supplying the Afghan military.

The rise of the Indian nationalist movement, however, led to the end of British hegemony in South Asia. Britain, weakened from war and soon divested of both political and military responsibility for the subcontinent, emerged from partition neither capable of nor particularly interested in assisting Afghanistan. The successor states, Pakistan and India, weakened from partition and poised against the other, likewise saw no reason to aid the Kabul regime. India, the legal inheritor of British obligations to Afghanistan, renounced those commitments shortly after independence. Meanwhile, the "Pushtunistan" dispute, whose complex origins are discussed herein in detail, precluded close relations between Pakistan and Afghanistan.

After the partition, only the United States remained as the potential benefactor of Afghanistan. Throughout the decade 1945–1955, the Afghan leadership and other regional governments courted American assistance. In time, the United States would move to support Pakistan and Iran as part of the worldwide containment effort. Successive administrations proved disinterested in Afghanistan since it possessed no strong conventional military forces, valuable strategic facilities, vital resources, or substantial economic worth yet was dangerously exposed to Soviet encroachment. Over time, the abject failure of American-sponsored development enterprises, aborted diplomatic initiatives, rejections of Afghan requests for arms assistance, and partisan support for Pakistan destroyed Afghan faith in the United States and prompted Daoud to accept the Soviet aid offers.

After those agreements, the United States suddenly took interest in Afghanistan and attempted to offset Soviet influence therein. Though offered alliance membership, Afghanistan had little choice but to support the nonaligned movement after 1956. A neutral stance promised continued aid from both blocs, while a shift of policy toward the West likely would have resulted in termination of Soviet assistance and might well have prompted countermeasures. The window of opportunity had closed.

Had Britain's relationship with Afghanistan been maintained or assumed by another power, Afghanistan could possibly have been spared the horrors of a quarter century of warfare. Such possibilities foundered on a series of misunderstandings and questionable strategic assessments, of which the decision for alliance with Pakistan ranks paramount. Denied access to the Western alliances and their accompanying economic assistance, Daoud faced a choice of continual military impotence, political frustration, and economic stagnation or a rapprochement with the Soviet Union. Confident that he could avert the dangers inherent in the latter, he mortgaged Afghanistan's economy to the U.S.S.R. and consigned the Afghan military to Soviet tutelage. Daoud's choice, however, paved the way for the Soviet invasion, with all its inherent consequences.

INTRODUCTION: BACKGROUND TO AFGHANISTAN, ITS HISTORY, AND PEOPLE

In the immediate aftermath of the Soviet invasion of Afghanistan, a former British officer wrote: "As one who has had considerable personal experience of engaging in military operations against the hillmen of those regions, I know exactly what the Russian army is up against. I firmly believe that the Russians have bitten off a lot more than they can chew. Let them stew in their own juice, and go on wasting a lot of military effort to no purpose."[1]

While his prediction that the war in Afghanistan would become a "Soviet Vietnam" proved correct, most strategic analysts thought that the Afghan *mujahidin* would fade away with the spring thaw. Such pessimism remained prominent even as the war progressed. Continued stalemate seemed palatable to the U.S.S.R. The Soviet government, apparently immune to public opinion, appeared capable of waging a sustained battle of attrition against the Afghans. They had, in fact, conducted similar successful campaigns before, in Central Asia and the Caucasus.[2] With no threat of popular protests or upcoming elections, the Soviet hierarchy not only could wage a prolonged struggle but could resort to forms of warfare not palatable to a Western democracy. The Soviet Union repeatedly violated Geneva protocols in the early years of the war, using various nerve gases, mustard gas, and other chemical/biological weapons in several provinces. Soviet and Afghan government (Democratic Republic of Afghanistan [DRA]) forces, supported by aircraft and helicopter gunships, directed their attacks against civilians, agricultural areas, water facilities, and livestock as well as the *mujahidin*.[3] Despite overwhelming technological superiority and the ability to wage a veritable war of extermination, the Soviet Union proved unable to suppress the *mujahidin* or sway the vast majority of Afghans from support of the resistance. Left with no hope for victory beyond the mass extermination of the population, the Soviet leadership ultimately determined that the price of retreat would entail less economic and political damage than would continuation of the war.

This recent episode was hardly the first time the Afghans have expelled a foreign invader from their soil. Aside from being a major staging area for assaults on the subcontinent, Afghanistan also lies astride the traditional east-west trade route to and from the Orient. Consequently, Afghanistan "has perhaps seen more invasions in the course of history than any other country in Asia, or indeed the world."[4] Persians, Scythians, Macedonians and Greeks, Huns, Mongols, Arabs, Turks, and Moguls all attempted to conquer Afghanistan, but none succeeded in permanently subduing the inhabitants. In time, the British supplanted the Moguls as the masters of India, and twice they would attempt to subdue Afghanistan. Despite disciplined armed forces, technological advantages, and expertise in military, government, and economic affairs, they would ultimately fare no better than those before them.[5]

The tenacity and resiliency of the Afghan population have consistently proven critical impediments to invasion. Afghan passion for independence, racial and personal pride, religion, ingrained self-reliance, social structure, legal systems and daily habits, and the geography and climate of their homeland have imparted a rugged individualism to the Afghans that is exceeded in no other people. Mohammed Ali, an Afghan writer, explains: "One of the most dominant characteristics of the Afghan is his intense love of independence. The Afghan patiently bears his misfortune or poverty but he cannot be made to reconcile himself to foreign rule. . . . Foreigners who have failed to understand this point and who have tried to deprive him of his national independence or personal freedom have had to pay heavily for the price of folly."[6]

While the Afghans have always refused to accept foreign rule, rarely have they proven amenable to a strong central government. Most tribes and villages have remained self-sufficient and autonomous, accepting central control only when in their material interest or when faced with overwhelming force. The traditional Loya Jirgah (National Grand Council), comprising influential tribal, religious, and urban leaders, established something of a precedent for unified central authority, but it met only during times of crisis. While local *jirgahs* practiced democracy in the villages, representative government remained an anomaly to most Afghans, who traditionally avoided contact with central government officials, fearing increased taxes, conscription, or other forced labor.[7]

The lack of central authority has rendered Afghanistan an easy state to invade. Indeed, while the Afghans can claim never to have been conquered, neither have they repelled an invader at the border or ousted one without protracted struggle. Afghanistan is perhaps the classic example of Machiavelli's "state of many princes," in that while easily entered, it has proven impossible to subdue. Whereas the peoples of Afghanistan tend to quarrel among themselves in the absence of external threats, resistance to outside intervention has traditionally spanned across religious, ethnic, and tribal lines. Though resistance has remained locally based, the disunity often has proven an advantage, as the aggressor is afforded no critical target whose destruction will spell the demise of the insurgency.

Afghanistan is not a homogeneous national state but a conglomeration of tribes and ethnic groups. The population of Afghanistan includes the Persian-speaking Tajiks, whose lands in the Oxus Plain are among the most fertile in Afghanistan and hence are vital to the national economy. The Turkic-speaking Uzbeks and Turkomen of the northwest, along with the Tajiks, rank among the most anti-Russian peoples of Afghanistan. The Mongolian-featured Hazaras, who inhabit the barren Central Highlands, remain alone among Afghanistan's major ethnic groups in professing Shi'a Islam. The Nuristanis, formerly known as Kaffirs, remain all but isolated in the mountains of the southeast, and the Baluchis and Brahui inhabit the desolate southwest. Several languages and innumerable dialects are spoken throughout the country.[8]

The predominant ethnic group in Afghanistan, comprising roughly half of the population, are the Pushtuns (at times called Pathans, Pakhtuns, Pashtuns, or Pakhtoons). Though some tribes live north of the Hindu Kush, the Pushtuns primarily live in the southern regions of the country. The inhabitants of a barren, infertile landscape, crisscrossed with mountains and deserts, many Pushtun tribes habitually raided the lowlands of the Indus Valley into the nineteenth century. They consider themselves "true Afghans" and have tended to regard neighboring peoples, whether within Afghanistan, India, or Persia, as incorrigibly inferior.

Within Afghanistan, the Pushtuns are divided into two main groupings: the Durranis and the Ghilzais. The Durranis long have dominated the political and economic life of modern Afghanistan. Some Pushtuns also inhabit modern-day Pakistan. They include, from northeast to southwest, Mohmands, Yusufzais, Afridis, Orakzais, Wazirs, and Mahsuds. Some of these peoples also inhabit parts of Afghanistan, and nearly all frequently migrate across the border.[9]

Pushtun customs, some of which contradict tenets of Islam, have tended to define Afghan society. They also have given Afghanistan its popular reputation for lawlessness and brutality. Pushtuns live by Pushtunwali, an unwritten system of values that governs resolution of disputes among individuals, families, and tribes. Basically an "eye-for-an-eye" system (or perhaps "two-to-ten eyes for an eye"), Pushtunwali mandates retribution for violations of personal or family *nang* (honor). Retribution can be obtained through seizure of livestock or acceptance of other payment but usually involves inflicting bodily harm upon the offender or next of kin. Securing appropriate *badal* (revenge) is an obligation rather than a choice, with nearest relatives compelled to seek retribution for the slain. (Indeed, stipulations for *badal* clouded Anglo-Afghan relations in the nineteenth century and precluded accommodation between the People's Democratic Party of Afghanistan and the *mujahidin*). In a way, Pushtunwali helps prevent crime, as few wish to commit murder for fear of revenge, but too often it perpetuates blood feuds between families that last for generations. Usually sparked by disputes over *zar, zan,* and *zamin* (gold, women, and land), such vendettas were often the most vicious among blood relatives. Indeed, the Pushtu word for cousin, *tarbur,* is the root of *tarburgalay,* a term that signifies extreme hatred.[10]

There are elements of mercy and kindness in the Pushtunwali. It mandates *melmastia,* requiring hospitality to visitors and guests, even strangers, without regard to personal inconvenience. *Nanawatai* extends that hospitality to include asylum, even to fugitives. Women, children, and members of the *ulama* are among those exempted from retribution. Mercy can also be granted through the intercession of a woman or *mullah* or simply if the intended victim begs forgiveness. The avenger, however, does not have to grant mercy; or necessarily follow any other rules of conduct. As with any feudal system, the effect of the Pushtunwali always has depended on the personality and moods of the individuals wielding the weapons.

The sharp contrast between *melmastia* and *badal* explains the dualism one encounters in reading of the Afghans. One can find Western accounts that describe the Afghans as the world's most outgoing, genuine, courageous, resourceful, and hospitable people and an equal number of others that portray Afghanistan as a land of sadistic brigands who, along with their scheming wives and knife-wielding children, delight in plundering hapless travelers when not abusing one another. Since violent incidents generally have remained more newsworthy than examples of generosity, even if more infrequent, and since the Afghans admittedly can be ingenious practitioners of torture, examples of more regrettable behavior have come to color the popular image of their nation. Yet, while one should not dismiss examples of barbarism, one should also note that invasions rarely leave any people in the mood to grant *melmastia* to the invader.[11]

As a result of the Pushtunwali, persistent inter- and intratribal feuding, and other socioeconomic factors, most Afghan males become acquainted with weapons in their early childhood and develop a keen sense of marksmanship. Centuries of practice have rendered them superb tacticians, who make excellent use of the rugged landscape. Over the centuries, the Afghans have acquired remarkable mechanical and ballistic aptitude, which allows them to make the best of captured equipment. They have also proven expert arms manufacturers and proficient arms thieves when that option is available to them. Furthermore, the proliferation of weapons across the nation has always allowed the Afghans to raise sizable forces with amazing speed.[12]

Generations of living amidst a hostile physical and social environment have imparted to the Afghans tremendous stamina and capacity for hardship. Their toughness and endurance are perhaps best exemplified in their national sport.

Buzkashi, often played between teams of more than 100, is not so much a team sport as a forum for displays of individual heroics. The players, mounted on horseback, attempt to carry a beheaded calf (young boys play with a goat) through the ranks of opposing horsemen and deposit it in a goal beyond. This dangerous "maelstrom of thundering hooves and flying fists, punctuated by wild yells as the opposing teams fight for possession of the carcass at full gallop," often produces several injuries and an occasional fatality.[13]

The low standard of living in Afghanistan has also proven an asset. Though possessed of tremendous natural resources, including one of the largest iron ore deposits in the world, transportation costs and government policy always limited development in Afghanistan. Though less than 10 percent of the land is suitable for farming and 40 percent at most can accommodate grazing, most Afghans remain engaged in subsistence agriculture.[14] While this has strengthened individual self-reliance, most Afghans also seem to have little difficulty abandoning their few possessions and once in the field take readily to survival there, subsisting for extended periods with little food and no amenities. On the other hand, invaders cannot live off the land, are susceptible to various diseases, and must import supplies across the limited transportation network, which is vulnerable to guerrilla attack. Afghanistan thus presents invaders with an impossible dilemma. Ali again explains: "Invade it [Afghanistan] with a large force, and you are destroyed by starvation, invade with a small force, you are overwhelmed by a hostile people."[15]

The combination of ballistic familiarity, tactical know-how, rugged endurance, and unyielding refusal to tolerate any sort of foreign rule has made Afghanistan a graveyard of armies. Though successive invaders, each possessed of greater technology than their predecessor, frequently routed Afghan forces in pitched battle, none ever succeeded in breaking the will of the Afghan people to resist. That determination ensured the independence of the Afghan state in the face of British and Soviet invasions and will likely remain Afghanistan's most valuable deterrent in the future. That resolve, often overlooked or underrated by Western policymakers, should be remembered in any analysis or assessment of Soviet, British, or American policy in the region.

NOTES

1. Brigadier F. Hughes, quoted in Schofield, *Every Rock,* p. 286.

2. Caroe, "Afghanistan: Strategic After-Effects," p. 131; Hyman, *Afghanistan under Soviet Domination,* pp. 162, 165, 183, 210; Malhuret, "Report from Afghanistan," p. 435; Baddeley, *Russian Conquest of the Caucasus,* pp. 129–134.

3. Department of State, Special Report No. 98, "Chemical Warfare in South Asia and Afghanistan," March 1982, pp. 6, 14–17, 23; Schofield, *Every Rock,* pp. 323–324; Amstutz, *Afghanistan,* pp. 172–176; Hyman, *Afghanistan under Soviet Domination,* pp. 96, 187–188 205–206; Collins, *Soviet Invasion of Afghanistan,* pp. 139, 146–148; Giradet, *Afghanistan,* pp. 41, 107–110, 164–165, 214, 233, 237–238;

Arnold, *Afghanistan,* p. 99. Soviet aircraft further dropped concentrations of butterfly mines across the country. These mines carried enough explosive to maim, but not enough to kill, their victims, apparently owing to realization that a wounded *mujahid* or civilian would disrupt resistance supplies and transport more than a dead one. These mines, often shaped to appear as toys or other innocuous items, have maimed thousands of curious or unsuspecting children, adults, and livestock.

In what has become perhaps the most commonly invoked example of atrocities in the Afghan war, on April 20, 1979, at Kerala, DRA forces murdered an estimated 1,170 Afghan males. To the grieving women left behind, a Soviet advisor offered the condolence: that "You can be sure that next year's potato crop will be a good one." It is interesting to note that during the Soviet conflict, resistance leaders expressed longing for the days when their forefathers had fought the "honorable" British. Several human rights groups documented similar executions of entire village populations. Amstutz (*Afghanistan,* pp. 145–146) documents two massacres, one in Ghazni and the other near Qandahar, and claims they are but the tip of the iceberg. .

4. Caroe, *Pathans,* p. 25.

5. Caroe, "Lecture to the Royal Institute of International Affairs," 4 February 1948, MSS.EUR F.203/4 (Olaf Caroe Papers); Barton, *India's North-West Frontier,* pp. 120–121; Gregorian, *Emergence of Modern Afghanistan,* pp. 20, 44–45.

6. Ali, *Afghanistan,* pp. 122–123; Arnold, *Afghanistan,* p. 2. Arnold, responding to an article that compared Afghanistan to a grain of wheat between two millstones, claimed the Afghans are more like ball bearings. Schofield, *Every Rock,* p. 118.

7. Payind, "Soviet-Afghan Relations," pp. 114–115; Dupree, *AUFS,* 4/6, p. 4; Dupree, *AUFS,* 9/4, pp. 14–15; Dupree, *AUFS,* 10/4, p. 2; Dupree, "Afghanistan, Problems of a Peasant-Tribal Society," pp. 3, 8; Griffiths, *Afghanistan,* pp. 166, 170–171, 176–179; Bhaneja, *Afghanistan,* pp. 32–35, 40; Wilber, *Afghanistan,* p. 141; Miller, *Khyber,* p. 100. *Jirgahs* did not vote per se but resolved issues through consensus. Miller claims they "repeated the excess of the Athenian agora, without the erudition of Athens, and with more than one Cleon to act as demagogue."

8. Del Croze, "Afghanistan Today," p. 33; Schofield, *Every Rock,* pp. 124–125; Dupree, "Afghanistan, Problems of a Peasant-Tribal Society," p. 5; Griffiths, *Afghanistan,* pp. 80–82, 87–90, 89fn, 196; Hyman, *Afghanistan under Soviet Domination,* pp. 9–10, 15; Gregorian, *Emergence of Modern Afghanistan,* pp. 34–39, 39fn. The predominant languages are Pashto and Dari, followed by a variety of Turkic dialects.

9. Hyman, *Afghanistan under Soviet Domination,* pp. 5–6; Schofield, *Every Rock,* pp. 123–124; Griffiths, *Afghanistan,* pp. 81, 92; Gregorian, *Emergence of Modern Afghanistan,* pp. 30–32. The Durranis are further subdivided into seven subtribes: the Achakzai, Alikozai, Alizai, Barakzai (from whom has descended the Mohammedzai clan, the most recent royal family), Ishakzai, Nurzai, and Popalzai (from whom the Sadozais originate). Ghilzais subtribes include the Ali Khel, Andar, Nassar, Suleiman Khel, Tarakhi, and Tokhi.

10. Poullada, "The Pushtun Role in the Afghan Political System," pp. 7–13; Cunningham, "Tribes of the North West Frontier of India," *World Review* February 1947, MSS.EUR D.670/28 (George Cunningham Papers); Arnold, *Afghanistan,* p. 76; Miller, *Khyber,* pp. 99–100; Griffiths, *Afghanistan,* p. 196.

11. Griffiths, *Afghanistan,* pp. 111–112. Perhaps one should conclude, as did John Griffiths, that the Afghans "were as likely to rob a rich visitor as they were to be generous to a poor one." Griffiths tells of encounters with villagers who do not hesitate

"to kill their last chicken" and then refuse all offers of recompense. Del Croze, in "Afghanistan Today" (pp. 48–49), describes the Afghans as patient, calm, with a good sense of humor, never angry, friendly, shy, and possessed of strong family values. For other positive portrayals, see Wilber, *Afghanistan*, p. 167; Squire, "Recent Progress in Afghanistan," p. 6; Squire, "Afghanistan and Her Neighbors," p. 68; Schofield, *Every Rock*, pp. 119–123, 145, 271–275; Barton, *India's North-West Frontier*, pp. 10, 17; MacMunn, "Real British Attitude toward Afghanistan," p. 469; Rawlinson, "Report on the Doorannee Tribes," 19 April 1841; Cunningham Papers, "Tribes of the North West Frontier of India," George Cunningham Papers. Sir Winston Churchill, on the other hand, called the Pathan tribesmen "amongst the most miserable and brutal creatures of the earth. Their intelligence only enables them to be more cruel, more dangerous, more destructive than wild beasts." He would later add that "every influence, every motive that provokes the spirit of murder among men, implores these mutineers to deeds of treachery and violence. . . . To the ferocity of the Zulu are added the craft of the Redskin and the marksmanship of the Boer. . . . Death by inches and hideous mutilation are the invariable measure meted out to all who fall in battle into the hands of the Pathan tribesman" (quoted in Schofield, *Every Rock*, pp. 118–119; Miller, *Khyber*, pp. 268–269). Of the more balanced perspectives, Montstuart Elphinstone, one of the first English travelers to Afghanistan, described them as having vices of "revenge, envy, avarice, rapacity and obstinacy; on the other hand they are fond of liberty, faithful to their friends, kind to their dependents, hospitable, brave, hardy, frugal, laborious and prudent; they are less disposed than the nations in their neighborhood to falsehood, intrigue and deceit" (*Account of the Kingdom of Caubal*, p. 253). The official British attitude changed little from Elphinstone's assessment over the years. See, e.g., Military Training Pamphlet No. 16, "Platoon Leading in Frontier Warfare" (1945, L/MIL/17/5/2258), which conceded Pathan strengths in "manliness, hospitality, a sturdy sense of independence and a good sense of humor" but also considered the Afghans fanatical, cruel, and treacherous. For an interesting modern contrast, compare the favorable impressions of Jason Elliot in *An Unexpected Light: Travels in Afghanistan* with the decidedly less favorable view of Ted Rall in *To Afghanistan and Back*.

12. Fletcher, *Afghanistan*, p. 190; Miller, *Khyber*, p. 101; Arnold, *Afghanistan*, p. 98.

13. Miller, *Khyber*, p. 45; Tabibi, "Aftermath Created by British Policy," p. 15.

14. Giradet, *Afghanistan*, pp. 152–154, 159–161; Griffiths, *Afghanistan*, pp. 131–132.

15. Ali, *Afghanistan*, pp. 122–123.

1

BRITISH POLICY TOWARD AFGHANISTAN IN THE NINETEENTH CENTURY: THE FIRST ANGLO-AFGHAN WAR

By the beginning of the nineteenth century, Great Britain had secured its grip on most of the Indian subcontinent. The British reduced the holdings of their assorted European rivals to a few isolated enclaves and, through outright conquest or forceful diplomacy, attained hegemony over most of the Indian princes. Profits from Indian trade would remain vital to the British economy, at times surpassing all other revenue of the Home government. Consequently, preservation of control in India remained paramount in British strategic planning for nearly 200 years.

The retention of naval supremacy in the Indian Ocean always remained the foremost concern. To this effect, Britain acquired several colonies along the seaward approaches to India. Bases at Aden, Suez, Singapore, and elsewhere helped preserve naval dominance while facilitating trade. Though some such colonies would later acquire some importance of their own, much of their significance remained linked to the protection of India.

With naval dominance ensured, strategic planners could focus on India's land frontiers. To the immediate north, India always seemed well protected by the Himalayas, the world's largest and most formidable mountain chain. To the east, the disease-infested swamps and jungles of Burma offered similar security. No invader ever breached either route until the mid-twentieth century, and even then Chinese and Japanese efforts, respectively, were limited and not entirely successful.

To the west of India lie the wastelands of Baluchistan and the Iranian plateau. The terrain and climate of these lands, believed by their few inhabitants to have been the place where God discarded the refuse of civilization, have made invasion difficult, though not impossible. From Alexander the

Great to the Saffavids, certain hardy conquerors crossed the badlands with their forces intact. Throughout the period of British hegemony, however, no similar invaders appeared.

The most commonly chosen avenue for invasion of India ran from the northwest, through modern-day Afghanistan. This route was not without major challenges. The Hindu Kush Mountains bisect the region. The few passes are difficult to negotiate, and they afford ideal ambush positions for the local inhabitants. Still, the northwest offered a practicable landward approach to the subcontinent. Given that nearly every successful invasion of India had come from that direction, British strategic planners would pay great attention to the Northwest Frontier, and to Afghanistan, throughout the duration of the Empire.

Though certain enlightened individuals espoused the idea of an Afghan state as early as the sixteenth century, as a political entity, Afghanistan dates from the reign of Ahmed Shah Durrani (1747–1773). An Abdali Pushtun, Ahmed Shah had commanded an elite cavalry contingent under Saffavid usurper Nadir Shah, which spearheaded the rout of the Moguls at Panipat and the infamous sack of Delhi in 1739. After Nadir's assassination in 1747, Ahmed assumed power in the Pushtun areas near Qandahar. He adopted the name "Dur-i-Durran" (Pearl-of-Pearls) and applied the name "Durrani" to the tribes of southwest Afghanistan as a measure of political unity. Over the next twenty years, he carved out a domain that eventually stretched from the Indus to the Oxus, from Kashmir to Khurastan. Ahmed Shah would leave a legacy that subsequent Afghan monarchs would try to emulate.

Ahmed Shah secured political authority through force of personality and reinforced it through a series of successful looting expeditions into north India. In 1761 he defeated the Maratha confederacy, also at Panipat. (In crippling Maratha power, he unintentionally facilitated the British conquest of the Indian interior.) Ahmed Shah shrewdly allocated captured booty and land grants to the Durrani chiefs, securing their acquiescence to his policies. In return, they continued to provide him military support.

Ahmed Shah established no permanent political system. The Durrani Empire remained more a tribal confederation buoyed by conquest than a modern nation-state. Lacking both an urban economic base and a royal army, Ahmed Shah could never force his rule on the tribes. His successors likewise would remain subject to their consent.[1]

Like other states that depended heavily on the personal magnetism of their leaders, the Durrani empire collapsed within a few decades of its founder's death. Ahmed Shah's son and successor, Timur Shah, quickly lost authority in outlying regions, and when his twenty-three sons battled upon their father's death in 1793, the empire disintegrated. Politics degenerated into a three-way battle between the rulers of Herat, Qandahar, and Kabul, with each city remaining hostile to the other two. Afghanistan experienced an "orgy of intrigue, treachery, torture and murder" wherein various pretenders attempted to unseat rivals through palace intrigues and military action in an "ever-shifting kaleidoscope of betrayal."[2] Afghanistan's cities lost between one-third and four-fifths of their populations over a fifty-year period.[3]

By the turn of the century, Timur's fifth son, Zaman Shah, had consolidated a small power base in southern Afghanistan, from which he attempted to restore his grandfather's empire. His threat to the surrounding states, former vassals to Ahmad Shah, caused many to court British assistance. Britain, fearful of incursions and desirous of expanded economic contacts, moved to support several local princes. Though Zaman Shah's usurpation eventually removed the threat, the British continued to extend their contacts and power in the northwest.

Afghanistan's period of misfortune coincided with the French Revolution and the Napoleonic Wars in Europe. Napoleon's campaign in Egypt had aroused British fears of an invasion of India. Then in 1801, the erratic Tsar Paul had ordered the Don Cossacks to march to the Indus, but they turned back when news of the tsar's assassination reached them at the Volga. The Treaty of Tilsit (1807) renewed British fears of direct Franco-Russian aggression. Though the hypothetical invading forces would have had to cross over 2,000 miles of hostile country just to get to India, British authorities thought enough of the threat to sign defensive alliances with the Persians and Sikhs. They also dispatched an emissary, Montstuart Elphinstone, to Peshawar to meet with the ruler of Kabul, Shah Shuja. Though the two men signed a treaty of "eternal friendship," Shuja's near-immediate usurpation (carried out by his brother) rendered the alliance meaningless. Thereafter, the British courted Afghanistan's seemingly more reliable neighbors. They maintained close ties with Ranjit Singh, whose disciplined Sikh army, modeled on Western lines, possessed of modern artillery and commanded by European officers, had earned their respect. The British also signed a comprehensive alliance with Persia in 1814, which stipulated mutual assistance against a Russian or Afghan attack.[4]

Continued Afghan instability presented its neighbors with opportunities for aggrandizement. Throughout the ensuing half century, Persia would often attempt to offset losses to Russia through expansion to the east. Ranjit Singh, meanwhile, captured the Afghan winter capital of Peshawar in 1823 and later added Baluchistan to his dominions. The losses of the Peshawar Valley, one of the richest tracts in all Pushtun territory, and of Afghanistan's outlet to the sea were political, economic, and psychological blows that subsequent Afghan rulers would attempt to reverse.[5]

In the late 1820s, Russia waged successful wars against the Persians and the Ottoman Empire. The treaties of Turkmanchai (1828) and Adriandople (1829) secured respective Russian gains. The Russian advance, however, seemed to many London politicians to threaten British economic and strategic interests. They grew fearful of Russian consolidation along the Hindu Kush, from which Russia could dominate Central Asian trade, threaten invasion, and foster rebellion in India. Tories and Whigs alike were already concerned with Russia when, in 1829, Colonel de Lacy Evans followed his *Designs of Russia* with publication of *Probability of an Invasion of British India*. Evans forewarned of Russian forces marching from the Caspian to Khiva, sailing down the Oxus, and resuming the march to India. Though such notions defied logistical reason, Evans's well-received works convinced more British officials of the necessity to take action to forestall Russian expansion.[6]

During Persia's war with Russia, however, Britain had not honored previous treaty commitments. Persia subsequently became a client of St. Petersburg. In 1837 the Russians encouraged Mohammed Shah Qajar to seize Herat, which his army invaded in November. Lord Palmerston, then the Home secretary, believed that Russo-Persian control of Herat would constitute a grave threat to regional security. He gave the governor-general of India, Lord Auckland, permission to take "measures that may appear to you desirable in order to contract [the] Russian advances." Palmerston left much to Auckland's discretion, allowing him the prerogative to "interfere decidedly in the affairs of Afghanistan."[7]

In the meantime, Afghanistan's internal dilemma had begun to abate after Dost Mohammed's accession in 1826. He consolidated a power base around Kabul and established a limited bureaucracy staffed by his sons and matrimonial allies, which reduced crime and corruption to manageable proportions. With a modicum of stability restored in eastern Afghanistan, he attempted to wrestle Peshawar from the Sikhs. In 1837 Dost's son, Akbar Khan, led an Afghan army to victory at Jamrud. Akbar, however, did not follow up his success with an advance to Peshawar, and the city remained in Sikh hands.[8]

Dost Mohammed held no animosity toward the British and, in fact, had expressed to Auckland a willingness to cooperate against the Russians and Persians, given a satisfactory settlement of Afghan disputes with the Sikhs. Dost's placating attitude earned him a visit from a British envoy, Sir Alexander Burnes. Like many other Britons, Burnes realized that Peshawar and its unruly environs had become a liability to the Sikhs and believed a restoration to Afghan control would bring stability to the frontier. While forceful diplomacy perhaps could have achieved a compromise, Burnes was officially on a commercial mission and was not empowered to negotiate a settlement. Nor would such prerogatives be forthcoming.[9]

Dost continually demonstrated amity for the British. Notably, he turned over to Burnes the private correspondence of the Russian envoy, Lieutenant Vitkevitch. Burnes duly noted the amir's conciliatory attitude and his rejection of numerous Russo-Persian overtures and repeatedly stressed potential benefits of an Afghan alliance in notes to Auckland. In one instance, he wrote the viceroy: "It remains to be considered why we cannot act with Dost Mohammed. He is a man of undoubted ability, who has at his heart a high opinion of the British nation. . . . [He] prefers the sympathy and friendly offices of the British."[10] Yet Anglo-Afghan relations could never reach fruition owing to Dost's quarrels with the Sikhs. Auckland remained unwilling to risk offending Ranjit Singh, whose European-modeled state, a British ally since 1806, seemed a more reliable partner, events at Jamrud notwithstanding. To Auckland, Dost's state seemed as weak and unreliable as those of his Qandahari or Herati rivals. Auckland thought Dost would be lucky, and should be content, to maintain sovereignty over his limited dominions. Auckland also believed that the continued division of Afghanistan was in the British interest, fearing attacks on India were Dost to unify it. Though Dost proved willing to accept nearly every demand Auckland could make, including the severance of relations with Persia and Russia, he could never countenance Ranjit's continued control of Peshawar, not only out of economic necessity and moral principle but also for fear of loss of face among the Pushtuns. Auckland's continued support for a Sikh presence in Peshawar eventually prompted Dost to cease his cold treatment of Vitkevitch and enter negotiations with the Russian in April 1838. The British reacted by supporting the Sikhs in a joint effort to replace the "unreliable" Dost with Shah Shuja.[11]

Auckland's decision was as much a product of the British attitude of the time as a logical choice between potential allies. A series of seemingly uninterrupted victories had given the early Victorians a sense of destiny that translated into overconfidence. Having never been more than temporarily checked by Asian armies, the British expected little trouble from the "barbarous" Afghans. Members of the civil service and military relished a chance to acquire laurels in Afghanistan; indeed, both army and East India Company regiments had to draw lots to see which would have the privilege to invade. The British, however, knew little of Afghanistan or its people. The only accounts available to them were the sketchy travelogues of assorted Central Asian explorers and traders. Burnes apparently learned little, as he assured Auckland that a token escort could ensure the establishment of a client regime. Virtually every official close to the crisis echoed this belief that Shuja could be restored without difficulty.[12]

The Simla Manifesto of October 1838 severed relations with Dost, berated him for collaborating with the Russian envoy and the Persians, and condemned his hostile intentions toward the Sikhs, the "ancient ally" of Britain. Curiously, the Persian siege of Herat had been lifted before the manifesto was written. The city had seemed on the verge of collapse until British Lieutenant Eldred Pottinger arrived and helped bolster the defenses. The poor performance of the Persian army, threats of direct British intervention, and an absence of tangible support from Russia forced the Shah to retreat in the late summer of 1838.[13]

The British nonetheless followed through on their plans to invade Afghanistan. Since Herat was hardly secure and Qandahar had recently allied with the Persians, the invasion still aimed at preventing Persian and/or Russian incursions into Afghanistan. In addition, Auckland faced crises elsewhere and hoped a strong show of force would lessen the threat of war with Nepal, reduce internal unrest across India, and perhaps have a sobering effect on Russia. Auckland's policy enjoyed the near-unanimous support of the Home government.[14]

In December 1838, the "Army of the Indus" went forward in what promised to be a brief, glorious campaign. The main force marched to Kabul via the Bolan Pass, a route four times longer than that through the Khyber but one that took it through Sind, where the British imposed further concessions upon the amir's already limited sovereignty. Along the march, the army suffered more from disease and the elements than from hostile action. As the army approached Qandahar, that city's rulers either fled or submitted to Shuja. After resuming the march to Kabul, a strong Afghan force in the fortress at Ghazni temporarily stalled the British advance, until a traitorous nephew of Dost helped the attackers breach an undefended gate in a daring night attack. Dost, who had expected a lengthy siege, fled to the north. On August 7, 1839, the Army of the Indus entered Kabul.[15]

From the beginning of the occupation, the Kabulis regarded the occupying forces with undisguised contempt. Shuja, viewed as a *watan ferosh* (literally "country seller," or traitor) from his arrival, attracted little support. His corrupt ministry only aggravated staggering inflation that had accompanied the invasion. Attempts to establish royal forces met with widespread desertion, and Shuja's army remained ill-disciplined rabble. This forced Auckland to retain a sizable British force in Kabul, despite the expenses. That force could also keep watch on Persia and the Russians, who then had an army advancing on Khiva.[16]

All the while, the British settled into occupation duties, brought forward their wives and children, and generally pursued their own way of life regardless of the circumstances. Their activities often constituted affronts to Islam and to Afghan society. While Kabul had acquired a debaucherous reputation prior to Dost's accession, Dost had later imposed strict laws against alcoholic beverages, intoxicating drugs, gambling, and prostitution. Now Burnes led the British contingent in various unsavory practices, availing himself of the "open, undisguised and notorious" traffic in Afghan women. Such behavior fostered greater resentment toward Shuja and his British supporters and prompted increased guerrilla attacks against them.[17]

Though attacks on the occupation force increased, British confidence remained high, bolstered by the surrender of the amir. Dost retreated into the Hindu Kush, where for more than a year he had raised armies as rapidly as the British dispersed them. Frustrated by his failures, he surrendered in the autumn of 1840. All his sons, save Akbar, followed him to exile in India. Though scattered uprisings continued to occur afterward, British-Indian forces responded with successful punitive expeditions, in which they often routed ten times their number of Afghans. With Herat secure, Sind and Qandahar subdued, and the Russians now retreating from Khiva, by mid-1841, Auckland's policy seemed a success. Buoyed by the positive overtones of messages from Kabul, Auckland turned his attentions to developments in China and the Middle East, leaving affairs in Kabul in the hands of the chief political officer, William MacNaughton.[18]

In this atmosphere of confidence, MacNaughton strove to lessen expenses. Throughout the occupation, the British had provided subsidies to the Ghilzais in return for noninterference with supply deliveries. MacNaughton terminated this arrangement, shortly after he transferred one of the garrison's two combat brigades to India. Within a few days, thousands of angry Ghilzais had "mobilized," isolating Kabul in the process. MacNaughton's move was among the most damning errors that ultimately led to the destruction of the Kabul garrison.

The besieged British faced several tactical disadvantages, most of which were their own fault. Initially they had occupied the Bala Hissar, Kabul's imperial fortress, but they abandoned it to Shuja and his harem and moved to a cantonment on the city's outskirts. One contemporary writer claimed the new position "must ever be spoken of as a disgrace to our military skill and judgment." The rough surrounding terrain, dotted with stone houses, provided the Afghans with avenues of approach, while occupation of hills to the north allowed them to pour fire from their *jezails* (which were, incidentally, superior to the British "Brown Bess" muskets) on the British positions with relative immunity. Most incredibly, the British left both the commissariat and the magazine one quarter mile beyond the walls of the cantonment. The early loss of the garrison's supplies ensured its eventual destruction.[19]

General William George Elphinstone, a veteran of Waterloo, was in command of the British forces. The elderly, gout-ridden general was so physically weak that he could scarcely mount his horse without assistance. Contemporaries labeled him "fit only for the invalid establishment on the day of his arrival." His infirmity rendered him useless in the crisis. He left tactical execution to Brigadier John Shelton. Another brave Napoleonic war veteran, his courage could not offset his tactical mistakes. In one particular counterattack, he formed his infantry in two squares, making them easy marks for Afghan snipers, and deployed his cavalry in the middle. When one square broke, horses and men became intertwined in complete disarray as all raced back to the cantonment. Though Shelton would prove more efficient on later occasions, neither he nor Elphinstone provided inspiration to the increasingly dispirited troops, as both commanders made no secret of their lack of faith in a successful outcome of the siege.[20]

Two events further weakened the British position. The onset of winter aggravated supply problems, while the arrival of Akbar brought reinforcements and determined leadership to the Afghan cause. The ever-optimistic MacNaughton attempted to negotiate with Akbar, offering to withdraw all British troops from Kabul if the Afghans would guarantee their safe conduct.

Shuja would be abandoned and Dost allowed to return. Akbar consented but later offered MacNaughton another deal, which promised a retained British presence in Kabul. MacNaughton, still hoping to rescue the situation, accepted the new offer. Akbar, in front of many influential chiefs, accused the political officer of treachery and shot him.[21]

With his forces facing imminent starvation, Elphinstone accepted Akbar's initial terms, which promised safe, unfettered passage to the border and adequate supplies of food. The army turned over its heavy weapons and began a retreat to Jalalabad on January 6, 1842. The troops and camp followers marched into an inverted hell of cold. Throughout the next week, many would die of exposure. Despite Akbar's promises, others fell to the bullets of Ghilzai tribesmen, who attacked the column all along the route. Initially content to finish off the wounded and ambush stragglers, the magnitude and daring of their attacks gradually increased. Within a week, 4,500 soldiers, along with over 12,000 camp followers, perished on the Kabul-Jalalabad road. Aside from a few officers, women, and children held personally by Akbar and the army's surgeon, who managed to reach Jalalabad, the Ghilzais annihilated the entire British contingent. The invasion of Afghanistan, soon dubbed "Auckland's Folly," had culminated in the worst disaster suffered by British armies in Asia until the fall of Singapore 100 years later.[22]

Though the invasion left a legacy of hatred, otherwise it proved but a minor setback that had few lasting consequences on British policy. In the fall of 1841, the Whigs had regained control of the Home government, which led Auckland to resign. Lord Ellenbourough was named as replacement. Though determined to retreat from the forward positions, Ellenbourough sanctioned further operations in Afghanistan to rescue besieged garrisons, restore army morale and reputation, and avenge the perceived treachery. Major General George Pollack's "Army of Retribution" forced the Khyber Pass to relieve the Jalalabad garrison, while another force under Major General James Knott rescued a brigade in Qandahar. Pollock's forces pushed on to Kabul, recovered Akbar's prisoners, and then burned the Kabul bazaar before departing in October 1842. British forces later pilfered artifacts from the revered tomb of Mahmud of Ghazni and leveled that city, where a small British garrison had also been annihilated. Both relief forces destroyed villages and the surrounding countryside, with notable examples occurring at Istalif and Charikar, where they executed some inhabitants.[23]

Though the Tripartite Pact was abandoned and Dost allowed to return to Kabul, British prestige suffered little. Politicians and military authorities wrote off the defeat, as did the Duke of Wellington, as attributable to the "grossest treachery and the most inconceivable imbecility." While other factors such as the weather, terrain, Afghan tenacity, and the mistaken belief that Shuja would command considerable support had also contributed to the disaster, since British forces always routed *lashkars* before, and soon did so again, the defeat would, indeed, seem an anomaly. The mutual bitterness that remained, however, would poison Anglo-Afghan relations and color the image of Afghanistan in other parts of the world well into the next century.[24]

The British emerged from the war with little but contempt for the Afghans. Throughout the next century, historians, poets, and novelists alike persistently attributed the British failure to flaws in Afghan character. Though a few Britons lauded Afghan military prowess, others found guerrilla tactics less than manly and derided the Afghans for not following European battlefield etiquette. Most decried the Afghans as sadists, who delighted in practicing hideous tortures upon their innocent victims. Many writers accentuated the stripping and mutilation of the dead, acts that seem to have repulsed the British more than the actual killings. The most commonly invoked derisive trait was sheer treachery. Many berated Akbar, who in their minds had not only been responsible for the murders of Burnes and MacNaughton but also agreed to the retreat, only to unleash the Ghilzais upon the column.[25]

The hardships imposed by the invasion and the atrocities committed by the "Army of Retribution" left the Afghans with similar animosities toward the British that would together preclude harmonious Anglo-Afghan relations. This resentment would increase when the British annexed the Sikh dominions in 1848. The Sikh state had become unstable following the death of Ranjit Singh in 1839. The British soon engineered its demise. The British commander, General Hugh Gough, proved the chief obstacle to success. Another Napoleonic retread, this "antique warhorse . . . thought of artillery as unsporting, effete, tactically useless and otherwise a liability." His well-disciplined infantry carried him through First Sikh War in 1845, but heavy casualties left the army near the breaking point. Though the British attempted to support a rump state, war soon began anew. In an ironic role reversal, the Sikhs bargained with Dost, promising him Peshawar and the surrounding area in return for Afghan support. Gough's tactics continued to produce near-Pyrrhic victories, notably at Chillianwala, but finally, with his replacement imminent, Gough brought forward the despised artillery and routed a combined Sikh/Afghan force at Gujerat. The Afghans fell back ignominiously on Kabul. The British soon annexed the whole of the Sikh dominions, including Baluchistan and Pushtun-occupied areas claimed by Afghanistan. Their continued presence in these areas would lead to decades of conflict with the tribal inhabitants and the Afghans who supported them.[26]

NOTES

1. Griffiths, *Afghanistan,* pp. 26–29; Gregorian, *Emergence of Modern Afghanistan,* pp. 43–49.

2. Miller, *Khyber,* pp. xiv, 11–12. Afghanistan's internal difficulties are perhaps best demonstrated by the fate of Futeh Khan, elder brother of the future Amir Dost Mohammed. Though a loyal commander of the ruler of Herat, Futeh was punished for one of his brother's adulteries, by being "first blinded, then scalped, then had the skin

pared from his body as if from an apple, and then had his limbs amputated, after which he was allowed to expire."

3. For details of the economic decline during this period, see Gregorian, *Emergence of Modern Afghanistan,* pp. 50–58; see also Newell, *Politics of Afghanistan,* p. 117; MacMunn, "Real British Attitude toward Afghanistan," pp. 472–473.

4. Norris, *First Afghan War,* pp. 7–11, 15–17; Gregorian, *Emergence of Modern Afghanistan,* pp. 92–97; Tabibi, "Aftermath Created by British Policy," pp. 41–42.

5. Ali, *Afghanistan,* p. 8; Miller, *Khyber,* pp. 14–15; Gregorian, *Emergence of Modern Afghanistan,* pp. 73, 79–80, 127; Fraser-Tytler, *Afghanistan,* pp. 306–307.

6. Norris, *First Afghan War,* pp. 22–30, 40–42, 74–76.

7. Miller, *Khyber,* pp. 19–21; Gregorian, *Emergence of Modern Afghanistan,* pp. 95–99, 99fn, 102fn; Norris, *First Afghan War,* pp. 79–83. Palmerston's policy had detractors. They discounted the immediate importance of Herat or thought Russia too backward to be an immediate threat.

8. Miller, *Khyber,* pp. 13, 16; Ali, *Afghanistan,* p. 14; Norris, *First Afghan War,* pp. 109, 114. Some sources claim Akbar retreated owing to an ammunition shortage, others assert he advanced to the city but was repulsed, while still more maintain that his advisors persuaded him not to advance. Norris claims the battle was simply more of a draw than an Afghan victory.

9. Norris, *First Afghan War,* pp. 56–57, 70–71, 119–124; Ali, *Afghanistan,* pp. 15–17. Burnes had met Dost in 1832, had been favorably impressed, and had argued for closer relations even then.

10. Quoted in Miller, *Khyber,* pp. 26–28.

11. Norris, *First Afghan War,* pp. 91–92, 106–109, 114–115, 120–121, 131–134, 145–149; Barton, *India's North-West Frontier,* pp. 125–127; Gregorian, *Emergence of Modern Afghanistan,* pp. 98–101, 100fn. Dost's position on Peshawar and British demands upon him make for interesting comparisons with American efforts to obtain a Pushtunistan settlement. See chapters 8, 12, and 13.

12. Ali, *Afghanistan,* pp. 2, 21, 37; Norris, *First Afghan War,* pp. 61–63, 184–186, 192–193. It was to Auckland's credit that he sent a more sizable force than recommended.

13. Norris, *First Afghan War,* pp. 162–163, 179–180, 214–216; Griffiths, *Afghanistan,* pp. 31, 31fn; Miller, *Khyber,* pp. 19–20, 33–34.

14. Though he cites a few objections (p. 228, e.g.), Norris demonstrates that there was a consensus among British officials in support of Auckland's policy (*First Afghan War,* pp. 117–118, 165–168, 176–178, 190–191, 200–201, 211, 218, 248).

15. Schofield, *Every Rock,* pp. 70–71; Ali, *Afghanistan,* pp. 31–32; Norris, *First Afghan War,* pp. 251–252, 286–290.

16. Norris, *First Afghan War,* pp. 249, 254, 260, 271–273, 284, 297, 312. Mass desertions among Shuja's forces make for an interesting comparison with subsequent People's Democratic Party of Afghanistan efforts to establish an effective military.

17. Kaye, *History of the War,* pp. 548–549; Schofield, *Every Rock,* pp. 72–73; Gregorian, *Emergence of Modern Afghanistan,* pp. 119–122.

18. Norris, *First Afghan War,* pp. 332–336, 353–354, 361–362.

19. Miller, *Khyber,* pp. 46–47, 59; Norris, *First Afghan War,* pp. 365–369.

20. Kaye, *History of the War,* pp. 218–227. Kaye claims: "It was a mockery to talk of his [Elphinstone's] commanding . . . in the quietest district of Hindostan." Norris,

First Afghan War, pp. 337–339, 373–374; Miller, *Khyber,* pp. 51, 59–63; Schofield, *Every Rock,* pp. 74–75.

21. Norris, *First Afghan War,* pp. 374–377; Miller, *Khyber,* pp. 64–67; Ali, *Afghanistan,* p. 41. According to Ali's account, MacNaughton was "murdered with his own pistol by Afghans in self-defense." MacNaughton's head was carried through the streets on a pole and his trunk impaled on a meat hook and displayed in the bazaar.

22. Schofield, *Every Rock,* pp. 77–80; Ali, *Afghanistan,* pp. 44–46; Norris, *First Afghan War,* pp. 379–381. The surgeon, Dr. Brydon, would become famous in Lady Butler's celebrated painting "Remnants of an Army."

23. Kaye, *History of the War,* pp. 630–640; Sale, *Journal,* pp. 80–82; Ali, *Afghanistan,* pp. 47–48; Griffiths, *Afghanistan,* p. 34. According to Griffiths, General Knott's forces butchered "every man, woman and child within the village of Killah-Chuk" in retaliation for an ambush of a detachment of his men.

24. Norris, *First Afghan War,* pp. 321–322, 359–360, 381, 387, 390–391, 394–398, 409–417. Though it became politically vogue among the Whigs to attack Auckland for underestimating economic expenses, ignoring the Afghan will to resist, and overestimating the Russian threat, such criticism belies bipartisan support that accompanied initial implementation of his plan. Norris also claims the criticism masks the very real gains that the advance into Afghanistan facilitated in the Middle East and China, where the Russians proved acquiescent.

25. See, e.g., Schofield, *Every Rock,* pp. 77–78, 98, 113, 200, 210; Miller, *Khyber,* pp. 69, 69fn, 74–77, 180–182, 188–189. Though some eyewitnesses claimed Akbar was distressed by the attacks and believed he could not control the Ghilzais' desire to exterminate every invader, other sources claim he encouraged the slaughter. Akbar's complicity remains a matter of question. Those who argue favorably note his protection of some 104 British officers, women, and children who surrendered along the march. The detractors of Akbar abhor the bribe that secured the prisoners' release and the extent of their captivity and accuse the Afghan prince of subjecting them to humiliation. Lady Sale noted how the local inhabitants cursed them routinely as he led them along the retreat route, rubbing their faces in the carnage. Yet Sale concluded that "Akbar said he would destroy the army and did, beyond that, he treated us well . . . honor has been respected."

26. Miller, *Khyber,* pp. 92–95; Schofield, *Every Rock,* p. 87; Ali, *Afghanistan,* p. 56; "Survey, Part III, The Indo-Afghan Frontier," L/P&S/12/1321.

2

BRITISH POLICY TOWARD AFGHANISTAN IN THE NINETEENTH CENTURY: THE SECOND ANGLO-AFGHAN WAR

Throughout the last century of the Romanov dynasty, Russia threatened the territorial integrity of Afghanistan, Persia, and the Ottoman Empire. At times, events in Europe and the Far East muted such threats. On occasion, they resulted in actual warfare. All three states lost sizable portions of territory, but fared better than the loosely organized *khanates* of Central Asia, many of which Russia absorbed over the course of the century.

In a manner reminiscent of the United States' westward march or Britain's seizure of Indian states, Russia justified the annexation of Asian territories as necessary actions to protect the border areas of civilization. Tsar Alexander II's foreign minister, Prince Alexander Gorchkov, explained:

The position of Russia in Central Asia is that of all civilized states which come into contact with half-savage, wandering tribes possessing no fixed social organization . . . the interests of security on the frontier, and of commercial relations, compel the more civilized state to exercise a certain ascendancy over neighbors whose turbulence and nomadic instincts render them difficult to live with. . . . We are compelled to reduce the tribes on our frontier to more or less complete submission. . . . in turn they are exposed to the aggression of more distant tribes. The state is obliged to defend them against these depredations. . . . The state . . . must abandon the incessant struggle and deliver its frontier over to disorder . . . or it must plunge into the depths of the savage countries, where the difficulties and sacrifices to which it is exposed increase with each step in advance. . . . The greatest difficulty is in knowing where to stop. . . . The Imperial Government . . . must allow anarchy to become chronic which paralyses all security and progress and involves distant and expensive expeditions at frequent intervals; or on the other hand it must enter on a career of conquest and annexation such as gave England her Indian Empire.[1]

Gorchkov's statement helps clarify the roots of Anglo-Russian hostility in the nineteenth century. Britain was content with a hold on India. Limited interests in expansion were confined to areas whose occupation would further protect the subcontinent and its trade. Russian aggrandizement, however, seemed a direct threat to India and the Empire.

Contemporary sources give support to both those who claim aggressive intent and those who see Russian activities as mere diversions or acts of regional defense. For example, in interviews with a British journalist, several Russian officers acknowledged the logistical barriers to invasion, voicing their inability "to understand Britain's perpetual state of terror on the Indian frontier." Mikhail Skobelev, the supreme commander of Russian forces in Central Asia, claimed he would "not like to be the commander of such an expedition. The difficulties would be enormous. . . . To invade India we should need 150,000 troops, 60,000 to enter India, and 90,000 to guard communications." Yet Skobelev did not always maintain that posture. On another occasion, he noted simply: "The stronger Russia is in Central Asia, the weaker England is in India and the more conciliatory she will be in Europe." He would later conclude: "It will be in the end our duty to organize masses of Asiatic cavalry and hurl them into India as a vanguard, under the banner of blood and rapine, thereby reviving the times of Tamerlane."[2]

Lack of information and irrational analysis at times led British planners to rabid overestimations of the capabilities of Russian armies. British fears of a Franco-Russian invasion in 1807, for example, seem unjustified, given that Napoleon and Tsar Alexander I could hardly have kept an army supplied across over 2,000 miles of inhospitable terrain for a strike at India. Even by the late nineteenth century, after Russia had seized much of Central Asia, an assault on India would still have encountered tremendous logistical obstacles. The invading armies could have been supplied along only one single-track railway, extending from the Caspian Sea, across a distance of approximately 2,200 miles. British planners at times acknowledged the geographic considerations that always limited the chance of success of an invasion of India through Afghanistan. They could not, however, readily dismiss possibilities of Russian aggression. Russia was an absolute monarchy and had had more than its share of eccentric and illogical rulers, who at times had implemented policies that representative nations would never have seriously considered. Throughout the nineteenth and even into the twentieth century, the Russian press publicized several plans for an assault on the subcontinent.

Fears of a direct Russian invasion, however, were not the sole determinant of British defense policy in Southwest Asia. The possibility of unrest within India reinforced British desires to keep Russia as far from the subcontinent as possible. British planners feared a Russian presence in a border region, notably Afghanistan, from which propaganda could be used to incite rebellion among the Indian populace. Afghan strategy harmonized with British policy in desiring to keep the Russians as far north as possible. The legacy of war, however, caused many Afghan rulers to regard the British as an equal threat to their independence. Furthermore, most Afghans desired to repatriate at least the Pushtun areas of the Northwest Frontier, if not all the dominions of the Durrani Empire. Mutual suspicion and conflicting desires precluded extensive Anglo-Afghan cooperation for much of the nineteenth century. Continued border conflict also reinforced the opinions of many Britons who thought direct occupation of Afghanistan superior to allowing the Afghans to serve as surrogate guardians of India's northwestern frontier.

Anglo-Afghan relations had remained sour into the early 1850s. Dost Mohammed refused to normalize relations with Britain and kept busy trying to reduce the internal chaos unleashed by invasion. Britain was similarly sidetracked by domestic strife and foreign policy developments elsewhere. Dual isolationist policies left relations sullen and devoid of substantive diplomatic interchange.

Relations improved when fears of Russo-Persian aggression re-emerged adjunct to the Crimean War. In 1855 Dost's heir apparent, Ghulam Haider Khan, concluded a treaty with the British, in which the two nations essentially "agreed to have the same friends." In the following year, Persian armies seized Herat. Dost called upon his British allies, who declared war on Persia and forced a retreat. In January 1857, Dost signed a more comprehensive alliance, in which Britain guaranteed the integrity of Afghanistan and agreed to provide Dost an annual subsidy.[3]

Fortunately for the Empire, the alliance coincided with the Indian Mutiny of 1857. Several commentators have claimed that had Dost supported the mutiny with an invasion, he might have driven the British from the subcontinent. Lord Frederick Roberts, writing shortly after the events, thought that no "part of the country north of Bengal could have been saved." Fears of an Afghan invasion so alarmed Sir John Lawrence, then chief administrator of the Punjab (and soon to be viceroy), that he proposed restoring all lands west of the Indus to Dost. While such fears seem a bit exaggerated, an Afghan attack would certainly have increased British difficulties. Yet Dost, mindful of his own weaknesses and the Persian threat, remained faithful to the alliance. Dost turned over many deserters to British authorities, while hundreds of frontier Pushtuns enlisted in British militia, marched on Delhi, and assisted in crushing its defenders.[4]

The Anglo-Afghan détente, however, faded amidst the dynastic turmoil that followed Dost's death in March 1863. Since Akbar and Ghulam had preceded Dost in death and his two eldest surviving sons were not of noble bloodline, Dost designated the third eldest, Sher Ali, as successor. Eleven of Sher's fifteen brothers, including the elder ones, refused to accept this edict. Fratricidal war gripped Afghanistan until 1868.[5]

Amidst this turmoil, Britain pursued the so-called "closed border" policy and avoided active interference in Afghanistan. Its chief advocate, Lawrence, summed up its logic as follows:

We object to any active interference in Afghanistan . . . in as much as we think such a measure would, under present circumstances, engender irritation, defiance and hatred in the minds of the Afghans, without in the least strengthening our power either for attack or defense. . . . We think it impolitic and unwise to incur any of the difficulties which would be entailed on Russia, if that power seriously thought of invading India, as we should certainly decrease them if we left our frontier and met them halfway in a difficult country and possibly in the midst of a hostile or exasperated population. We foresee no limits to the expenditure which such a move might require, and we protest against the necessity of having to impose additional taxation on the people of India. . . . Should a foreign power, such as Russia, ever seriously think of invading India from the without or, what is more probable, of stirring up the elements of dissatisfaction or anarchy within it, our true policy, our strongest security, would then, we conclude, be found to lie in previous abstinence from entanglements at either Kabul, Kandahar, or any similar outpost.[6]

Lawrence essentially argued that occupation of Afghanistan would be so costly to the Russians as to virtually prohibit an invasion of India. It would therefore be foolish for Britain to attempt to conquer Afghanistan and incur the same difficulties.[7]

Criticism of the closed border policy grew as the frontier tribes continued to defy British authority.[8] Such criticism increased further with renewed Russian advances. Following the setbacks of the Crimean War, Alexander II again charted Russia on an expansionist course. The Central Asian *khanates* collapsed one by one. Tashkent was taken in 1865, Bokhara was forced to accept Russian suzerainty in 1866, and Samarkand fell in the spring of 1868. Though the indigenous people proved tough fighters, they were handicapped by the lack of protective terrain and undermined by political infighting between the regional states. The Russian high command did not shirk from employing barbaric measures to subdue them and to keep them pacified.[9]

Following the fall of Bukhara, the Russian press called for a drive on Herat. England voiced displeasure to St. Petersburg. After five years of sporadic negotiations, both nations signed an agreement in January 1873 that roughly defined the Russo-Afghan border along the Oxus. Within a few months, however, Russia was again on the move, occupying Khiva in 1873 and Khokand in 1875. Certain expansionists in St. Petersburg began to argue for an advance to the Hindu Kush, noting how occupation of northern Afghanistan would provide both a defensive frontier for Central Asia and a springboard for penetration into India.[10]

The British also began to reconsider their position. Sir Henry Rawlinson, a veteran of the First Anglo-Afghan War and an avowed Asian expert, came to champion a new "Forward Policy." In 1875 he published *England and Russia in the East,* which for the most part argued that Russian moves in Central Asia would ultimately lead them to Herat, "the key to India." Using Herat as a base, Russia would establish control over Afghanistan and foment revolution in India. Having portrayed Afghanistan as a gateway of danger, it followed that Rawlinson sought a safe defense in the occupation of Herat and the establishment of a forward boundary across the "scientific frontier" of the Hindu Kush. He also sought local peace through direct occupation of the frontier and "taming" of the Pushtun tribes.

England and Russia in the East demonstrates the vacillations and contradictions of British strategic discourse in Asia. At times, it declares a Russian invasion of India a near certainty. Later it discounts Russian designs on the subcontinent, claiming their advance in Asia a roundabout method of securing goals in Europe. Still, many influential politicians, especially among the Tories, became convinced that the security of India depended on extension of the frontier to the Hindu Kush, "the great natural boundary of India." Some called for the establishment of a major British garrison at Quetta and the courting of an Afghan alliance.[11]

Russian aggrandizement also aroused fears in Kabul. Though Sher Ali was among the most Anglophobic of Afghan rulers, the Russian advance nonetheless predisposed him to an arrangement with the British. In 1869 and again in 1873, Sher requested an agreement, to include an offensive and defensive alliance, an annual subsidy, acknowledgment of his ascendancy, and recognition of his son's similar right. The "closed border" viceroys, however, held firm to their policy of nonintervention. They offered Sher Ali a subsidy and the right to import weapons but, while claiming support for Afghan independence, refused to provide him assurances against Russian aggression. For his part, Sher Ali forbade the stationing of a British resident in Kabul, claiming popular resentment left him unable to guarantee the safety of an envoy.[12]

British policy changed following the election of Benjamin Disraeli's Tory ministry in 1874. Lord Salisbury, Disraeli's secretary of state for India, saw advantage in an alliance with Afghanistan. He directed the viceroy, Lord Lytton, to offer Sher Ali a guarantee against outside aggression and recognition of his favorite son, Abdullah Jan, as heir apparent. Lytton would also endeavor to establish permanent British diplomatic representation in Kabul.[13]

Lytton's tactless diplomacy, however, fired Sher Ali's volatile personality and soured potential partnership. Without requesting permission, Lytton sent notice to the amir that a diplomatic mission would soon arrive in Kabul. Sher Ali, already angered over a British-negotiated settlement of a border dispute that awarded much of the Seistan to Persia, ignored the mission. The British occupation of Quetta in 1876 would further anger the temperamental Afghan ruler. While designed to guard against a hypothetical Russian advance through Herat and the Bolan Pass, to Sher Ali the occupation seemed no less a threat to his independence than Russian moves to the north. The following year of "barely civil correspondence" increased Sher's anger to the point where he began to consider "the pros and cons of launching an anti-British *jihad*." Only renewed Russian pressure mitigated Sher's loathing for the British.[14]

In the spring of 1877, war broke out between Russia and the Ottoman Empire. The Russians soundly defeated the Turks and pressed for a humiliating peace, until a consortium of European powers, led by Britain and Germany, intervened. The decisions of the Berlin Conference eventually forced Russia to accept a more lenient peace.[15]

In the summer of 1878, however, the Russians disregarded earlier pledges to leave Afghanistan outside their sphere of influence and dispatched a diplomatic mission to Kabul, apparently in effort to influence the proceedings at the Congress of Berlin. There is no evidence that Sher Ali desired the Russian mission. In fact, he attempted to postpone its arrival. Repeated delays prevented the Russians from reaching Kabul until July 22, nine days after the Treaty of Berlin had been signed. The arrival of the mission, however, ultimately provoked the Second Anglo-Afghan war, though not before another series of misunderstandings and recriminating accusations between Lytton and Sher Ali.[16]

While the Russian mission was in Kabul, Abdullah Jan died. At this point, Lytton sent word to the amir, demanding diplomatic representation for Britain and threatening military action in the event of rejection. This turned Sher Ali's depression to rage. He ordered the British mission repulsed at his frontier. While the British determined their next move, the Russian envoy offered Sher Ali an agreement that promised: "if any foreign enemy attacks Afghanistan, and the Amir . . . asks the assistance of the Russian government, the Russian government will repel the enemy." Sher Ali accepted the secret Russian offer.[17]

In the meantime, Lytton proposed to eliminate any problem by invading and dismembering Afghanistan, establishing a scientific frontier in the process. Sher Ali's refusal to apologize and accept a British mission fired another round of mutual insults that gave Lytton the pretext to call for a declaration of war, which came on November 21, 1878. Russia, then isolated in Europe, did not wish to risk war with Britain and reneged on its commitment. Russian emissaries informed Sher Ali that the tsar deemed it "impossible to assist you with troops now." When the Russian mission left Kabul in December, Sher Ali departed with it, abdicating to his son, Yakub Khan.[18]

In May 1879, a three-pronged force invaded Afghanistan. Neither flanking group met serious resistance. The center group, commanded by Lord Roberts, overcame assorted logistical problems and difficult terrain to rout the defenders of Peiwar Kotal. Following the battle, Yakub, who had been imprisoned by his father for the last five years, met Roberts. Yakub's political position matched his physical infirmity. Having little other choice, he signed the Treaty of Gandomak on May 26, 1879.

Gandomak was the most humiliating treaty ever signed by an Afghan ruler. Ostensibly an alliance, the treaty promised Yakub a subsidy and assistance against outside aggression. But Yakub was also forced to acknowledge British annexation of the Khyber and Kurram Passes, the adjoining frontier districts, and Baluchistan. The British compelled Yakub to accept a permanent British resident in Kabul and to subjugate his foreign policy to their discretion, making him, in effect, their vassal.[19]

Gandomak officially ended the hostilities, and a British political mission, headed by Lord Louis Cavagnari, arrived in Kabul. Peace, however, proved illusory.[20] Several hundred Herati soldiers were stationed in the Afghan capital, and they had not been paid in a year. Though Lytton offered payment, Cavagnari, seemingly oblivious to the danger, turned down the offer. On September 2, he cabled to Lytton: "All well in the Cabul Embassy." Shortly thereafter, the Heratis attacked the residency. By nightfall of September 3, Cavagnari and the whole of his escort were dead.[21]

The British assembled an army of retribution that, after delays to round up its decommissioned pack animals, marched on Kabul. Roberts engaged a hastily assembled Afghan force at Charasia. The result was typical of clashes between a well-equipped, disciplined force and what is best described as an armed mob. Roberts's force, comprising Highland Scots, Ghurkas, and loyal Pushtun troops, routed the Afghans in a brief engagement. Three days later, they entered Kabul, whereupon Yakub abdicated.[22]

Roberts declared martial law and imposed harsh punishments upon the Kabulis. His purpose was twofold: as fitting punishment for "treachery and insult" and as insurance against recurrent uprisings. He ordered the Bala Hissar, "the symbol of the power of the Afghans," demolished. To make the Afghans pay for the occupation, he imposed heavy fines that drove many citizens to abject poverty. Roberts made frequent use of the death penalty. Some of the public hangings, such as those of the ringleaders of the attack on the residency, appear justifiable. Yet critics seem equally justified in condemning the execution of Afghans whose only crime was to resist invasion. To a certain extent, Roberts's Draconian methods sowed hatreds that led to a renewed siege in December 1879. Then again, those measures so weakened the Afghans as to ensure the survival of his force.[23]

While attempting to avoid an uprising, Roberts prepared for such a contingency. When rebellion materialized, he withdrew his forces within a formidable bastion at Sherpur, wherein he had stored enough supplies to last well into the next year. When an Afghan messenger demanded his surrender, Roberts, instead of begging for safe passage home, gave him "a Victorian version of McAuliffe's reply to the Germans at Bastogne." Eventually he launched a surprise attack that threw the Afghans into complete disarray. By the time a relief force arrived, Roberts was again in control of Kabul.[24]

Near-disaster at Maiwand Pass, near Qandahar, soon offset Roberts's success. On July 27, 1880, a 25,000-man Afghan force, commanded by another of Sher Ali's sons, Ayub Khan, attacked a British brigade one-tenth its size. That brigade, hobbled by oppressive heat, overladen pack animals, and a confused command structure, broke ranks under the onslaught. The brigade suffered some 1,100 casualties before reaching safety in Qandahar.[25]

Meanwhile, Gladstone's Liberal opposition had made use of the Afghan issue, among others, to oust Disraeli and with him Lytton. Gladstone's triumph led to abandonment of the Forward Policy. Following the uprising in Kabul, Lytton himself had come to favor a withdrawal from eastern Afghanistan, given a suitable replacement for Yakub. Abdur Rahman Khan seemed the only realistic alternative. The son of Afzal Khan and grandson of Dost Mohammed, Abdur Rahman had led troops against Sher Ali in the civil war of the 1860s, scoring three notable victories before finally being forced to flee to Samarkand. Abdur Rahman became disenchanted with Russia during his twelve-year exile and recrossed the Oxus, hoping to secure the throne. Lytton and his Liberal successors hoped this man of "violent temper . . . and forceful personality" would restore domestic tranquility to Afghanistan.[26]

In the aftermath of Maiwand, the British offered Kabul and its environs to Abdur Rahman. Though Abdur Rahman did not want a truncated state, he accepted the offer for the time being. He consigned his foreign policy to British tutelage and agreed to conduct diplomatic relations with them only, in return for British subsidies, a promise of nonintervention in Afghan internal affairs, recognition of the independence of the tribal belt between Afghanistan and India proper, and a "guarantee" against outside aggression. The British thereby assumed responsibilities they had repeatedly denied to Sher Ali.[27]

Despite his incantations regarding the rights of Afghans and the inhuman behavior of the Kabul garrison, Gladstone still allowed "Butcher Roberts" to strike at Ayub to restore British prestige in the Qandahar area. Roberts marched his force over 300 miles in just twenty-three days, through intense daytime heat and equally severe night cold, across some of the world's most forbidding terrain. Reaching Qandahar, he wasted little time in attacking Ayub, broke his fortified positions, and sent his army reeling toward Herat. The British forces suffered only minimal casualties. Roberts's stunning victory, however, could not rescue failed strategic policy.[28]

Despite an expert commander, appropriate tactics, suitable logistical preparations, and high-quality troops and equipment, the British had still failed to subdue the Afghans. Universal resentment of the populace to outside authority, coupled with their stamina and military prowess, promised only continued war for the occupying force. In March 1881, the British abandoned all ideas of a retained presence in Afghanistan and withdrew from Qandahar, leaving it to Abdur Rahman. They also offered him Herat, if he could conquer it from Ayub. Having apparently learned their lesson, the British would leave Afghanistan as a "buffer state." Though various issues would provoke future tensions between the two states, the evidence suggests that they never again seriously considered invading Afghanistan.

While the Second Anglo-Afghan War did modify policy, it did nothing to improve bilateral relations or Afghanistan's general reputation. British correspondence echoed that of the first war in deriding the Afghans as barbarians.

Sher Ali and the pathetic Yakub replaced Akbar Khan as objects of derision, with the former spurned as a treacherous ingrate and the latter berated as an ostensible ally turned traitor. Most Britons, in fact, believed that Yakub had delighted with the assault on the residency, "if not, as many believed, actually being party to it."[29]

The cumulative effects of the wars also produced lasting effects on Afghan society. Though always xenophobic to a degree, prior to the first war, the Afghans demonstrated no particular animosity toward Europeans. Diplomats and civilian travelers alike encountered pronounced hospitality and Islamic respect for Christian beliefs. The 1839 invasion, however, changed those attitudes, and the second reinforced them. Russian advances in Central Asia, meanwhile, aroused similar resentment and fears. By the end of the nineteenth century, Europeans would be "considered not only infidels, but also enemies who threatened Afghan independence."[30]

The Anglo-Afghan wars left a legacy of hatred and suspicion, reaffirmed strong tribal and religious influence in the affairs of state, and ensured continued outrages along the frontier. The wars also brought economic hardships, eventually prompting most educated Afghans to blame the British for the country's continued backwardness. Despite common fears of the Russians, the residue of popular anti-British prejudice would limit cooperation well after the ruling elite had adopted a more favorable stance.[31]

NOTES

1. Prince Gorchkov's Statement of 21 November 1864, quoted in Fraser-Tytler, *Afghanistan*, pp. 319–320.

2. Gregorian, *Emergence of Modern Afghanistan*, pp. 108–111. Citing many Russian sources, he claims that even cautious leaders who discounted invasion of India as utterly impractical recognized the propaganda value of such suggestions. Miller, *Khyber*, pp. 147–152, 232–234. An engineering officer told the British journalist: "You give so much attention to the fact of certain centers being what you call 'keys,' that you altogether overlook the vast distances separating them from the places they are supposed to protect."

3. Ali, *Afghanistan*, pp. 57–60.

4. Gregorian, *Emergence of Modern Afghanistan*, pp. 84–85, 104; Wolpert, *Roots of Confrontation*, pp. 58–59; Arnold, *Afghanistan*, pp. 4–5; Barton, *India's North-West Frontier*, p. 131; Fraser-Tytler, *Afghanistan*, p. 307; Miller, *Khyber*, pp. 122, 126–127, 130–135. Herbert Edwardes had proposed a similar course several years earlier. Lawrence had then opposed the idea, claiming the Afghans, whose "name is faithlessness, even among themselves," would not uphold the treaty. Now, Edwardes dissuaded Lawrence, arguing that such an offer would only whet Dost's appetite and guarantee invasion.

5. Schofield, *Every Rock*, p. 93; Barton, *India's North-West Frontier*, p. 133. Akbar and Ghulam died in 1846 and 1858, respectively.

6. Quoted in Ali, *Afghanistan*, pp. 67–68.

7. Curiously, Lawrence's policy was based as much on loathing for the Afghans as a rational assessment of the military situation. Though some politicians and military men favored actively cultivating the friendship of Afghanistan, Lawrence demurred, noting: "I do not myself see how a truly friendly feeling can be established between the Afghans and the English government in India, when we bear in mind the character of these people and the history of our connection with them during the last thirty years." See Gregorian, *Emergence of Modern Afghanistan*, pp. 103–107.

8. Fletcher, *Afghanistan*, p. 246; Qureshi, *Anglo-Pakistan Relations*, p. 184; Khalizad, *Security of Southwest Asia*, p. 135; Barton, *India's North-West Frontier*, pp. 56–57, 93–94. The outrages of the tribes prompted British authorities to launch forty expeditions against them between 1849 and 1879 alone.

9. According to Skobelev: " I hold it as a principle that in Asia the duration of the peace is in direct proportion to the slaughter you inflict on the enemy." Quoted in Miller, *Khyber*, p. 232. See also Gorchkov's statement of 21 November 1864, quoted in Fraser-Tytler, *Afghanistan*, pp. 319–323: "Asiatics respect only visible and palpable force." Barton, *India's North-West Frontier*, p. 59; Schofield, *Every Rock*, p. 93.

10. Gregorian, *Emergence of Modern Afghanistan*, pp. 108–111. General D.A. Milutin headed the expansionist group.

11. "Survey of Anglo-Afghan Relations, Part III, The Indo-Afghan Frontier," L/P&S/12/1321; Miller, *Khyber*, pp. 150–155, 165; Gregorian, *Emergence of Modern Afghanistan*, pp. 107, 141. Sir Bartle Frere was another Forward Policy advocate. Rawlinson believed Indian hostility to Britain ran deep: "It may truly be said that we are living upon a volcano in India, which at any moment may explode and overwhelm us."

12. "Survey of Anglo-Afghan Relations, Part III, The Indo-Afghan Frontier," L/P&S/12/1321; Gregorian, *Emergence of Modern Afghanistan*, pp. 89, 106–108; Ali, *Afghanistan*, pp. 62–63, 79; Tabibi, "Aftermath Created by British Policy," p. 48; Barton, *India's North-West Frontier*, pp. 131–132.

13. Ali, *Afghanistan*, p. 71; Miller, *Khyber*, pp. 159–60; Dupree, *AUFS*, IV/3, p. 7; Gregorian, *Emergence of Modern Afghanistan*, pp. 109–112. Disraeli considered Russian advances in Central Asia decoys designed to obtain the real objective of the Turkish straits but nonetheless thought strength in India a tremendous asset for Britain.

14. In 1876 Sher sent an emissary, Said Nur Mohammed, to Peshawar. Said repeatedly insulted the British representatives, arrogantly implying that protection of Afghanistan was their duty while insisting that diplomatic representation in Kabul was out of the question. As fate would have it, the elderly Said died during the "negotiations." Sher, suspecting foul play, flew into a rage and again considered the possibility of war with Britain. Lytton, believing Sher in contact with the Russians, broke off contact with Afghanistan. "Survey of Anglo-Afghan Relations, Part II," L/P&S/12/1321; Miller, *Khyber*, pp. 160–163; Ali, *Afghanistan*, pp. 74–81.

15. Gregorian, *Making of Modern Afghanistan*, pp. 112–113, 112fn. The British attempted to use the offices of the Turks, who had long been interested in the establishment of an anti-Russian Islamic pact, to succor alliance with Afghanistan. A Turkish mission, calling Russia "the enemy of all Mohammedian states," tried to ease the amir's Anglophobia, to no avail. Sher wrote: "The English look to nothing but their own interests and bide their time. Whosoever's side they see strongest for the time they turn to him as their friend. I will not waste precious life in entertaining false hopes from the English and will enter into friendships with other governments."

16. Dupree, *AUFS*, IV/3, p. 8; Kakar, *Afghanistan*, pp. 9–11. Though certifiable in his Anglophobia (which likely originated in childhood experiences between 1839 and 1842), Sher was not a Russophile. Kakar claims he called them "self-centered devils." See also Ali, *Afghanistan*, p. 92; Gregorian, *Making of Modern Afghanistan*, pp. 113–114, 113fn.

17. Miller, *Khyber*, pp. 165–168; Ali, *Afghanistan*, pp. 83–88.

18. Kakar, *Afghanistan*, p. 11; Ali, *Afghanistan*, pp. 93, 124. Sher died the following February in Mazar-i-Sharif, according to Ali, "of a broken heart."

19. Ali, *Afghanistan*, pp. 74, 97–98, 125; Tabibi, "Aftermath Created by British Policy," p. 49; Miller, *Khyber*, pp. 170–173; Kakar, *Afghanistan*, p. 12.

20. Ali, *Afghanistan*, p. 100; Miller, *Khyber*, pp. 174–182; Schofield, *Every Rock*, pp. 95–97. Roberts noted that the Afghans "had not had the sense of defeat sufficiently driven into them. [A] peace made now, before they had been thoroughly beaten, would not be a lasting one, and would only end in worse trouble in the near future." Fearing the fates of Cavagnari and the mission, Roberts, when called upon to make a toast, "could scarcely utter a word." Lawrence is alleged to have uttered on their departure: "They will all be murdered every one of them."

21. The siege of the Kabul residency witnessed among the most incredible displays of heroism and audacity ever put on by troops of the Empire. A force of perhaps eighty made the siege a British version of the Alamo, dispatching many times their number of Heratis with shot, sword, and bayonet. After holding off the attackers for hours, they charged thrice into the face of fire in a vain effort to capture two field guns. The Heratis eventually overwhelmed the defenders, but not before suffering roughly 600 casualties. Not surprisingly, a huge bronze statue of the commanding officer is one of the most imposing sculptures in the Royal Army Museum, Chelsea.

22. Miller, *Khyber*, p. 191; Ali, *Afghanistan*, p. 101; Sykes, "Afghanistan: The Present Position," p. 143.

23. Miller, *Khyber*, pp. 192–193; Ali, *Afghanistan*, pp. 103–104; Kakar, *Afghanistan*, p. 13. Roberts's actions were not entirely negative. For example, he supplied Kabuli medical needs at a hospital and dispensary. He also maintained the discipline of his forces, avoiding the debauchery that fueled the 1841 uprising.

24. Miller, *Khyber*, pp. 193–200; Schofield, *Every Rock*, pp. 98–99. Roberts's tactical abilities, his attention to logistics, and his knowledge of the fundamental connections between politics and strategy deserve his ranking among Britain's finest soldiers. Unlike many of them, he also knew how to improvise. He kept his troops well trained and spirited, and they in turn respected him. Perhaps "no general ever commanded so much loyalty and personal devotion as did 'Bobs.'"

25. Miller, *Khyber*, pp. 208–210; Ali, *Afghanistan*, p. 116. Maiwand now tends to be remembered for one of three anecdotal episodes: (1) The fictional Dr. Watson was supposedly wounded there. (2) A white mongrel mascot named Bobby barked defiantly at the head of its battalion, until they had all been killed or fled. Wounded and taken prisoner, Bobby was later repatriated and received a medal from Queen Victoria personally for his gallantry. (3) An Afghan girl named Malalay made a flag of her veil and led the Afghans forward in Joan of Arc fashion, shouting: "My love! If you do not taste the martyrdom of the field of Maiwand, by God you will have to lead an ignominious life."

26. Miller, *Khyber*, pp. 203–205; Kakar, *Afghanistan*, p. 6; Schofield, *Every Rock*, p. 100; Barton, *India's North-West Frontier*, pp. 140–141.

27. Kakar, *Afghanistan,* pp. 51–53; Schofield, *Every Rock,* p. 100; Gregorian, *Making of Modern Afghanistan,* pp. 115–117.

28. Miller, *Khyber,* pp. 211–217. Night cold was especially tough on the poor Scots, "whose kilts were an open invitation to frostbite in the most sensitive parts of their anatomy" Ali, *Afghanistan,* pp. 118–119. The battle took place on September 1, 1880.

29. Kakar, *Afghanistan,* p. 18. Though accused of being "indifferent to the fate of the envoy and his companions," it subsequently came to light that Yakub has sent his son and his commander-in-chief, among others, in effort to dissuade the Heratis, but all had been unsuccessful.

30. Gregorian, *Emergence of Modern Afghanistan,* pp. 118–119, 345; Barton, *India's North-West Frontier,* pp. 150–151, 277.

31. MacMunn, "Real British Attitude toward Afghanistan," p. 475. Even this die-hard imperialist admitted the wars left a regrettable trail of hatred behind them. Squire, "Afghanistan and Her Neighbors," p. 70; Quddus, *Afghanistan and Pakistan,* p. 32; Gregorian, *Emergence of Modern Afghanistan,* pp. 126–127.

3

---•◦•◦•---

THE REIGN OF ABDUR RAHMAN: AFGHANISTAN AS A "BUFFER STATE"

Abdur Rahman took over a state that had once again fallen into anarchy. In his own words: "The first thing I had to do was to put an end to these numberless robbers, thieves, false prophets, and trumpery kings. I must confess that it was not an easy task, and it took 15 years of fighting before they finally submitted to my rule or left the country, either by being exiled or by departing to the next world."[1]

Abdur Rahman executed his political opponents, as well as common criminals, through a variety of methods deliberately designed to frighten other would-be troublemakers into submission. His methods allegedly included "throwing down mountain-side . . . cutting in pieces . . . hanging by hair and skinning alive . . . boiling woman to soup and man drinking it before execution . . . burying alive . . . throwing into soap boilers . . . tying to bent trees and disrupting . . . blowing from guns" and other methods that "cannot be described." Minor offenders, if not blinded, amputated, or punished through exposure and starvation, received "sewing together of upper and lower lips, rubbing snuff in the eyes, [or] hanging by heels for a week." Even Afghan writers question Abdur Rahman's excessive penalties and lack of mercy. More often than not, his intrigues and his cruelties overshadowed his accomplishments, and, along with continued tribal incursions into the settled districts of India, maintained the negative popular image of Afghanistan in the West.[2]

Moral repugnance, however, should not mask Abdur Rahman's achievement of restoring domestic order to Afghanistan. He established a strong absolutist government, in which his power was restrained only by his own devotion to the Shari'a. The "Iron Amir" created a civil service, a police force, and an extensive system of informants who kept him abreast of threatening developments. He maintained a consultative inner council, composed primarily of the sons of regional officials, which served not only as a gauge of popular opinion but also as a cache of hostages that ensured the loyalty of the provincial chieftains. He attacked the policies of the uneducated Afghan *mullahs* and ultimately forced them to pass examinations before allowing them to perform state functions. He exploited tribal rivalries, matrimonial alliances, and religious differences to strengthen his influence. On one occasion, he ordered the forced migration of thousands of Ghilzais to the north, not only to weaken them, but to also undermine the strength of the Tajiks.[3]

Most importantly, Abdur Rahman strove to form a dependable national army. Earlier monarchs, as well as the tribesmen themselves, had recognized the need to adopt European military technology. Dost Mohammed had hired European officers who imposed regimental organization, introduced uniforms, and formed specialty units of artillery, cavalry, and musketeers. Their overall impact, however, was minimal. The army remained of feudal character, its resources limited, its troops ill-disciplined conscripts, and its officers political loyalists rather than trained professionals. Sher Ali likewise endeavored to modernize his army, promoting increased domestic armaments production, furthering organizational reform, and sponsoring the translation of military textbooks into Pashto. Through use of British subsidies, he increased the army to three times the size of Dost's and instituted regular payment for the troops, but the outbreak of war with Britain terminated his embryonic programs.[4]

While aware that a modern military establishment would increase his nation's deterrent, Abdur Rahman did not need an army to protect Afghanistan's borders. The people themselves could ensure continued Afghan independence. A modern standing army would instead provide a source of domestic power with which to ensure tranquility at home. Though he inherited a force "weak in administration, discipline, logistics, and armaments," by the mid-1880s, Abdur Rahman had created an army of some 50,000 to 60,000 men that, while perhaps incapable of a successful campaign against a foreign power, was superior to any tribal *lashkar*. Organized into divisions, brigades, and regiments of infantry, cavalry, and artillery, it was supported by logistical depots at Kabul, Qandahar, and Herat and a small domestic war industry. Led by the "Red Chief," Ghulam Haider Charkhi, the army conducted some fourteen major sorties against internal opposition during the course of Abdur Rahman's reign, proving a critical element in the amir's efforts to restore central authority in Afghanistan.[5]

In 1886 Charkhi's forces crushed a rising of the Ghilzais and pacified eastern Afghanistan. Abdur Rahman then forced the tribes that remained recalcitrant to migrate to the north. The following year, the amir's cousin, Ishaq Khan, attempted to usurp the throne but, following a defeat, fled across the Oxus. In the early 1890s, Abdur Rahman invoked Sunni-Shi'a hatreds to promote a pacification campaign in the Hazarajat. Many of the vanquished Hazaras were sold into slavery after the brutal campaign, which contributed greatly to the modern legacy of ethnic prejudice in central Afghanistan. The coup de grace came in 1896, when the army conquered Kafirstan (later of Kipling fame). Abdur Rahman never "became king" (his son, Habibullah, would be declared king of Afghanistan in a 1905 treaty with Britain), but he forcibly converted the inhabitants to Islam, renaming the area Nuristan.[6]

Cognizant of Afghanistan's impotence relative to Russia and India, but aware of his country's value to both, Abdur Rahman maintained a neutral foreign policy. Though he distrusted the British, he despised the Russians, whom he thought Islamophobes. Believing Russian aggression more likely than a third British invasion, he accepted British control of his foreign affairs in exchange for subsidies that allowed him to build his army. It was, in his own words, "better to be a pawn of London and Calcutta than a serf of St. Petersburg."[7]

Despite this limited correlation of strategic goals, Abdur Rahman avoided extensive involvement with London and Delhi. He did not accept British offers to send military instructors to Afghanistan and refused to dispatch his officers abroad, fearing they would acquire European vices or, worse, loyalties to alien interests. He warned (in words prophetic to those familiar with the 1979 Soviet invasion) that "a neighboring power, by offering military officers from its army, under the pretense of teaching the Afghan soldiers British military tactics, might also teach them to attend to foreign interests."[8]

With maintenance of national independence his overriding goal, Abdur Rahman adopted isolationism as the basis of his policy. He reasoned that by avoiding contact with modernizing influences, Afghanistan would remain undesirable and hence safe from foreign incursion. According to the Amir:

Many of my officials who think themselves very wise keep on advising me to introduce railways and telegraphs, saying that it is impossible to get the full benefit of the minerals and other products. But I again advise my sons and successors not to listen to these people. Of course, I know myself that what they say is quite true, but, at the same time, they do not consider that by making the country easily accessible, foreign powers would not find so much difficulty in entering and spreading themselves over our country. The greatest safety of Afghanistan lies in its natural impregnable position. Allah has given us every peak of the mountains for a fortress of nature, and foreigners know that the Afghans, being born warriors, can go on fighting for ever and ever, as long as they can hide themselves behind the stones and do not have to face the enemy in the open field. There is no doubt that the day will come when railways and telegraphs will be most beneficial, and when they will be welcomed in the country, and that day will be when we see that we have a great army, strong enough to fight our neighbors, but until we are strong enough to hold our own, we must not weaken the strength of our hilly country with our own hands. We must not make the mistake once made by the man who killed the goose that laid golden eggs every day, thinking that he would get all the eggs at once, which he did not."[9]

Fearing limitations on his autonomy, Abdur Rahman refused to allow Britain to station diplomatic personnel in Kabul and spurned most of their offers of development aid. Though he wanted to improve the economy, he refused to sanction any measures that threatened his sovereignty. Most notably, he rejected plans to extend the Indian railway and telegraph systems to Afghanistan, believing such would expedite a British or Russian invasion.[10]

In keeping out modernizing influences, Abdur Rahman, unlike the Indian princes, preserved complete internal autonomy, without British residents or garrisons. Yet, Afghanistan still suffered many of the disadvantages of colonialism without accruing any of the benefits. Unlike India and Pakistan, to which Britain left a modern transportation infrastructure, a professional civil service and a disciplined military establishment, Afghanistan underwent little forced modernization and remained economically and bureaucratically backward. Abdur Rahman thus bequeathed a challenge to his successors: to find a method of modernization that would neither impose undue subservience to a foreign power nor risk domestic turmoil.

British policy toward Afghanistan remained a subdivision of its policy toward Russia. It mirrored the logic of the closed border system, in that the continued independence of the buffer states along the periphery of India was to be maintained, so as to keep Russia off the Indian glacis. That the buffer state idea also harmonized with the Liberal refutation of aggressive war seems more a coincidence than a foundation of policy. Despite periodic fulminations on the rights of the Afghans, Gladstone and his Whig opponents alike recognized the value of India to the British Empire and did not intend to endanger it. During the last decades of the nineteenth century, successive British governments proved willing to allow Afghanistan's borders to be redrawn repeatedly in order to protect vital interests.[11]

Following the British retreat from Qandahar, a new round of Russian expansion in Central Asia tested Anglo-Afghan relations. In February 1884, the Russians annexed Merv. Barely 150 miles from the Afghan border, Merv was another of Rawlinson's "keys" to the defense of India. Its fall aroused considerable popular excitement ("Mervousness") in London. The Gladstone government dispatched an emissary to St. Petersburg, who obtained the assurance that a future Anglo-Russian border commission would delineate Afghanistan's "inviolate" northern border. The respite was temporary. In March 1885, heedless of British warnings, the Russians moved against Panjdeh oasis. The Afghan defenders, outnumbered and outgunned, fought bravely, but the tsarist troops overwhelmed them. Russian newspapers called for a drive on Herat.[12]

General preparations began for what seemed an inevitable war between Russia and Great Britain. Gladstone, chastising the Russian aggression, obtained a 6.5-million-pound war credit. Two Indian army corps were mobilized and directed to the Afghan frontier. The British sent weapons to the Afghans, increased Abdur Rahman's subsidy, and dispatched engineers to bolster the defenses of Herat. Neither great power, however, desired a confrontation that could have precipitated a global war. Following the election of a Conservative ministry in June 1885, Russia was offered a diplomatic escape. Britain ignored their guarantee of Afghan integrity and independence and ceded Turkestan to Russia, securing peace through the sacrifice of Afghan territory. Abdur Rahman, beset with internal troubles, was powerless to oppose the settlement.[13] Throughout the next two decades, more European-staffed boundary commissions further delineated Afghanistan's borders. Abdur Rahman forfeited more territory and gained only the unwanted Wakhan corridor, a narrow strip of mountains that permanently separated India and Russia, as recompense.[14]

In 1893 the British sent Sir Henry Mortimer Durand, foreign secretary to the government of India, to meet with Abdur Rahman and define India's border with Afghanistan. That November, the two nations signed an agreement that called for its delineation. Essentially a ratification of the Treaty of Gandomak, the resultant Durand Line divided the Pushtun tribes roughly (and sometimes literally) in half. Whether viewed from a perspective of regional economics, ethnography, or basic geography, the line seems illogical. The line has only recently functioned as an international border in a modern sense. Heretofore the inhabitants of the area routinely crossed the border unfettered.[15]

In his autobiography, Abdur Rahman repeatedly states that he never considered any Pushtun areas permanently ceded to Britain and thought the resultant border but a temporary assignment of spheres of influence. His signature can be attributed to two factors. First, the British offered to increase his allowances of money and weapons. Second, Abdur Rahman felt compelled to comply. British forces had already occupied some frontier villages, and the Viceroy Lord Landsdowne had refused to allow any more arms deliveries to Afghanistan, barring agreement. Beset by domestic disturbances, Abdur Rahman could not risk renewed conflict with Britain. Other analysts add that Abdur Rahman's acceptance should be in part attributed to confusion. Fraser-Tytler, for example, suggests he "did not really take in all the implications of the line drawn on the map before him, but was too conceited to say so."[16]

The agreement did nothing to alleviate British difficulties with the tribes. Regarding the trans-Durand tribal regions as Afghanistan irridenta, Abdur Rahman attempted to exert limited authority over the area. He also desired to acquire access to the sea through restoration of Baluchistan to his dominions. Despite official friendship with Britain and written assurances against interference, Abdur Rahman constantly intrigued with the tribes throughout his reign, prompting riots, raids, and sometimes full-scale rebellion.[17]

The Pushtuns remained vulnerable not only to the amir's exhortations but also to the incantations of assorted *pirs, faqirs,* and *mullahs* throughout the history of the frontier. Intertribal feuding usually ensured that those intent on violence could recruit members of a war party for limited engagements.

Intertribal jealousies, however, also curtailed the extent of authority and usually prohibited extensive uprisings. In 1897, however, a certain Saddullah, known to the British as the "Mad Mullah," incited the greatest frontier uprising to date. Pushtun tribesmen flocked to the standards of this leader, who claimed the ability to turn British bullets to water and stop cannon with the wave of a hand and whose thirteen-year-old traveling companion claimed to be the last descendant of the Moguls. Within a few weeks, Saddullah's forces had overrun several British-Indian outposts, besieged others, and prompted desertions of many militia units.[18]

A composite group of British-Indian troops, dubbed the Malakand Field Force, marched to relieve the besieged forces. The tribes held a numerical advantage and fought on familiar terrain, and the British faced severe logistical obstacles. Still, the Pushtuns could not withstand the onslaught of well-disciplined troops. The British forces, equipped with modern artillery, machine gun detachments, and the new Lee-Enfield rifle, routed the tribesmen in open battle. When the Pushtuns resorted to guerrilla tactics, General William Lockhart responded with a scorched earth campaign. Lockhart's seizure of tribal herds and flocks proved decisive, forcing the *jirgahs* to surrender. The five-month campaign temporarily checked tribal military power but at a cost of 1,150 British and Indian casualties.[19]

Similar campaigns occurred frequently during the last fifty years of British rule on the frontier, prompting effort to bring tranquility to the region. Not long after the Saddullah campaign, on November 9, 1901, the Viceroy Lord Curzon detached the Pushtun areas from the civil administration of the Punjab and created the North West Frontier Province (NWFP). He divided the province between the settled districts, which were administered much like any other area in India, and the "tribal areas." He withdrew British garrisons from the latter, leaving them to British-officered tribal militia. Specially appointed political agents attempted to maintain the peace in the tribal areas, while keeping the army garrisons in the settled districts abreast of threatening developments. Curzon summoned Lord Kitchener, fresh from victories in the Sudan and South Africa, to reorganize the Indian army. Kitchener implemented a rotation policy that improved the combat readiness of the troops who garrisoned the frontier, while his program of road building allowed the garrisons to react quickly to any tribal threat.[20]

Though Curzon's administration imparted a number of benefits to the Pushtuns, uprisings occurred throughout the first decade of the twentieth century that rivaled previous ones. British forces remained in a perpetual state of war with the tribes. Though punitive expeditions always achieved their immediate military objectives, they also aroused resentment and lust for revenge and left the tribesmen even more unwilling to accept British policies, even when in their immediate interest.

British efforts to subdue the tribal territories perpetuated Anglo-Afghan prejudice and helped preclude rapprochement. Their relationship remained peculiar and satisfactory to neither state. The Viceroy Lord Morley explained the dichotomy of Anglo-Afghan relations circa 1900:

> The extraordinary and unparalleled anomaly of the relations with Afghanistan and the British government has often been described: how we are bound to defend the Amir's country, yet are forbidden to take a single step for defense within its border . . . how we give the Amir an annual subsidy of 18 lakhs, yet are not allowed to place a European agent at his capital; . . . how even our advice is resented; how we give the Amir arms . . . yet must make the best of much unfriendly behavior. . . . Evidently so singular a position is only tolerated or upheld for peculiarly strong reasons, arising from the belief in the minds of Afghan and British rulers equally that each of them requires and receives some valuable considerations from the other.[21]

British policy in northwest India had evolved into a three-tiered proposition, all of which involved the maintenance of sizable garrisons near the frontier. On the strategic level, British forces remained a deterrent to Russian ambitions in the region. On the local, tactical level, those same forces served to guard the settled districts of the Indus Valley from tribal outrages. Finally, British garrisons could also be called upon to confront a frontier-wide *jihad*. Overall policy toward Afghanistan, however, presented British planners with a difficult dilemma. On the one hand, since Afghanistan provided a buffer between Russia and India, Britain wanted Afghanistan sound and able to stand up to Russian aggression. On the other hand, Britain did not want Afghanistan so strong that it would, in conjunction with the tribes, threaten India itself. The vacillations in British policy evident through the ensuing half century stem from these conflicting objectives.

Abdur Rahman's isolationism found favor in some circles in Delhi and London. While Forward Policy advocates long favored extending the Indian railroad and telegraph systems to Kabul and Qandahar, later authorities rejected a number of schemes for the integration of Afghanistan into the subcontinent communications network, fearing such would make a Russian invasion feasible and more tempting. A poor Afghanistan, dependent on India, seemed preferable to a prosperous one that might prove recalcitrant or a target for Russian aggression. Other officials further opposed measures that strengthened Abdur Rahman's regime, arguing that the stronger the tribes and the weaker the central authorities, the greater the deterrent value of Afghanistan. Speaking in 1905, the prime minister summarized these views, adding logistical considerations:

> Russia is making steady progress towards Afghanistan and railways [are] under construction which could only be strategic. . . . A war on the North-West Frontier would be chiefly a problem of transport and supply. We must therefore allow nothing to be done to facilitate transport. Any attempt to make a railway in Afghanistan in connection with the Russian strategic railways would be regarded as an act of direct aggression against us. . . . As long as we say resolutely that railways in Afghanistan should only be made in time of war, we can make India absolutely secure. But if, through blindness

or cowardness, we permit the slow absorption of the country, if strategic railways are allowed to creep close to our Frontier, we shall have to maintain a much larger army.[22]

Given these preclusions, shared by both Afghans and Britons, and continued frontier outrages, there remained little incentive for extensive Anglo-Afghan cooperation.

NOTES

1. Quoted in Wilber, *Afghanistan,* p. 166. "I had to put in order all those hundreds of petty chiefs, plunderers, robbers, and cutthroats who were the cause of everlasting trouble in Afghanistan." Abdur Rahman, *Life of Abdur Rahman,* II, p. 177.

2. Miller, *Khyber,* pp. 223–226, quoting a chapter from a work by Frank Martin, the chief engineer to Abdur Rahman. See also Ali, *Afghanistan,* pp. 132, 141; Barton, *India's North-West Frontier,* p. 135. Barton claims the *chahi siyah* (black well) was the worst torture, wherein victims were left to die among corpses, reptiles, and vermin, with food and water lowered at intervals to prolong the agony. Gregorian (*Emergence of Modern Afghanistan,* p. 138fn) chronicles amputations and mutilations and one case of a man who outraged a woman and was thereafter frozen into an icicle. The amir remarked, "He would never be too hot again."

3. Abdur Rahman, *Life of Abdur Rahman,* II, p. 190. "My sons and successors should not try to introduce new reforms of any kind in such a hurry as to set the people against their ruler, and they must bear in mind that in establishing a constitutional government, introducing more lenient laws, and modeling education upon the system of Western universities, they must adopt all these gradually as the people become accustomed to the idea of modern innovations, so that they will not abuse the privileges and reforms given to them." Kakar, "Trends in Modern Afghan History," in Dupree and Albert, *Afghanistan in the 1970's,* p. 15; Fraser-Tytler, *Afghanistan,* p. 172; Franck, *Afghanistan between East and West,* p. 2; Gregorian, *Emergence of Modern Afghanistan,* pp. 132–135.

4. Gregorian, *Emergence of Modern Afghanistan,* pp. 74–78, 84–89, 88fn, 104, 127–128; Ali, *Afghanistan,* p. 72. Dost's army numbered approximately 15,000 men.

5. Gregorian, *Emergence of Modern Afghanistan,* pp. 140–141; Kakar, "Trends in Modern Afghan History," p. 15. Abdur Rahman allocated 50,000 ponies and pack mules for transport, and his army even had a band, complete with Scottish bagpipes.

6. Ali, *Afghanistan,* pp. 132–133. Had Ishaq Khan followed up when a wing of national troops broke, he could have carried the day. Charkhi, however, rallied his forces and broke the ranks of the insurgents. Abdur Rahman showed no mercy to the vanquished. Those of Ishaq's followers not killed outright were blinded with quicklime. For a detailed discussion of Abdur Rahman's campaigns, see Kakar, *Afghanistan.*

7. Abdur Rahman, *Life of Abdur Rahman,* II, pp. 175, 182. The Brititsh, Abdur Rahman wrote, "are really anxious to see Afghanistan a strong and independent Government—a true ally and barrier to protect the Indian Empire of their noble Queen." But "the Russians, quite contrary to the English, want to see Afghanistan divided into pieces and very weak, if not entirely cleared out of their way to India." See also pp. 260–271; Newell, *Politics of Afghanistan,* p. 48; Gregorian, *Emergence of Modern Afghanistan,* p. 125; Squire, "Afghanistan and Her Neighbors," p. 69.

8. Abdur Rahman, *Life of Abdur Rahman,* IIp. 196.

9. Abdur Rahman, *Life of Abdur Rahman,* II, pp. 77–78. See also Gregorian, *Emergence of Modern Afghanistan,* pp. 126, 153–155. "[Abdur Rahman's] hope was that Afghanistan's natural barriers and primitive communications, underdeveloped economy and political isolation, would be assets in preserving their independence. Inaccessibility, for instance, would permit the most effective use of the Afghan fighting forces and traditional tactics of warfare; difficult communications would make the operation of foreign armies in Afghanistan both costly and precarious; economic underdevelopment might deter the 'greedy temptations' of British India and Russia. At times, Abdur Rahman compared Afghanistan to a swan on a lake, with an "old tigress" (Britain) on one side and a pack of wolves (Russia) on the other. "The water is deep and Enshallah, will remain so." On another occasion, Afghanistan became a goat between a lion and a bear.

10. Newell and Newell, *Struggle for Afghanistan,* p. 36; Arnold, *Afghanistan,* p. 3; Barton, *India's North-West Frontier,* p. 140; Gregorian, *Emergence of Modern Afghanistan,* pp. 142–148, 155, 161; Ali, *Afghanistan,* p. 142; Miller, *Khyber,* p. 228. He did enact some modernist reforms. For example, he hired some foreign technicians, from nations with no overt political ambitions in the region, to explore Afghan mineral resources. He provided interest-free loans to enterprising Afghans who wished to start businesses and supported government workshops. Abdur Rahman also standardized the coinage, facilitated the collection of taxes, and improved road maintenance and the postal service. He built public toilets in Kabul and provided donkeys to remove the refuse from the city. He also ordered increased production of soap.

11. Miller, *Khyber,* pp. 203–205. While Almighty God might have been moved to profound grief and terrible anger by the British occupation of Afghanistan, it did not follow that He would fail to appreciate the vital necessity of protecting British India or that He was unable to bestow His blessing on the idea that Afghanistan remain a British sphere of influence.

12. Dupree, *AUFS,* 4/3, pp. 9–10; Sykes, "Afghanistan: The Present Position," p. 144; Miller, *Khyber,* pp. 233–234; Ali, *Afghanistan,* pp. 119, 136. Skobelev had earlier captured Geok Tepe, where his troops dispatched some 10,000 Turkomen women and children with edged weapons.

13. Ali, *Afghanistan,* pp. 135–136; Schofield, *Every Rock,* p. 105; Dupree, *Afghanistan,* pp. 422–423; Miller, *Khyber,* pp. 235–238.

14. For discussion of the boundary delineations, see Wilber, *Afghanistan,* pp. 174–177; Hyman, *Afghanistan under Soviet Domination,* pp. 39–40; Ali, *Afghanistan,* pp. 149–150; Dupree, *AUFS,* 4/3, pp. 9–11; Wakman, *Afghanistan,* pp. 8–9. The specific boundary along the Oxus itself was not specified, leading to several disputes, most notably in 1926, until in 1948 the *thalweg* became the official boundary.

15. Kaur, *Pak-Afghanistan Relations,* pp. 11–13. Britain's treaties with Dost Mohammed had agreed to respect his territorial integrity but did not specify a boundary. Fraser-Tytler, *Afghanistan,* p. 188; Wolpert, *Roots of Confrontation,* p. 66; Barton, *India's North-West Frontier,* p. 65. The line left the tribal areas unadministered and open to Afghan penetration, local and foreign intrigue, and arms traffic. The settled areas remained susceptible to raids into the plains (Caroe, *Pathans,* p. 382). Caroe is among the few who argue that the Durand Line "is far less arbitrary than it may appear," though even he admitted "the agreement did not describe the line as the boundary of India, but as the frontier of the Amir's dominions and the line beyond

which neither side would exercise interference." Curiously, the negotiations were carried out in secret, and no account of them was ever published. A more critical view appears in Arnold, *The Fateful Pebble*, p. 35fn. Arnold claims Durand "meandered his way from covey to covey of upland birds in pursuit of each day's sport and a just international boundary, in that order."

16. Wolpert, *Roots of Confrontation*, pp. 65–66; Khalizad, *Security of Southwest Asia*, pp. 137, 164fn; Barton, *India's North-West Frontier*, p. 138. Abdur Rahman wrote that "the Viceroy was so insistent on this matter that he addressed a letter to me which was practically an ultimatum to the effect that the Indian government cannot wait for indefinite promises of uncertain date" (Ali, *Afghanistan*, pp. 140–141). Ali claims the British threatened to use Ayub Khan, then resident in India, as a threat to Abdur Rahman's throne. Curiously, Abdur Rahman never signed a map delineating the Durand Line. Fraser-Tytler, *Afghanistan*, p. 188; Rahman, *Life of Abdur Rahman*, p. 158; Dupree, "Durand Line of 1893," pp. 79–80; Tabibi, "Aftermath Created by British Policy," p. 57; Kaur, *Pak-Afghanistan Relations*, pp. 25–27, 197. Kaur thinks confusion arose from language difficulties and differences on the concept of a boundary between a "feudal ruler" and a "modern nation state." Griffiths, *Afghanistan*, p. 57. Abdur Rahman also specified a number of areas to which he renounced his claims. It was important to later Pushtunistan disputes that historians could argue that the agreement was obtained under threat.

17. Abdur Rahman's desire to access to the sea can be noted in his own words (*Life of Abdur Rahman*, II, pp. 211–212): "Afghanistan ought to secure a footing upon the ocean, and have a port for its own steamers. . . . I always had a great fancy for a little piece of this sandy desert (Baluchistan), unimportant at present but of great value if annexed to Afghanistan in order to bring the country in touch with the ocean. . . . If the friendship now existing between Great Britain and Afghanistan grows in strength and becomes properly cemented . . . it would be very easy for her to give this little piece of land to the Afghan government . . . there is no doubt that the country would soon grow rich and prosperous, and it would never be wanting in gratitude to Great Britain for such a concession." Gregorian, *Emergence of Modern Afghanistan*, pp. 157–158. Abdur Rahman gave payments to tribal leaders and gifts of rifles and ammunition. One source claims he sold them 80,000 rifles, obtained through British subsidies. He wrote *Taqwim-ud-Din*, in which he stressed the importance of *jihad* in Muslim life, and held "theological seminars" in Kabul, at which he reveled in anti-British fulminations. Abdur Rahman never actually called for *jihad*, nor did the Afghan army ever join in an uprising. When the tribes did move, he turned his back: "What you have done with your own hands you must now carry on your own backs." Such actions allowed British agents to label him "duplicitous" and "faithless." Schofield, *Every Rock*, p. 110; Barton, *India's North-West Frontier*, p. 67; Miller, *Khyber*, pp. 237–40, 259–261; Dupree, *AUFS*, 1/4, pp. 14–17. Durand said of Abdur Rahman: "If it were not for the fact that his fall would . . . give Russia an opening, I should not be sorry to see him driven out of the country." Another British authority felt that "Abdur Rahman owes us his throne. . . . He has no right whatever to resent any action that we may see fit to take with regard to the tribes and countries which . . . form no part of his dominions" (quoted in Kaur, *Pak-Afghanistan Relations*, p. 23).

18. Miller, *Khyber*, pp. 100, 265–271, 265fn; Schofield, *Every Rock*, pp. 110–111. Miller notes that Winston Churchill, who covered the campaign for the *Daily Telegraph*, compared Saddullah with the eleventh-century monk Peter the Hermit, whose

THE REIGN OF ABDUR RAHMAN

oratory had helped launch the Crusades. Churchill would report the battles with a good deal of nonchalance, noting, "One man was shot through the breast and pouring with blood; another lay on his back kicking and twisting. The British officer was spinning round just behind me, his face a mass of blood, his right eye cut out. Yes, it was certainly an adventure."

19. Miller, *Khyber,* pp. 273–280; Schofield, *Every Rock,* p. 114; Barton, *India's North-West Frontier,* pp. 48, 191. Another shortage of transport animals held up the campaign for some time. Bulls, horses, camels, and mules were seized, and along with their owners marched in the frontier without proper clothing. Many animals and owners perished, but "there was no extremist politician to exploit the peasants' grievances." Lack of attention to animal transport and problems of supply occurred repeatedly in frontier campaigns.

20. Ali, *Afghanistan,* pp. 146–147; Miller, *Khyber,* pp. 250–254, 288–291; Schofield, *Every Rock,* pp. 149–150, 159, 179–180, 194–197; Barton, *India's North-West Frontier,* pp. 50–51, 57–58, 68, 80, 214–215. Curzon's efforts were only one failed effort to bring order to the frontier. Attempts to adopt the "Sandeman System," which successfully established indirect rule in Baluchistan, proved a failure in the tribal belt. The judicial system proved equally unsuited to tribal life, as it ran counter to the Pathan emphasis on satisfaction for the victimized rather than punishment of the infractor. Christianity also failed to attract new converts on the frontier. Indeed, there "was something almost comical about extolling the virtues of turning the other cheek among a people whose most cherished article of faith was two eyes for an eye." The India Arms Act of 1906 was perhaps the most foolish effort to bring stability to the frontier. It outlawed gun ownership for inhabitants of the settled districts but made no similar provision for the tribal areas. Intended to stop crime, it instead left border villages at the mercy of raiding parties. The government of India signed agreements with the tribes that allowed for the continued production of weapons in exchange for noninterference with commerce. The government justified the policy, claiming it would reduce theft and leave the tribes with inferior weapons. The policy ultimately left law enforcement authorities outgunned by the tribes, which only worsened with the advent of major gun-running operations through the Persian Gulf area. French and German arms merchants delivered weapons to the tribes via a network of quasi-piratical middlemen, until the Royal Navy abruptly closed the route in 1909. The Frontier forces gradually rearmed and were again superior by 1914. See Miller, *Khyber,* pp. 296–297, 303–305.

21. Quoted in "Survey of Anglo-Afghan Relations," Part I, L/P&S/12/1321.

22. Gregorian, *The Emergence of Modern Afghanistan,* pp. 152–153, 202–203, 206, 206fn. British military authorities tended to favor a more active defense policy vis-à-vis Afghanistan. After the signing of the Anglo-Russian convention in 1907, ideas to incorporate Afghanistan in the railway system gained renewed prominence. Some even contended that the rapprochement had brought an end to the necessity of a buffer state policy, and suggested diplomatic recognition of Afghanistan on an equal footing as a prelude to increased economic involvement.

4

THE RISE AND FALL OF AMANULLAH: A LESSON IN MODERNIZATION

Habibullah, who succeeded Abdur Rahman in 1901, proved less brash and extreme than his father. Habibullah reduced the use of severe punitive measures and curbed the activities of the intelligence apparatus, though from time to time he still eliminated domestic opposition in dramatically cruel fashion. Habibullah continued to strengthen central authority, most notably its tax collection capability. He refined judicial and administrative policies and even created Afghanistan's first parliament, though it was but an advisory council with thirty appointed members and did not survive his reign. He promoted some limited modernization schemes, to achieve a semblance of economic self-sufficiency, but refused to sanction development that would facilitate invasion of Afghanistan.[1]

Like his father, Habibullah recognized the importance of a reliable army. He expanded officer recruitment among national minorities and increased pay for officers and enlisted men alike. In an effort to establish a loyal and efficient officer corps, he founded the Royal Military College (*Madrasse-ye Harbi-ye Sirajieh*) in 1904. A limited number of recruits, almost all of upper-class origin, received training in the core sciences, mathematics, religion, and various aspects of military science, primarily from Ottoman officers. Together with the civilian graduates of Habibiya College (also founded in 1904), these cadets became members of an embryonic Afghan intelligentsia.[2]

Initially, Habibullah's policies toward Britain were cold and aloof. He refused to reaffirm the treaty commitments of his father, sacrificing his subsidies in the process. Like Abdur Rahman, Habibullah regarded the trans-Durand Pushtun regions as Afghan territory stolen by British thieves, and he pursued an irredentist, obstructionist frontier policy. Afghan officials helped spark a series of uprisings, notably those of the Mullah Powindah and the Mahsuds in 1901–1902, the Zakka Khel Afridis from 1904 to 1908, and the Mohmands in 1907–1908.[3] Habibullah also sought to increase contacts with Russia. From 1900 to 1907, Russo-Afghan trade increased threefold. Habibullah did not establish formal diplomatic relations with Russia, however, despite several overtures from St. Petersburg.[4]

In time, Habibullah came to recognize the advantages of a more conciliatory policy toward Britain. With some misgivings, he reaffirmed the Durand Treaty in an agreement signed March 21, 1905. The British retained control of Afghan foreign policy but reinstated the provision of subsidies and allowed for munitions deliveries from India. The treaty also acknowledged Habibullah as the "Independent King of Afghanistan."[5]

The need for proper relations with Britain increased as the "Great Game" wound down in the early twentieth century. Japan's victory in the Russo-Japanese War of 1904–1905 prompted the Russians to seek an entente with London. The growing might of Germany, a more serious and immediate threat, proved an even greater reason for agreement. In light of the German menace, Anglo-Russian cooperation made more sense than continued saber rattling over Central Asia. The St. Petersburg Convention of 1907 sanctified the accord, dividing Persia into three spheres of influence, with Britain in charge of the southern sector and in control of the Gulf. It also consigned Afghanistan to Britain's sphere of influence.[6]

The Anglo-Russian Convention offended and frightened the Afghans, who feared that the agreement might lead to eventual partition. Though the final article had stipulated his consent, Habibullah saw no advantage in signing the convention and never did. The Anglo-Russian entente, however, restricted Afghan policy options and eventually prompted another interlude of Anglo-Afghan cooperation. Following Habibullah's visit to India in 1907 and the cessation of the 1908 campaigns on the frontier, Anglo-Afghan relations improved steadily. Britain would once again acquire the favor of an Afghan ruler at a most advantageous time.[7]

During the First World War, Habibullah declared Afghanistan neutral and restrained tribal incursions into India. His policy was a pragmatic response to geographic, economic, and strategic considerations. Though sympathetic to the Central Powers, Afghanistan could not risk war with both England and Russia simultaneously, regardless of ideological motivations, popular sentiments, or any desire to acquire territory at the expense of India.

Maintaining neutrality was not easy. When the Ottoman Empire joined the Central Powers in October 1914, the Caliph declared the war a *jihad*. In denying his appeal, Habibullah risked accusation as a heretic. Continued loyalty to the Allies aroused bitterness and resentment among the country's tribal and religious leaders and among the emerging intellectual elite.

Nasrallah, the younger brother of Habibullah and commander-in-chief of the army, headed the conservative opposition.[8] His anti-British stance made him popular among the *ulama* and the tribes. Habibullah's eldest son, In-ayatullah, likewise supported the conservatives. Mahmud Tarzi led the modernists. Tarzi had studied in the Ottoman Empire, where he became a convert to the ideas of the Young Turk movement. After his return to Afghanistan in 1902, he began publication of the modernist Persian-language journal *Siraj al-Akhbar Afghaniyah*. Tarzi wielded considerable influence over Habibullah's third son, the future King Amanullah, who had married his daughter, Souraya.[9]

In September 1915, a joint German-Turkish mission arrived in Kabul, in an effort to enlist Afghanistan among the Central Powers and prompt major uprisings among the tribes. With the avowed approval of the kaiser and the sultan, the emissaries promised Habibullah postwar territorial annexations including most of present-day Pakistan and sections of Central Asia. In early 1916, Habibullah appeased the mission and his domestic opposition, signing a tentative declaration of war against the Allies. Afghanistan's entry into the war, however, was made conditional on the arrival of 100,000 Turkish troops and massive quantities of equipment and financial support. Habibullah's signatures "might just as well have been forgeries." Habibullah would write to King George of England: "I can assure you that we will remain neutral and keep our pledges to the last." George would later reply: "I have been much gratified to learn . . . how scrupulously you have maintained the attitude of strict neutrality which you guaranteed."[10]

The Revolutions of 1917 and Russia's subsequent abandonment of the Allied cause revived thoughts among the Afghan opposition of entrance into the war. Lenin's anti-imperialist fulminations and his revocation of the Anglo-Russian Convention removed the prospect of a two-front war and weakened Habibullah's arguments for continued neutrality. The Bolshevik disclosure of secret Allied wartime understandings that forecast the complete dismemberment of the Ottoman Empire aroused modernists and traditionalists alike as evidence of British duplicity and lack of sympathy for Muslim interests. Despite internal pressures, Habibullah maintained a neutral course.[11]

Habibullah's adherence to neutrality allowed the British high command to commit thousands of troops on the Western front, in Palestine, and in Mesopotamia that would otherwise have had to garrison the frontier. Though he could not prevent scattered tribes and local *mullahs* from launching occasional raids, prompt British action thwarted those limited incursions. The Afghan king recognized that his policy had benefited the Allied war effort and hoped he would be rewarded in the peace. At least one Afghan writer even claims that Habibullah secured secret concessions from the British that promised complete Afghan independence following the war.[12]

Habibullah sought his rewards in early February 1919, when he requested the Viceroy Lord Chelmsford to sanction "a written agreement recognizing the absolute liberty, freedom of action and perpetual independence of Afghanistan." Though some Britons supported the idea and thought increased

Anglo-Afghan contacts beneficial, the official response merely thanked Habibullah for his loyalty while dismissing his request. Habibullah had seen no consignments when a still-unknown assailant assassinated him on February 20.[13]

Following the assassination, Nasrallah announced his claim to the throne from Jalalabad. Amanullah, however, was in Kabul, in control of the army and the treasury. He charged his uncle with Habibullah's murder (a claim made believable by Nasrallah's quick assumption of power), imprisoned him along with most of his followers, and claimed the throne for himself. Though he had temporarily disrupted his opponents, Amanullah's hold on power remained insecure, as widespread suspicion of complicity in his father's murder undermined his legitimacy.[14]

An opportunity for Amanullah to bolster his popular appeal and solidify his domestic position arose amidst unrest in India. During the First World War, the Indian National Congress pursued a cooperative policy, supporting the Allied war effort in expectation of political rewards in the aftermath. The passage of the Montague-Chelmsford Act of 1919 granted limited internal sovereignty but bitterly disappointed nationalist leaders, who had expected more extensive legislation. The accompanying Rowlatt Acts, which severely restricted civil liberties, only increased Indian ire.

Indian disappointment with the reforms and disgust with the Rowlatt Acts spawned protests across the subcontinent. In April 1919, a large number of protesters gathered in the Jallianwala Bagh in Amritsar. General R.E. Dyer, denied the opportunity to serve on the Western front due to a serious groin injury, resolved to teach a lesson. Dyer ordered the crowd to disperse. When they did not, his Ghurka troops sealed the only entrance and fired repeatedly on the unarmed crowd, killing an estimated 400 and injuring 1,200 more. Dyer's action served only to unite formerly disinterested parties to Mohandas Ghandi's nationalist movement and triggered widespread disturbances.[15]

Amanullah seized the opportunity presented by Amritsar. He launched what is now known as the Third Anglo-Afghan War, ostensibly as a *jihad* to free the Pushtun tribes in India from British imperialism. Three Afghan armies mobilized for invasion, hoping that upheaval in India would prompt extensive tribal support. The Afghan forces, comprising some 50,000 men, were poorly trained and ill disciplined. Their weapons were obsolete, and much of their aged ammunition was as dangerous to the firer as any target. There were few competent leaders, no general staff, and very little organization. The Afghans consequently fared poorly in the month-long campaign.[16]

The northernmost battle group advanced toward the Peshawar districts, prompting scattered tribal upheavals. When its only encounter with Indian troops ended in rout, however, tribal agitation quieted. The central army under Nadir Shah fared better, securing some local successes and prompting several tribesmen, including some British-paid militia, to flock to his standards. He besieged Thal, but the arrival of a relief force under Dyer quickly rectified the situation. Nadir's forces put up scarcely more resistance than had the protesters at Amritsar before fleeing for their lives. The southernmost force never even crossed the border. Instead, British forces attacked and captured Spin Baldak.

Despite their victories, British authorities, fearing that a continuation of hostilities might unleash more rioting in India, did not press the war to a decisive conclusion. Facing similar unrest in Ireland and Egypt, supporting intervention in Russia, and nursing a drained treasury, the British could ill afford another protracted Afghan campaign. Most importantly, the troops, some of whom had fought for four years in Europe, were tired of war. One mutiny did occur, when part of a brigade detrained and simply waited for another going the opposite direction.[17]

The performance of the Afghan army left Amanullah equally desirous of peace. British bombers, though obsolete models, terrorized the Afghan army and tribal auxiliaries throughout the conflict and eventually raided Kabul and Jalalabad. Though the bombing apparently did little besides frighten Amanullah's harem, it nonetheless provided a reminder to Amanullah of the technological inferiority of his forces. In late May, Amanullah requested an armistice. The British quickly obliged.[18]

Peace talks dragged on for several months and came close to breaking down, as Amanullah insisted on complete independence of Afghan foreign policy. Finally, the British conceded to his demand. The Treaty of Rawalpindi, signed August 8, 1919, guaranteed full sovereignty to Afghanistan. A more comprehensive treaty would confirm Afghan independence on November 22, 1921.[19]

Independence changed Anglo-Afghan relations fundamentally. Afghanistan was no longer circumscribed within a sphere of British influence. Britain terminated its policy of providing Afghanistan with annual subsidies and refused to allow Amanullah to import weapons and munitions. In addition, the treaty classified the Durand Line as a "frontier" rather than simply a line of influence. While it acknowledged the interests of both nations in tribal affairs on both sides of the border, the British interpreted the treaty stipulations as confirmation that the Durand Line was an international border in the modern sense.[20]

The treaties did not bring lasting or even temporary peace to the frontier. Approximately 20,000 Indian Muslims, upset by the vindictive treatment accorded the Ottoman Empire by the Allied powers and led to believe that Afghanistan would offer them a better existence, sold their lands and fled India in the summer of 1920. Though Amanullah offered ideological support to the "Khalafat movement," it proved little more than a nuisance to the Afghan authorities, who had to turn the pilgrims back. Attempts to reclaim their belongings upon their return to India sparked some of the worst communal violence theretofore seen.[21]

Like his father and grandfather, Amanullah fomented rebellion among the Pushtuns. Even after signing the Treaty of Rawalpindi, he continued to disseminate anti-British propaganda, increased arms shipments to the tribal areas, and allowed *lashkars* to operate from Afghan bases. Throughout the 1920s, the tribes conducted a series of raids against the settled districts, in which an estimated 1,100 civilians were killed. The Wazirs and Mahsuds staged the most notable uprisings. In the 1919–1920 punitive campaign against them, Indian army troops suffered some 2,000 casualties, making it the most costly frontier campaign in history. The Mahsuds, however, lost twice that number and had to surrender. Steady artillery bombardment and repeated air strikes likewise persuaded the Wazirs to come to terms.[22]

Amanullah's government signed treaties of friendship with Turkey and Iran and established relations with Germany, France, Italy, and several other nations. The most significant aspect of his foreign policy, however, was his increased intimacy with the Soviet Union. In May 1919, the U.S.S.R. became the first nation to recognize Amanullah's government. Buoyed by Soviet promises to free the Central Asian *khanates* of Khiva and Bukhara, return the Panjdeh area to Afghanistan, and provide economic assistance, Amanullah sought close relations. Similar pledges made to Iran and Turkey to return lands stolen by the corrupt tsarist regime, along with frequent denunciations of the British Empire and European imperialism in general, made the amir optimistic.

In the summer of 1921, Afghan and Soviet representatives signed a treaty of friendship, in which the Soviets promised Afghanistan a 1-million-ruble-per-year subsidy, guaranteed the independence of Khiva and Bukhara, and sanctioned use of Soviet transit facilities for Afghan export. The U.S.S.R. also agreed to provide military and technical assistance to the Afghan armed forces. The Afghans in turn agreed to abstain from any political agreement or alliance deemed prejudicial to Soviet interests and allowed the Soviets to establish five consulates in Afghanistan.[23]

The Soviets fulfilled few promises. Little economic aid proved forthcoming, and their actions in Bukhara and Khiva would gradually convince Amanullah "that his Bolshevist friends were merely waiting for a propitious moment to liquidate him and set up a Soviet government in Kabul." Beginning in October 1919, Amanullah sent support to Khiva and Bukhara in its struggle with the Red Army. After both states were defeated in September 1920 (they were eventually annexed in 1924), Amanullah granted support to *basmachi* (a Russian term meaning "bandits") resistance groups. Motivated by religious as well as political sentiments, the *basmachi* waged indigenous rebellion against the Soviets for over fifteen years, often operating from Afghan sanctuaries (in a manner not unlike later *mujahidin* use of Pakistan). Without protective terrain and substantial foreign support, however, Soviet forces eventually overwhelmed the disunified resistance movement.[24]

Amanullah's increased connections with the U.S.S.R., his militant support for the Khalifat movement and other pan-Islamic groups, and the continued perpetration of tribal outrages had brought Anglo-Afghan relations to new lows in the early 1920s. Gradually, Soviet behavior induced Amanullah toward a neutral policy. Unable to confront Moscow while simultaneously ignoring or offending Delhi, Amanullah ceased his provocative frontier campaign and signed a new treaty with Britain that prohibited Soviet consulates in eastern Afghanistan. It also established legations at the respective capitals and facilitated shipment of construction materials and other goods intended for development projects. The British allowed arms deliveries to Afghanistan again, but they did not reinstate any subsidies. Anglo-Afghan relations remained proper during the remainder of Amanullah's reign but were never cordial. British-Indian forces remained on alert along the Northwest Frontier, and the Indian army command developed several contingency plans for use in the event of another Afghan invasion.[25]

Afghan relations with the U.S.S.R. fluctuated. In November 1925, Soviet troops chased out an Afghan garrison and occupied Urtatagai Island in the Oxus. Subsequently, the Soviets withdrew, after a third-party settlement awarded the island to Afghanistan. In August 1926, the two nations signed a treaty of neutrality and nonaggression, which called for both parties to abstain from any economic sanctions directed against the other and to refrain from interference in one another's internal affairs. It also reaffirmed both nations' commitments not to enter into alliances or political agreements directed against the other. Following the treaty, Afghan-Soviet relations steadily improved. By the late 1920s, the Soviets maintained the largest foreign presence in Kabul. Soviet technicians helped construct highways and light industry, while Moscow provided Amanullah with gifts of aircraft, telegraph lines, and other heavy equipment.[26]

Though the British periodically attempted to undermine Amanullah's regime, the king eventually proved his own undoing. Like his father-in-law, Amanullah was convinced that rapid modernization was an absolute necessity for Afghanistan. Inspired by superficial knowledge of Kemal Ataturk's programs in Turkey, he implemented a series of reforms in 1924. His legal code (*nizam nameh*) alienated many Afghans. Earlier educational reforms, which brought French and German instructors to Afghanistan and allowed for the education of Afghans abroad, had aroused suspicions of some conservative elements. The new code further limited the legal and educational prerogatives of the *mullahs*. The establishment of schools for girls (supported and supervised by the king's wife and mother-in-law) provoked more resentment, as did laws concerning child marriage, female inheritance, and other aspects of gender relations. The code also proscribed a *hashtnafti* conscription system, in which one in every eight male citizens became liable for military service. The usurpation of traditional male prerogatives and enforced conscription proved too much for some to take.

Rebellion broke out in the south among the Ghilzai Mangals, who marched on Khost. Hired German pilots dropped leaflets on the *lashkars,* which did not slow the illiterate tribesmen. The rebels turned back only when similarly employed Russians dropped bombs. Violence continued for nine months, however, as the army proved incapable of suppressing the revolt. Amanullah had to offer payment to Wazir, Afridi, and Mohmand *lashkars* to augment his forces. They eventually subjugated the Mangals, but not without great cost in life and income. The revolt consumed two years' worth of government earnings and forced Amanullah to postpone several projects and withdraw the objectionable sections of his legal code.[27]

Though left economically weak and politically discredited, Amanullah did not abandon hope to modernize Afghanistan. In December 1927, he journeyed to India, Egypt, several European countries, the Soviet Union, Turkey, and Iran. He returned to Kabul in July 1928, more determined than ever to westernize his country regardless of conservative sentiments. He embarked once again upon a reform program, this one more radical than the first. In advocating the total emancipation of women, universal education, separation of religious and secular affairs, and other economic, political, and military reforms, Amanullah attempted to transform Afghanistan from a premodern kingdom into a progressive, westernized state. His impatient, impulsive efforts sparked indignation that turned into a mass uprising and eventually cost him his throne.[28]

Amanullah continued Abdur Rahman's efforts to modernize the judicial system, again curbing the authority of the *mullahs* while stressing criminal justice as an affair of state rather than the responsibility of individuals. Through the termination of feudal allowances and the establishment of local administrative divisions (*alaqadari*), he assaulted not only the *ulama* but also the entire local power structure. Amanullah even curtailed his own powers, dissolving his grandfather's feudal councils and proposing a 150-member elected Parliament, based on the Iranian constitution.

Amanullah renewed attacks on patriarchy as well. Encouraged by his queen, who dramatically removed her veil on the palace steps, Amanullah left the decision to wear *purdah* to individual women rather than their husbands. The king again allowed for the education of women, sanctioning travel abroad for such purposes. He prohibited arranged marriages, proposed a minimum age law for prospective brides, dismissed bigamists in government service, and voiced general opposition to traditional polygamy. Perhaps most foolishly, Amanullah ordered all inhabitants of and visitors to Kabul to wear Western clothes and sport short haircuts. This seemed not only an affront to Islam but also to Afghan pride. While any one of these reforms would have aroused discontent, such dissent could perhaps have been managed. By assaulting the entirety of the established social norms (even allowing women to style their hair!), however, Amanullah alienated every segment of the Afghan nation, save a few Westernized inhabitants of the cities.

Amanullah also proposed a number of other less controversial reforms, which called for improvements in medical services, education, sanitation, the police, hotels, and parks. Afghanistan's dearth of capital, however, caused by the 1924 revolt, earlier projects, and the European journey meant that few plans were implemented and few tangible gains were achieved. Increased taxes and customs duties, passed despite the already grim economic situation, alienated merchants and villagers alike.[29]

Amanullah not only moved too rapidly, without necessary finances and without the existence of any social groups that would support such reforms, he also moved without an efficient central administration. Though Amanullah's efforts to improve education increased the pool of trained administrators slightly, there remained a considerable dearth of competent bureaucrats. Strict laws designed to prevent extortion did little but alienate lesser officials, as Amanullah had no funds with which to compensate them for the loss of *baksheesh*. His subsequent request for every official to sacrifice one month's salary for the state further undermined already limited loyalty.[30]

Most importantly, Amanullah failed to maintain a modern army, free of tribal control, which could thwart popular resistance. While his immediate predecessors paid close attention to army reform, Amanullah neglected the sympathies and interests of the armed forces throughout his reign and allocated few funds to defense. Even after the Mangal Revolt had demonstrated the army's weakness, Amanullah undertook no immediate reforms. The officers remained improperly trained, the soldiers underpaid, equipment obsolete, and overall organization rudimentary. Near the end of his tenure, Amanullah established a military academy and a staff college, sent some fifty officers to Turkey for training, and brought in Turkish advisors to assist in a modernization program. He also ordered munitions, aircraft, trucks, and other hardware and hired German, Soviet, and Italian instructors, but few reforms had been incorporated by the time of his ouster. Compulsory conscription laws, which also lowered the enlistment age and increased the length of service, only increased desertion rates.[31]

Amanullah's reform programs produced widespread outrage in the countryside. The king's amity with the Soviet Union had never been popular and seemed further proof of his purported abandonment of Islam. Rumors abounded concerning the conduct of the king and queen in Europe even before the start of the modernization programs. British propagandists encouraged the trend by distributing pictures of Souraya in revealing European evening gowns and others spliced to show her apparently nude and surrounded by European men. Several *mullahs* soon charged the king himself with having "danced, drunk alcoholic beverages, even eaten pork." While the British were certainly desirous of Amanullah's downfall and may have assisted in bringing it about, their machinations were not the root of his demise. Rather, his own "gross ignorance of the realities of tribal power in his own country" precipitated his ouster.[32]

Rebellion began in October among some Ghilzai tribes. The army, ill equipped for a winter campaign, failed to suppress the insurgents. Habibullah Kalakani, more commonly known as Bacha-i-Saqao (Son of the Water-Carrier) assumed leadership of the rebellion in the vicinity of Kabul. A Tajik of humble birth, Bacha had worked as a teashop server before being imprisoned for eleven months for breaking into a shop. After brief employment as a gardener, he served three years in the army, deserted during the rebellion of 1924, and became a highwayman. Over time, he developed a Robin Hood reputation for his attacks against government officials and generosity to the poor. Though defeated in an initial assault, he soon gained the support of traditionalists, and in late November his forces entered the capital.[33]

Throughout December, battle raged in Kabul. Bacha's ranks, swelled with deserters, gradually conquered the city. Amanullah eventually repealed most of his controversial reforms, including those on *purdah*, female education, and European dress, but could not save his throne. The Russians advised him to stay, promising support, but the amir abdicated to his brother, Inayatullah, and abandoned Kabul in early January 1929. Inayatullah abandoned Kabul three days later, along with most foreign embassy staff. Amanullah fled to Qandahar, where he launched several attempts to reconquer the capital, but only a few tribes proved willing to offer him support, and some of his closest advisors deserted to the rebels. Amanullah ultimately fled to Italy in April.[34]

Never pro-Soviet, Afghanistan emerged from the Amanullah episode with increased animosity toward her northern neighbor. Anti-Soviet sentiments would remain strong throughout the ensuing decades. Amanullah's failed reforms and forced exile also left a lasting impression on those who would succeed him. His failure graphically illustrated the difficulty inherent in attempting to modernize the devoutly Islamic and fundamentally tribal Afghan state. Yet Afghanistan's future rulers could not pursue Abdur Rahman's policy of avoiding modernization. Future attempts to alter the Afghan economy or social structure would have to be gradual but would still require substantial foreign assistance. The reconstruction of the army, necessary both to restore order in the country and to enforce any controversial legislation, would likewise require outside support. Afghanistan's need for modernization assistance for her army and economy and common anti-Soviet sentiment would foster increased Anglo-Afghan cooperation throughout the ensuing decades.

NOTES

1. "Survey of Anglo-Afghan Affairs, Part II," L/P&S/12/1321; Ali, *Afghanistan*, pp. 143–144, 148, 153; Miller, *Khyber*, p. 308; Wakman, *Afghanistan*, pp. 12–16; Gregorian, *Emergence of Modern Afghanistan*, pp. 181–183, 188–193, 198–199, 202–204, 212–213; see also Jewett, *American Engineer in Afghanistan*. Habibullah was more introverted and more receptive to Western influences than his father. He is said to have enjoyed cooking, photography, and tennis. Perhaps his most remarkable achievement, however, was his fathering of an estimated 200 children.

2. Gregorian, *Emergence of Modern Afghanistan*, pp. 183–187; Adamec, *Afghanistan's Foreign Affairs*, p. 13; Del Croze, "Afghanistan Today," p. 43. Beyond the two colleges, education remained under control of the *ulama*. Even the curriculum at Habibya and the Madrasse was heavily weighted to religious studies.

3. Miller, *Khyber*, pp. 292–293, 297–298, 301–303; Barton, *India's North-West Frontier*, pp. 66, 72–74, 141, 213–215.

4. Gregorian, *Emergence of Modern Afghanistan*, pp. 195–196, 206.

5. Ali, *Afghanistan*, pp. 147–151; Miller, *Khyber*, pp. 308–309; Wilber, *Afghanistan*, pp. 19–20; Sykes, "Afghanistan: The Present Position," p. 147. The British negotiating team had hoped to acquire Habibullah's permission to extend rail and telegraph links from Peshawar to Jalalabad and to secure his acceptance of British equipment and officers for training purposes. The amir refused and instead discussed "an impossible request for a strip of land on the Baluch coast, for the purpose of founding an Afghan seaport."

6. Caroe, *Wells of Power*, pp. 64–69; Miller, *Khyber*, p. 292; Dupree, *AUFS*, 4/3, p. 12.

7. Gregorian, *Emergence of Modern Afghanistan*, pp. 207–208, 207fn, 211.

8. Ali, *Afghanistan*, p. 153; Gregorian, *Emergence of Modern Afghanistan*, pp. 179–180, 192. In November 1894, Lord Curzon had traveled to Afghanistan, where he met Abdur Rahman. The two men formed a friendship almost immediately, and Curzon convinced the amir to visit England. The amir later declined to go but sent Nasrallah, giving him the advice to "take care . . . especially when ladies are present . . . not to spit and not to put fingers into your nose." Whether Nasrallah's etiquette failed him or not is not clear; however, he did not secure an ambassador for Afghanistan at the Court of St. James. Anglo-Afghan relations plummeted as Abdur Rahman attributed the failure to British politicians and thereafter increased agitation on the Indian Frontier. Nasrallah never forgave the British for the snub.

9. Kakar, "Trends in Modern Afghan History," in Dupree and Albert, eds., *Afghanistan in the 1970's*, p. 26; Arnold, *Afghanistan*, p. 47; Gregorian, *Emergence of Modern Afghanistan*, pp. 199, 204, 216–221, 224.

10. Hauner, *India in Axis Strategy*, pp. 71–72; Barton, *India's North-West Frontier*, p. 141; Miller, *Khyber*, p. 312; Ali, *Afghanistan*, pp. 151–152; Wakman, *Afghanistan*, p. 15; Adamec, *Afghanistan's Foreign Affairs*, p. 33; Sykes, "Afghanistan: The Present Position," p. 148

11. Gregorian, *Emergence of Modern Afghanistan*, pp. 221–224, 222fn.

12. Ali, *Afghanistan*, p. 152; Miller, Khyber, pp. 311–313; Barton, *India's North-West Frontier*, pp. 1–2, 75–76, 108, 142, 216, 291. Barton believes that had Habibullah unleashed *jihad*, "the British might have been hard put to it to hold India." This is probably an overstatement, but his neutrality, which can be compared with that of Dost Mohammed during the Great Mutiny, did ease British defense requirements considerably.

13. Arnold, *Afghanistan*, p. 5; Gregorian, *Emergence of Modern Afghanistan*, pp. 225–226. Arnold believes that Habibullah asked not just for independence but for a return of British-held Pathan territories to Afghanistan.

14. Sykes, "Afghanistan: The Present Position," pp. 150, 170; Ali, *Afghanistan*, p. 155. Nasrallah died in prison shortly after Amanullah's takeover. Inayatullah would later claim that Amanullah's fall in 1929 owed to "the curse of the departed spirit" of Habibullah. He is not alone in believing that Amanullah and his mother were behind

the death of the king. See Arnold, *Afghanistan,* pp. 5–7. Arnold argues that the swift takeover bespeaks prior planning. He notes how two men (Taj Mohammed and Abdur Rahman Ludin), sentenced to death by Habibullah for an earlier assassination attempt, were freed by Amanullah. He claims that Ludin and Amanullah were acting with Soviet assistance and collusion and that Amanullah expected Soviet support against a potential British counterattack.

15. Wolpert, *Roots of Confrontation,* pp. 91–92. Sir Olaf Caroe, then a minor official in the Indian government, claims the mob had killed a woman and ignored dispersal orders, but even this unabashed imperialist does not excuse Dyer's action. Caroe's Unfinished Autobiography, MSS.EUR F.203/78, Olaf Caroe Papers.

16. Fletcher, *Afghanistan,* pp. 189–193; Ali, *Afghanistan,* p. 156; Barton, *India's North-West Frontier,* pp. 291–292; Miller, *Khyber,* p. 318. Miller described the Afghan army as "little more than a mob of bandoleer-festooned ragpickers."

17. Miller, *Khyber,* pp. 318–325; Sykes, "Afghanistan: The Present Position," p. 151.

18. General Staff, "The Third Afghan War," pp. 132–133. There is considerable debate as to the damage caused by the British BE2c aircraft (which incidentally operated at such low altitudes as to allow the tribesmen to fire down upon them as they flew). Schofield claims the bombers hit the tombs of Abdur Rahman and Habibullah by mistake (*Every Rock,* p. 152). Gregorian claims the bombers destroyed military facilities at Jalalabad and Kabul (*Emergence of Modern Afghanistan,* p. 230). Sykes claims the bombs hit the palace ("Afghanistan: The Present Position," p. 151).

19. Miller, *Khyber,* pp. 338–339, 339fn. The following March, Amanullah received Sir Francis Humphries as the first British minister in Kabul since the ill-fated Cavagnari. Humphreys's staff held quite a party on their six-week anniversary in Kabul, simply because they had not been murdered. General Staff, "The Third Afghan War," p. 136. "Many instances can be quoted in which nations, defeated in war, have laid claims to a larger degree of success than later history records, but it is seldom that a nation has gone so far as to claim victory when it has been defeated."

20. Qureshi, *Anglo-Pakistan Relations,* pp. 186, 208fn; Squire, "Afghanistan and Her Neighbors," p. 69; Tabibi, "Aftermath Created by British Policy," pp. vi, 59; Wilber, *Afghanistan,* pp. 20–21; Dupree, "Durand Agreement of 1893," pp. 83–84; see also "Policy in Regard to Afghanistan," C.P. 36(34), Memo by the Secretary of State for War, February, 1934, L/WS/1/299, ff. 45–47. The treaty stated that "the Afghan government accepts the Indo-Afghan frontiers accepted by the late Emir."

21. Wolpert, *Roots of Confrontation,* pp. 94–95; Sayeed, *Pakistan, the Formative Phase,* p. 51; Schofield, *Every Rock,* p. 153; Barton, *India's North-West Frontier,* pp. 156–157, 161; Gregorian, *Emergence of Modern Afghanistan,* pp. 235–236. Communal feelings remained high on the frontier during the interwar years. In the Rangila Rasul case, for example, which bears similarities to the recent Salman Rushdie affair, a pamphlet ridiculing the Prophet, printed by a Hindu, evoked waves of violence in the late 1920s.

22. Barton, *India's North-West Frontier,* pp. 41, 53, 77–80, 158–159, 217–219, 291–292. Barton claims that the Wazirs and Mahsuds alone killed 293, wounded 392, kidnapped 461, and looted 200,000 pounds of property from 1919 to 1920 and killed 153 more through 1921. He further notes that the tribes continued to receive Afghan support after the treaty of November 1921 was signed. Barton also claimed, "There

can be no doubt that Afghan intrigues during the Great War, followed by the jihad of 1919, had turned the political aspirations of the tribes more than ever to Kabul."

23. Gregorian, *Emergence of Modern Afghanistan,* pp. 232, 238; Wilber, *Afghanistan,* p. 179; Arnold, *Afghanistan,* pp. 10, 16; Amstutz, *Afghanistan,* pp. 11–12; Watt, "Sa'adabad Pact," p. 296. For the text of the treaty, see Shapiro, *Soviet Treaty Series 1921–1928, Vol. I,* pp. 96–97.

24. Benningsen, "Soviet Union and Muslim Guerilla Wars," pp. 302–303; Gregorian, *Emergence of Modern Afghanistan,* pp. 235–236. Khiva and Bukhara had lost their sovereignty in the late nineteenth century and remained rather like the Indian princely states, devoid of independent external relations and host to Russian garrisons. Amanullah had granted diplomatic recognition to them, hoping to unite Central Asia into a pan-Islamic confederation or that the independent *khanates* would provide a buffer for Afghanistan against Soviet expansionism. Sources differ widely as to the extent of Amanullah's support for the *basmachi.* According to Arnold (*Afghanistan,* pp. 11–16), many anti-Soviet Bukharans defected to the *basmachi,* including the commissar of war, chief of police, and head of the Cheka. Stalin executed the only faithful Central Asian Communist leader as a "bourgeois nationalist" 4. See also Amstutz, *Afghanistan,* pp. 371–372.

25. Gregorian, *Emergence of Modern Afghanistan,* pp. 236–238, 262; "Survey of Anglo-Afghan Affairs, Part II, 1919–1947," L/P&S/12/1321; Sykes, "Afghanistan: The Present Position," p. 154.

26. Ali, *Afghanistan,* p. 160; Wilber, *Afghanistan,* p. 180; Dupree, *AUFS,* 4/3, p. 13; Watt, "Sa'adabad Pact," pp. 297–298; There is reason to believe that the Oxus Island incident was deliberately provoked so as to force Afghanistan into accepting the subsequent treaty. See Amstutz, *Afghanistan,* pp. 12–13.

27. "Survey of Anglo-Afghan Relations, Part II, 1919–1947," L/P&S/12/1321; Gregorian, *Emergence of Modern Afghanistan,* pp. 241–243, 247, 255. Miller, *Khyber,* p. 342; Barton, *India's North-West Frontier,* p. 145; Newell and Newell, *Struggle for Afghanistan,* p. 38. The rebellion was led by Pir-i-Lang, the Lame Mullah. His primary grievance concerned laws that created schools for girls and restricted male control over wives and daughters.

28. General Staff Report, "Summary of Events in Afghanistan," 1 July 1928–30 June 1929, L/P&S/12/1637; Wilber, *Afghanistan,* p. 154; Gregorian, *Emergence of Modern Afghanistan,* pp. 246–247, 257–258. His visits to Turkey and Iran, where he witnessed the modernizing processes of Ataturk and Reza Shah, particularly moved Amanullah. In the words of one journalist, he "became infected with the germ of the West so seriously as to lose his sense of proportion." Ali states simply: "He forgot the maxim that Rome was not built in a day" (*Afghanistan,* p. 163).

29. General Staff Report, "Summary of Events in Afghanistan," 1 July 1928–30 June 1929, L/P&S/12/1637; Newell, *Politics of Afghanistan,* p. 56; Kakar, "Trends in Modern Afghan History," in Dupree and Albert, *Afghanistan in the 1970's,* pp. 16–18. According to Sir Francis Humphreys, Amanullah violated safe conducts given to religious and tribal leaders visiting Kabul, conducting a series of open and clandestine executions. See Griffiths, *Afghanistan,* p. 50; Bhaneja, *Afghanistan,* pp. 17–18; Gregorian, *Emergence of Modern Afghanistan,* pp. 248–254, 250fn, 269–274, 270fn. The Loya Jirgah, curiously, accepted many of the proposed reforms. They proved most hostile to the social reforms, especially laws that governed marital consent and education for women.

30. Gregorian, *Emergence of Modern Afghanistan,* pp. 248, 253, 260, 271; Sykes, "Afghanistan: The Present Position," p. 156.

31. General Staff Report, "Summary of Events in Afghanistan," 1 July 1928–30 June 1929, L/P&S/12/1637; Sykes, "Afghanistan: The Present Position," p. 156; Griffiths, *Afghanistan,* p. 50; Bhaneja, *Afghanistan,* pp. 18–19; Gregorian, *Emergence of Modern Afghanistan,* pp. 252, 255–256, 260, 271, 273. Poor training and inadequate pay and medical facilities remained key problems. There was also friction between older established officers and new foreign-trained commanders. In refusing to allow the influential families to keep their sons from military service through bribes, Amanullah helped ensure their hostility. When the Pushtuns opposed conscription laws, he recruited from ethnic minorities, which further alienated tribal leaders.

32. Fletcher, *Afghanistan,* p. 224; Griffiths, *Afghanistan,* pp. 103–104; Gregorian, *Emergence of Modern Afghanistan,* pp. 263–267, 267fn, 292. While there is no direct proof that the British distributed the pictures, only they had the technological capabilities, and the incentive, to do so.

33. Humphreys to the Secretary of State for Foreign Affairs, India Office, 27 January 1929, L/PO/5/30, f. 196; "Leading Personalities in Afghanistan," Office of the Secretary of State for Foreign Affairs, 9 February 1929, L/PO/5/30, ff. 108–122.

34. "Survey of Anglo-Afghan Relations, Part II, 1919–1947," L/P&S/12/1321; "Extract from Lady Humphreys' Diary of Recent Events in Kabul," L/PO/5/30, ff. 102–103; General Staff Report, "Summary of Events in Afghanistan," 1 July 1928–30 June 1929, L/P&S/12/1367.

5

NADIR SHAH AND HASHIM KHAN: THE DAWN OF ANGLO-AFGHAN COOPERATION

In January 1929, Bacha-i-Saqao became the first Tajik ruler in modern Afghan history. Neither he nor the *mullahs* he appointed as advisors, however, demonstrated any aptitude for government.[1] Faced with a multitude of internal challenges, but lacking a stable source of income, Bacha resorted to extortion and terror to maintain his hold on power. Bacha loyalists confiscated private property, pilfered public facilities, and executed many presumed political opponents. Shortly before his departure from the capital, the British minister wrote: "None was safe, houses were pillaged indiscriminately, women were ravished, and a reign of terror was established unprecedented in the annals of bloody Afghan history."[2]

Domestic chaos provided both the British and the Soviets with opportunities to influence Afghan politics. Though some individuals and organizations within the Soviet administration favored recognition of the bandit-king, others recognized his limitations and valued Amanullah's traditional anti-British stance. Stalin ultimately turned his back on the peasant usurper and sent an 800-man force, comprising Red Army soldiers disguised as Afghans, to assist Amanullah. Though supported by aircraft, artillery, and machine gun detachments, these "volunteers" were checked by Bacha's forces. Mindful of Amanullah's defeats in the south and hostile international opinion, the Soviet force subsequently withdrew.[3]

The British also saw little hope in a Tajik peasant bringing lasting stability to Afghanistan. Previous experiences, however, warned against direct intervention. Thus, while outwardly professing neutrality, the British championed the return of Nadir Shah. Nadir, hero of the Third Anglo-Afghan War and former war minister, had fallen out of Amanullah's favor in 1924 when he refused to lead troops against the Mangal rebellion. Effectively exiled as ambassador in Paris, he had remained in France thereafter but retained a reputation as a capable and honest statesman. His reputation and military experience promised the best hope for a return to stability.[4]

Courted by both Bacha and Amanullah, Nadir refused to support either and instead sought power himself. The British facilitated Nadir's transit to the frontier and provided him a grant of 175,000 pounds and 10,000 Enfield rifles. Nadir and three of his younger brothers, Hashim Khan, Shah Mahmud Khan, and Shah Wali Khan, advanced their newly recruited *lashkars* on Kabul. Bacha defeated their forces in April and again in June, but constant pressure from the north, the south, and the central highlands gradually sapped his strength. Economic mismanagement, personal debauchery, battle casualties, and numerous executions heightened resistance to his rule and left Bacha increasingly unable to attract new recruits. British authorities, meanwhile, turned blind eyes to Nadir's recruitment of Wazir and Mahsud tribesmen from the Indian side of the Durand Line. This augmentation proved decisive when Nadir's brothers resumed the offensive. Bacha was captured and eventually executed along with many of his followers. The tribal chiefs and other influential Afghans proclaimed Nadir king.[5]

Nadir Shah assumed power amidst a nation that had reverted to anarchy. From his bases in the northern provinces, *basmachi* leader Ibrahim Beg conducted campaigns against the Soviets without regard for Kabul authorities. The Ghilzai tribes, all but independent since 1928, continued to resist central authority, while Herat remained under the control of a Bacha loyalist. Nadir faced this situation with a bankrupt treasury, no bureaucracy, and no national army. To mend the damage caused by the civil war, Nadir needed cooperation from the British. For that reason, his accession marks a key turning point in the history of Anglo-Afghan relations.[6]

Nadir's first priority was reconstruction of the armed forces. To that end, he sought and received British financial assistance and weapons, with which he rebuilt the national army. The former war minister continued to strengthen his forces throughout his reign. By 1933 the Afghan army numbered over 40,000 compared with 12,000 under Amanullah. Its strength would reach 70,000 on the eve of the Second World War. To increase the reliability and efficiency of the armed forces, Nadir dispatched army and air force officers abroad for training, mostly to India, Turkey, France, and Germany, and opened a military preparatory school, *Makhab-i-Ihzariah*, in Kabul. As in Abdur Rahman's time, the army's primary purpose remained not defense against external aggression, but internal security. Nadir used the army to restore domestic order in a series of campaigns.[7]

To secure his hold on the throne, Nadir appeased conservative forces within the country. Aware that the Afghan people would reject another attempt at rapid modernization, he limited reform efforts to a cautious program that carefully adhered to the tenets of Islam. He reinstated *purdah* and passed numerous declarations that relegated authority to religious officials. The constitution, given Loya Jirgah approval in 1931, cited its legitimacy in Hanafi law. Though it officially created a constitutional monarchy with a bicameral legislature, Parliament provided consultative advice only, which the ministers, Cabinet, and king could ignore. Nadir retained the right to declare war, to appoint and remove Cabinet members, to veto legislative actions, and to promulgate laws unilaterally. The chief significance of the assembly, as during Abdur Rahman's reign, was in bringing many chieftains to Kabul, thereby cutting down on local agitation.[8]

On the surface, Nadir's foreign policy reflected his public statements, which declared neutrality "the best and most useful policy" for Afghanistan. Yet beneath the rhetoric of Islamic solidarity and neutralism, Afghan policy in the 1930s favored Britain over the Soviet Union. Nadir endeavored to maintain appropriate relations with the U.S.S.R., recognizing that a hostile Stalin could conceivably support separatist or tribal uprisings, perhaps involving Amanullah. In June 1931, Nadir renewed the 1926 Treaty of Neutrality and Non-Aggression. He also offered no support to the *basmachi* and instead aided in the capture of Ibrahim Beg.[9] Yet one of Nadir's first acts was to dismiss all Soviet advisors and technicians brought in by Amanullah. He kept economic contacts limited thereafter, though the worldwide depression forced occasional exceptions. Soviet influence in the Afghan army and air force, meanwhile, disappeared.[10]

Nadir and his brothers, who would rule Afghanistan through 1953, realized the Soviet Union was the only immediate threat to continued Afghan independence. They saw Britain content with its hold on India, a hold that itself was unstable. They similarly realized that economic modernization was vital to their country and saw cooperation with India beneficial to that end. Nadir further considered the tribes a hindrance to centralization and development and saw them as a danger to the longevity of his reign. Thus, improved relations with Britain would provide Afghanistan with the fiscal capability to enact modernization, expanded trade and development opportunities, an efficient army with which to maintain internal order, cooperative assistance against the tribes, and a measure of protection against Soviet aggression. Some sources curiously indicate that members of the ruling family believed cooperation would someday be rewarded with intimate relations, perhaps even federation, with an autonomous Muslim state in north India.[11]

Most British authorities similarly desired a strong government in Afghanistan that would serve as a buffer to Soviet expansion, decrease the likelihood of tribal uprisings, and foster economic cooperation. They were willing to resume provision of subsidies to Kabul, if Nadir's regime proved cooperative. In exchange for continued support, Nadir remonstrated interference in the trans-Durand tribal regions, abandoning the aggressive nationalism of his immediate predecessors. The British minister to Kabul, Sir Richard Maconachie, summarized Nadir's tribal policy: "Since the demands of internal reconstruction will absorb the whole resources of the Government for many years to come . . . there is to be no interference in areas beyond the Afghan frontiers, and Amanullah Khan's 'irredentist' attitude . . . is to be definitely abandoned. Such a policy accords with common sense, and there seems to be no reason to doubt its sincerity."[12]

Nadir also reaffirmed the Treaty of Rawalpindi in May 1930 and concluded several other agreements with Indian authorities.[13]

The Anglo-Afghan rapprochement proved of importance as the North West Frontier Province (NWFP) gradually drifted into the rising tide of the Indian Nationalist movement. While the Montague-Chelmsford reforms of 1919 had established a central legislature and granted a modicum of political authority to most provincial governments in India, the frontier Pushtuns were denied such reforms. British authorities claimed the frontier's strategic location and turbulent history left it "singularly inappropriate" for reform, a decision initially supported by many Indian nationalists.[14] The omission, however, offended Pushtun dignity and led to a decade of political upheaval, in which the NWFP became an ideological battleground for both indigenous parties and the leading factions of the Indian nationalist movement.[15]

In response to the exclusion of the NWFP, two leading frontier personalities, the half-brothers Khan Sahib and Abdur Ghaffar Khan, founded an opposition party. Known as the "Frontier Jirgah" (or the "Afghan Jirgah") at its inception, it became the leading provincial party during the interwar years, ultimately adopting the name *Khudai Khidmatgaran* (Servants of God). Ghaffar Khan later organized regiments of Pushtuns who served the party as its paramilitary force. To affect uniforms, they covered their clothes in vegetable dye or brick dust, becoming known as the "Red Shirts" (*Surkh Posh*), a sobriquet often erroneously applied to the party as a whole.[16]

In late 1929 (after some initial hesitation), the *Khudai Khidmatgaran* formally united with the Indian National Congress in a political alliance born of expediency rather than common ideology. The Congress, the only effective nationalist opposition group at the time, provided the *Khudai Khidmatgaran* with financial support and organizational assistance in exchange for the Khan brothers' cooperation against the British in the civil disobedience movement. Other Muslim parties had feared Congress, but the *Khudai Khidmatgaran* saw them as valuable political and economic allies, especially as Congress was willing to respect their regional autonomy and identity. As long as the *Khudai Khidmatgaran* cooperated on vital political questions, the Congress authorities, though at times openly dissatisfied, were willing to let it "pursue its regional brand of nationalism"[17]

At times, Ghaffar Khan espoused pacifism, had party members swear never to take revenge, and refused to wear European clothes, earning the nickname "Frontier Ghandi." He even advocated consideration of Hindus as "People of the Book" alongside Jews and Christians. At other times, however, Ghaffar Khan seemed to draw more inspiration from the Haji of Turangzai than

Ghandi. Little evidence exists to support claims that the Pushtun rank-and-file accepted Ghandian principles of nonviolence, inner purity, and passive resistance. On the contrary, the Red Shirts were organized along regimental lines, wore military insignia, routinely drilled, and, according to virtually every contemporary source, were inclined toward violence.[18]

Long-term *Khudai Khidmatgaran* goals remain obscure. While a devoted social reformer, generally supportive of the lower classes and opposed to the great landholders, Ghaffar Khan's political philosophy, espoused in vague generalities, was ever-shifting. He clearly opposed British rule, which he regarded as the root of all difficulties, but wavered as to its replacement. Nehru and Ghandi claimed they promised the Khan brothers regional autonomy in a federated India. Sir Olaf Caroe, the last governor of the NWFP, believed Ghaffar Khan and Sahib were convinced that the Pushtuns would "rule the roost" in a united India, in which they would impose a "Pathan form of communism." Sir William Barton typified British sentiments in decrying the entire movement as "little Soviets," deriding Ghaffar Khan as "a fanatical agitator whose object was to raise both border and cis-border Pathans against the British and drive them beyond the Indus." Though oft labeled a puppet of Kabul, there is no evidence to indicate that Ghaffar Khan supported the Afghan regime prior to 1947. During the 1930s, a few organizations and individuals envisioned reunion of Afghanistan and the NWFP. While Ghaffar Khan occasionally spoke of the Afghan people as one, more often he championed regional autonomy within a federated India. During the Second World War, he remained in contact with Axis representatives and the Afghan opposition, voicing a willingness to merge the NWFP with Afghanistan. Throughout 1947, he claimed that he had always wanted an independent "Pushtunistan" that would maintain intimate relations with a united India or later Pakistan. After partition, he alternately supported Kabul and Karachi, demanding independence as often as autonomy, even voicing support for the PDPA shortly before his death in 1986. Ghaffar Khan's constantly shifting allegiance, coupled with his remarkable capacity for exaggeration, left his political philosophy an enigma. Perhaps the difference between autonomy and independence was of no relevance to the Pushtuns or was lost somewhere in translation. Then again, perhaps Ghaffar Khan's flexible ideology as well as his dictatorial handling of the *Khudai Khidmatgaran* should lead one to conclude that he was less interested in philosophical formalities than in securing power by any means available.[19]

Whatever their political goals, *Khudai Khidmatgaran* behavior rarely resembled a pacifist movement. On April 23, 1930, British-Indian authorities responded to anti-government activity in Peshawar by placing the Khan brothers in confinement, which prompted widespread demonstrations. Indian Army troops supported by four armored cars attempted to restore order. The armored cars used machine guns against the brick-throwing crowd and ran over at least six demonstrators, but the troops were withdrawn the following day and the insurgents took over the city. For the next nine days, governmental activities all but ceased.[20]

On May 4, British troops reoccupied Peshawar and restored order in the city. Peshawar itself remained quiet thereafter, but the entire summer would pass before order was restored throughout the district. In June and in August, Mohmand and Afridi *lashkars* marched on the city. Battles raged throughout the summer, with many citizens actively helping the rebels, giving them food and shelter, sometimes even joining in the attacks. Though the attacks were uncoordinated, the damage was nonetheless extensive. Finally, with the Afridis disrupting all communications, district officials placed the city under martial law and called in reinforcements, which managed to quell the uprising by October.[21]

The British learned several lessons from the uprising. It demonstrated serious failings in contingency plans and a shortage of available security forces (though it must also be noted that the chief commissioner had suffered a nervous breakdown in the midst of the violence). The general staff and provincial officials recommended greater expenditures and preparedness.[22] Such reforms were implemented and would pay dividends when Ghaffar Khan again used local grievances, coupled with an apparent impasse at the Round Table talks in London, to bring Peshawar to the brink of rebellion. The *Khudai Khidmatgaran* scheduled a meeting for January 1, 1932, but the authorities struck preemptively with mass arrests in December, which removed the leadership and forestalled insurrection. Revenue collection in January was a record. The contrast with April 1930 was dramatic. Ghaffar Khan spent the next three years in prison and remained barred from the frontier until 1937. By the time he returned, a provincial assembly had been functioning for four years.[23]

The 1930 uprising, however, also demonstrated flaws in British political policy and helped convince British authorities to reverse their position on democratic reforms in the NWFP. Several factors induced such a decision, including the insistence of Ghandi, who made the inclusion of the frontier a prerequisite for an all-India settlement made the same arguments. A moderate frontier politician, Abdul Qaiyum Khan. The Home government declared the NWFP a governor's province in 1932 and a legislature was elected that served the settled districts until 1936. Tribal policy remained under central control of the governor. Greater reforms were implemented following the Government of India Act of 1935, wherein the NWFP received the same provisions as other provinces (save that the governor remained the arbiter of tribal policy). The combined efforts of the governor, Sir George Cunningham, and Qaiyum, who became for a time his chief minister, kept Peshawar and its surrounding districts relatively tranquil for the remainder of the decade.[24]

Throughout the frontier disturbances, the Afghan government offered no assistance to the agitators and pursued a policy that the British themselves labeled "Anglophile." One British official explained: "The present ruler, King Nadir Shah, has honorably lived up to his engagements and shown himself most fair and loyal. Indeed he has kept his firebrands on his side of the border much better than we have ours. It is greatly due to his influence that the Red Shirt movement has not spread into independent territory to a greater extent than it has."[25]

Other contemporary British commentators noted how "the tribes were coldly advised to make their peace with the British" and that "for the first time the Afghan government had ceased to encourage the warlike, fanatical tribesmen to give trouble to the British." Such behavior aroused British hopes for an eventual end to the perpetual violence on the frontier.[26]

Such cooperation, however, also fueled domestic opposition in Afghanistan. The presence of British weapons in Kabul had spawned accusations of undue subservience to London following Nadir's assumption of power. When the government of India "found it impossible to avoid publishing . . . the details of the grant" given to Nadir, they opened possibilities for agitators to label him a puppet of Delhi. The Indian press only fired these rumors with repeated praise of the regime, especially statements that thanked Nadir for cooperation "in dealing with the tribal problem on our common borders." British retribution against the tribes, often accompanied by warnings threatening action against those hostile to the Kabul regime, gave even more impetus to those who labeled Nadir another *watan-ferosh*.[27]

Such domestic opposition, rather than reluctance among the leadership, prohibited extensive cultural, military, and economic contacts with Britain and necessitated a cautious and overtly Islamophile Afghan policy. Though British authorities expressed willingness to provide the Afghan regime with greater support, Nadir's regime often responded in roundabout ways to the offers, fearing that acceptance would arouse popular indignation. Nadir repeatedly declared solidarity with the tribes and cited long-standing moral obligations to supply them allowances. Noting how the cessation of payments could provoke rebellion, the British also conceded the necessity to continue providing funds to key frontier leaders and to reward those who had helped Nadir take the throne. But while recognizing that Nadir could not terminate relations with the trans-Durand tribes, the British still expected continued cutbacks and cooperation.[28]

Opposition to Nadir centered on Amanullah, whose capacity for desperate gambles kept Delhi and Kabul alert to possible coup attempts. The ex-king's activities aroused suspicion of plots involving foreign governments, dissident governors, and tribal leaders. The British kept a 500-page file on Amanullah's movements, most notably a series of "pilgrimages to Mecca," which routed through Rome, Berlin, and other out-of-the-way capitals, between 1931 and 1934.[29] The Charkhi brothers, Ghulam Nabi, Ghulam Siddiq, and Ghulam Jilani, headed the in-country opposition. Sons of Abdur Rahman's commander-in-chief, they had fallen out of favor with Habibullah, but Amanullah had restored them to prominence, and they remained among his leading supporters. Nabi, who ostensibly led the Soviet-backed effort to oust Bacha-i-Saqao, participated in a variety of subversive activities, arrogantly challenging Nadir's right to the throne, until Nadir ordered him executed.[30]

In 1933 a series of anti-government incidents occurred. On June 6, a Charkhi supporter killed Nadir's brother, Mohammed Aziz, the Afghan envoy to Germany, in Berlin. The assassin confessed that his action was in protest against Afghan official policy that facilitated British consolidation in the NWFP at the expense of Pushtun independence. In September, a man broke into the British legation in Kabul and killed three employees. In the aftermath, Nadir ordered Ghulam Jilani and several other alleged conspirators executed for treason and sedition, along with the assassin.[31]

On November 8, 1933, the one-year anniversary of Nabi's execution, a sixteen-year-old boy, Abdul Khaliq, assassinated Nadir as the king handed out awards at a high school graduation. While some claim assassination was part of a wider plot, it seems more likely that the act was a simple case of *badal*. Still, had Abdul Khaliq failed, further efforts to assassinate Nadir would likely have followed.[32]

In the aftermath of the assassination, War Minister Shah Mahmud used his considerable power to secure the accession of Nadir's twenty-one-year-old son, Zahir Shah. For the next thirteen years, the reserved Zahir left affairs of state to another uncle, Prime Minister Hashim Khan. Hashim quickly enacted retaliatory measures, which decimated the domestic opposition. He continued to rule Afghanistan with a firm hand until his resignation in 1946.

Nadir's death did not prompt a change in Afghan policy. Instead, Hashim proved even more willing to cooperate with Britain than his brother. Hashim had served as ambassador to the Soviet Union during Stalin's consolidation of power and knew well of the purges and forced collectivization programs. He developed "an intense dislike for all things Russian" and remained suspicious of Soviet intentions. Hashim also knew that Afghanistan could not lag behind while the rest of the world modernized. Like his deceased brother, he hoped frontier cooperation would be rewarded with economic and military assistance.[33]

British authorities continued to express satisfaction with Afghan policy, often noting a general spirit of friendship and desire for peace on the frontier. Both sides assumed greater responsibility for tribes within their borders. Hashim's government agreed to bar "Indian rebels" from Afghan soil and vowed to "prevent the Afghan tribes along the Indian border from participating in acts hostile to British authority." Representatives at a series of conferences discussed concerns ranging from the extradition of criminals to the monitoring of trans-border trade. Proposals called for the establishment of bilateral commissions on tribal affairs and Indian assistance in the establishment of Afghan border police.[34] This continued cooperation prompted a steady improvement in Anglo-Afghan relations. One contemporary analyst noted simply: "British relations with Kabul have never been more friendly than at present."[35]

Repeated outbreaks of tribal violence, however, dominated reporting and overshadowed the Anglo-Afghan rapprochement. Such uprisings were the work of the tribes themselves, not the Afghan authorities. Along with the aforementioned Red Shirt agitation of 1930, Mohmands from both sides of the frontier conducted a sporadic campaign of violence from 1932 to 1935. The Haji of Turangzai (who had participated in the 1897 uprising and several others since that time—and was once a teacher of Abdul Ghaffar Khan) and his son, Badshah Gul, led their *lashkars,* allegedly including Red Shirts, on a series of raids, eventually prompting a British invasion in force in September 1935. A force of over 30,000 troops managed to crush the uprising, but even then renewed violence, again ascribed to the Red Shirts, occurred sporadically thereafter.[36]

The worst outbreak of insurrection in the history of the NWFP plagued Wazirstan in the late 1930s, when Haji Mirza Ali Khan, the infamous "faqir of Ipi," led his followers in a guerrilla campaign. The war originated in the so-called "Islam Bibi" incident of 1936. Following a Sikh attack on a mosque in Lahore, Wazir tribesmen abducted a Hindu girl in Bannu, forced her to convert and marry a Muslim, and renamed her Islam Bibi. Her original husband brought the case to court, where the jury ignored hostile protesters and favored him, ultimately reuniting the couple. The *faqir,* whose hatred for the British was enormous, seized the incident. Citing the irrevocability of Muslim conversion, he called for *jihad.* He raised a *lashkar* and engaged British forces even before the trial had formally concluded. A punitive mission managed to disperse most of the hostiles in the late 1936, but the *faqir* remained at large, and for the next three years, Indian forces chased his elusive forces through the mountains in a campaign that witnessed little mercy.[37]

The nature of the war helped maintain the popular image of the Afghans. The *faqir,* no signatory of the Geneva Convention, was not averse to terror tactics. The Pushtuns made excellent use of their knowledge of the terrain and their seemingly limitless patience to spring ambushes upon British lines of communication and avoided direct confrontation with organized forces. Despite technological developments (most notably the widespread use of aircraft) and tactical improvements in the Indian army and the fact that the *faqir*'s forces apparantly never surpassed 800 to 1,000 men at any one time, the Wazirs still kept some 40,000 to 50,000 British-Indian troops in the field for over two years, including 10,000 dedicated to guarding supply routes. Through December 1937, the British had suffered almost 1,000 casualties and spent over 1.5 million pounds in the Wazirstan campaign.[38]

During the same period, the Afghan government had as much if not more trouble with the tribes as the British did. Nadir's successful invasion heightened desires among the trans-Durand tribes to again participate in king making and attracted numerous pretenders who desired to lead the attack. Just a few years after Nadir's ascension, Wazir and Mahsud *lashkars,* convinced of profits to be had in Afghanistan and showing a "fine impartiality" in their avowed support of a bastard son of Amanullah, joined domestic dissidents in hopes of again ransacking Kabul. They defeated local Afghan forces and besieged Matun, the capital of Khost Province. Only the combined efforts of Afghan and British civil and military authorities convinced them to return.[39]

Hashim's efforts to expand his authority fanned continued suspicions of subservience to British interests, which, along with economic incentives, fostered a series of revolts throughout the late 1930s. In the spring of 1938, for example, Shami Pir, a Syrian "holy man" and a distant relative of Amanullah, arrived in India. He soon had Wazir and Mahsud *lashkars* ready to march on Kabul, but Afghan troops, supported by ten aircraft, checked their advance. After British aircraft joined the fray, British authorities offered Shami Pir a 20,000-pound bribe and promised continued air strikes if he refused. He accepted, and they flew him out of the country.[40]

By the late 1930s, nearly half of the Indian army remained on the Northwest Frontier, not so much to guard against Soviet or Afghan invasion but to curtail tribal raiding and increasingly to contain outbreaks of communal violence.[41] By 1939 the government of India paid 885,790 rupees per year to the tribes, but military action was often needed to enforce the peace. Britons and Afghans advanced proposals designed to bring greater peace to the frontier. Disarmament proposals were dismissed as expensive and difficult to implement. Some even advocated construction of a barbed-wire rendition of the Great Wall along the administrative boundary, similar to what Italy had erected along the border of Libya and Egypt. Others saw the continued construction of schools, roads, irrigation systems, hospitals, and other facilities along the frontier as essential to give the tribes alternatives to raiding.[42]

Improvement of any sort, however, depended on cooperation from Afghanistan, and for the first time, the Afghan government was willing to collaborate on frontier matters. The advent of the Muhsahiban dynasty and its recognition of both the threat posed by outside agitators and the advantages to be had through cooperation with British India had brought considerable change to the strategic situation along the Northwest Frontier. Such policy also promised extensive collaboration on more expansive strategic issues. Opportunities for even closer relations would continue to expand through the next decade.

NOTES

1. Ali, *Afghanistan,* pp. 163, 172. Four of Bacha's eight Cabinet members were illiterate. According to Dupree (*AUFS*, 4/8, p. 10), this "Andy Jackson of Afghanistan" (minus the administrative ability, education, and competence) held court in the lapis lazuli-tiled bathrooms of Amanullah's palace and cockfights in the large reception rooms.

2. Humphreys to the Secretary of State for Foreign Affairs, India Office, 20 January 1929, L/PO/5/30, f. 221; see also General Staff Report, "Summary of Events in Afghanistan," 1 July 1929–30 June 1930, L/P&S/12/1637; Gregorian, *Emergence of Modern Afghanistan,* pp. 275–277, 280–281. Political opponents were "either blown up from the cannon's mouth, or shot down; others were either beaten, bastinadoed, impaled, bayoneted, or starved to death."

3. General Staff Report, "Summary of Events in Afghanistan," 1 July 1929–30 June 1930, L/P&S/12/1637. The report claims that there were Russian dead found at the battle site. Gregorian, *Emergence of Modern Afghanistan,* pp. 278–279; Amstutz, *Afghanistan,* pp. 14, 421fn; Squire, "Afghanistan and Her Neighbors," p. 69.

4. "Leading Personalities in Afghanistan," Office of the Secretary of State for Foreign Affairs, 9 February 1929, L/PO/5/30, ff. 108–122; Ali, *Afghanistan,* pp. 167–169. Nadir and his brothers were descendants of both Ahmed Shah Durrani (on their mother's side) and Dost Mohammed (on their father's).

5. General Staff Report, "Summary of Events in Afghanistan, 1 July 1929–30 June 1930," L/P&S/12/1637; "Survey of Anglo-Afghan Relations, Part II, 1919–1947," L/P&S/12/1321; Barton, *India's North-West Frontier,* pp. 146, 220; Griffiths, *Afghanistan,* p. 51; Ali, *Afghanistan,* p. 165; Gregorian, *Emergence of Modern Afghanistan,* pp. 285–290; Arnold, *Afghanistan,* p. 18.

6. General Staff Report, "Summary of Events in Afghanistan," 1 July 1930–30 June 1931, Simla, Government of India Press, 1931, L/P&S/12/1637, ff. 21–34; Ali, *Afghanistan,* pp. 171–172; Dupree, *AUFS,* 4/3, pp. 13–14; Fletcher, *Afghanistan,* p. 228; Fraser-Tytler, *Afghanistan,* p. 230. The coldest winter in thirty years further aggravated the plight of the Afghan people and state.

7. General Staff Report, "Summary of Events in Afghanistan," 1 July 1930–30 June 1931, L/P&S/12/1637; Bhaneja, *Afghanistan,* pp. 19–20; Barton, *India's North-West Frontier,* p. 148; Gregorian, *Making of Modern Afghanistan,* pp. 297, 313. Though Nadir also established a national police force, soldiers performed their duties while recruits received training in England. The army also staffed military hospitals and was theoretically responsible for medical services in the remote areas of the country. Nadir himself claimed the army's purpose was "to foster national unity and ensure progress."

8. Wilber, *Afghanistan,* pp. 160–161; Newell, *Politics of Afghanistan,* p. 59. Unlike many previous Afghan kings, Nadir could depend on four brothers to handle crucial government posts. Mohammed Hashim was appointed prime minister and minister of the interior. Shah Wali became ambassador to London, after serving as minister of war and commander-in-chief. Shah Mahmud thereupon became minister of war. Mohammed Aziz was named ambassador to the Soviet Union and later became ambassador to Germany. Gregorian, *Emergence of Modern Afghanistan,* pp. 294, 299–301, 300fn, 305; Bhaneja, *Political Modernization,* pp. 21–22, 27.

9. In June 1930, Soviet forces crossed the border and drove some forty miles into Afghanistan in pursuit of Beg. Given that the *basmachi* had caused many problems in north Afghanistan, Nadir eventually sent an army north, which drove Beg across the border, where he was captured and executed by the Soviets.

10. Adamec, *Afghanistan's Foreign Relations,* pp. 202–204; Amstutz, *Afghanistan,* p. 15; Arnold, *Afghanistan,* p. 20; Ali, *Afghanistan,* p. 173; Gregorian, *Emergence of Modern Afghanistan,* pp. 321–323, 330–332, 376. In March 1936, Hashim Khan extended the pact for ten years.

11. Extract from Annual Report, "Afghanistan, 1931," L/PS/12/3155, ff. 125–126; Fletcher, *Afghanistan*, p. 232; Fraser-Tytler, *Afghanistan*, pp. 236, 256–257. He summarized that the "frontier policy of the Afghan government would be actuated by a desire for peace on both sides of the frontier and a spirit of true friendship towards his Majesty's government."

12. Quoted in Adamec, *Afghanistan's Foreign Policy*, p. 201 (from India Office Annual Report, 1930). Later (p. 212), Adamec argues that the Afghans did not want to lose their "tribal buffer" and were embarrassed by their inability to help the tribes. It seems more likely that the continuation of subsidies and occasional protest against British policies were sops to tribal *maliks* designed to preserve the peace, and the cordiality between Britain and Afghanistan was more than superficial.

13. Gregorian, *Emergence of Modern Afghanistan*, p. 322; Wilber, *Afghanistan*, p. 181.

14. This attitude was perhaps best conveyed by the subsequent Simon Commission (quoted in Rittenberg, *Ethnicity*, p. 47), which declared "the inherent right of a man to smoke a cigar must necessarily be curtailed if he lives in a powder magazine."

15. Cunningham, "Reforms," pp. 95–96; Caroe, Unfinished Autobiography, MSS.EUR F.203/78 (Olaf Caroe Papers); Schofield, *Every Rock*, p. 222; Rittenberg, *Ethnicity* pp. 48–50. George Roos-Keppel, the chief commissioner of the NWFP, effectively blocked extension of self-government to the frontier, arguing that strategic concerns and the frontier's economy precluded such risk, despite the *jirgah* tradition. His immediate successor, Sir Hamilton Grant, favored giving the NWFP some sort of representative institutions (in the wake of the Khalifat movement), but Grant's term in office was brief and his successor reverted to conservative policy.

16. Caroe, Review of H.V. Hodson's *Great Divide*, MSS.EUR F.203 (Olaf Caroe Papers); Mitchell, *Sir George Cunningham*, pp. 64–65. The Khan brothers came from a well-to-do family near Peshawar. Sahib received a medical degree in England, where he took an English wife. He later served as a medical officer in the Guides. Their sister married the Haji of Turagzai, a noted frontier agitator. There is considerable debate as to when the party was actually founded, owing in part to the many names by which the party was known in its early years. In 1919 Ghaffar invoked agitation against the Rowlatt Acts and would probably have tried to rally the tribes to Afghan banners had not their forces been so thoroughly routed in the Third Anglo-Afghan War. Ghaffar Khan spent three years in prison from 1921 to 1924, during which time he was "either bound in fetters or grinding corn, according to prison rules." See Schofield, *Every Rock*, pp. 223, 247. Calling the entire party "Red Shirts" is incorrect. Not all *Khudai Khidmatgaran* were Red Shirts, and other organizations, even other militia, existed within the party. The nickname caused many problems, including a tendency to associate the movement with the Bolsheviks. British officials regularly associated pan-Islamic movements with Bolshevism and in this case saw the Red Shirts as political statements. In actuality, few members had ever heard of Marx. See Wolpert, *Roots of Confrontation*, p. 94; Fletcher, *Afghanistan*, pp. 211, 249. This misnomer was all the more unfortunate as their "red" uniforms were more a dingy plum-cum-brick color. See Caroe, *Pathans*, pp. 431–434; Barton, *India's North-West Frontier*, pp. 114–115.

17. Rittenberg, *Ethnicity*, pp. 150–153: "A gulf exists between the Congress and the *Khudai Khidmatgaran* movement, and they are not one. In this connection Khan Abdul Ghaffar Khan . . . has gone so far as to state that they are not Congressmen

but have an alliance with the Congress and could sever their relations with the Congress at any time as they liked."

18. Extract from an Unfinished Autobiography by Sir Olaf Caroe, MSS.EUR F.203/78 (Olaf Caroe Papers); Cunningham, "Speech to the Royal Institute of International Affairs," 13 June 1946, MSS.EURD.670/25; Rittenberg, *Ethnicity,* pp. 75–77, 83; Caroe, *Pathans,* pp. 432–434; Adamec, *Afghanistan's Foreign Relations,* p. 299, fn 99; Schofield, *Every Rock,* pp. 224–226; Andrews, *Challenge of the Northwest Frontier,* pp. 88–89. Ghaffar Khan wrote: "Non-violence is not a new creed to a Muslim though Mahatma Ghandi has revived it when it was forgotten. It was followed by the Prophet all the time he was in Mecca, persecuted for his faith in one God. It has been followed by other Muslims, who had wished to throw off the yoke of oppression."

19. Wylie to the Secretary of State, India Office, 6 October 1942, L/P&S/12/1789; Extract from an Unfinished Autobiography by Sir Olaf Caroe, MSS.EUR F.203/78 (Olaf Caroe Papers); Cunningham, "Speech to the Royal Institute of International Affairs," 13 June 1946, MSS.EUR D.670/25. Cunningham thought the Pathans unlikely to tolerate being disciplined from Congress. He also noted, "All talk of Afghanistan as part of Pakistan had disappeared." Dupree, *Afghanistan,* p. 488. Ghandi claimed: "Even before the Congress ministry came into being . . . Ghaffar Khan had on his brain Pathan independence in internal affairs" (telegram from the Press Information Bureau, 1 July 1947, L/P&S/12/1811, f. 53). Nehru echoed the opinion that Ghaffar Khan sought full autonomy within India and opposed Afghan interference along the frontier (*ITOP,* XI/502, p. 889). Dupree, "Durand Line of 1893," in *Current Problems in Afghanistan,* p. 85fn; Quddus, *Afghanistan and Pakistan,* p. 94; Khalilzad, *Security of Southwest Asia,* pp. 137–140. Included among the organizations that espoused reunion was Anjumani-Islahi-Afghanin (Fletcher, *Afghanistan,* p. 249). Caroe called Ghaffar Khan "half-educated," "addicted to his slogans," and "a bit mad" (Caroe to Mountbatten, 8 May 1947, Governor's Report, MSS.EUR F.203; Olaf Caroe Papers). Caroe, Lecture to the Royal Institute of International Affairs, 4 February 1948, MSS.EUR F.203/4 (Olaf Caroe Papers); Barton, *India's North-West Frontier,* pp. 114, 179, 182, 222; Mitchell, *Sir George Cunningham,* pp. 65, 72, 74. As early as 1938, Sahib had reported to the Central Assembly that the tribes would unite to form a Pathan republic that would control the area from the Indus to the Durand Line. This means an "imperative necessity" to absorb the frontier in India. Rittenberg, *Ethnicity,* pp. 51–64, 100–103. Pakhtuns were deeply concerned about events across the border in a way they were not about events in India. Afghanistan was still the paramount symbol of their past glories, political aspirations, and sense of honor as a people. The *Anjuman-i-Islah-al-Afghania,* for example, used the royal Afghan emblem on the cover of its journal, *Pakhtun,* until 1930. Its leaders spoke of Pakhtuns and Afghans as forming one nation and metaphorically called the Afghan Amir their king. See Rittenberg, *Ethnicity,* p. 73.

20. Estimates on casualties vary. A dispatch motorcycle rider who accompanied the force against orders was killed.

21. "Report of the Peshawar Disturbances Enquiry Committee, 1930," L/MIL/17/13/98; Extract from an Unfinished Autobiography by Sir Olaf Caroe, MSS.EUR F.203/78 (Olaf Caroe Papers); "Report on the Administration of Martial Law in the Peshawar District from the 16th of August, 1930 to the 23rd of January, 1931," by the Chief Commissioner, NWFP (Caroe) 7 February 1931, L/P&S/12/3125; Memo, Caroe to the Foreign Office, Delhi, 4 April 1931, L/P&S/12/3125; "The Military

Occupation of Peshawar City, 4 May 1930," by Caroe, 27 October 1930; photographs, attached to letter, E.B. Howell to J.C. Watson, Secretary, Political Dept., India Office. L/P&S/12/3215. Caroe claims there were 12 deaths in the initial disturbance, while Ghaffar Khan claimed "over 200." The armored car crews were exonerated, incidentally, on grounds they were "following proper tactics to maintain platoon formation." The photographs clearly show an armored car afire, a dispatch rider's shattered bicycle, and many stones and bricks in the road. Rittenberg, *Ethnicity*, pp. 78–81, 84, 87–88. The magnitude of the uprising was attested to by Lord Irwin, who wrote the secretary of state in August, "The whole of Peshawar district as far as Attock must be considered in a state of war."

22. Caroe, then deputy commissioner, argued for such, "otherwise big sums of revenue arrears . . . will have to be written off as irrecoverable and a permanent increase in heinous crime must be expected if steps are not taken to chain or remove those who desire to profit by the present malaise. . . . The ordinary processes of law are not sufficing and will never suffice to restore authority unless accompanied by measures which will show the determination of Government to control subversive activities." Quoted in Rittenberg, *Ethnicity*, p. 107.

23. Rittenberg, *Ethnicity*, pp. 117–119, 123–124.

24. Extract from an Unfinished Autobiography by Sir Olaf Caroe, MSS.EUR F.203/78 (Olaf Caroe Papers); Cunningham, "Reforms," pp. 98–99. Caroe also claims Qaiyum was the architect of the Pathan/British synthesis that eventually became the bulwark of Pakistan. Barton, *India's North-West Frontier*, pp. 167, 170, 223, 293. Barton claims that Qaiyum was not popular, being suspected of too close a connection to British authority. Rittenberg, *Ethnicity*, pp. 81, 84, 123, 126, 135, 140–142. In the February 1937 elections, the Frontier Congress won a plurality, but not a majority of legislative seats. Cunningham attempted to support Qaiyum in a coalition government, but following considerable infighting, a Congress inspired no confidence vote, and Qaiyum's death, the governor allowed the *Khudai Khidmatgaran* to assume power in September.

25. Gregorian, *Emergence of Modern Afghanistan*, p, 329, quoting Sir Michael O'Dwyer; see also pp. 321–322.

26. Ibid., pp. 328–330; Political Department Paper 6644/35, September 1935, L/P&S/12/1721, ff. 157–158; Barton, *India's North-West Frontier*, p. 147; Sykes, "Afghanistan: The Present Position," pp. 159–160. Nadir's restraint may have stemmed from Ghaffar Khan's alleged ties to Amanullah or from fears that the *Khudai Khidmatgars* might unite the northwest regions of India and eventually attempt to absorb Afghanistan.

27. "Survey of Anglo-Afghan Relations, Part II, 1919–1947," L/P&S/12/1321; see L/P&S/12/1575, generally; Kakar, "Trends in Modern Afghan History," in Dupree and Albert, eds., *Afghanistan in the 1970's*, p. 30; Adamec, *Afghanistan's Foreign Relations*, pp. 194–195, 207; India Office Annual Report, 1933, National Indian Archives, 41F, 1930; 25F, 1934; 730F, 1933.

28. Memo, Chief Secretary to the Government of the NWFP, 3 August 1933, L/P&S/12/1651, ff. 83–85. Nadir sometimes rejected offers of British trade because their products were simply too expensive compared with Indian or Japanese products. Telegram, Fraser-Tytler to the Government of India, 24 September 1939, L/P&S/12/1762, 4739/39, f. 160; Political Department Paper 6644/35, September 1935, L/P&S/12/1721, ff. 157–158.

29. L/P&S/12/1575.

30. "Survey of Anglo-Afghan Relations, Part II, 1919–1947," L/P&S/12/1321; Adamec, *Afghanistan's Foreign Policy,* pp. 192–197. Ghulam Nabi was once ambassador to the Soviet Union. He also was active among the tribes of southern Afghanistan during the Red Shirt agitation.

31. Translations of *Islah,* 13, 15, and 16 September 1933, L/P&S/12/1658, ff. 25–30. The dead employees included the garage superintendent and two Afghans. The Afghan press portrayed the assassin as an insane, drunken fornicator who wanted to introduce "free love, unlawful drinks and loose-living . . . to destroy and ruin all Mohammedans." He allegedly confessed that his assault stemmed from a belief that "the British have secretly acquired Afghanistan."

32. "Survey of Anglo-Afghan Relations, Part II, 1919–1947," L/P&S/12/1321; Sykes, "Afghanistan: The Present Position," p. 159; Kakar, "Trends in Modern Afghan History," p. 31; Arnold, *Afghanistan,* pp. 21–23. Abdul Khaliq is often listed as having been Ghulam Nabi's son, though according to Adamec, Nabi was merely the employer of the boy's father (see *Afghanistan's Foreign Policy,* p. 198; citing *Islah,* 26 December 1933, 28 December 1933, and the National Indian Archives, 559F, 1933).

33. Lancaster, Weekly Intelligence Survey, 10 May 1946 and 6 September 1946, L/P&S/12/1849; A.E.F. Dundas, "Precis on Afghan Affairs, 1927–1936"; Squire, "Afghanistan and Her Neighbors," p. 70; Gregorian, *Emergence of Modern Afghanistan,* pp. 351–352, 356–357. An intense nationalist, Hashim encouraged the study of Afghan history and culture and Pushtu language and literature and established organizations to promote such endeavors. Hashim proclaimed Pashto the official language in 1937.

34. "General Note on Policy on the Northwest Frontier" [n.s., n.d.] L/P&S/12/1721, ff. 240–253; Minute Paper, January 30, 1936 [n.s.], L/P&S/12/1721, f. 116; Letter, Maconachie to the Foreign Secretary, GOI (Howell), 27 January 1932, L/P&S/12/1607, 1641/32; Kabul Embassy to GOI, 17 August 1945, L/P&S/12/1603, f. 33; Fraser-Tytler to GOI External Affairs Dept., 17 April 1945, f. 63; Adamec, *Afghanistan's Foreign Affairs,* pp. 230–231; Hauner, *India in Axis Strategy,* p. 87.

35. Barton, *India's North-West Frontier,* p. 195.

36. Ibid., pp. 109, 171–175. For an account of battles during the Mohmand campaign, see Schofield, *Every Rock,* pp. 163–166.

37. Mitchell, *Sir George Cunningham,* pp. 60–61; Miller, *Khyber,* pp. 357–358; Dupree, *AUFS,* 1/4, p. 17; Barton, *India's North-West Frontier,* pp. 17, 90, 99, 176–177, 186, 224–225. Forty to fifty thousand troops were needed to occupy a territory one third the size of Switzerland. Rittenberg presents a curiously different story, in which the girl eloped with a Muslim lover, took the name Islam Bibi, and her parents regained custody of her (*Ethnicity,* p. 160, citing Official History of Operations on the Northwest Frontier of India, 1936–1937, Delhi, 1943).

38. Military Training Pamphlet No. 16, "Platoon Leading in Frontier Warfare, 1945," L/MIL/17/5/2258. The pamphlet also includes "22 points on animal mastership," in which one's mules are deemed one's "second best friend," to be looked after with as much care as your rifle. Military Training Pamphlet No. 6, "The Support of Land Forces by Aircraft in Tribal Warfare on the Western Frontier of India, 1940," L/MIL/17/5/2247; Adamec, *Afghanistan's Foreign Relations,* pp. 210–211; Barton, *India's North-West Frontier,* pp. 60, 199–200, 236–240; Mitchell, *Sir George Cun-*

ningham, p. 66; Rittenberg, *Ethnicity,* p. 161. Livestock were frequent targets of the pilots, a policy followed by the Soviets during their invasion of Afghanistan.

39. "Latest Information about the Khost Agitators" [n.s.] 8 March 1933, L/P&S/ 12/1651, ff. 69–70; see L/P&S/12/1739, generally; Cunningham, "Speech to the Royal Institute of International Affairs," 13 June 1946, MSS.EUR D.670/25. He stated simply that "Afghanistan had more trouble with her tribes than we with ours" (MSS.EUR D.670/17 George Cunningham Papers).

40. "Extract from War Cabinet Conclusions" (W.P.[G][39]4), 11 September 1939, L/P&S/12/1762, ff. 207–209;" Mitchell, *Sir George Cunningham,* pp. 67–69; Adamec, *Afghanistan's Foreign Relations,* pp. 227–228; Barton, *India's North-West Frontier,* pp. 146–147, 220–221, 241–244; Caroe, *Pathans,* pp. 408–409.

41. Schofield, *Every Rock,* p. 155; Editorial by Captain G.T. Hawkins, *Times,* 21 November 1946, L/P&S/12/1185; Adamec, *Afghanistan's Foreign Policy,* pp. 208– 209. While garrisons of scouts and *Khassadars* (frontier police) guarded the expanded road network, Indian army regiments in the settled districts served as operational reserves. Contemporary British generals compared the "Modified Forward Policy" with the frontier strategy of the Romans, wherein auxiliary forces served as police and a tripwire defense, alerting the reserve legions to major incursions. The British constructed roads and forts along the frontier, which proved of immediate tactical value but brought resentment from the tribes, who saw not only roads, but industry, schools, and even hospitals as threats to their traditional independence. .

42. "Tribal Disarmament in Afghanistan," note by Military Department [n.s., n.d. (1944?)] L/WS/1/98, ff. 1–6; Barton, *India's North-West Frontier,* pp. 208, 222 252– 259, 263–265; see also Cabinet, India and Burma Committee, Paper I.B.(47)47, "Constitutional Developments—Attitude of Afridis Letter from the Governor of the North-West Frontier Province to the Private Secretary to the Viceroy," 11 April 1947, *ITOP,* X/128, p. 205.

6

AFGHANISTAN IN THE SECOND WORLD WAR AND THE ORIGINS OF THE "LANCASTER PLAN"

As early as 1931, Nadir Shah inquired as to the British position in the event of a Soviet attack on his country. British authorities proved reluctant to offer firm assurances, as they considered Afghanistan's northern provinces "absolutely indefensible." They felt the Soviets could conquer those areas with relative ease, regardless of Afghan defense measures. Furthermore, no political or economic incentives mandated British guarantees. Yet while the British remained noncommittal, they were at least conciliatory, claiming they valued the territorial integrity of Afghanistan and would regard a threat to it in a serious light. In the official reply, British Minister Sir Richard Maconachie downplayed the likelihood of a Soviet attack to Afghan officials. Yet he also stated that any Soviet attack would be regarded as a direct threat to British interests and would be met with economic sanctions and diplomatic pressure, if not military measures.[1]

Like many nations in the 1930s, Afghanistan sought a degree of security through membership in international organizations. Afghanistan entered the League of Nations in 1934, shortly after the Soviet Union joined. Though failure in the Ethiopian crisis quickly destroyed Afghan faith in the organization, Afghanistan was not alienated from ideas of collective security.[2]

On July 7, 1937, representatives of Afghanistan, Iran, Iraq, and Turkey signed the Saadabad Pact. A treaty of nonaggression and friendship, it remains the only alliance Afghanistan ever entered. The Saadabad Pact provided for general consultation on regional disputes and stipulated similar discussion in the event of aggression by nonmembers. The pact prohibited interference in the internal affairs of member states and promoted cooperation in dealing with subversives. Though all members shared common distrust of the U.S.S.R., in the wake of Fascist aggressions, the Saadabad Pact met with Soviet as well as British approval.[3]

For the Afghan government, the pan-Islamic overtones of the pact placated conservative opposition at home, and membership lessened the likelihood that any regional power would support a return of Amanullah. It also increased cultural and economic contacts and led to a temporary settlement of a border dispute with Iran. Finally, membership facilitated the provision of Turkish military assistance. By 1939 the Turks maintained a sizable military mission in Kabul. Though a small step, the Saadabad Pact was nonetheless a definite one, indicative of the political goals and national sentiments of the member nations, all of whom supported the establishment of an Islamic bloc along the southern border of the U.S.S.R. As an American official would subsequently note, "In a real sense this could be regarded as a precursor to the Baghdad Pact, except for the fact that Afghanistan did not join the latter."[4]

Though willing to consider regional security arrangements, Hashim Khan's government also sought to further develop and expand the Afghan armed forces. While the guerrilla potential of the population remained Afghanistan's primary deterrent, continuation of Nadir's modernization plans increased that deterrent while augmenting internal security capabilities. By 1939 Hashim had overseen expansion of the curriculum at the military academy, opened artillery, cavalry, and infantry officers' schools, and continued the foreign education of officers in India, the U.S.S.R., Turkey, Italy, Germany, and Japan. About 150 Turkish officers, along with a few Germans and Italians, provided in-country training. The air force was enlarged, some mechanized and motorized units formed, and a department of logistics established.[5]

Over time, more and more British authorities came to support increased military assistance to Kabul. Some favored provision of modern weaponry, including machine guns, tanks, and aircraft, to help improve internal security, pacify the tribes, and thereby bolster the defense of the subcontinent. Others favored increased economic contacts. When Hashim Khan requested a 2.5-million-pound loan from London in 1935, however, the British rejected his proposal. Evidence suggests that Britain's economic difficulties, still severe in the midst of the Great Depression, rather than scattered dissension from those who feared that Afghanistan would allow her surplus weapons to filter down to the frontier, precluded offers of military assistance and greater cooperation on development.[6]

Britain's reluctance to make a greater commitment led Hashim to solicit other sources. Though the Japanese, Italians, Turks, Poles, Czechs, and Iranians all responded to some degree, Hashim received the most enthusiastic responses from the Germans. Afghan-German relations had deteriorated under Nadir. The assassination of Mohammed Aziz in Berlin and delays surrounding the trial and execution of the assassin aroused suspicions that the Weimar Germans still preferred Amanullah.

Relations improved following the Nazi seizure of power. Germany's allegedly pro-Islamic stance in the First World War and an apparent lack of imperial designs on the area made intimate relations politically desirable. German personal discipline, technological expertise, and willingness "to work for moderate wages in conditions of extreme discomfort" further appealed to the Afghan leadership. Finally, unlike the British and other Western allies, Hitler's Germany proved willing to offer favorable credit terms and to accept payments in raw materials, in an effort to secure political leverage among the Afghans. In late 1936, the Afghan and German governments, the latter on order from Hitler himself, signed a secret protocol promising increased economic contacts and the delivery of arms to Afghanistan. Another agreement signed the following year granted Organization Todt rights to supervise road construction and aviation facilities development, while other concessions granted German firms rights to natural resource exploitation and industrial development. Then in August 1939, Afghanistan and Germany signed a ten-year comprehensive economic agreement, in which Germany became Afghanistan's chief supplier of economic and military assistance. On the eve of World War II, over 100 German technicians were supervising a variety of commercial projects in Afghanistan, while other officials helped train the army and the police.[7]

The increased Afghan-German contracts spurred Britain to action. Hashim and Minister of the Economy Abdul Majid Zabuli visited London in 1937 and obtained a 500,000-pound development loan, which partly balanced German commitments. Continued fear of Soviet aggression, meanwhile, sustained Afghan desires for strategic cooperation with British India. Discussion on a mutual cooperation pact commenced in mid-1939, prompted by Afghan inquiries following British guarantees of Poland's territorial integrity. Britain did not actually ally with Afghanistan, fearing adverse Soviet reaction and doubting its ability to enforce any such guarantee in the wake of defense commitments elsewhere. Still, in the months preceding the outbreak of the Second World War, the British sold aircraft and armaments to the Afghans and offered to train Afghan officers. The respective Chiefs of Staff secretly discussed modernization of the Afghan army and its integration into subcontinent defense plans, where it could "take its place in future years as the first line of defense of India."[8]

Afghan fears heightened in the aftermath of the Nazi-Soviet Pact to the point where Hashim even considered allowing British garrisons in Kabul and Herat. Despite any evidence of logistical preparations for such an assault, the British considered a Soviet invasion of Afghanistan and India a distinct possibility. In December 1939, following the Soviet assault on Finland, two British officers, Brigadier G.N. Molesworth and Major A.S. Lancaster, arrived in Kabul, where they conducted an inspection of the Afghan army. Molesworth found leadership in short supply. Afghan officers, he claimed, were afflicted with "oriental chicanery, indolence, ignorance and incapacity." Their "idiotic" war plans seemed to have been composed overnight and, such as they existed, were wholly inadequate. Their armaments requests seemed but "a stupendous and fantastic list of war material," and their attraction for modern equipment, Molesworth wrote, amounted to "children playing with expensive and half-comprehended toys." He ultimately dismissed the army as "little more than a facade and of little value off the barracks square," concluding that, for the immediate future, "to expend time, energy, and money on such a concern . . . is sheer waste." Yet Molesworth still acknowledged that, if invaded, the Afghans would resist as a nation and believed they wanted to be allied "in the real sense of the word." He thought long-term agreements offered a good probability of favorable political return and recommended that Britain continue to supply arms and training, provided the equipment and officers were available.[9]

In early 1940, the Foreign Office recommended giving Hashim a secret guarantee against "indisputable aggression by Soviet forces" and even thought promise of "some measure of assistance by land forces in India, in addition to air support," worthwhile. They acknowledged, however, that no guarantee could include the security of the northern border. The War Cabinet likewise remained fully cognizant of Britain's inability to offer Afghanistan realistic assistance in the event of attack and remained reluctant to offer firm guarantees of Afghanistan's territorial integrity. Prime Minister Winston Churchill eventually took the initiative in offering Hashim further arms purchases, technical assistance, and training. The prime minister also stressed Britain's concern for the territorial integrity of the Afghan state, believing such policy would bolster Hashim's government, help pacify the tribes, undermine Axis influence, and improve British relations with Muslim states elsewhere.[10]

Stalin ignored German urgings to exploit Allied weaknesses in the Gulf region and ultimately withdrew most of his troops from Central Asia following the fall of France. Once the Soviet threat to Afghanistan dissipated, extensive German-Afghan connections chilled Anglo-Afghan relations. The Germans, hoping to discomfit the British, offered Hashim a restored Durrani Empire in exchange for Afghan intervention in India. Early German victories led some members of the Afghan hierarchy to consider their options in the event of a Russian collapse. Abdul Majid, for example, at times voiced support for a "Berlin-Baghdad-Kabul Axis" in return for military hardware, a guarantee of Afghanistan's northern border, and territorial aggrandizement up to the Indus River. In conversation with Axis agents, he reportedly considered "whether or not he should turn away from the present Afghan government."[11]

Though geographic and logistical considerations rendered such possibilities remote, Axis intrigues in Afghanistan nonetheless unnerved the British.

So, too, did Afghan efforts to continue their economic contacts with Berlin. Some British officials came to believe Afghanistan would join Germany in an attack on India were the Soviet Union to collapse. British Indian forces constructed a number of anti-tank obstacles all along passages through the frontier, and some units carried out exercises (War Plan Pink) that presumed German forces would be warmly welcomed in Afghanistan.[12]

In October 1941, Britain and the U.S.S.R., tired of what they considered undue Afghan sympathy for Hitler, issued a joint demand for the expulsion of all nonofficial Axis nationals from Afghanistan. Hashim's government, aware that the Allies had crushed rebellion in Iraq in April and partitioned Iran in August and cognizant of Afghanistan's dependence on India for imports, had little choice but to comply. Hashim avoided the onus of the decision by calling a Loya Jirgah, which agreed to appease the Allies but stipulated that Afghanistan would tolerate no more infringements on its neutrality. In the official reply, Hashim complained, with some justification, of how little note had been taken of his nation's efforts to curtail propaganda, quell tribal raids, arrest known agents, and pursue a genuinely neutral policy.[13]

As in the First World War, Afghanistan's neutrality allowed Britain to decrease its Indian garrisons and send expeditionary forces to various fronts. It also freed forces for internal pacification operations, which proved critical when renewed independence agitation threatened the British position in the subcontinent. In September 1939, following the invasion of Poland, the Viceroy Lord Linlithgow had declared India at war with Germany. This act, made without consultation of Congress opinion, enraged the party. The Japanese advance through Southeast Asia further aroused aspirations for independence and practically forced Churchill to re-examine the Indian situation. The prime minister dispatched Sir Stafford Cripps to India with a War Cabinet declaration that promised postwar reforms. Cripps conceded the Congress demand for an elected assembly to frame a constitution, thereby committing the British government to a policy of complete independence for India. His proposal also allowed the various provinces and states to achieve dominion status independently of the union, if they desired.[14]

Congress rejected Cripps's offer. Their official response attacked the proposal's insistence on continued British hegemony over subcontinent defense, but other provisions influenced the decision. Congress would not approve a plan that did not grant immediate concessions, made no allowances to bring democracy to the princely states, and conceded provincial independence, effectively allowing for the "Balkanization" of India.[15]

After it became evident that the British were not going to concede immediate independence, Congress passed the "Quit India" resolution on August 8, 1942. Though a renewed campaign of civil disobedience began, Government of India authorities arrested most of the key party leaders and managed to contain the scattered disturbances. Churchill's government did not reconsider the Indian question again during the war.[16]

The North West Frontier Province also remained remarkably quiet throughout the conflict. Shortly after the outbreak of war in 1939, Khan Sahib's *Khudai Khidmatgaran* government (which had been elected in 1937) resigned in accordance with Congress' noncooperation tactics. Their efforts to discomfit British authorities met with little success. Instead, the frontier witnessed six years of relative peace. Wazirstan was never completely calm, but following a minor outbreak in the wake of events in Iraq, by late 1941, even the stubborn faqir of Ipi had gone into hiding, and remained of little trouble thereafter.[17] Following still another arrest of Ghaffar Khan on October 27, 1942, Congress activity all but disappeared.[18] The British governor found Pushtun dislike of Germans, Italians, Japanese, and Congress "hearty and genuine." The Afridis, for example, made a spontaneous gift for victims of the London Blitz, and the Mahsuds offered to enlist en masse to fight the Japanese "and those Hindus who sympathize with the Japs" on the sole condition that they be allowed to retain whatever booty they might acquire. Some local religious authorities threatened frontier agitators who fought the British instead of the Nazis.[19]

Most Pushtuns supported the war effort and resented Congress' not-so-subtle sympathy for the idol-worshipping Japanese. Still more attacked the personal character of the *Khudai Khidmatgaran* leaders. Some resented the marriage of Abdul Ghaffar Khan's son to a Parsi and Khan Sahib's daughter to a Sikh-turned-Christian flight lieutenant. Governor Cunningham supported this trend with an anti-Congress propaganda campaign and was looking to form a Muslim League ministry as early as 1940 but could not owing to "selfish ambitions and private feuds" among the party leadership.[20]

Throughout the war, Axis propaganda in the region proved ineffective. Intelligence and espionage operations suffered from the same failings that hindered efforts elsewhere. German agents demonstrated remarkable ignorance of area affairs. A chronic lack of secrecy further allowed Afghan authorities and the British to employ effective countermeasures. The German Foreign Office *Auswaertiges Amt,* its Nazi party counterpart *Aussenpolitische Amt,* and the *Abwehr,* military intelligence, implemented divergent plans, occasionally duplicating or undermining the other's endeavors. Japanese and Italian efforts did little but add to the confusion. For example, the *Auswaertiges Amt,* frustrated by Hashim's neutrality, devised a plan to restore Amanullah. The German Foreign Office planned to send Ghulam Siddiq through Soviet Central Asia, where he would recruit an army and march on Kabul. *Aussenpolitische Amt* and *Abwehr* officials opposed the plan, as it depended on Soviet cooperation, would waste all previous efforts to court the current regime, and, if it failed, would merely drive Afghanistan to alliance with Britain. Hitler, who personally was unimpressed with the Amanullah clique, ordered the project scrapped. The Italian minister Pietro Quaroni, meanwhile, had developed a plan for a major insurrection among the frontier tribes. The Germans, however, believing Britain on the verge of surrender, rejected the idea, claiming "they did not want to diminish further the prestige of the whites in the Middle East or India."[21]

During the summer of 1942, German forces pushed the Soviets back toward Stalingrad and the Caucasus, Rommel's Afrika Korps drove through Egypt toward El Alamein, and the rejection of the Cripps Mission forecast a distinct possibility of revolution in India. Fearing that the Germans would soon be on their border, some members of the Afghan government "attempted to get one leg on the Axis side of the fence," hatching plans for cooperation in the event of a Soviet collapse. Abdul Majid, for example, promised to mobilize 500,000 tribesmen if and when German forces reached Afghanistan's vicinity. The finance minister, however, had been long at odds with the government over fiscal policy and had no significant following among the frontier Pushtuns. Hashim, on the other hand, while willing to utilize German development assistance and technological expertise, had always been anti-Nazi. He remained a stalwart supporter of the Allied cause throughout the war and rejected several German proposals, "most damaging to Britain." He pursued policies in Britain's interest, without implying abject subservience to London. Sir Giles Squire, who assumed the Kabul ministry in 1945, claimed Hashim's policy was "of the greatest advantage to us and I do not think it has even been generally and adequately recognized." Such policy helped bring Anglo-Afghan relations closer than they had been before.[22]

Shortly after the German invasion of the Soviet Union, the U.S.S.R. had closed its border with Afghanistan. The subsequent occupation of Iran eliminated Afghanistan's last contact with the Axis, leaving British India as Afghanistan's sole supplier of provisions. The loss of other contacts made it easier for all Afghans to accept British assistance. The British, assisted by the United States, used the opportunity to succor favor, sending the Afghans food supplies and manufactures as well as a smattering of military hardware. Hashim's government, for its part, arrested dozens of frontier agitators, including several Indian nationalist leaders, and deported most of them to India.[23]

Following the great turning point victories of 1942–1943, the Afghan government showed little hesitation in making public admissions of its friendship with the Western Allies. Hashim actually requested an alliance with Britain and the United States in 1943, but the Allies, fearful of upsetting relations with the U.S.S.R. and claiming "Afghanistan has little to offer us in return," turned him down. Despite the rejection, Hashim continued to argue for increased economic and educational contacts. Through 1944 and 1945, the government-supervised Afghan press ran numerous pro-Allied articles, expressing thanks for economic assistance and desires for future cooperation. Examples of the changing Afghan attitude include the hiring of three English teachers at Kabul University, an exchange of publications with the Royal Asiatic Society of Bengal, a grant of watering rights to the British military cemetery at Maiwand, and, perhaps most notably, the removal of the picture of

Dr. Brydon (the survivor of 1841) from the cover of national grade school textbooks.[24]

A number of trends and events heightened Afghan desire for cooperation after the war. The war had left Afghan development programs a shambles. Most German-sponsored development projects had been terminated shortly after ground breaking. With popular discontent rising, the ruling family recognized the necessity for modernization, without which their very hold on power would be threatened.

Military weakness further necessitated cooperation with the West. In 1945 an uprising of the Safi tribe, caused by government attempts to enforce conscription, erupted in southern Afghanistan. Though a minor revolt by most standards, the army experienced great difficulty in containing it. Ultimately, the government had to arm other tribes and abandon the conscription idea to contain the rebellion.[25]

Additional events heightened Afghan fears of the U.S.S.R. The Soviets, perturbed over Anglo-American inroads in Afghanistan and soon ousted from northern Iran, routinely bullied Hashim and his successor (from May 1946), Shah Mahmud, for economic concessions. They also increased espionage activities in northern Afghanistan amidst renewed negotiations over the Oxus boundary. Though the "agent provocateurs" sent across the Afghan border found few converts amidst the former *basmachi,* they, along with the ongoing negotiations, nonetheless served as a reminder of the northern menace. Facing both internal and external threats, the Afghan government attempted to secure close military relations with British India. The British responded accordingly.[26]

Improved Anglo-Afghan military relations owed much to the work of the military attaché in Kabul, Lieutenant Colonel A.S. Lancaster. A career officer with an intimate knowledge of his assigned country (Lancaster surveyed the Afghan military with Brigadier Molesworth in December 1939), Lancaster was well respected among the Kabul leadership. By 1945 he still acknowledged that the Afghan army lacked the technical and administrative skills necessary to wage modern war. Officers lacked professionalism, the supply system was rudimentary at best, most equipment was over ten years old, and while excellent physical specimens, the illiterate and poorly disciplined Afghan conscripts were largely ignorant of modern warfare. Overall, he thought the army incapable of waging war against more than a third-class power. Mohammed Daoud, then war minister, conceded to the attaché that ignorance, laziness, religious conservatism, and the lack of efficient administration were serious obstacles to improving the Afghan armed forces. Yet Daoud still desired procurement of British technical and training assistance and even hoped to send Afghan officers to Sandhurst after the war.[27]

Lancaster further admitted that Afghanistan was impossible to defend in a conventional sense and indeed thought it foolish for the Afghan army to plan to meet a Soviet invasion in open battle. He believed an army of 50,000 was all Afghanistan could afford and conceded that their main purpose would be internal security. Lancaster nonetheless championed the idea of supplying Afghan military needs through India and integrating the Afghan army into subcontinent defense plans. He wrote:

There are few diplomats in Kabul who realize that penetration into the military sphere is important. . . . [The army is] the one thing that really matters . . . on which the Royal Family and the government have to rely for the stability of the country.[28]

Lancaster realized that provision of the army's supplies would secure Britain considerable political influence, at a minimal cost, while increasing Afghanistan's deterrent against potential aggression.

Lancaster arranged a visit to India for an Afghan military mission in the winter of 1944–1945. Shortly thereafter, British Indian and Afghan authorities signed a comprehensive agreement in which the British agreed to provide equipment and training for the Afghan armed forces. The "Lancaster Plan" offered Afghanistan some 30 million rupees' worth of equipment and services, at a cost of only 15 million, payable in ten installments, on easy credit terms. British officers were soon assigned to Afghan army units, and equipment began to arrive from India. In 1946, 150 Afghan officers and noncommissioned officers were dispatched to India for one-year's training. A second group followed in 1947.[29]

By early 1947, the Afghan army had become heavily dependent on Britain for supplies, instructors, and technical assistance. The British also secured a dominant influence over the Afghan air force, selling the Afghans properly conditioned, second-line aircraft at reasonable prices. The entire Afghan air force was equipped with British planes, and its pilots were all British trained.[30]

For the first time since the early nineteenth century, the governments of Afghanistan and Britain were resolved to a policy of cooperation. Most Afghans, not just government officials, were well disposed toward London (and the allies, including the United States). Mahmud's regime envisioned further economic cooperation, was extremely happy with the arrangements to supply and train the army, and hoped to continue such liaison. Daoud bluntly stated that Anglo-Afghan and Indo-Afghan relations had never been better. Yet Britain's position in the region was about to crumble. In the aftermath of the partition of India, Britain would no longer be willing, able, or even interested in providing protection and assistance to Afghanistan. The successor states, Pakistan and India, would share a similar lack of interest. Less than ten years later, Daoud, as prime minister, would mortgage Afghanistan's independence in an aid package with the Soviet Union.

NOTES

1. "Relations with Afghanistan," Memo for the Cabinet by the Secretary of State for Foreign Affairs and the Secretary of State for India, October 1932, L/P&S/12/1558, ff. 90–94; John Simon to Maconachie, 17 October 1932, L/P&S/12/1641, f.

16; Maconachie to the Secretary of State for India, 1 December 1932, L/P&S/12/1640, f. 4; Foreign Office to Kabul, 17 October 1932, FO 371/22257; "Policy in Regard to Afghanistan," Memo by the Secretary of State for War, C.P. 36(34), February, 1934, L/WS/1/299, ff. 45–47; Hauner, "Significance of Afghanistan," p. 243; see also Minute Paper, E.F. Crombie (Military Secretary, Kabul), 1 December 1939, L/P&S/12/1762, f. 48; Report by Brig. Gen. G.N. Molesworth of Conversations with Hashim Khan, 13–16 December 1939, L/P&S/12/1763, ff. 308–340; Lancaster to Fraser-Tytler, Report of Interview with Mohammed Daoud, 22 October 1940, L/P&S/12/1763, ff. 37–41.

2. Adamec, *Afghanistan's Foreign Relations*, p. 216; 300fn. In the 1920s, British authorities opposed Afghan entry into the League, claiming membership "might hamper our traditional and effective methods of dealing with certain kinds of border trouble."

3. Dupree, *Afghanistan*, p. 479; Asopa, *Military Alliance*, p. 34; Gregorian, *Emergence of Modern Afghanistan*, pp. 376–377; Watt, "The Sa'adabad Pact," p. 302; Fraser-Tytler, *Afghanistan*, pp. 251, 304. Fraser-Tytler provides a text of the agreement in Appendix VI, pp. 330–332. The pact was automatically renewed every five years.

4. Scholars remain divided on the impact and importance of the Saadabad Pact. Evan M. Wilson (Harry S Truman Library, Oral History Interviews, p. 59) commented that "the Iranians always attached a great deal of importance to this relationship, although more in the direction of Turkey, because, as you know, Reza Shah was a great admirer of Ataturk." Kirk (*Survey*, pp. 489–490) hails the pact as "a regional bloc strong enough to withstand Great Power interference whether from the growing Mediterranean ambitions of Fascist Italy or from the traditional Middle Eastern rivalry of Britain and Russia." Adamec (*Afghanistan's Foreign Relations*, pp. 233–234) claims the Afghans were unenthused with the pact. Gregorian (*Emergence of Modern Afghanistan*, pp. 377–378) claims "the actual and potential benefits of the Saadabad Pact were limited," owing to the military weakness of the alliance members, border disputes, and Shi'a-Sunni divisions. Fletcher's thesis (*Afghanistan*, p. 237), which calls it "a harmless piece of mutual non-aggression that nevertheless marked the first time that either the Turks or the Afghans had shown any friendship for their Persian neighbors," is perhaps the most accurate.

5. O'Ballance, "Afghanistan," pp. 226–227; Gregorian, *Emergence of Modern Afghanistan*, pp. 371–372, 381. While better than any *lashkar*, however, the army remained deficient in many ways. For example, while officially a volunteer force, the government allocated regional quotas to local *jirgahs*, who compelled the enlistment of often unwilling, and unfit, "volunteers." The army's equipment also remained a menagerie of German, British, Italian, and Czech designs.

6. "Survey of Anglo-Afghan Relations, Part II, 1919–1947," L/P&S/12/1321; Fraser-Tytler to the Secretary of State for Foreign Affairs, 16 November 1938, L/P&S/12/1683, ff. 29–30; Fraser-Tytler to the Foreign Office, 27 November 1937, L/P&S/12/1683, ff. 22–23; Minute Paper, E.F. Crombie (Military Secretary, Kabul), 1 December 1939, L/P&S/12/1762, f. 48; see also WO 208/15, Report by Brig. Gen. G.N. Molesworth of Conversations with Hashim Khan, 13–16 December 1939, L/P&S/12/1763, ff. 308–340; Lancaster to Fraser-Tytler, Report of Interview with Mohammed Daoud, 22 October 1940, L/P&S/12/1763, ff. 37–41; Hauner, *India in Axis Strategy*, pp. 80, 147–148. During the same period, the Soviets offered the Afghans modern

weaponry, training, and extensive economic contacts, but Hashim's government turned them down.

7. Hauner, *India in Axis Strategy,* pp. 72–79. He claims the value of the 1936 agreement 15 million reichmarks and the 1939 treaty 55 million. Adamec, *Afghanistan's Foreign Policy,* pp. 199–200, 221–227, 238; Gregorian, *Emergence of Modern Afghanistan,* pp. 379–380, 383; Maillart, "Afghanistan's Rebirth," pp. 226–227.

8. Minute Paper, E.F. Crombie, Military Secretary, Kabul, 1 December 1939, L/P&S/12/1762, f. 48; Kabul to Foreign Office, 7 July 1939, R/12/I/113; Kabul to the Secretary of State, 18 July 1939, FO 371/23632; "Survey," Part II, L/P&S/12/1321. Hashim and Majid, in addition to seeking closer economic cooperation, also came "to sound the British government on the idea of a port." By the late 1930s, Hashim's regime even expressed willingness to improve road communications to India. Hauner, *India in Axis Strategy,* pp. 89–90, 147; Barton, *India's North-West Frontier,* p. 150.

9. Report of Conversation with Hashim Khan, by Brig. Gen. G.N. Molesworth, 13–16 December, 1939, L/P&S/12/1763, ff. 308–340; see also Hauner, *India in Axis Strategy,* pp. 144–147.

10. Hauner, *India in Axis Strategy,* pp. 135–136, 147–155, citing FO 371/24768: WP(G)(40) 94, 12 March 1940, CAB 65 WM(39)12, 11 September 1939; WO 106/5169, 29 September 1939; Foreign Office to the Kabul Embassy, R/12/I/113, 14 September 1939; Kabul Embassy to the Foreign Office, 24 September 1939, R/12/I/113, and other documents; see also Hauner, "Significance of Afghanistan," pp. 242–243.

11. L/P&S/12/1656; Kirk, *Survey,* p. 143; Gregorian, *Making of Modern Afghanistan,* pp. 384–387, 389, 389fn; Adamec, *Afghanistan's Foreign Policy,* pp. 238, 245–246, 255. While trying to succor the Afghan regime, the Nazis also considered plans to restore Amanullah and encouraged the Soviet Union to invade Afghanistan. Later, however, Majid informed Hashim of the secret discussions, and the Afghan government reaffirmed its neutrality and subsequently ignored Iraqi urgings for Afghanistan to join their uprising in accordance with the Saadabad Pact.

12. "Afghanistan—General Situation," January–June 1941 [n.s.] L/P&S/12/1778, ff. 2–9; India Office Minutes, "Approach by Afghan Government to the Axis" [n.d., 9 March 1942?], L/P&S/12/1789, ff. 173–174; Gregorian, *Emergence of Modern Afghanistan,* pp. 384–389, 389fn; Squire, "German and Italian Conspirative Work in Afghanistan" (Interview with Italian Minister Quaroni), 11 December 1943, L/P&S/12/1805, ff. 11–20; Sykes, "Afghanistan: The Present Position," p. 162; Schofield, *Every Rock,* pp. 229–231. Furthermore, the British remained upset that the Afghans allowed for the continuation of German cultural activities, which often provided a cover for propaganda, while refusing similar rights to Britain. British planners foresaw mechanization and airpower allowing German armies to move rapidly across the Russian steppe, through Afghanistan, and into India. The Germans also envisioned armored thrusts through Afghanistan and charged Organization Todt with construction of roads and bridges that would permit such passage.

13. "Approach by Afghan Government to the Axis" [n.s., n.d.; 9 March 1942?]), L/P&S/12/1789, ff. 173–174; "Afghanistan—General Situation," January–June 1941, L/P&S/12/1778, ff. 2–9; Wylie to Caroe, 24 June 1943, L/P&S/12/1789, ff. 77–79; Wylie, Report of Interview with Hashim Khan, 20 February 1943, L/P&S/12/1789, ff. 104–108; "Expulsion of Axis Nationals from Afghanistan," U.S. National Archives, 740.0011, 1939/24927; Barton, *India's North-West Frontier,* p. 1101; Dupree, *Af-*

ghanistan, pp. 481, 491. Only 10 of 180 Germans were allowed to stay. Newell, *Politics of Afghanistan,* p. 64; Adamec, *Afghanistan's Foreign Affairs,* pp. 252, 257–258. In the immediate aftermath, Hashim rode a crest of nationalism to invoke a new conscription system for all males over the age of seventeen and a new tax for the purchase of military hardware. Curiously, the American ambassador opposed these plans. "Any effort to force the Government of Afghanistan to expel the Axis Legations or . . . drastically to reduce their staffs is inexpedient and would be considered by the Afghans as an unjustified infringement upon their sovereignty with resultant bitterness toward all the Allied governments. Though US views Axis activity with concern, maintenance of Axis legations entirely a matter of decision for the GOA. US will not attempt to force the GOA to sever relations. This attitude . . . is occasioned by firm confidence in the friendship of Afghanistan." Secretary of State (Hull) to Engert, 5 June 1943, FRUS, 1943, IV, pp. 38–39.

14. Qureshi, *Anglo-Pakistan Relations,* pp. 20–21; Zeigler, *Mountbatten,* p. 351.

15. *ITOP,* I/587; Brown, *United States, India and Pakistan,* pp. 105–107. Though the League rejected the proposal for falling short of their demand for Pakistan, provincial independence provisions still encouraged Pakistan advocates.

16. In official correspondence, Linlithgow produced a very different picture, calling the movement "by far the most serious rebellion since that of 1857, the gravity of which we have concealed from the world for reasons of military security" (*ITOP,* II/662). Throughout 1943–1945, the government of India kept busy, responding to serious food shortages, which seem to have contributed to the lessening of political activism.

17. "Summary of Events on the North West Frontier," 1937–1946, MSS.EUR D.670/17 (George Cunningham Papers). Cunningham wrote of traveling unescorted through Ahmedzai territory in 1941, stopping for roadside tea. He later discovered that one of his tea companions was a notorious highwayman, Sabar Gul, with a 20,000-rupee bounty on his head. Wavell, "Report on Operations in Waziristan, 25 May 1940–30 September 1941," L/MIL/17/13/126, and October 1941–31 December 1942.

18. "Summary of Events on the North West Frontier," 1937–1946," MSS.EUR D.670/17 (George Cunningham Papers); Barton, *India's North-West Frontier,* pp. 180–181, 294; Mitchell, *Sir George Cunningham,* pp. 62–63; Cunningham to Linlithgow, NWFP Governor's Report No. 9, 9 May 1942, *ITOP,* II/40, p. 58; War Cabinet Paper W.P.(45)218, "Recent Ministerial Changes in Certain Indian Provinces," 5 April 1945, *ITOP,* V/374, p. 831; Cunningham to Linlithgow, NWFP Governor's Report No. 15, 8 August 1942, *ITOP,* II/471, p. 626; Cunningham to Linlithgow, 28 September 1942, *ITOP,* III/43, p. 55; Linlithgow to Amery, 7 October 1942, *ITOP,* III/74, p. 105; Cunningham to Linlithgow, NWFP Governor's Report No. 21, 9 November 1942, *ITOP,* III/156, p. 222; Cunningham to Linlithgow, NWFP Governor's Report No. 22, 23 November 1942, *ITOP,* III/209, p. 293; Home Department to Secretary of State, Government of India, 5 September 1942, *ITOP,* II/697, pp. 904–905; Cunningham, "Speech to the Royal Institute of International Affairs," 13 June 1946, MSS.EUR D.670/25. The *Khudai Khidmatgaran* was the only branch of the Congress party not outlawed, largely at Cunningham's insistence. His tactful policy helped curtail disruption. The tribes gave the emissaries particularly hostile receptions. The *Khudai Khidmatgaran* officially called off the campaign in April 1943 (Rittenberg, *Ethnicity,* pp. 169–171).

19. "Summary of Events on the Northwest Frontier," 1937–1946, MSS.EUR D.670/17 (George Cunningham Papers). According to Cunningham, the tribes believed the Afghan regime was supportive of Axis intrigues. "In my opinion, the Afghans had warned [Ipi] not to give us trouble; if this is correct, it shows that the Afghans can stop this kind of nuisance if they really want to." See also Schofield, *Every Rock,* pp. 232–234, which recounts the story of an elderly Mahsud who entered a recruiting station clutching old World War I medals, wanting to beat the Germans again.

20. Cunningham to Linlithgow, 25 July 1942, *ITOP,* II/326, p. 458; Cunningham to Linlithgow, NWFP Governor's Report No. 13, 8 July 1942, *ITOP,* II/237, p. 353fn; Cunningham to Linlithgow, NWFP Governor's Report No. 16, 24 August 1943, *ITOP,* IV/89, pp. 186–187. The Pushtuns regarded Ghandi's fondness for "spinning" as "women's work" and for street-cleaning as utterly undignified. Cunningham was especially delighted when a group in Peshawar dressed a stork in a "dhoti" as a "cruelly true caricature" of Ghandi and paraded it through the streets. The exhausted stork died the next day (Rittenberg, *Ethnicity,* pp. 170–173).

21. "German and Italian Conspirative Work in Afghanistan," Interview with the Italian minister Pietro Quaroni by Squire, 11 December 1943, L/P&S/12/1805, ff. 11–20; Report of Interview with Italian Minister Pietro Quaroni, by Engert, 8 December 1943, *FRUS,* 890.00/253; Adamec, *Afghanistan's Foreign Policy,* pp. 240–243, 260. He adds that individuals within these organizations, upset at having been sent to an area of "petty hostilities" but given license by Nazi ideology, launched individual attempts to become a "Teutonic Lawrence of Arabia." Gregorian, *Emergence of Modern Afghanistan,* pp. 384–385, 384–385fn; Hauner, *India in Axis Strategy,* pp. 160–161, 164–166, 168–170; Ambassador in the United Kingdom (Winant) to the Secretary of State, 11 June 1943, *FRUS,* 1943, IV, pp. 40–42. After the Italian surrender, Quaroni said the "Prime Minister who completely dominates the government has been consistently hostile to the Axis." Quaroni also accused the Germans of "being extremely stupid and bungling in their methods and ready to be led up the garden path by every petty intriguer." Charge in Afghanistan (Thayer) to the Secretary of State, 29 September 1943, *FRUS,* 1943, IV, pp. 50–51.

22. Wylie to the Secretary of State for Foreign Affairs, India Office, 6 October 1942, L/P&S/12/1789; Incoming Telegram, Kabul, 21 October 1942, L/P&S/12/1789, ff. 147–148; India Office Minutes [n.d., 9 March 1942?], L/P&S/12/1789, ff. 173–174; Wylie to Caroe, 24 June 1943, L/P&S/12/1789, ff. 77–79; Hauner, *India in Axis Strategy,* pp. 75, 81, 91, 155; Squire, "Afghanistan and Her Neighbors," p. 70. Engert to Secretary of State, 20 July 1943, *FRUS,* 1943, IV, pp. 25–27.

Abdul Majid was a Tarakai Pashtun but had long lived in Herat, where he had become a successful businessman. Hashim's neutrality may also in part have been due to the Afghan government's sizable investments in the United States. Hashim did not want to lose this nest egg.

23. Eden to Lord Moyne (Minister of State, Cairo), 18 April 1944, L/P&S/12/4626; "Afghanistan—General Situation," January–June 1941, L/P&S/12/1789, ff. 2–9. The British allowed German supply deliveries to go through but intercepted the payments. See Hauner, *India in Axis Strategy,* p. 138; also see L/P&S/12/1573; Adamec, *Afghanistan's Foreign Policy,* p. 253; Wilber, *Afghanistan,* p. 182.

24. Wylie, Report of Interview with Hashim Khan, 20 February 1943, L/P&S/12/1789, ff. 104–108; "Survey of Anglo-Afghan Relations, 1919–1947," L/P&S/12/1321; Cunningham, in the *Statesman,* 4 January 1949, L/WS/1/1169, f. 57; L/P&S/

12/1665, in general; Kabul to the Foreign Office, 20 August 1943, L/P&S/12/1558, 6205/43, and 23 October 1943, 6057/43; Squire to Eden, 13 October 1944, L/P&S/12/1789, ff. 21–22, and 19 May 1944, ff. 26–27; Squire, "Afghanistan and Her Neighbors," p. 70; Squire, "Recent Progress in Afghanistan," pp. 8–9.

25. Gregorian, *Emergence of Modern Afghanistan,* pp. 390, 391fn, 396; Hauner, "Significance of Afghanistan," p. 241; Squire, "Recent Progress in Afghanistan," p. 17. Russia flooded the *karakul* market, Namibia apparently also increased competition, and the Afghans lost many animals in the snowstorms of the winter of 1945–1946. Military Attaché's (Kabul) Summary of Intelligence for the Fortnight Ending 11 May 1947, L/P&S/12/1850; "Survey of Anglo-Afghan Relations, Part II, 1919–1947," L/P&S/12/1321.

26. Squire to Bevin, 25 April 1946, L/P&S/12/1556, f. 35 and generally; Squire to Bevin, 13 April 1946, R/12/166; Squire to Bevin, 7 June 1946, R/12/166. Squire to Bevin, 7 December 1946, R/12/166; L/P&S/12/1597, in general; L/P&S/12/1598, in general; Military Attaché in Kabul, Weekly Intelligence Summary, 17 May 1947, 31 May 1947, 6 September 1946, and 9 November 1946, L/P&S/12/1849; Crichton to Lt. Col. R.R. Burnett, Secretary, External Affairs Department, GOI, 30 December 1945, L/P&S/12/1811, ff. 308–314; Wilber, *Afghanistan,* pp. 175, 182; Dupree, *Afghanistan,* pp. 512–516; Arnold, *Afghanistan,* p. 29. Ultimately, the Russians and Afghans dispatched a commission that in 1946 specified that the *thalweg* of the Oxus would be the official boundary. In April 1947, a joint delegation began to delineate the border, completing their work in September 1948.

27. Lancaster, Report of Interview with War Minister Daoud Khan and Chief of the General Staff Assadullah Khan, 10 June 1947, L/WS/1/986, ff. 149–156 (also in L/P&S/12/1821); Lancaster, "Annual Review—Afghan Army," 1 January 1948, L/P&S/12/1667, ff. 3–20; Lancaster to His Majesty's Minister at Kabul, Report of Interview with General Daoud, 22 October 1940, L/P&S/12/1763, ff. 37–41, 8–14. Though he believed the Afghans were playing up to Western fears to secure aid, he added that "the Afghan fears appear to be genuine." He claimed to have "no doubt . . . as to where Afghan sympathies lie; they are with the Anglo-American bloc and not with Russia." Squire ("Recent Progress in Afghanistan," p. 11) agreed with Lancaster's assessments. During the war, members of the Turkish military mission to Afghanistan expressed similar criticism to Colonel Lancaster. The Turks derided the Afghan troops as bigoted and unwilling to learn and the officers as corrupt, illiterate, and lazy. They claimed that they "were tired of attempting to produce efficient officers from ill-educated cadets in the Afghan Military College." One told Lancaster that "even if they were to stay for one thousand years he doubted whether any definite or permanent results could be obtained." Lancaster noted that the Turks never established close relations with the Afghans but preferred European company. He attributed this to their relative ir-religion, modern dress, treatment of women, and use of alcohol. Report by Lt. Col. A.S. Lancaster to the Legation at Kabul, 24 January 1941, L/P&S/12/1763, ff. 18–25; Report by Lancaster to the Chief of the General Staff, Delhi, 26 March 1943, L/P&S/12/1560, ff. 8–14.

28. Military Attaché in Kabul, "Half-Yearly Report on the Afghan Army," 16 September 1946, L/P&S/12/1667, ff. 33–46.

29. Military Attaché, Kabul Legation, "Annual Review Afghan Army," 1 January 1948, L/P&S/12/1667, ff. 3–20; Peshawar Weekly Intelligence Report, 12 April 1947, L/P&S/12/3201; Military Attaché in Kabul, Weekly Intelligence Summary, 6 Septem-

ber 1946 and 9 November 1946, L/P&S/12/1849; A.S. Lancaster, Military Attaché at Kabul, Report of Interview with War Minister Daoud Khan and Chief of the General Staff Assadullah Khan, 10 June 1947, L/WS/1/986, ff. 149–156; Squire to Bevin, 12 and 14 May 1949, FO 983/46; "Survey," Part II, L/P&S/12/1321; Squire, "Recent Progress in Afghanistan," p. 11.

30. Chiefs of Staff Committee, "Afghanistan—Strategic Importance," COS(47) 182(0), L/WS/1/986, ff. 141–148 (early 1947); Lancaster, "Annual Review—Afghan Army," 1 January 1948, L/P&S/12/1667, ff. 3–20; A.S. Lancaster, Military Attaché at Kabul, Report of Interview with War Minister Daoud Khan and Chief of the General Staff Assadullah Khan, 10 June 1947, L/WS/1/986, ff. 149–156. The Soviets would do much the same later.

7

AFGHANISTAN, BRITISH STRATEGY, AND THE DECISION TO PARTITION INDIA

During the years immediately preceding partition, several individuals of various nationalities and religious persuasions advanced proposals designed to establish some form of central government within a united India. Debate continues to rage as to whether one of these proposals could have secured a unitary state and prevented the extensive human carnage that accompanied and followed partition. At the heart of the issue were Muslim fears that a successor government controlled by the predominantly Hindu Congress Party would reduce their community to subservience. In one rival camp, Mohammed Ali Jinnah and the Muslim League refused to accept any federation that would have given the Congress undisputed control of any central legislature. On the other hand, Congress leaders, notably Jawaharlal Nehru, demanded extensive powers since Congress represented a majority of the subcontinent's population. Given a more conciliatory Nehru, a more accommodating Jinnah, or a more forceful British presence, perhaps some sort of compromise could have been imposed. Then again, an attempt to enforce unity on unwilling participants might have produced even greater dislocation and violence.

During the early years of the independence movement, efforts were made to foster Hindu-Muslim accord. Mohandas Ghandi, the spiritual leader of the Congress, accepted British legislation that guaranteed Muslim representation in government through a system of separate electorates. Ghandi, however, would isolate himself after a series of violent communal incidents in 1920 and often thereafter left the Congress in control of younger, more radical men, led by Nehru. During the next two decades, these Congress radicals would alienate Jinnah by repeatedly demanding the elimination of separate electorates and the establishment of a strong central government. Ultimately Jinnah converted to the idea of two separate states, wherein the Muslim and Hindu communities would live according to their own respective beliefs and traditions.[1]

Cognizant of increased Muslim demands for a separate state in the northwest of India, the Afghans watched constitutional developments in India with interest and sought to coordinate events therein with their own political goals. Certain British officials also saw opportunities to strengthen Indian ties to Afghanistan. In the weeks prior to the outbreak of the Second World War, Sir William Barton, a man with nearly twenty years' experience on the frontier, wrote of Afghanistan:

The country is landlocked, its foreign trade, except on the Russian side, has to move nearly 1500 miles to the sea across India; in such conditions rapid expansion is impossible. The obvious remedy is a port and an approach corridor on the Arabian Sea. To have such a port is an ambition of the Afghan Government. Why does not Britain offer the concession? Doubtless as a quid pro quo the Afghan Government would give Britain special trade facilities.[2]

Given that access to a port had been an ambition of the Afghan government since the days of Dost Mohammed, Barton felt that such an offer would earn Hashim's gratitude and secure Afghan support against the Axis. The Afghan hierarchy read Barton's suggestions with interest. Most British officials, however, would prove an unreceptive audience.[3]

In the summer of 1940, shortly after publication of Barton's article, Hashim Khan's government expressed concern for the future of their coreligionists in India, especially the Pushtuns of the North West Frontier Province (NWFP). In a series of dispatches, they indicated desires to reabsorb the Pushtuns and pressed for Afghanistan to be given a corridor to the sea when British authority lapsed.[4] The British bluntly dismissed these claims, chastising the Afghans for having been deluded by Axis propaganda. Churchill's government never intended to permit the reunification of all Pushtuns. They refused to countenance proposals that suggested a transfer of power to more than one authority and dismissed any notion of Afghanistan having a right to participate in, or even to be kept informed of, India's constitutional proceedings. As one official would state, "Afghanistan had better understand that one way or another the British government is going to see that India's frontiers remain inviolate."[5] Such policy did not change with the Labour victory of July 1945 and would continue even after the decision for partition.

The proposed withdrawal from India did elicit considerable debate on future strategy among British political and military authorities. Such discussion, however, produced no fundamental change in policy, which remained inappreciably different from what it had been in the nineteenth century. The primary British concern centered not so much on the loss of India per se but on the repercussions a hasty withdrawal would have elsewhere. A disgraceful, chaotic evacuation would cause Britain to lose "trade, strategic advantages, and prestige" and might encourage rebellion in other colonies. Furthermore, Britain's position in the Middle East precluded an abandonment of the sub-continent without finding a permanent solution to Muslim concerns.[6]

Virtually every Briton wanted to keep India united. Many expressed moral or sentimental obligations to leave India intact, either for the inhabitants' sake or simply as a lasting testament to the Empire. The Cabinet Defense Committee and the Chiefs of Staff, however, stressed the maintenance of a united India as vital to the defense (and economy) of the region. A unified India, an orderly transfer of power, and a bilateral alliance would, they argued, leave Britain's strategic position undamaged. India's military assets, including its seemingly limitless manpower, naval and air bases, and expanding pro-duction capabilities, would remain accessible to London. India would thus remain of crucial importance as a base, training ground, and staging area for operations from Egypt to the Far East.[7]

To ensure this eventuality, Lord Montgomery and the Chiefs of Staff em-phasized the need of "taking every possible step to persuade India to remain within the Commonwealth." The Cabinet concurred that India's continued importance in imperial strategy mandated enrollment in that organization. The governments of the other Commonwealth nations agreed that "every endeavor should be made to persuade India to retain association with the British Commonwealth," noting that India's departure would diminish the political, economic, and military strength of the organization and dampen its authority and prestige worldwide.[8]

The Chiefs of Staff felt Commonwealth membership would make strategic arrangements palatable to independent India. Ideally, Britain and India would enter into an alliance requiring mutual support in event of third-party ag-gression. They envisioned the creation of a Strategic Reserve, under dual authority of the British and Indian governments, details of which they left to subsequent discussions. The Chiefs hoped India would continue to provide regiments for duty abroad, participate actively in any war in which the Com-monwealth became involved, and take direct action "in [the] event of a threat developing in any of the neighboring territories."[9]

Most British military planners believed they would retain immediate lev-erage with the new Indian government, reasoning that the Indian army would require the continued service of British officers, technical specialists, and maintenance personnel, even if combat contingents were withdrawn. India's limited naval and air forces would likewise require supplementation from the Royal Navy and Royal Air Force in order to provide adequate defense. Such service could only be undertaken given safeguards for their employment, presumably involving joint Anglo-Indian control.[10]

Some British political and military leaders questioned the Chiefs' emphasis on India's adherence to the Commonwealth. For example, Lieutenant Gen-eral Sir Archibald Nye, the governor of Madras, noted the problems of nationalizing the armed forces and India's relative lack of industry, as he argued that India had nothing to offer besides trade, which it would facilitate regardless of Commonwealth membership. He concluded that India would simply accrue the advantages of Commonwealth membership while pursuing a totally independent policy.[11]

Sir David Monteath, the permanent under-secretary of state for India and Burma, thought it likely that India would remain in the Commonwealth but would shape its defense policy on neutral lines rather than parallel with the strategic interests of Great Britain. The lengthy struggle against British imperialism would predispose Indian leaders to, at least, an independent foreign policy. He thought it unlikely that Indians would share the same sentiments common to the "White Dominions" (Australia, New Zealand, Canada, and South Africa) and felt spreading this "club spirit" to people of the oriental race and modes of thought nearly impossible. Opposition to colonialism would cause conflict with other members, leaving India more an embarrassment than source of strength.

While various inducements could perhaps persuade India to remain within the Commonwealth, membership itself would be no guarantee of strategic advantage. India could take from the organization without giving in return. For example, though officially a member of the Commonwealth, Ireland had eliminated the position of governor-general in 1937 and proclaimed a sovereign, independent, democratic state, in a move tantamount to secession. The Irish redefined their interdominion agreements, equating them with typical international understandings, and declared their ability to "remain neutral in a war declared by the King." In the Second World War, Eire remained neutral and barred Allied shipping from southern Irish ports at the height of the Battle of the Atlantic, despite its Commonwealth membership. In event of another war, India might be no more wholehearted than Eire had been.[12] Sir Gilbert Laithwaite, the deputy under-secretary of state for Burma, provided another example:

What one would fear would be that we might get a sound paper relation with India, but that in practice her position would tend to resemble that of Italy in the Triple Alliance before the war of 1914—completely bound on paper, hesitant when the moment came and possibly disposed to await until the issue of the struggle turned decisively one way or the other before deciding whom to back.[13]

Signs of future discord were evident before partition. In his speeches, Nehru emphasized an intention not to associate with any major bloc and desires to remove Indian troops from foreign stations and British troops from India. Congress repeatedly protested the use of Indian troops in support of the Dutch in Indonesia, and further conflict loomed over Commonwealth policy in Iraq, Ceylon, Burma, Malaysia, and South Africa. Congress also complained bitterly of defense expenditures that overburdened the Indian economy. Though several political leaders recognized these factors and acknowledged the frail nature of Commonwealth relationships, most of Britain's military leaders continued to adhere to literal interpretations of the Commonwealth agreements and to attach great significance to India's membership in the organization.[14]

Since the main danger to India still seemed to come from the northwest, the Chiefs continued to value Afghanistan as a buffer state. As long as the Soviets could be kept behind the Hindu Kush, their capacity for subversive activities would be limited, the likelihood of a surprise attack would be minimal, and the Indian army would have time to deploy in depth against such an unlikely eventuality. British planners reasoned that a Soviet attack through a hostile Afghanistan would require seven times as many troops as would an assault staged after a hypothetical consolidation of forces and within that nation. Afghanistan constituted a major obstacle to aggression and could not be allowed to fall readily.[15]

The Afghans were themselves concerned about the strategic consequences of the British withdrawal from India. Traditional fears of Russia intensified. Afghanistan's leaders recognized that Britain had helped perpetuate their nation's existence by refusing to tolerate major incursions against it and feared that a Hindu government devoid of British presence would not be an effective counterbalance. They also feared that the absence of British-Indian support would leave the Afghan army unable to stop a major tribal uprising. For these reasons, the Afghans stated early on the need to reorient policy and made a sustained effort to discuss future frontier policy concurrent to the independence proceedings.[16]

In intermittent bilateral discussion from November 1944 to February 1946, Afghan officials reiterated their intentions to cooperate on tribal affairs and promised to maintain a policy of noninterference as long as the British remained in India. They sought economic and military assistance and proposed a treaty of alliance and nonaggression. Hashim's government, however, also sought British assurances against annexation of the tribal areas and proposed that the NWFP be allowed to join with Afghanistan, if India were granted independence. The Afghans again requested that they be given access to the sea by a corridor through Baluchistan, which they agreed to return to British control in time of war. While British officials acknowledged the Afghan government's concerns surrounding future economic relations with India, they dismissed the proposals as impractical and unwarranted.[17]

The vast majority of British officials were cognizant of Afghan interest in frontier affairs and willing to acknowledge that Afghanistan would play a prominent role in any potential solution to the area's problem. For example, in a Cabinet paper, the secretary of state for India and the secretary of state for foreign affairs concluded that the "handling of tribal affairs in the North West Frontier of India is inseparable from the conduct of relations with the Afghan government." The External Relations Department of the government of India concurred that Anglo-Afghan relations were "inextricable from the conduct of the tribal problem." Sir Olaf Caroe, the last British governor of the NWFP, and his predecessor, Sir George Cunningham, similarly advised that tribal affairs "not be considered in isolation, but only with reference to our relations with Afghanistan and to the political situation in India." Yet all opposed incorporation of any part of India into Afghanistan.[18]

Caroe opposed territorial concessions and dismissed the Baluchistan port idea as impractical. Yet he still thought proposals for the establishment of "free-transit and free-warehousing facilities at Karachi and Bombay on the lines that were under consideration before the war" viable, beneficial policy. Others advanced suggestions to increase the quality and availability of trucks and railroad cars operating between the border and Karachi, provide warehouse facilities for Afghan goods, and establish repair and maintenance centers.[19] Some officials thought immediate planning would benefit the successor governments and favored negotiations with Afghanistan. Monteath believed that "the time has come to start discussions on the formal basis between the Afghan Government and the Government of India." Given that the Indian settlement would likely take a while to resolve, he wrote: "I feel that we ought to get to grips with Afghan questions as soon as possible whilst the Afghans are holding out the hand of friendship. . . . Otherwise, the Afghans, following precedent, may be driven to turn about and toy with the Russians."[20] Even the War Department, which insisted that any constitutional changes in India not involve a reduction in its territories, still thought Afghanistan's friendliness mandated a sympathetic response.[21]

Yet when the Afghans offered similar policy proposals to the Labour government in August 1946, Lord Pethick-Lawrence, the secretary of state for India and Burma, opposed reopening this "awkward question" on which the British had "no definite policy" at this "most inopportune time for consultations." Throughout the ensuing months, the Afghans continued to stress their preference for a unified India, voiced desires to expand relations with Britain, and expressed anxiety concerning Indian politics, the future of frontier relations, the communal violence, and possible Soviet aggression in the wake of British withdrawal. British policy toward Afghanistan, however, remained inflexible.[22]

In November 1946, Caroe, later a chief architect of Anglo-American defense policy in Southwest Asia, wrote: "If Pathan nationalism can be aligned with India as a whole without introducing unnecessary rifts . . . much will have been done to produce a stable . . . frontier. . . . We need a bulwark and not a sandbank torn by tides from without and shifted by streams from within."[23]

Perhaps such a bulwark could have been established had Britain or the major Indian political parties entered negotiations with Afghanistan. Discussion of economic, political, and military issues might have circumvented decades of frontier conflict. Though the Afghan government repeatedly indicated a desire to continue close cooperation with British India, during the months ahead, Afghanistan's strategic concerns would be all but ignored as officials struggled to implement partition. Like other strategic issues, frontier matters would ultimately be left to the successor governments.

With their electoral victory in the summer of 1945, the Labour Party inherited the standoff between Congress and the League. The Viceroy Lord Wavell tried to bring the two parties together and avoid partition. He called a conference at Simla, where he soon discovered no basis for agreement existed. Jinnah feared that Congress could use Muslim loyalists to circumvent all proposals for reserved seats, separate electorates, or other constitutional safeguards. Jinnah's stance owed much to events in the NWFP.

The Muslim League had long struggled to organize on the frontier but remained handicapped by a lack of economic support, charismatic leadership, and an appealing platform. Attacks against the *Khudai Khidmatgaran* alleging bias toward Hindus seemed of little substance, while dire predictions of impending Hindu tyranny seemed preposterous, even insulting to the Pushtuns. With the outbreak of war and the resignation of the Sahib ministry, however, *Khudai Khidmatgaran* popularity waned, opening a political door for the League.[24]

In 1943, in the wake of popular dissatisfaction with the *Khudai Khidmatgaran,* Aurangzeb Khan of the League formed a provincial government. During its brief interim, however, the ministry earned a reputation for mismanagement and blatant corruption, through manipulation of appointments and licenses, interference with the judicial process, and, most importantly, misappropriations of food rations.[25] Even Cunningham criticized the ministry for having "far less sense of duty to the public than their Congress predecessors had."[26]

The *Khudai Khidmatgars* regained popularity through attacks on the discredited Aurangzeb. In March 1945, the Frontier Congress spearheaded a no-confidence vote, and two days later, Cunningham asked Sahib to return to office. The Indian National Congress leadership approved an exception in allowing Sahib to reassume office even before the war had ended.[27]

During the war, the League had not supported the Quit India campaign. While Congress leaders were imprisoned, Jinnah proved able to consolidate and strengthen League support, at the expense of smaller regional parties. In the national elections of 1945–1946, Congress received the votes of over 90 percent of the non-Muslim electorate and carried all the non-Muslim majority provinces. Yet the League captured 412 of the 482 provincial seats reserved for Muslims and formed governments in Sind and Bengal. Thanks to Jinnah's efforts, the League had joined Congress as one of the dominant parties in India.[28]

In the 93-percent-Muslim Northwest Frontier Province, however, the League suffered a stinging defeat. Despite continued efforts to slander the *Khudai Khidmatgaran* as Hindu puppets and a personal tour by Jinnah himself in November, the *Khudai Khidmatgaran* won thirty of fifty seats, including nineteen of thirty-six reserved for Muslims. Caroe (who became governor after the elections) and Cunningham both attributed the victory to superior Congress organization and a basic appeal that was better oriented toward the masses. In addition, Cunningham claimed, the very concept of Pakistan had no appeal to the average Pushtun villager, "to whom suggestion of Hindu domination is only laughable. . . . India's communal troubles still seemed distant . . . and the Frontier Congress no less a Muslim party than the League."[29] The NWFP would remain an anomaly that would plague efforts at compromise.[30]

In another effort to effect compromise, the Home government dispatched a Cabinet Mission to India in March 1946. After a series of interviews and conferences, which brought nationalist leaders no nearer consensus, the mission issued a statement that rejected Pakistan as impractical, claiming such a division would ruin the economy and treble defense requirements, without solving the communal problem. While decrying Pakistan, the plan still acknowledged Muslim apprehensions in proposing a three-tiered federal government for India. The intermediate regional governments, composed of groups of provinces and/or states, were key to the arrangement. The mission allocated the provinces so that Muslims held a slim majority in two of the three groupings, which mitigated Hindu predominance at the center by requiring a majority vote from representatives of both communities on questions of communal interest.

For a time, the Cabinet Mission Plan seemed to have a chance of success. Both leading parties accepted the plan, albeit with reservations. On July 10, however, Nehru delivered a speech that alienated Jinnah permanently. Citing the situation in the NWFP as an example, Nehru declared that Congress had made no commitment to a binding plan and demanded that the constitution allow for changes in the grouping scheme. To Jinnah, to allow provinces and states to change groupings would allow for splinter parties such as the *Khudai Khidmatgaran* to undermine the system safeguards. Jinnah would remain convinced that Congress would attempt to use its Muslim loyalists to abrogate constitutional guarantees at the first opportunity.[31]

Jinnah withdrew his acceptance of the Cabinet Mission Plan, abandoned the idea of further negotiations, and declared August 16 "Direct Action Day." This spawned severe communal rioting in Calcutta, in which an estimated 4,400 were killed, 16,000 injured, and 100,000 left homeless. In October and November, the violence spread to Bombay, the United Provinces, and Bihar. The spread of communal violence soon overshadowed political discussion, ensured that there would be no compromise, and aroused fear of civil war. Though Congress passed a series of conciliatory resolutions aimed at regaining League trust, Jinnah dismissed their peace offerings as "evasions, equivocations and camouflage." He called upon the British government to declare the Cabinet Mission Plan failed and to create Pakistan.[32]

By late 1946, Wavell claimed to be amidst another Palestine, where the choices were to "withdraw in danger and ignominy" or "stomp on without power." Wavell had lost the respect of the Congress, if not the League as well, and seemed incapable of any creative political policy that might save the situation. To Prime Minister Clement Attlee, Wavell appeared to view the transfer process as little more than a military withdrawal. The prime minister told King George that Wavell's plans savor "too much of a military retreat and [he] does not realize it is a political problem and not a military one." The transfer of power, however, was much more than a political move. Attlee himself stressed the need to keep India unified when he directed Wavell's replacement, Lord Louis Mountbatten, to conduct negotiations "in accordance with Indian Defense requirements" and "to impress on the Indian leaders the importance of avoiding a break in the continuity of the Indian army, and to point out the need for continued collaboration in the security of the Indian Ocean."[33] Mountbatten would attempt to find a political compromise that satisfied these requirements, but in the end could not prevent the partition of India from producing serious strategic ramifications.

Following his arrival in India on March 22, Mountbatten used economic, demographic, and strategic arguments as he attempted to dissuade Jinnah from partition. The viceroy pointed to the already strained financial situation of the Muslim majority areas, noting how such difficulties would be exacerbated by separation from India. He further argued that partition offered no solution to the communal problem, as the creation of national boundaries would leave sizable minorities in both new states, regardless of the peculiarities of division. Finally, Pakistan would face strategic hardships. It would have to create armed forces from the fractured infrastructure of the Indian army, build munitions factories and logistical bases to support them, and be strong enough to face both India and the Soviet Union in the interim. Mountbatten claimed he "could not possibly recommend to His Majesty's Government that they should take on such a severe liability as the moth-eaten Pakistan was bound to be."[34]

Mountbatten later wrote that he spent most of his time with Jinnah "going around the Mulberry bush." Jinnah did not even attempt to counter these arguments but remained insistent on Pakistan. He threatened to respond to any attempt to impose the Cabinet Mission Plan with civil war. Mountbatten thought Jinnah both vain and naive, yet he could neither dismiss Jinnah's sentiments nor deny his authority.[35]

In the meantime, communal violence threatened to erupt in the NWFP. Following the 1946 election, support for the *Khudai Khidmatgaran* had again declined. Ironically, the man who most revitalized the League cause in the NWFP was Jawaharlal Nehru. Nehru toured the province in mid-October 1946 against the wishes of Wavell, some members of Congress, and especially Governor Caroe.[36]

Hostile demonstrators met Nehru at the Peshawar airport. Shots were fired at the plane. The next day, a group of Wazir leaders bluntly insulted the

Pandit, decrying Hindus as *hamsayas* (serfs or tenants). Later, tribesmen threw pots filled with dung at the Congress leaders. One doused Sahib in "night-soil." That evening and twice on the following day in Malakand, crowds stoned Nehru's car. On the final occasion, Nehru, Sahib, and Ghaffar Khan were all injured, Nehru having been hit in the head with a brickbat. Shots from escorting troops dispersed the protesters, or else Nehru might have been killed.[37]

Nehru had hoped his visit would crush the two-nation theory. Instead, it served only to inflame communalism. Prior to Nehru's visit, the Pakistan idea had few adherents on the frontier, where the Pushtuns had little fear of Congress. Nehru's visit, however, legitimized allegations of potential Hindu domination and accomplished in a few days what League agitators had failed to do for years. The path was now open for the League to exploit the anti-Hindu sentiments of the population.[38]

Following the visit, atrocities against frontier Hindus increased.[39] Mounting food shortages further aggravated the communal situation and undermined confidence in the government. Attacks within Peshawar increased and soon spread to villages east and south of the city. Continued riots took many lives and ruined property. League provocateurs led protests in which they dragged effigies of Sahib through the streets and burnt them in the bazaars. Sahib responded by throwing League supporters in jails, filling them to capacity. On the pretext of protecting Hindus, the ministry brought several thousand armed Red Shirts to Peshawar. League "Green Shirts" responded with huge processions. Caroe soon thought his primary task as governor was simply "to prevent the disintegration of the Northwest Frontier."[40]

On April 21, 1947, Mountbatten flew to Peshawar in hopes of diffusing the situation. A tremendous crowd, numbering between 50,000 and 100,000 Pushtuns, met the viceroy. Mountbatten climbed to the top of a railroad embankment, in full view of the crowd. Initially the Pushtuns expressed hostility. Mountbatten, however, was either clever or fortuitous enough to have worn a green shirt, which not only seemed to glorify Islam but was also part of the uniform worn by Pushtun troops in the Burma campaign. Taunts turned to shouts of "Mountbatten *zindabad*."[41]

Mountbatten's experiences on the frontier convinced him of the necessity of partition. The sheer size of the crowd clearly demonstrated League strength. Several provincial officials and delegations reinforced that fact. A mixed group of British and Indian civilian and military personnel accused Sahib's government of judicial improprieties and unfair food rationing policies and stressed the need for fresh elections. Sahib later admitted to being "guilty of certain things," supposedly done with the "best of intentions." While in Peshawar, Mountbatten received over 3,000 mailings, of which the majority "expressed no confidence in the Congress government." He concluded that "an upsurge in communal feeling . . . is finding its vent in agitation against a Ministry which is regarded as being dominated by the essentially

Hindu Congress." He laughingly dismissed Sahib's accusations, which blamed the disturbances on Caroe's machinations.[42]

By the last week of April, Mountbatten and his staff were convinced that a united India could not be achieved without the risk of a complete breakdown of authority. Delaying the transfer of power only invited more chaos.[43] Knowing that Jinnah would remain insistent on Pakistan and fearing wholesale slaughter if the NWFP Pushtuns were loosed on the subcontinent in its name, Mountbatten was left with little choice but partition. Convinced that he had to take action or risk civil war, he declared the Cabinet Mission Plan dead.[44]

While Jinnah's continued recalcitrance amidst the intense communal violence led Mountbatten to opt for partition, the viceroy did not want the principle of self-determination to undermine the strategic welfare of the subcontinent. He also wanted to keep India within the Commonwealth. Mountbatten saw political advantages, mostly in terms of enhanced global prestige, in maintaining Commonwealth connections with the subcontinent. Adherence would further provide a measure of security for India, Pakistan, and the neighboring states and would make accession palatable to the princes and the tribes.

Mountbatten's able Indian assistant, V.P. Menon, supplied the viceroy with a compromise solution. Menon suggested that partition could be conceded, and a transfer of power enacted, provided both successor states remained in the Commonwealth. Jinnah had already indicated that Pakistan would not secede and would appeal to the other member nations if Britain attempted to exclude it. Mountbatten supported using the "Pakistan threat" as a lever to help India "take the plunge." He thought India would hesitate to abandon the Commonwealth if Pakistan retained membership and felt confident that he could "persuade Congress to accept Dominion status provided . . . the actual transfer of power would be secured substantially earlier than June, 1948." An early transfer of power would enhance British prestige both within India and abroad and terminate British responsibilities for law and order within the subcontinent.[45]

Had India remained a single nation under Congress control, it almost certainly would have seceded from the Commonwealth. The Congress leadership, possessed of many grievances against the British, wanted a clean break. After conceding Pakistan, however, Congress found the advantages of Commonwealth membership outweighed sentimental inducements to charter a course alone. With only the League in the Commonwealth, Congress would have been compromised in relations with the Western bloc as a whole. Divorced entirely from the Empire, India would have lost trading privileges and would also have surely lost some of the 1.178 billion pounds owed it in war debt (though, in fact, India never received these funds). Perhaps most importantly, the League had already requested the retention of British military personnel and continued receipt of equipment and supplies for Pakistan's armed forces. Congress wanted similar arrangements, if only to avoid allow-ing Pakistan qualitative superiority.[46]

The British proved willing to grant concessions to make Commonwealth membership ideologically acceptable to Congress. The king, for example, accepted the elimination of the words "Emperor of India" from his title. His Majesty's Government also conceded Congress' demand that India should inherit the international rights and obligations of the old government, assum-ing a concurrent agreement with Pakistan over division of assets. These con-cessions combined to secure Congress' acceptance of Menon's plan.[47]

The Chiefs of Staff reconsidered the strategic implications of a divided India after Mountbatten conceded partition. While they acknowledged that the partition "has affected the position of the Indian Continent in respect to war and to all questions of defense," strategic imperatives and expectations still did not change. With Commonwealth membership of both successor states assured, the Chiefs continued to stress procurement of the "active co-operation of the Armed Forces of both Dominions and the use of reserves of manpower and of the industrial potential, which they can provide." The Chiefs hoped that the successor states would pursue a common defense pol-icy, preferably through a combined central command organization. They fur-ther expected both the Indian and Pakistani armies to "accept the obligation to participate actively in the defense of India in the event of a threat devel-oping in any of the neighboring territories, including the possibility that this might entail employment of some of their forces outside their own terri-tory."[48]

Certain British officials also considered the effects a divided India would have on Afghanistan. Some opposed the formation of Pakistan entirely and suggested allowing Kabul to absorb all Indian territories up to the Indus. Barton claimed the latter opinion extended to "a highly placed member of the League," who stated:

If necessary we should be prepared to hand over the Frontier up to the Indus to the Afghan government, with which we should construct an offensive and defensive alli-ance. The Afghans would then be responsible for the peace of the borderland. The additional resources they would derive from the settled districts of the NWFP and Sind would enable them to increase their forces and provide funds for the economic de-velopment they have already planned. Holding both sides of the tribal belt now split by the Durand Line, they would be in a better position to control the tribes as a whole than is the case under the present system.[49]

Such opinions apparently remained confined to a small coterie of powerless individuals.

The vast majority of British officials, citing economic as well as strategic concerns, opposed incorporation of any part of India into Afghanistan. Since strategic conceptions remained unaltered even after the decision for partition, the tribal areas, long considered of crucial importance to India's security, would not be readily surrendered. A paper from the External Affairs Department of the government of India typifies these sentiments, in claiming, "changes in the political status of India cannot alter geographic factors which govern her security."[50] Maintenance of the status quo remained the goal of British frontier policy.

A few officials, including the secretary of the External Affairs Department of the government of India, Hugh Weightman, thought immediate planning on frontier-related issues would be beneficial to the successor governments.[51] While cognizant of Afghan desires for continued cooperation, the majority of British officials saw no reason for any change in strategic policy vis-à-vis Afghanistan or the frontier. They instead thought it best, given the continued communal violence, the other concerns of the Indian leaders, and possible reactions by the U.S.S.R., to relegate those issues to some future discussion. Though ultimately slated for discussion within the Joint Defense Council, the hostilities that accompanied partition ensured that Afghanistan's defense requirements would not be filled or even dutifully examined.

NOTES

1. Qureshi, *Anglo-Pakistan Relations,* pp. 11–15, 19, 26); Wolpert, *Roots of Confrontation,* p. 105; Khan, *Story of the Pakistan Army,* p. 10; Brown, *United States, India and Pakistan,* pp. 101–103, 127; Aziz, *Britain and Pakistan,* p. 26. In March 1940, the League passed the Lahore Resolution, demanding an independent Pakistan. Recent studies, however, indicate that Jinnah remained undecided on independence or autonomy and might have lessened his demands and accepted some sort of federation given a suitable, resolute proposal, perhaps as late as 1946.

2. Barton, "Northwest Frontier and the War," pp. 1103.

3. Ibid., pp. 1102–1103. Barton, incidentally, thought it likely, if Pakistan were formed, "that in the end it would be united to Afghanistan" (*India's North-West Frontier,* p. 13). He noted that British officials had considered granting Afghanistan a free trade area in Karachi. Note also Squire, "Recent Progress in Afghanistan," pp. 17–18.

4. "Afghanistan—General Situation, January–June 1941" [n.s], L/P&S/12/1778, ff. 2–9; Viceroy to the Secretary of State, 3 March 1942, R/12/169, ff. 4–5; Fraser-Tytler to the Secretary of State for Foreign Affairs, 28 June 1940, L/P&S/12/3155, f. 52. Like Barton and Squire, Fraser-Tytler wanted to concede Afghan access to the sea. See also *ITOP,* I/225, p. 308.

5. *ITOP,* I/256, pp. 347, 347fn6; Squire, "Afghanistan and Her Neighbors," p. 71; Kaur, *Pak-Afghanistan Relations,* p. 30. While they never committed to a specific course, the British did at times assure Hashim that he would be consulted in determining the future political status of the area. In 1942 the Cripps Mission informed the Afghan regime that their opinions would be sought at the appropriate time, and as late as 1945, officials of the government of India agreed to keep Kabul informed. Other documents claim Afghanistan had no right even to timely information about constitutional developments in India. See External Affairs Department, GOI to the Viceroy, 7 August 1940, L/P&S/12/3155, f. 61; *ITOP,* I/251, 294–297; Wylie to the

Viceroy and Secretary of State for Foreign Affairs, 6 March 1942, R/12/169, ff. 7–10; Foreign Office to Kabul, 30 June 1945, R/12/169, f. 12. Wylie, discussing the future Afghan role in the transfer of power process, stated, "I agree, of course, that they [the Afghans] have no right to receive such warning" of constitutional developments in India. It would remain the policy of the Labour government that the NWFP constituted an integral part of India, having been recognized as such in the 1921 Anglo-Afghan Treaty. See India and Burma Committee, I.B.(47) 40th Meeting, 3 July 1947, *ITOP,* XI/486, pp. 870–871; see also Cabinet, Meeting of Ministers on Indian Questions, 13 March 1947, *ITOP,* IX/530, p. 942.

6. Minutes of Viceroy's Twenty-Seventh Staff Meeting, *ITOP,* X/339, pp. 658–9; Wavell to Pethick-Lawrence, 13 July 1946, Enclosure 1, "Note on the Results to the British Commonwealth of the Transfer of Political Power in India," *ITOP,* VIII/26, p. 51; Cabinet C.M.(46) 59th Conclusions, 17 June 1946, *ITOP,* VII/557, pp. 963–965; Listowel to Mountbatten, 30 April 1947, *ITOP,* X/255, p. 486. Listowel exemplified these sentiments, noting, "It is important that British troops should leave India as an organized force. . . . There would be world-wide criticism of the British if they withdrew from India . . . and left the country . . . in a mess."

7. Wavell to Pethick-Lawrence, 13 July 1946, Enclosure 1, *ITOP,* VIII/26, pp. 50–51, 55; Cabinet Defense Committee Paper D.O.(46) 104, 4 September 1946, *ITOP,* VIII/254, pp. 415–416; Laithwaite to Turnbull, 10 October 1946, *ITOP,* VIII/425, p. 689; Cabinet, Defense Committee, Paper D.O.(46) 68, 12 June 1946, "India—Military Implications of Proposed Courses of Action," *ITOP,* VII/509, pp. 889–891; Major-General Hollis to Monteath, 4 October 1946, *ITOP,* VIII/408, pp. 659–662; Chiefs of Staff Committee, "The Strategic Value of India to the British Commonwealth of Nations," COS(46)229(0), 8 September 1946, L/WS/1/985, ff. 41–52.

8. Cabinet Defense Committee, D.O.(46) 26th Meeting, 2 October 1946, *ITOP,* VIII/398, p. 646; Hollis to Monteath, 4 October 1946, *ITOP,* VIII/408, p/ 659; Cabinet, Chiefs of Staff Committee, C.O.S.(46) 143rd Meeting, 20 September 1946, *ITOP,* VIII/339, p. 547; Sargent to Monteath, 7 December 1946, *ITOP,* IX/173, p. 307; Cabinet, Chiefs of Staff Committee, C.O.S.(46) 133rd Meeting, 30 August 1946, *ITOP,* VIII/224, p. 350: "From the military point of view, it is nearly as vital as anything can be that India remains with the Commonwealth."

9. Hollis to Monteath, 4 October 1946, *ITOP,* VIII/408, pp. 659–660; Chiefs of Staff Committee, Paper C.O.S.(47)59(0), 18 March 1947, *ITOP,* IX/544, pp. 976–977.

10. Cabinet Defense Committee, Paper D.O.(46) 104, 4 September 1946, *ITOP,* VIII/254, p. 416; *ITOP,* V/346, pp. 769–775; Chiefs of Staff Committee, Paper C.O.S.(47)59(0), 18 March 1947, *ITOP,* IX/544, pp. 966–967. The Chiefs assumed that the "Indianization" of the armed forces would require at least twenty years to implement. During the interim, India would have to rely on British assistance for her security needs.

11. Nye to Mountbatten, 2 May 1947, *ITOP,* X/282, pp. 558–561.

12. Monteath to Sir E. Machtig, 8 November 1946, *ITOP,* IX/17, p. 32; Turnbull to Donaldson and Anderson, 4 October 1946, *ITOP,* VIII/409, pp. 664–666; see also Viceroy's Conference Paper VCP 153, 5 August 1947, *ITOP,* XII/343, 534.

13. Laithwaite to Turnbull, *ITOP,* VIII/425, pp. 689–690.

14. Monteath to Hollis, 31 October 1946, *ITOP,* VIII/537, p. 850; Wavell to Pethick-Lawrence, 19 September 1946, *ITOP,* VIII/332, p. 540; *ITOP,* VIII/371fn;

Wavell to Pethick-Lawrence, 12 February 1947, *ITOP*, IX/383, p. 682; Monteath to Pethick-Lawrence, 1 October 1946, *ITOP*, VIII/394, p. 641; Croft to Turnbull, 9 April 1946, "Note on the Defense Implications of Pakistan," *ITOP*, VII/78, p. 198. Croft raised the issue, later repeated, of whether Commonwealth defensive interests would be better served through an alliance with Pakistan, rather than a neutral or hostile India. Connell, *Sir Claude Auchenleck*, p. 849.

15. Joint Planning Staff, COS Committee, "Afghanistan—Strategic Importance," 26 November 1946, JP(46)194(Final), L/WS/1/985, ff. 18–20; Report of the Joint Planning Staff, "Afghanistan—Strategic Importance," 26 March 1947, JP(46)210, L/WS/1/986, ff. 166–180; Joint Intelligence Sub-Committee, Chiefs of Staff Committee, "Threats to India's Land Frontiers," 15 April 1946, JIC(46)10(0), L/WS/1/987, ff. 91–99.

16. Note by Government of India, External Affairs Department [n.d., March 1946?], *ITOP*, VII/15, pp. 30–32; Crichton to Burnett, 4 October 1945, L/P&S/12/1811, ff. 343–351; *ITOP*, I/256; Barton, *India's North-West Frontier*, p. 298. Afghan fears were heightened by their belief that the Indians were in general a cowardly lot, ruled by the Moguls and British for centuries. The British likewise believed an independent India under the pacifistic Congress would not accept obligations to Afghanistan.

17. "Proposal of the Royal Afghan Government, November 1944," L/P&S/12/1811, ff. 262–286; "Afghanistan and the North West Frontier Province," Note by R.H.S. Allen, 28 May 1947, L/P&S/12/1811, ff. 144–145.

18. Cabinet Paper C.P(46)329, 30 August 1946, *ITOP*, VIII/228, p. 362; Note by Government of India, External Affairs Department [n.d., March 1946?], *ITOP*, VII/15, pp. 30–32; *ITOP*, VI/190; Record of Meeting between Ismay, Caroe, et al., 14 April 1947, *ITOP*, X/141, 233; Cunningham, "Tribes of the North West Frontier of India," *World Review*, February 1947, MSS.EUR D.670/28 (George Cunningham Papers). Cunningham thought it possible for a Muslim government to come to grips with the tribal problem and saw Afghanistan as the key to a peaceful, prosperous future. See also Crichton to Squire, 24 April 1947, *ITOP*, X/213, p. 413; GOI External Affairs and Commonwealth Relations Department to the Secretary of State, 30 June 1947, *ITOP*, XI/431, p. 799: "The Afghan government has a natural and lively interest in seeing a satisfactory arrangement emerge from the discussions with the tribes. . . . We have always recognized that both India and Afghanistan are interested in the welfare and development of the tribes inhabiting their respective zones of tribal territory."

19. L/P&S/12/1777, in general. Note by Caroe, 27 January 1945, ff. 392–394.

20. Note by Sir D. Monteath, 29 October 1945, L/P&S/12/1811, f. 340; Record of Meeting between Ismay, Caroe, Weightman, et al., 14 April 1947, *ITOP*, X/141, p. 233.

21. Memo, Government of India War Department, 19 April 1945, L/P&S/12/1811, f. 398.

22. Cabinet, India and Burma Committee, Paper I.B.(47) 39, "Future Relations between India and Adjacent Countries," *ITOP*, X/2, pp. 3–4; Caroe to Mountbatten, 22 March 1947, *ITOP*, X/1, p. 2. Neither the Cabinet Mission nor Attlee's Statement of February 20, 1947, made any explicit reference to the future status of the frontier. Draft Telegram, Secretary of State to the Viceroy [n.d., early 1947]; Military Attaché's Weekly Intelligence Report for the Week/Fortnight Ending 1 February 1947, 22 February 1947, 29 March 1947, 3 May 1947, and 22 May 1947, all L/P&S/12/1850.

23. Caroe to Nehru, 7 November 1946, *ITOP*, IX/11, p. 22.

24. Rittenberg, Ethnicity, pp. 156–157, 174–175. The party was disdainfully called the "Motor League" because its adherents spent more time visiting one another than promoting the party. Cunningham had considerable doubts about the Frontier League, especially its self-serving, fractionalized leadership. (He referred to any possible coalition as a "bathroom majority," so precarious it might fold whenever one member went to the toilet.) He feared failure would revive the *Khudai Khidmatgaran*, which it in fact did.

25. Rittenberg, Ethnicity, p. 179. The Sahib government of the late 1930s had engaged in similar actions but never so openly or on so grand a scale. With the League in charge, it was "Everyone for himself and the devil take the hindmost. Corruption with a capital C is writ large on the face of the Frontier administration and almost everybody who had anything to do with the administrative machinery there bothers about just one thing—how to feather his own nest."

26. Cunningham to Linlithgow, NWFP Governor's Report No. 10, 24 May 1943, *ITOP*, III/730, p. 1006. Cunningham admitted, "There is no doubt that the name of the Muslim League administration is simply mud nowadays owing to the scandalous way in which they buy votes." Cunningham to Wavell, 24 June 1943, 24 June 1943, *ITOP*, IV/549, p. 1046; Cunningham to Wavell, 9 October 1945, *ITOP*, VI/134, pp. 318–319; Cunningham to Wavell, 9 February 1943, *ITOP*, IV/366, p. 708; Cunningham to Wavell, 2 July 1945, *ITOP*, V/560, p. 1190; Cunningham, "Speech to the Royal Institute of International Affairs," 13 June 1946, MSS.EUR D.670/25. Here he deemed the ministry "undignified and discreditable." Gupta, *North West Frontier Province Legislature,* pp. 207–208.

27. Rittenberg, Ethnicity, pp. 182–183.

28. *ITOP*, II/740; Moore, Escape from Empire, pp. 79–80; Brown, *United States, India and Pakistan,* p. 138. The League also won fourteen nonreserved seats. In 1937 they won but 109 seats total. In the Punjab, the League won more seats than any other party, but not a majority.

29. Caroe to Wavell, Governor's Report No. 6, 23 March 1946, MSS.EUR F.203 (Olaf Caroe Papers); Cunningham to Wavell, 27 February 1946, *ITOP*, VI/479, pp. 1085–6; Note of Meeting between the Cabinet Delegation, Wavell, Mr. Qaiyum and Sir M. Sa'adullah, 2 April 1946, *ITOP*, VII/40, pp. 47–49; Caroe to Wavell, 9 June 1946, *ITOP*, VII/479, p. 852; Cunningham, "Speech to the Royal Institute of International Affairs," 13 June 1946, MSS.EUR D.670/25; Cunningham, "Summary of Events on the Northwest Frontier," MSS.EUR D.670/17 (George Cunningham Papers); Gupta, *North West Frontier Province Legislature,* pp. 173, 177–178; Schofield, *Every Rock,* pp. 240–241; Sayeed, *Pakistan, the Formative Phase,* pp. 135, 135fn. The *Khudai Khidmatgaran* victory, however, was not as impressive as the delegate count might imply. The League polled a slightly larger number of Muslim votes that Congress, and the popular vote was almost equal. The League also emerged the clear choice of the province's non-Pushtun Muslims.

30. Rittenberg, *Ethnicity*, p. 200 Caroe noted interestingly, "If the Muslim League up here had had the sense to substitute Pathanistan for Pakistan, they would certainly have done a good deal better." Rittenberg continues: "It was not that the Pakhtuns enthusiastically embraced the Indian National Congress' vision of a unified India with a strong central government. If anything, they expected strong constitutional safeguards, much like those the League had demanded before adopting the Pakistan res-

olution. Rather, most favored the Frontier Congress because they believed it faithfully reflected their ethnic interests."

31. Statement by the Cabinet Delegation and the Viceroy, 25 May 1946, *ITOP*, VII/376, pp. 688–689, and, 16 June 1946, *ITOP*, VII/550, pp. 954–955. Paragraph 8 of the June 16 declaration stated that if one party refused to join the interim government according to the proposal, the viceroy would proceed regardless with those willing to accept the idea. Full Version of Pandit Nehru's Press Conference of 10 July 1946, *ITOP*, VIII/16, pp. 25–27; Wavell to Caroe, 29 July 1946, *ITOP*, VIII/87, p. 39. Wavell himself believed that this Nehru's "intemperate speeches," more than anything else, ruined the chance of compromise. Wavell to Pethick-Lawrence, *ITOP*, IX/107, p. 196. Nehru, Wavell claimed, "always loses his head in front of a large audience." Wavell, like Jinnah, was convinced that the Congress intended to destroy both the grouping system and the League with it. According to Wolpert (*Roots of Confrontation*, p. 110), Nehru later acknowledged his speech as one of his worst political blunders that in effect "threw all the work of the Cabinet Mission onto the rubbish pile of history." Yet Nehru was also aware that Jinnah had extracted concessions himself and could not have known that the heretofore-legalistic barrister would resort to "direct action" (see Sayeed, *Pakistan, the Formative Phase*, pp. 147–148).

32. Wavell to Pethick-Lawrence, *ITOP*, VIII/208, p. 323; Sir A. Clow (Bombay) to Wavell, 3 October 1946, *ITOP*, VIII/399, pp. 648–649; Cabinet, India and Burma Committee, Paper I.B.(46) 35, 11 November 1946, *ITOP*, IX/25, pp. 45–49; Statement by Pethick-Lawrence, Casualties in Communal Disturbances in India, September 2–November 18, 1946, *ITOP*, IX/102, p. 188; see also Zeigler, *Mountbatten*, p. 353; Connell, *Sir Claude Auchenleck*, pp. 348–350; Stephens, *Pakistan*, p. 112. Some estimates put the Calcutta death toll at or near 20,000. *Dawn*, 26 January 1947, *ITOP*, IX/309, pp. 554–556; Resolution of the All-India Muslim League Working Committee of 31 January 1947, *ITOP*, IX/333, pp. 588–592.

33. Wavell to Pethick-Lawrence, 22 November 1946, *ITOP*, IX/77, p. 141; Wavell to Pethick-Lawrence, 3 February 1947, *ITOP*, pp. 596–598; Wheeler-Bennett, King George VI, pp. 709–710 (recorded in the king's diary); Attlee to Bevin, 2 January 1947, *ITOP*, IX/243, p. 445; Khan, *Story of Pakistan Army*, p. 18; Attlee to Pethick-Lawrence, 18 March 1947, *ITOP*, IX/543, pp. 972–973; Zeigler, *Mountbatten*, pp. 355, 359, 373; Campbell-Johnson, *Mission with Mountbatten*, p. 31.

34. Minutes of the Viceroy's Seventh Staff Meeting, 3 April 1947, Addendum, "A Few Questions That the Viceroy Might Ask Mr. Jinnah Regarding Pakistan," *ITOP*, X/64, pp. 100–101; Viceroy's Personal Report No. 3, 17 April 1947, *ITOP*, X/165, p. 301.

35. Uncirculated Record of Discussion at Viceroy's Staff Meeting, 11 April 1947, *ITOP*, X/119; Record of Interview between Mountbatten and Jinnah, 9 April 1947, *ITOP*, X/105, pp. 163–164; Viceroy's Personal Report No. 3, 17 April 1947, *ITOP*, X/165, pp. 299–300. Mountbatten wrote that "he gives me the impression of a man who had not thought out one single piece of the mechanics of his own great scheme, and he will have the shock of his life when he really has to come down to earth and try and make his vague idealistic proposals come to life." Mountbatten later described Jinnah as the most difficult and unreasonable man with whom he had ever had to deal. "I regard Jinnah as a psychopathic case; in fact until I had met him I would not have thought it possible that a man with such a complete lack of administrative knowledge or sense of responsibility could achieve or hold down so powerful a position."

36. Nehru to Caroe, 26 October 1946, ITOP VIII/520, pp. 818–819; Nehru to Wavell, 19 March 1947, *ITOP*, IX/549, p. 989; Pethick-Lawrence to Wavell, 15 November 1946, *ITOP*, IX/42, p. 81; Barton, *India's North-West Frontier*, pp. 112, 186, 202–203, 247. "The frontier visit of Nehru in October 1946, more than anything else, made partition inevitable." According to Caroe (Review of Hodson's *Great Divide*, MSS.EUR F.203; Olaf Caroe Papers), Ghandi and Maulana Azad both tried to persuade Nehru not to go. Weightman tried "to induce some appreciation of the explosive potentialities of the Frontier, of the fanatical savagery of the tribes, of their lust for money and of the fearsome danger of promoting party factions there." But he concluded Nehru "cannot rid himself of the last lingering belief that our subconscious objective is to impede progress, and doubts our ability to appreciate the psychology of the tribal area" (Weightman to Abell, 15 February 1947, *ITOP*, IX/405, p. 723). Congress often claimed that the British did not desire peace on the frontier but deliberately provoked the tribes, using continued unrest to justify the maintenance of British forces in India and the high percentage of income allocated to the defense budget. Nehru "wanted to change the system of control and "overturn the feudal social structure" by reducing the number of troops in the area and halting the system of allowances. Talk of a regime of brotherly love amidst tribesmen reared with firearms and sworn to uphold family honor at all costs, however, had little chance of success, and suggestions of a cessation of allowances only begged for violent retaliation.

37. Nehru to Caroe, 26 October 1946, *ITOP*, VIII/520, pp. 820–821; Wavell to Pethick-Lawrence, 22 October 1946, *ITOP*, VIII/492, p. 766; Caroe to Wavell, 23 October 1946, *ITOP*, VIII/498, pp. 787–791. Nehru did not visit the area again. Schofield, *Every Rock*, pp. 242–244; Miller, *Khyber*, p. 366. Miller describes Nehru's predicament at the airport with flare: "A strong police cordon just managed to hold back an angry sea of tribesmen brandishing black war flags and screaming epitaphs at the loathsome Brahmin who had the effrontery to think he and his cow-worshiping ilk were going to sway the true sons of the Prophet."

38. Cunningham to Wavell, 9 August 1945, *ITOP*, VI/11, pp. 42–43; Record of Meeting between Wavell, the Cabinet Delegation and the Provincial Governors, 28 March 1946, *ITOP*, VII/17, p. 44; Cunningham to Wavell, 27 February 1946, *ITOP*, VI/479, pp. 1085–1086; Mountbatten to Nehru, 30 April 1947, *ITOP*, X/259, p. 493; Note of Meeting between Cabinet Delegation, Wavell and Sahib, 1 April 1946, *ITOP*, VII/34, p. 74. Nehru accused the political officers of prearranging the demonstrations and of having "intentionally imperiled his life." League agitators, rather than British or local authorities, had prepared the tribes beforehand. Caroe to Wavell, 9 September 1946 and 23 October 1946, MSS.EUR F.203 (Olaf Caroe Papers). Caroe claimed the "attitude of the Khan brothers and their sons to Nehru was almost homosexually pathological." He added, "But Nehru was, or could be, so attractive!"

39. Caroe to Wavell, 22 February 1947, Governor's Report, MSS.EUR F.203 (Olaf Caroe Papers). In one notable instance, a Muslim gang kidnapped a Sikh girl whose husband had been murdered in an earlier incident and forced her to convert and marry a Muslim. Sahib took her to his home in Peshawar, from which she announced, in the presence of her Muslim husband, a desire to return to her family and Sikhism. League mobs thereupon ransacked Sahib's house. The League mob ransacked Sahib's garden and broke all his windows. Sahib was not harmed and remained "brave as a lion," going out on his porch "to tell the crowd what he thought of them." The police curiously disobeyed orders to disperse the mob. They did not mutiny but simply went

through the motions, demonstrating no desire to interfere with the affair. This new "Islam Bibi" played to the League's hand, giving them another vehicle through which to arouse the passions of the frontier.

40. Caroe to Wavell, 22 February 1947 and 8 March 1947, and Caroe to Mountbatten, 22 March 1947, Governor's Reports, MSS.EUR F.203 (Olaf Caroe Papers); Caroe to Mountbatten, 31 March 1947, *ITOP*, X/41, p. 61; Mountbatten to Pethick-Lawrence, 9 April 1947, *ITOP*, X/107, p. 166; Minutes of the Viceroy's Third Miscellaneous Meeting (Situation in the N.W.F.P.), 16 April 1947, *ITOP*, X/162, pp. 286–287; Minutes of the Second Day of the First Governor's Conference, 16 April 1947, *ITOP*, X/158, p. 277; Caroe to Mountbatten, 31 March 1947, *ITOP*, X/41, p. 61; Cabinet, India and Burma Committee, Paper I.B.(46)41, 5 December 1946, *ITOP*, IX/156, 270; Pethick-Lawrence to Attlee, *ITOP*, IX/255, 470; Caroe to Wavell, 22 August 1946 and 23 January 1947, MSS.EUR F.203 (Olaf Caroe Papers). Already Caroe was reporting Congress manipulation of supply channels, packing of juries, using *jirgahs* instead of proper courtroom procedures, and other totalitarian practices. Congress workers rationed government-supplied cloth and sugar, rewarding political allegiance rather than allocating according to need. Congress also withdrew prosecution, withheld bail, ordered cases dropped or retried, or negotiated out of court, even in murder cases. Gupta, *North West Frontier Province Legislature*, pp. 193–194; Stephens, *Pakistan*, pp. 152–153; Mitchell, *Sir George Cunningham*, pp. 126–127; Moore, *Escape from Empire*, pp. 239–240.

41. Scott to Abell, 28 April 1947, *ITOP*, X/247, pp. 476–477; Zeigler, *Mountbatten*, pp. 375–376. Sahib, for his part, called off a counterdemonstration of Red Shirts, which would likely have provoked bloodshed.

42. Mountbatten to Nehru, 30 April 1947, *ITOP*, X/259, pp. 491–494; Viceroy's Personal Report No. 5, 1 May 1947, *ITOP*, X/276, pp. 537–540.

43. Viceroy's Personal Report No. 5, 1 May 1947, *ITOP*, X/276, p. 537; Viceroy's Personal Report No. 6, 8 May 1947, *ITOP*, X/354, p. 686; see also Connell, *Sir Claude Auchenleck*, pp. 867–870, 881–884.

44. Minutes of Viceroy's Ninth Miscellaneous Meeting, 1 May 1947, *ITOP*, X/264, p. 508; Viceroy's Personal Report No. 14, 25 July 1947, *ITOP*, XII/228, pp. 333–334. Mountbatten subsequently noted that his "visit to the NWFP confirmed me in the view that they would join Pakistan." Though he regretted that Jinnah forced him "to give up the idea of a united India," he admitted that Muslim fears have some foundation. Note by Cunningham, 18 February 1945, L/P&S/12/1811, ff. 395–397; Zeigler, *Mountbatten*, pp. 380, 386.

45. Mountbatten to Ismay, 11 May 1947, *ITOP*, X/409, p. 774; Minutes of Viceroy's Twenty-Fourth Staff Meeting, 1 May 1947, *ITOP*, X/272, p. 523; Zeigler, *Mountbatten*, p. 406; see also Record of Interview between Mountbatten and Ghandi, 9 July 1947, *ITOP*, XII/43, pp. 50–52; Cabinet, India and Burma Committee, I.B.(47) 25th Meeting, 19 May 1947, *ITOP*, X/485, p. 897.

46. Viceroy's Personal Report No. 11, 4 July 1947, *ITOP*, XI/506, p. 897; Record of Interview between Mountbatten and Rajagopalachari, 11 April 1947, *ITOP*, X/121, p. 195; Record of Interview between Mountbatten and Jinnah, 7 April 1947, *ITOP*, X/92, pp. 149–150; Record of Interview between Mountbatten and Baldev Singh, 16 April 1947, *ITOP*, X/161, p. 286; Pillai, *Political Triangle*, pp. 15–16; Connell, *Sir Claude Auchenleck*, pp. 887, 912.

47. Cabinet, India and Burma Committee, I.B.(47) 25th Meeting, *ITOP*, X/485,

p. 897; Mountbatten to Listowel, 9 June 1947, *ITOP,* XI/115, pp. 119–120; Cabinet, India and Burma Committee, Paper I.B.(47)99, 13 June 1947, *ITOP,* XI/188, pp. 346–347; Mountbatten to Listowel, 14 June 1947, *ITOP,* XI/202, pp. 394–395; Cabinet, India and Burma Committee, I.B.(47) 31st Meeting, 17 June 1947, *ITOP,* XI/244, pp. 480–481; Record of Interview between Mountbatten and Bhabha, 23 April 1947, *ITOP,* X/202, p. 377; Mountbatten to Ismay, 8 May 1947, *ITOP,* X/357, p. 696; Commonwealth Relations Office to British High Commissioners in Canada, Australia, New Zealand and South Africa, 1 August 1947, *ITOP,* XII/311, p. 466. Though Jinnah argued otherwise, Liaquat eventually abandoned the argument over successor rights, claiming greater interest in securing a "fair proportionate division of assets." Nehru would eventually proclaim India a republic, while declaring India's desire to continue her full membership in the Commonwealth of Nations.

48. Listowel to Attlee, Enclosures 1 and 2, India—Defense Requirements, 24 July 1947, *ITOP,* XI/219, pp. 319–321.

49. Sir William Barton, in the *Daily Telegraph,* 23 May 1947, L/P&S/12/3280; Extract from Peshawar Weekly Intelligence Summary No. 10, 8 March 1947, L/P&S/12/3280, ff. 38. Barton acknowledged, however, that Afghanistan would be left exposed to Russia and would likely encounter Indian resentment as well.

50. Government of India, External Affairs Department, to the Secretary of State, 30 June 1947, *ITOP,* XI/431, p. 799. External Affairs also urged Pakistan to settle policy regarding defense of the region, suggesting some form of association with the tribes similar to the arrangements made with the princely states. They hoped Pakistan "would appreciate the wider aspects in which the whole Commonwealth cannot fail to be interested" and would pursue some form of common policy, suggesting discussions on "obligations devolving on them under the Anglo-Afghan treaty." See also Listowel to Mountbatten, 1 August 1947, *ITOP,* XII/310, pp. 463–465, which noted "the need for a strong and independent buffer state between the Commonwealth and the Soviet Union." Congress and League officials agreed with this policy. Krishna Menon wrote: "The one thing we both thought fundamental was that, in any partition . . . the outer line of India must remain intact" (Menon to Mountbatten, 14 June 1947, *ITOP,* XI/201, p. 390). (Curiously the Anglo-Afghan treaty did not expire when those of the Indian princes did.)

51. Record of Meeting between Ismay, Caroe, Weightman, et al., 14 April 1947, *ITOP,* X/1.

8

---·•··•··•·---

THE TRANSFER OF POWER ON THE NORTHWEST FRONTIER AND THE ORIGINS OF THE "PUSHTUNISTAN" DISPUTE

Following the decision for partition, the fate of the North West Frontier Province (NWFP) remained to be determined. The viceroy feared that any frontier government, if perceived as Hindu dominated, invited a *jihad* that would witness unimaginable atrocities. With the maintenance of order his primary concern, Mountbatten reasoned that the overwhelmingly Muslim province should go to Pakistan, regardless of its *Khudai Khidmatgaran* ministry. Mountbatten was, in fact, prepared to dismiss Sahib, but the Home government rejected that idea, fearing unfavorable Congress reaction.[1]

Caroe had earlier recommended holding a general election in the NWFP to ascertain to whom power should be transferred. To leave the decision to the provincial legislature or to the Constituent Assembly representatives would give the province to Congress. Mountbatten agreed that an announcement of an impending election would ease the tension but realized that the Congress hierarchy would resent such a move. Nehru did, indeed, object to a proposal for fresh elections, claiming such would constitute a victory for League terrorism. Mountbatten found a way out of the dilemma through referendum.[2]

Mountbatten manipulated Nehru's democratic principles and persuaded the Pandit to accept a vote on whether the NWFP would join India or Pakistan. The viceroy stressed how divergence of opinion in the NWFP necessitated a plebiscite, carefully adding that His Majesty's Government would never agree to any transfer of power if the situation in the province remained indeterminate. Nehru ultimately agreed that it was desirable to ascertain the will of the people. He was, in his own words, "intellectually in favor of a referendum." Jinnah approved as well, sensing certain League victory.

Mountbatten thus avoided Congress resentment over dissolving the ministry without reason and ultimately secured League sovereignty on the frontier.[3]

Mountbatten persuaded Nehru to accept the plebiscite as part of the overall independence plan. Caroe's dismissal was also part of the package. Congress deemed him hand-in-glove with the League. Nehru clearly resented Caroe's disapproval of his visit to the frontier and may have still harbored resentment from 1930, when Caroe, as deputy commissioner in Peshawar, had played a role in "large-scale shooting and killing of peaceful demonstrators" during the *Khudai Khidmatgaran* uprisings. Nehru cited a lack of cooperation with Sahib to argue that the governor be requested to resign. The party press went so far as to proclaim an "anti-Caroe day." Even one of Caroe's subordinates, Lieutenant Colonel Dudley Gordon Herriot de la Fargue, the chief secretary of the NWFP, informed Mountbatten that Caroe was "biased against his Congress government." De la Fargue further claimed that Caroe "had lost the confidence of all fair-minded people in the Province" and deemed his continuation in office "a menace to British prestige."[4]

During the subsequent weeks, Mountbatten oft expressed his support for Caroe. He described him as loyal, competent, and honest and claimed to have a high opinion of Caroe's "capacity, integrity and selfless devotion to duty." Mountbatten, however, desired to transfer power in the NWFP "in the most peaceful and dignified manner possible." Fearing a hostile reaction from Congress if he arranged for a referendum without dismissing Caroe, Mountbatten made plans to replace him with Lieutenant General Sir Robert Lockhart.[5]

Mountbatten thought it preferable to invite a resignation, citing ill health, which "in a way is true as he (Caroe) is obviously suffering from strain and is very tired." Officially Caroe went on leave at his own bequest. Caroe later wrote that he felt satisfied to have kept the tribes controlled and was not "in any way sore about this affair." Listowel, however, later wrote that Caroe was highly strung and "prone to suffer these aspersions on his impartiality less easily than a man of more equable temperament." Mountbatten, Listowel claimed, "no longer has confidence in Sir Olaf Caroe as a Governor fully competent to hold the situation" in the NWFP.[6]

After having secured referendum in the NWFP, Mountbatten made one final change to the partition plan. The initial draft of the plan, which Ismay had delivered to London on May 1, had allowed all provinces to join one dominion or be divided between India and Pakistan. It also allowed all the provinces, including the NWFP, the option of independence. On May 9, Ismay queried Mountbatten concerning the possibility of an independent NWFP. Mountbatten replied early on the tenth that this was the first he had heard of such a suggestion. Later that day, he dispatched two telegrams, both of which apologized for earlier "incorrect" statements and disparaged the idea of an independent state on the frontier. Mountbatten also wrote the secretary of state for India, claiming "I do not consider that [the] Frontier

Province should be given [the] option of remaining independent since obviously it could not possibly stand by itself." The next day, Mountbatten apologized again and sent Ismay amendments, arguing that the error could be easily corrected.[7]

In a statement delivered the same day, Nehru criticized the plan for granting independence options to the provinces and the princely states. He claimed such would result in the "Balkanization of India and lead to a complete breakdown of authority." He further insinuated that the British did not sincerely desire to leave India but were maneuvering it into multiple partitions so as to retain influence through support of those states that would remain in the Commonwealth.[8]

By May 12, Mountbatten, cognizant of Nehru's objections and equally ill disposed to options for provincial independence that allowed for dozens of potential separatisms, argued for the elimination of all such options. On May 13, Menon presented a new draft, which drew on the earlier plan in calling for an early transfer of power to dual dominion status, the partition of the disputed provinces of Bengal and the Punjab, and a referendum in the NWFP but eliminated independence options for all provinces. It also expressed hope that all the states would join one of the two dominions, dismissing the idea that they could maintain direct relations with His Majesty's Government.[9]

This move was a drastic change. From the Cripps Mission onward, earlier independence plans had always allowed provincial independence. Early on May 10, in his first note denouncing an independent NWFP, Mountbatten wrote of independence for Bengal and/or the Punjab as a "practicable proposition." Nehru had acquiesced to such possibilities earlier, as had Jinnah, who still envisioned an independent Bengal.[10]

When confronted with Mountbatten's proposed revisions, the India and Burma Committee at first supported the provincial independence option, demanding strict adherence to the broad outlines of the Cripps offer. The committee argued that since the choice of independence would be given to the princely states the remainder of India should be allowed a similar choice. They felt the option desirable for Bengal and also the Punjab, where independence seemed a remedy to Sikh concerns.[11]

Mountbatten responded that it was "essential that we should not turn over [power] to more separate units than was absolutely necessary." The provincial independence option would only give credence to a variety of separatist movements, while reinforcing princely designs on dominion status. He reminded the Cabinet how they had objected to the concept of Pakistan for the damage it would do to the Indian economy and defense establishment, which further fragmentation would only exacerbate. If India were divided into several small states, he argued, the separated parts would be vulnerable to attack from without and tempted to wage war against one another. With partition inevitable, Mountbatten now desired a peaceful transition to two governments that kept initial disputes to a minimum and doors to reunification open. That, he argued, could only be achieved without an independence option, as anything less than a clean break would produce enmity from the League or Congress. Thus, the independence option could not be offered selectively to Bengal or the Punjab. Ultimately, such arguments persuaded the Home government to withhold the independence option. A new policy statement was issued with the assent of the party leaders. Mountbatten would later attribute the onus of the decision to those leaders, who "have decided not to permit [provincial] independence," rejecting such ideas "as a matter of general principle."[12]

The announcement of impending referendum brought relative calm to the frontier. Sensing certain defeat, Sahib's ministry reacted strongly against the proposal. Voicing fears that the Pushtuns would be swamped in Punjabi-dominated Pakistan while admitting that union with Hindustan was impractical, the *Khudai Khidmatgaran* demanded the voters' choices be altered, replacing the Hindustan option with the choice of an independent "Pushtunistan."[13]

Ironically, Caroe, who would later vehemently decry the Pushtunistan idea, apparently played a major role in its ascent. During the debates over the Cabinet Mission Plan, Caroe advised Ghaffar Khan to propose a "Pathan national province," so as to frighten Congress and League leaders into accord. Ghaffar Khan professed fury at the mere suggestion. Only later did he start propaganda "on a theme which I (Caroe) advised them to take up months ago . . . a Pathan national province under a coalition." As the date of the referendum approached, Caroe's chief secretary, among others, suggested expanding the voters' choices to include Pushtunistan. Caroe himself conceded that "many advocates of Pathanistan are sincere and some of Jinnah's local supporters are not without sympathy for the idea." But while the governor believed lasting peace more likely if the third option were included, he also thought it impossible for the League to concede such a possibility.[14]

The *Khudai Khidmatgars* presented Mountbatten their requests for the Pushtunistan option. Responding to questions on possible frontier independence at the June 4 press conference, Mountbatten voiced no personal opposition to provincial independence, stating: "If they can get the High Commands of the two parties to agree to it, and if they want to vote for independence, I will agree." But he added that "the question of whether a province could decide her independence was not raised specifically in the case of the NWFP when the plan was drawn up. It was raised as a matter of general principle and it was turned down as a matter of general principle by the leaders of both parties."[15]

Caroe thus informed the Sahib ministry that the possibility of frontier independence had already been considered and rejected by the Congress hierarchy. Ghaffar Khan, however, continued to oppose a referendum that turned on communal issues. He also claimed Congress support for Pushtunistan. Mountbatten countered that he had removed the independence option for all provinces in direct response to Congress requests. Mountbatten later wrote Nehru, noting how it "was at your written request that the option for Provinces to vote for independence was taken out." The option could not now be offered without League approval, which was out of the question. The viceroy expressed further surprise and indignation at alleged Congress support for Pushtunistan since Nehru had agreed that the NWFP could never survive on its own.[16]

In early May, meanwhile, Afghan Foreign Minister Mohammed Ali had again inquired as to the future status of the tribal areas. He asked that the NWFP be given not only the option of independence but also of reunification with Afghanistan. On May 9, Sir Giles Frederick Squire, the British minister in Kabul, returned a negative reply. Ali admitted disappointment, claiming he expected more after three years of discussion of the issue. Though he reiterated that Afghanistan would make no trouble as long as the British remained in India, Ali warned that should the successor government attempt to coerce the tribes, Afghanistan would become involved in conflict, "with consequences no one could foresee."[17]

Throughout the early summer, the government-controlled Afghan press decried how the Pushtuns living between the Durand Line and the Indus had not been provided with independence and reunification options. Several Afghan officials, including King Zahir Shah, reaffirmed Afghan interest in ascertaining how changes in the Indian constitution would impact the political future of the tribes. On June 13, Ali again informed the Foreign Office of his country's dissatisfaction with the referendum, again suggesting expansion of the voters' choices. In so doing, he described the nineteenth-century British annexation of the Pushtun areas as "an arbitrary dismemberment of Afghanistan." He maintained that common history, ethnology, and political loyalty mandated that the Pushtuns on the Indian side of the Durand Line be given the option of reunification. A short while later, the Afghans offered to send a diplomatic mission to Delhi to discuss common concerns "in a friendly manner."[18]

The External Affairs Department countered that the Pushtuns, domiciled in India for generations, were Indian nationals or, in case of the tribal areas, "British protected persons." Since the frontier inhabitants were not Afghan subjects, the fate of the province was solely an internal concern of the government of India, one in which "the Afghan government has no *locus standi*." The department expressed indignation at what they perceived as Afghan ingratitude, claiming "India is more entitled to expect Afghan goodwill than Afghan intervention in her internal affairs." They warned that a hostile propaganda campaign would jeopardize the continued flow of military equipment and economic assistance from India.[19] In the midst of the constitutional debate, the Foreign Office rejected immediate discussion and ultimately dismissed the Afghan mission proposal as unwelcome interference in India's internal affairs, claiming "the appropriate time for discussing these common problems will be after the new Governments of India and Pakistan come into being; it is not now."[20]

On July 5, the day before the NWFP referendum commenced, British officials informed the Afghan government of the rejection of Ali's proposals. While official statements acknowledged Afghan economic, strategic, and ethnological interests in the area, they maintained that the NWFP was an integral part of India, citing "overriding economic and strategic considerations which make it essential that the NWFP should remain within one of the two states into which India will be divided." They again noted that undue Afghan interference in the area might result in the termination of military and economic assistance. On July 10, Ali gave Squire an ominous reply that promised "a legacy of disagreement" with the successor authorities.[21]

The Afghans made one final attempt to open frontier discussions before independence. On July 15, Prime Minister Shah Mahmud expressed his interest in the frontier Pushtuns and confided his fears relating to the expiration of existing agreements to Squire. Squire urged the prime minister to meet with Jinnah in the near future to discuss common concerns, suggesting they issue a joint statement confirming continued tribal autonomy. Squire felt they could also discuss steps to ensure cooperation between Pakistan and Afghanistan and thereby prevent the tribes from playing one against the other. He saw no reason why Pakistan could not guarantee continued tribal autonomy and no outright annexation of tribal territory.[22]

The External Affairs Department, however, continued to oppose the idea of Afghanistan sending an emissary to discuss frontier matters, claiming such action would only cause Afghan leaders to assume "that their claim to voice in future status of [the] frontier areas is still open to discussion." The secretary of state for foreign affairs agreed, but added that since Mahmud was to pass through Delhi on his way to London and had indicated a friendly attitude, there might be advantage to his meeting with Indian officials. The government of India eventually agreed that discussions might be worthwhile. Mahmud, however, was unable to meet anyone of consequence when he arrived.[23]

The *Khudai Khidmatgars* chose to boycott the referendum, effectively conceding the outcome to the League. On July 20, Mountbatten reported the foregone conclusion: 289,244 votes were cast for Pakistan compared with but 2,874 for India. Considering the voters' religion, the atmosphere of communal violence, and the curious facts that the ballot boxes were green for Pakistan and red for India and placed beside a Koran and a Sikh holy book, respectively, the outcome is hardly surprising. The boycott had some success, as voter turnout was considerably less than the 375,989 who voted in the most recent general election, yet since the total electorate in the NWFP was 572,798, the British and the League could still claim that over half (50.49 percent) of the eligible voters opted for Pakistan. Still, a sizable segment of the population remained unpersuaded by these arguments. The referendum was open only to eligible voters residing in the settled districts. The tribal territories and princely states were ignored. Thus, fewer than 600,000 out of a population of over 4 million were eligible to vote, and less than 10 percent of the total population of the NWFP had voted for incorporation with Pakistan.[24]

The *Khudai Khidmatgars* voiced scattered criticisms of the conduct of the referendum, claiming it improperly administered. Though the *Khudai Khidmatgars* seemed "determined to fight for power with any means at their disposal," Sahib did not proclaim independence, nor did serious disturbances materialize. When he declined to resign, Cunningham, chosen to return as governor by the Pakistanis, quietly replaced him on August 22. Pakistani sovereignty over the NWFP had been secured.[25]

Mountbatten, like most British officials, had adamantly opposed an independent Pushtunistan, believing that its economy could not survive without Indian subsidies and that it would constitute a security risk to the subcontinent. He felt that boundary readjustments were similarly out of the question. Yet, he also saw a continued "need for a strong and independent buffer state between the Commonwealth and the Soviet Union" and to that end supported discussion among Commonwealth governments designed to ensure Afghan independence. He claimed that frontier affairs were "very much in the minds of both successor governments" but assumed those problems could be discussed later, since Jinnah and Nehru had agreed to discuss strategic concerns with the Chiefs of Staff in the Joint Defense Council. Since both successor states had retained Commonwealth membership, Mountbatten assumed India and Pakistan would pursue appropriate policy toward Afghanistan and offered his services to help procure consensus. Listowel agreed that matters of cultural assistance, customs exemptions, provision of transit facilities, and other issues also could be discussed later, "with a view to common policy being put jointly to the Afghan government."[26] Though External Affairs advocated discussions with the Afghans on "transit facilities and customs exemptions for Afghan goods, the supply of military equipment . . . the provision of instructors and training facilities for the Afghan forces, and financial, economic and cultural assistance," since Pakistan seemed willing to continue the established policies, Mountbatten saw no need for immediate discussions. He believed a general statement from Jinnah would suffice until opportunities for meetings with the Afghans arose.[27]

The League, however, was unwilling at first to consider itself the successor to treaty obligations relating to the Pushtuns and Afghanistan, since India had been designated as inheritor of all international rights and obligations of the colonial government. Had such attitudes persisted, they would have destroyed the basis of the British plan to keep the frontier inviolate. Mountbatten, however, pointed out that denial of these obligations might invoke tribal disturbances and Afghan irredentism and ultimately persuaded Jinnah to confirm that Pakistan would assume the pertinent treaty obligations of British India.[28]

In a statement delivered July 30, Jinnah declared Pakistan would continue to honor all previous arrangements with the Pushtuns until representatives of the new government met with the tribal *jirgahs*. Jinnah added that Pakistan would not interfere with traditional regional autonomy, appealing "to all the different elements in the Frontier Province and in the tribal areas to forget past differences and join hands with the Government of Pakistan in setting up a truly democratic state." He further claimed that Pakistan "can only frame a constitution wherein the Frontier will be an autonomous unit and in which the Frontier people will be their own masters." Jinnah also expressed "every intention and desire to have most friendly relations with the Government of Afghanistan." Through the last few months of his life, Jinnah would often repeat these sentiments. In retrospect, Jinnah's words seem empty rhetoric, as Pakistan would within seven years declare tribal territory an integral part of the state, while their policies aimed at subverting Pushtun sectionalism, rather than promoting autonomy.[29] Instead of friendly relations, the fate of the NWFP became a crucible of conflict for Afghanistan and Pakistan. Pushtunistan protest would last in some form for decades and ensure continued friction between the two states. The continued controversy played a prominent role in the eventual alienation of Afghanistan from the West.

NOTES

1. Mountbatten to Nehru, 30 April 1947, *ITOP*, X/259, p. 494; Viceroy's Personal Report No. 5, 1 May 1947, *ITOP*, X/276, pp. 534–535. Mountbatten thought the province "the greatest danger spot in India and the bone of contention between Congress and the Muslim League." Record of Interview between Mountbatten and Jinnah, 9 April 1947, *ITOP*, X/105, pp. 163–164; Cabinet, India and Burma Committee, Paper I.B.(47)27, "India: Transfer of Power to More than One Authority," by the Secretary of State for India, *ITOP*, IX/480, p. 830: "The political objections to the inclusion of the North-West Frontier in Pakistan appear to be very much less and the practical necessities of the situation make a strong case for its inclusion."

2. Caroe to Wavell, 22 February 1947 and 8 March 1947, and Caroe to Mountbatten, 22 March 1947, Governor's Reports, MSS.EUR F.203 (Olaf Caroe Papers); Minutes of the First Day of the First Governors' Conference, 15 April 1947, *ITOP*, X/147, p. 253; Minutes of the Viceroy's Third Miscellaneous Meeting (Situation in the NWFP), 16 April 1947, *ITOP*, X/162, pp. 291–292; Viceroy to Secretary of State, 5 May 1947, R/3/1/151, ff. 103–104; Mountbatten to Ismay, 3 May 1947, *ITOP*, X/300, p. 599; Mountbatten to Ismay, 5 May 1947, *ITOP*, X/317, p. 622.

3. Minutes of the Viceroy's Third Miscellaneous Meeting (Situation in the NWFP), 16 April 1947, *ITOP*, X/162, p. 288; Minutes of the Viceroy's Tenth Miscellaneous Meeting, 8 May 1947, *ITOP*, X/350, pp. 672–673; Record of Interview between Mountbatten and Nehru, 22 April 1947, *ITOP*, X/193, p. 362; Minutes of the Viceroy's Fourth Miscellaneous Meeting (Situation in the NWFP), 18 April 1947, *ITOP*, X/171, p. 318. Sahib's bravado led him to state that he "would be prepared for an election at any time."

4. Viceroy's Third Miscellaneous Meeting, 16 April 1947, *ITOP*, X/162, pp. 286–

287. Sahib accused Caroe, in the presence of Mountbatten, of disregarding his advice and calling conferences without inviting him. Caroe acknowledged that he had, on occasion, disregarded Sahib's suggestions, on the posting of officials, for example. Caroe disliked Congress for historical reasons. Though the governor blamed the communal trouble squarely on the League agitators he opposed the *Khudai Khidmatgars,* going so far as to equate the Red Shirts with Hitler's SS and another new militia, the Young Pathans, with the SA. Caroe to Mountbatten, 17 May 1947, *ITOP,* X/474, p. 875; Record of Interview between Mountbatten and Caroe, 14 April 1947, *ITOP,* X/143, p. 235; Minutes of Viceroy's Fourth Miscellaneous Meeting, 18 April 1947, *ITOP,* X/171, pp. 316–317; Record of Interview between Mountbatten and Lieutenant Colonel de la Fargue, 11 April 1947, *ITOP,* X/122, pp. 196–197. De la Fargue, however, also believed that a free election would return Congress to power. Zeigler (*Mountbatten,* pp. 375–377) claims Caroe was partial to the Muslims and that Mountbatten dismissed him in order to get a governor who was truly neutral. Nehru to Wavell, 19 March 1947, *ITOP,* IX/549, pp. 988–989; Nehru to Mountbatten, 4 June 1947, *ITOP,* XI/61, p. 123. Ghandi likewise favored Caroe's dismissal. See also Record of Interview between Mountbatten and Ghandi, 2 June 1947, *ITOP,* XI/24, p. 48. League leaders opposed Caroe's dismissal; see Liaquat Ali Khan to Mountbatten, 11 June 1947, *ITOP,* XI/143, p. 268.

5. Minutes of Viceroy's Third Miscellaneous Meeting, 16 April 1947, *ITOP,* X/162, pp. 290–291; Viceroy's Personal Report No. 3, 17 April 1947, *ITOP,* X/165, p. 303; Mountbatten to Listowel, 1 May 1947, *ITOP,* X/275, pp. 530–531; Mountbatten to Caroe, 6 June 1947, *ITOP,* XI/96, p. 173. Mountbatten later wrote that he was "convinced of Caroe's essential straightforwardness and desire to handle the very difficult situation on the Frontier in the most impartial and statesmanlike manner," but added, "Personal considerations are a small thing compared to the public weal." Mountbatten to Ismay, 3 May 1947, *ITOP,* X/300, p. 600; Mountbatten to Ismay, 6 May 1947, *ITOP,* X/328 pp. 635–636; Listowel to Attlee, 12 May 1947, *ITOP,* X/417, pp. 793–794.

6. Viceroy's Personal Report No. 3, 17 April 1947, *ITOP,* X/165, p. 303; Listowel to Attlee, 12 May 1947, *ITOP,* X/417, pp. 793–794; Extract from an Unfinished Autobiography by Sir Olaf Caroe, in Conjunction with P.L. Mehra, MSS.EUR F.203/77 (Olaf Caroe Papers); Review of H.D. Hodson's *Great Divide,* (Olaf Caroe Papers); Minutes of Viceroy's Fortieth Staff Meeting, 9 June 1947, *ITOP,* XI/108, p. 203; Caroe to Mountbatten, 13 June 1947, *ITOP,* XI/181, p. 334; Caroe to Mountbatten, 23 June 1947, *ITOP,* XI/310, pp. 579–580.

7. Ismay to Mountbatten, 9 May 1947, *ITOP,* X/365, p. 702; Mountbatten to Ismay, 10 May 1947, *ITOP,* X/380, pp. 728–729; Mountbatten to Ismay, 10 May 1947, *ITOP,* X/399, p. 753; Minutes of the Viceroy's Thirty-First Staff Meeting, 12 May 1947, *ITOP,* X/414, p. 781; Mountbatten to Ismay, 13 May 1947, *ITOP,* X/429, p. 807, Moore, *Escape from Empire,* pp. 272–275 Apparently, Mountbatten simply "overlooked the fact that the draft that Ismay took to London offered the option of independence to the NWFP," for which Ismay blamed the Viceroy's lack of attention to detail. Viceroy to Secretary of State, 10 May and 11 May 1947, L/PO/6/125, f. 61 and f. 52 (also R/3/1/151, f. 49); Mountbatten to Ismay, 11 May 1947, L/PO/6/125, f. 51; Caroe to Mountbatten, L/PO/6/125, f. 50 (also R/3/1/151, f. 59). Caroe concurred, noting, "I agree that option for Frontier province is out of the question, as such suggestion apart from other considerations would stimulate ideas of Afghan ir-

redentism." Memorandum by the Secretary of State for India, "Viceroy's Suggested Amendments to Draft Statement," 12 May 1947, I.B.(47)66, L/PJ/10/79. The secretary also thought independence unsuited to the deficit province.

8. Minutes of Viceroy's Twenty-Seventh Staff Meeting, 7 May 1947, *ITOP,* X/339, 657; Note by Nehru, 11 May 1947, *ITOP,* X/406, pp. 767–771; Note by Nehru, 11 May 1947, *ITOP,* X/402, p. 756; Nehru to Ismay, 19 June 1947, *ITOP,* XI/264, pp. 509–510.

9. Mountbatten to Ismay, 13 May 1947, *ITOP,* X/430, pp. 809–812; Abell to Mieville, 20 May 1947, *ITOP,* X/495, p. 923.

10. Record of Interview between Mountbatten and Nehru, 8 April 1947, *ITOP,* X/96; Minutes of Viceroy's Ninth Miscellaneous Meeting, 1 May 1947, *ITOP,* X/264, pp. 509–12; Mountbatten to Ismay, 10 May 1947, *ITOP,* X/380, p. 729; Mountbatten to the Secretary of State for India, 10 May 1947, L/PO/6/125, f. 61.

11. Cabinet, India and Burma Committee, Paper I.B.(47) 71, "Draft Statement of Policy," by the Secretary of State for India, *ITOP,* X/475, pp. 876–878. The committee saw "no reason . . . that the NWF would stand out for independence." Ismay to Mountbatten, 15 May 1947, *ITOP,* X/449, p. 834.

12. Cabinet, India and Burma Committee, Paper I.B.(47) 27, "India: Transfer of Power to More than One Authority," by the Secretary of State for India, 4 March 1947, *ITOP,* IX/480, pp. 847–848; Viceroy's Personal Report No. 5, 1 May 1947, *ITOP,* IX/276, p. 542; Minutes of Second Day of the First Governors' Conference, 16 April 1947, *ITOP,* X/158, pp. 273–274; Cabinet, India and Burma Committee, I.B.(47) 25th Meeting, 19 May 1947, *ITOP,* X/485, pp. 896–899; Cabinet, India and Burma Committee, I.B.(47) 25th Meeting, 19 May 1947, *ITOP,* X/485, p. 898; Proceedings of a Press Conference held in Council House, New Delhi, 4 June 1947, *ITOP,* XI/60, pp. 116, 120. "After discussing this particular point with the leaders of both the parties I [Mountbatten] find that the leaders do not wish to have any other option than to join one or the other of the constituent assemblies for the good and sufficient reason that they do not wish this plan to encourage what I might call 'Balkanization.'"

13. Viceroy's Personal Report No. 6, 8 May 1947, *ITOP,* X/354, p. 682; Viceroy's Personal Report No. 7, 15 May 1947, *ITOP,* X/451, p. 837; Text of Broadcast of Mr. Jinnah, 3 June 1947, *ITOP,* XI/47, p. 98; Mountbatten to Ghandi, 12 June 1947, *ITOP,* XI/156, p. 290; Caroe to Mountbatten, 8 June 1947, Governor's Report, MSS.EUR F.203 (Olaf Caroe Papers); Telegram, Caroe to Mountbatten, 4 June 1947, *ITOP,* XI/65, p. 126; Lockhart to Mountbatten, 3 July 1947, *ITOP,* XI/475, p. 849; Lockhart to Mountbatten, 16 July 1947, *ITOP,* XII/130, p. 190.

14. Caroe to Mountbatten, 5 June 1947, *ITOP,* XI/83, pp. 151–152; Caroe to Sir J. Colville (Bombay), 22 May 1947, *ITOP,* X/512, p. 944; Caroe, Lecture to the Royal Institute of International Affairs, 4 February 1948, MSS.EUR F.203/4 (Olaf Caroe Papers); Caroe to Mountbatten, 22 May 1947, Governor's Report, MSS.EUR F.203 (Olaf Caroe Papers); Minutes of First Day of First Governors' Conference, 15 April 1947, *ITOP,* X/147, p. 252. Caroe believed that had the Pushtunistan idea been advanced prior to Nehru's visit, it might have become a rallying cry that saved a united India. Instead it seemed a desperate attempt to distance the *Khudai Khidmatgars* from the Congress and too late to have any effect.

15. Proceedings of a Press Conference Held in Council House, New Delhi, 4 June 1947, *ITOP,* XI/60, pp. 116–120. Answers to questions given by Mountbatten at a

press conference, June 4, 1947. At the press conference, Mountbatten claimed the idea for frontier independence had never been raised. In fact, such options had been proposed by the *Khudai Khidmatgars* and the Afghans and even mentioned by members of the Home government. Caroe to Mountbatten, 5 June 1947, *ITOP*, XI/83, p. 151fn; Record of Interview between Mountbatten and Sahib, 5 June 1947, *ITOP*, XI/81, p. 150; Mountbatten to Sir F. Burrows (Bengal), 21 May 1947, *ITOP*, X/509, p. 941; Mieville to Abell, 28 May 1947, *ITOP*, X/552, p. 1013; Cabinet, India and Burma Committee, I.B.(47) 28th Meeting, 28 May 1947, *ITOP*, X/553, p. 1014; Mountbatten to Burrows, 18 May 1947, *ITOP*, X/478, p. 889.

16. Mountbatten to Nehru, 17 June 1947, R/3/1/151, 17 June 1947, f. 131; Statement of 3 June, *ITOP*, XI/45, p. 93; Caroe to Mountbatten, 4 June 1947, *ITOP*, XI/65, pp. 126, 127fn; Viceroy's Personal Report No. 8, 5 June 1947, *ITOP*, XI/91, p. 162; Kripilani to Mountbatten, 17 June 1947, *ITOP*, XI/228, pp. 440–441; Mountbatten to Kripilani, 17 June 1947, *ITOP*, XI/236, p. 459; Mountbatten to Nehru, 17 June 1947, *ITOP*, XI/237, p. 460; Statement by Abdul Ghaffar Khan, 24 June 1947, *ITOP*, XI/321, p. 595.

17. Squire to Weightman, 5 April 1947, *ITOP*, X/82, pp. 135; Squire to Crichton, 9 May 1947, L/P&S/12/1811, f. 147.

18. Squire to the Secretary of State, 11 June 1947, *ITOP*, XI/140, pp. 262–263; Secretary of State to Squire, 16 June 1947, *ITOP*, XI/212, p. 415; Secretary of State to Squire, 20 June 1947, *ITOP*, XI/272, pp. 526–527. Squire attempted to satiate Kabul by claiming that the tribes would be free to negotiate new agreements, adding that this freedom included the right not to negotiate. This did not dissuade Afghan opinion from believing that the tribes would be coerced into joining India or Pakistan. See also Squire to Weightman, 5 April 1947, *ITOP*, X/82, pp. 135–136; Military Attaché's Summary of Intelligence for the Week Ending 29 March 1947, 31 May 1947, and 6 June 1947, L/P&S/12/1850; Squire to the GOI External Affairs and Commonwealth Relations Departments, 23 June 1947, *ITOP*, XI/309, pp. 577–578; Squire to Bevin, 23 June 1947, R/12/178, f. 21; Squire to GOI External Affairs and Commonwealth Relations Departments, 27 June 1947, *ITOP*, XI/377, p. 707. Squire initially considered reception of such a mission "wholly beneficial in removing misunderstandings" and hoped the government of India could receive it. Squire later tempered his position, thinking the Afghans could be permitted to visit "ostensibly to discuss future diplomatic relations" only if secret dealings with the tribes could not "cut the ground from underneath Afghan agitation." He still noted that the Afghans, given the publicity and excitement, would "have to take some action if only to placate public opinion" if their mission request were denied. Caroe to Mountbatten, 25 June 1947, *ITOP*, XI/342, p. 633. Caroe expressed hostility to the proposed mission, which he felt would interfere with "crucial Indian constitutional and political issues," disturb the tribes, and disrupt the referendum. Telegram Lockhart to the Foreign Office, Delhi, 25 June 1947, R/12/178, f. 23. Lockhart and other frontier administrators also considered the mission undesirable, as it would have an unsettling effect on tribes and interfere with the referendum.

19. GOI External Affairs Department to the Secretary of State, 29 June 1947, *ITOP*, XI/395, pp. 731–732; GOI External Affairs Department to the Secretary of State, 30 June 1947, *ITOP*, XI/431, pp. 799–800. The reply claimed that Afghanistan had since 1893 agreed to refrain from interference in the tribal areas and had reaffirmed this in the treaty of 1921. They further claimed that Afghan historical arguments, if

pushed back far enough, could justify India claiming Afghanistan. See also Barton, *India's North-West Frontier,* p. 19; Foreign Office to London, 30 June 1947, R/12/178, f. 40.

20. External Affairs Department and Commonwealth Relations Department to the Secretary of State for India, 30 June 1947, L/P&S/12/1811, f. 81, and 29 June 1947, f. 82; Foreign Office, Delhi, to the Secretary of State for Foreign Affairs, London, 30 June 1947, R/12/178, ff. 35–37. The Foreign Office thought either U.S. pressure, a cessation of aid, or a reminder of their own fears regarding Russian aggressive intentions would sober the Afghans.

21. Listowel to Mountbatten, 5 July 1947, *ITOP,* XI/517, pp. 909–910; Squire to the Secretary of State, 11 July 1947, *ITOP,* XII/70, pp. 107–108, 107fn; Secretary of State for India to Squire, 7 July 1947, L/P&S/12/1811, ff. 62. The official Afghan reply, citing the three conflicts with Britain and the subsequent treaties, argued that Britain had seized Afghan territory, and "their transfer to India therefore is arbitrary act out of keeping with British sense of justice." The Afghan press continued to call for self-determination, criticizing the British refusal to participate in friendly negotiations. Squire replied that Afghanistan should "look forward not backward" and seek the friendship of the successor states, which "was of vital importance to Afghanistan." Squire to Bevin, 5 July 1947, R/12/178, ff. 48–49; Bevin to Squire, 7 July 1947, R/12/178, f. 63; Military Attaché's Summary of Intelligence for the Week Ending 11 July 1947, L/P&S/12/1850.

22. Squire to GOI External Affairs and Commonwealth Relations Department, 16 July 1947, *ITOP,* XII/132, p. 192. Squire realized that Afghan pride had been hurt by the refusal to host their mission. He suggested renaming the NWFP as Pushtunistan. See also Squire to Bevin, 19 July 1947, R/12/178, f. 95. Squire acceded to "some force in the Afghan argument as far as the tribal areas are concerned," especially since Annex 4 of the 1921 treaty had acknowledged the interest of the Afghan government in the trans-Durand tribes.

23. Foreign Office, New Delhi, to the Secretary of State for Foreign Affairs, London, 16 July 1947, R/12/178, f. 92; GOI External Affairs and Commonwealth Relations Department to the Secretary of State, 16 July 1947, *ITOP,* XII/142, pp. 200, 200fn; GOI External Affairs and Commonwealth Relations Department to Squire, 20 July 1947, *ITOP,* XII/177, p. 266. According to a note by Sir Archibald Carter (15 September 1947, L/P&S/12/1812) and a telegram (Viceroy to Secretary of State, 25 July 1947, L/P&S/12/3282, f. 4), Mahmud made his own reservations and did not allow enough time to meet with Jinnah and Nehru.

24. Mountbatten to Listowel, 20 July 1947, *ITOP,* XII/187, p. 277; Poster for the Referendum in the NWFP, R/3/1/151, f. 252; Viceroy's Personal Report No. 14, 25 July 1947, *ITOP,* XII/228, pp. 333–334; Fletcher, *Afghanistan,* p. 251; Kaur, *Pak-Afghanistan Relations,* pp. 197, 203fn.

25. Lockhart to Mountbatten, 23 July 1947, *ITOP,* XII/211, pp. 306–307, and 9 August 1947, *ITOP,* XII/394, pp. 617–618. Lockhart expressed fear that the faqir, who had been a benefactor of Congress financial support, might declare himself "Amir of Waziristan" and "make things difficult for Pakistan by creating as much disturbance as possible." Minutes of the Viceroy's Twenty-Third Miscellaneous Meeting, 29 July 1947, *ITOP,* XII/278, pp. 406–408; Lockhart to Mountbatten, 1 August 1947, *ITOP,* XII/327, p. 493; Mountbatten to Lockhart, 6 August 1947, *ITOP,* XII/363, p. 560; Lockhart to Mountbatten, 9 August 1947, *ITOP,* XII/392, pp. 615–66;

Cunningham to Mountbatten, 14 August 1947, *ITOP,* XII/481, p. 727fn; Sayeed, *Pakistan, the Formative Phase,* pp. 247, 271–273; Mitchell, *Sir George Cunningham,* pp. 129–134.

26. Extract from Viceroy's Personal Report No. 16, 16 August 1947, L/P&S/12/3282, f 23; Extract from Letter, Mountbatten to Listowel, 16 August 1947, L/P&S/12/3282, f. 22; Listowel to Mountbatten, 1 August 1947, *ITOP,* XII/309, p. 463; Listowel to Mountbatten, enclosing "North West Frontier Tribal Area and Afghanistan," 1 August 1947, *ITOP,* XII/310, pp. 464–465; Cabinet, India and Burma Committee, Paper I.B.(47) 66, "Viceroy's Suggested Amendments to Draft Statement," by the Secretary of State for India, 12 May 1947, *ITOP,* X/415, p. 783. Mountbatten also thought the present an inappropriate time to enter negotiations with Afghanistan. An independent NWFP would be a tempting target for Russian intrigue and might "encourage irredentist ideas in Afghanistan." Cabinet, Meeting of Ministers on Indian Questions, GEN 174/1st Meeting, 13 March 1947, *ITOP,* IX/530, p. 942. Mountbatten also thought economic and transit difficulties would be exacerbated "unless Sind, the Punjab and the NWF were grouped under one government."

27. Mountbatten to Listowel, 4 August 1947, *ITOP,* XII/336, p. 510; Mountbatten to Listowel, 16 August 1947, *ITOP,* XII/488, pp. 741–742; Extract from Letter, Mountbatten to Listowel, 16 August 1947, L/P&S/12/3282, f. 22; Memo, Mountbatten to Listowel, 1 August 1947, L/P&S/12/3282.

28. Mountbatten to Listowel, 2 July 1947, *ITOP,* XI/463, p. 832; Cabinet, India and Burma Committee, I.B.(47) 40th Meeting, 3 July 1947, *ITOP,* XI/486, pp. 870–871; Listowel to Mountbatten, 5 July 1947, *ITOP,* XI/517, pp. 910, 910fn; External Affairs and Commonwealth Relations Department to Squire, 5 August 1947, *ITOP,* XII/350, pp. 543, 543fn. For a time, the common legal view was that all treaties would expire "except those relating to Customs, transit and communications." Her Majesty's Government and the government of India initially saw no reason not to inform the Afghans of this, but on August 8, 1947, the External Affairs and Commonwealth Relations Department informed Squire that "the Government of Pakistan would be grateful if you would not repeat nor inform the Afghans even informally."

29. *ITOP,* XII/365, 562fn; Mountbatten to Listowel, *ITOP,* XII/336, pp. 509fn, 510; Extract from the *Times of India,* 31 July 1947, L/P&S/12/1812, f. 231. Jinnah promised the Pathans would enjoy similar same self-government as any other part of Pakistan and that he would "[continue] all treaties, agreements and allowances until new agreements are negotiated." See also Tabibi, "Aftermath Created by British Policy," pp. 67–71; Translation of *Islah,* 9 May 1949, FO 983/37.

9

THE STRATEGIC RAMIFICATIONS OF THE PARTITION OF INDIA FOR BRITAIN, THE SUCCESSOR STATES, AND AFGHANISTAN

On August 15, 1947, crowds in every major city across the subcontinent greeted independence with enthusiasm. One of the few Indians who did not share their euphoria was Ghandi. He feared that partition "would leave a legacy of war," with the Pakistani and Indian armies battling one another.[1] The factors that precluded the establishment of a unified successor state would indeed ensure that India and Pakistan would pursue military strategies hostile to one another, regardless of Commonwealth membership. Such policies would have a pronounced lack of correlation with British strategic goals and a dramatic effect on Afghanistan.

Though he accepted concession of Pakistan, hoping to reduce the violence, Mountbatten still thought it possible to include Jinnah in an interim government. The viceroy hoped partition would prove an "anesthetic" that would prompt "saner councils" to cooperate once the complications became evident. Mountbatten was not alone in believing that he could reunify India. Throughout the British hierarchy, hopes remained that the difficulties incurred would demonstrate a necessity for continued cooperation and ultimately lead to reunification.[2]

Mountbatten initially thought Pakistan and India could be declared separate dominions, but with a central defense council resembling a Combined Chiefs of Staff and a single army. Jinnah and Liaquat Ali Khan, however, persisted in demanding the partition of the armed forces, fearing Pakistan would be absorbed if left without its own military establishment. Liaquat argued that the preponderance of Hindu officers in the defense establishment would allow any unified army to be controlled by Congress and leave Pakistan "a house of cards," devoid of real political power. Jinnah insisted that the "transfer of power to [the] Pakistan and Hindustan Governments must mean a division of the defenses as a *sine qua non* of such a transfer and the defense forces should be completely divided—and in my opinion can be divided before June 1948—and the states of Pakistan and Hindustan should be made absolutely free, independent, and sovereign."[3]

Liaquat and Jinnah both realized that the division of the army was the crux of partition. Their insistence on division was a "rapier thrust at the very heart of a unitary India."[4]

Once Mountbatten conceded partition, Liaquat and Jinnah repeatedly threatened to derail the agreement if an army was not available at Pakistan's disposal prior to the transfer of power. They forced Mountbatten to choose whether to risk League ire in an attempt to maintain one army, which appeared to be disintegrating amidst the backdrop of communal violence, or attempt to divide the army into two coherent forces. Foregoing his earlier reservations, Mountbatten appointed Chandulai Trivedi, governor of Orissa and friend to both Liaquat and Nehru, to supervise an Armed Forces Reconstitution Committee. In a span of just eight days, Trivedi obtained concessions from both parties that outlined the procedures and technicalities of division.[5]

Thereafter, Mountbatten pinned postpartition strategic issues on the generation of good feeling. Though the Chiefs of Staff had opposed allowing defense issues to go by default and lobbied for immediate negotiations with Indian leaders on the entire breadth of defense questions, Mountbatten believed that Britain would stand the best chance of securing lasting commitment to the Commonwealth through "the introduction of complete autonomy, with no reservations" and maintained that discussions not commence until the new states had established themselves.[6] Ismay thought that after independence, Britain could demonstrate the strategic vulnerability of the successor states, convince them of the need for Commonwealth support, and then open discussions on strategic requirements in the context of mutual assistance. Ismay added that Jinnah and Nehru, while fully occupied, had expressed desires to meet with the Chiefs of Staff after partition.[7] The India and Burma Committee accepted Ismay's and Mountbatten's advice and left the timing and method of approach for securing future defense-related agreements "for political decision."[8]

Foiled of his plans to retain one army for both successor states, Mountbatten attempted to ensure cooperation among the national commands. The Independence Bill established a Joint Defense Council (JDC), consisting of Auchinleck, left in the role of supreme commander, the governors-general, and the respective ministers of defense, and encharged it with the actual division of the armed forces. Mountbatten buoyantly noted impending discussions between Indian and Pakistani leaders and the Chiefs of Staff, in expressing his belief that the JDC could prevent hostilities until April, leaving eight months in which to create common defense arrangements.[9] Ismay echoed this optimism, voicing "hope that the Joint Defense Council . . . may in time develop into a body which will foster unity of doctrine, unity of equipment and unity of policy between India and Pakistan."[10] Auchinleck, however, among others, had few doubts that once in power, Congress would attempt to render the JDC impotent and undermine Pakistan.[11]

While Mountbatten had hoped that partition would provide an anesthetic, the atrocities that accompanied partition, boundary disputes in Bengal and the Punjab, and difficulties regarding the accession of certain princely states, most notably Kashmir, heightened political and religious differences and left neither Congress nor the League in any mood to compromise. The division of the armed forces evoked further resentment. Though Auchinleck tried to divide impartially, his suspicions of Congress proved correct. Pakistan was cooperative, but India, in possession of the stores, balked and delayed and ultimately retained many goods promised to Pakistan. Congress leaders eventually accused Auchinleck of favoring Pakistan and further claimed that Pakistani behavior, evidenced by the continued communal violence and the tribal invasion of Kashmir, precluded cooperation. Congress soon argued for the abolition of the JDC. Auchinleck knew that disbandment would leave "no hope at all of any just division of assets . . . belonging to the Indian army." Faced with Indian intransigence, however, the commander-in-chief, who originally had until April 1948 to complete his task, had little choice but to disband the JDC on November 30, 1947, regardless of League objections.[12]

With continued Commonwealth membership ensured, Mountbatten and other British officials had hoped for eventual reunification of the subcontinent or at least common defense policy among the successor states. But instead of a united India, supported by a single army, two mutually antagonistic nations emerged, with the divided remnants of that force poised against one another. All attempts to circumvent Clausewitzian logic through a system of two states with one army or two states, two armies, and one command had proven illusory. The civil service, government, and economic system were similarly disrupted. The myriad philosophical, political, religious, and personal differences of the Indian and Pakistan leaders that prompted partition also ensured that bitter animosity would remain. Pakistan and India would not consider a joint defense strategy and have since remained more concerned with defense against each other than any external threat. Though Mountbatten continued to work for improved relations, he could neither overcome the animosity between the rival states nor drastically alter their foreign policy goals.

While the British withdrawal changed the balance of power in South Asia, it also altered the strategic dilemma of the Empire. The Chiefs of Staff had desired to preserve as much of the old strategic balance as possible. The Chiefs had assumed that, from within the Commonwealth, India and Pakistan would pursue strategic policy similar to that of the colonial government and thought that both would cooperate in the creation and maintenance of strategic reserve forces. They further assumed that British personnel would retain access to naval and air bases thought vital for Indian Ocean defense and communications with the Far East.

Commonwealth membership, however, brought the successor states economic benefits, improved ties with the West, and a modicum of security without in any way restricting their foreign or strategic policies. While many British officers remained with the Indian and Pakistani armed forces, training and organizing them along the lines of the old Indian regiments, no agreement allowed Britain to control the deployment of troops as before. Lingering anticolonialism left the Indian leaders particularly ill disposed to participation in Commonwealth defense activities. India's postwar financial situation further mandated reductions in the defense budget. Unable to force India to follow the old strategic policies or even divert funds from internal reform, Britain would be deprived of the manpower pool with which it had long supported the Empire and the Chiefs' primary requirement could not be filled.

The loss of political control of India, however, eliminated much of the *raison d'être* of the Empire. Continued Commonwealth membership of Pakistan and India, together with British economic interests in the Middle East, Pacific, and Indian Ocean regions, legitimized continuation of many old strategic policies, but with India no longer the Jewel of the Empire or even an active member of the Commonwealth, its defense no longer remained the overriding concern of planners in Whitehall. Considerations of Atlantic and European defense policy dominated British strategic considerations in the postwar era, while even within the region strategic interests gradually shifted away from the subcontinent toward the Suez and the oil-rich Persian Gulf area. This would have tremendous consequences not only for Pakistan and India, but also for Afghanistan.[13]

Throughout independence discussions, the Chiefs of Staff had voiced continued support for the territorial integrity and internal stability of Afghanistan. They hoped military aid to Afghanistan would continue and even planned to send additional supplies and instructors. The Chiefs were unable to undertake any program until after the transfer of power, however, and had to hope that the successor governments would see the need for a benevolent policy. The partition plan, however, left Britain in no position to ensure any such continuum. The Chiefs suggested a joint approach be made to Afghanistan, with reference to the tribal situation, but until such points were raised in the JDC, Britain could do nothing. They would ultimately prove unable to prevent the demise of the Lancaster Plan and the attendant decline of Western influence in Afghanistan.[14]

Shortly after partition, Afghanistan abrogated all treaties made with British India and challenged Pakistani claims to have inherited the treaty rights of the colonial government. Throughout the ensuing years, the Afghan government, with support of elements of the *Khudai Khidmatgaran* and assorted frontier agitators, demanded the establishment of an independent Pushtunistan. To support their claim, the Kabul regime argued that Afghans had historically controlled the region. The Treaty of Gandomak and the Durand Line agreement had been obtained through force, or threat of force, and therefore were invalid. They noted how, since the mid-nineteenth century, every Afghan ruler had considered the fate of the trans-Durand Pushtuns a matter of national interest. None had ever recognized the Durand Line as an international boundary or even considered it more than a delineation of zones of control, and all had fought to restore the British-controlled territories to Afghan suzerainty.[15]

The Pakistanis, supported by the British, countered that while Durrani had held India up to Delhi, his control was weak and lasted only a few years. Historical arguments stretched *ad absurdum* could justify Pakistani absorption of Afghanistan, since in earlier times Afghanistan had fallen under Indian suzerainty. Pakistan discounted any notion that Abdur Rahman had signed the Durand Line agreement under duress and noted that the boundary was repeatedly validated in treaties of 1905, 1919, 1921, and 1930. British officials in particular stressed that the 1921 and 1930 treaties, which confirmed Afghan independence, also confirmed the border in the modern sense.[16]

British authorities frequently reaffirmed their view that Pakistan had, under international law, inherited the rights and duties of British India. The Afghans in turn argued that they had accepted the treaty given certain facts and could absolve themselves when those facts changed. The British dismissed this *rebus sic stantibus* argument, claiming international law "affords no warrant for the view that the substitution of one country for another as a party to a treaty affords any automatic ground . . . to justify the other party in regarding the agreement as being at an end." To support such an argument, however, they cited such precedents as the division of the Kingdom of Norway and Sweden in 1905 and the separation of Austria and Saxony in 1845. In fact, partition was a unique event, and while some international experts supported the belief that successor nations inherit the rights of their predecessor, others supported the Afghan position.[17]

There is no denying an affinity between the Pushtuns of the North West Frontier Province (NWFP) and those in Afghanistan. Pushtuns on both sides of the border share common ethnicity, customs, literature, folklore, history, sentiments, and language. An Afghan writer would note: "The contiguance of the province with independent territory and Afghanistan, the free inter course between the people on both sides of the borderline, the simplicity of their ideals, customs and mode of life, and especially their descent from the common stock, strongly distinguish the people of our province from those of the rest of India."[18]

Certainly the racial and linguistic affinities of the Pushtun tribes were closer to the Durranis and Ghilzais than to the peoples of Pakistan or India. While there was little national consciousness among the tribes, evidence suggests that many favored political arrangements with Afghanistan to intimate relations with India or Pakistan. While they claimed independence of both states, cultural and religious ties often rendered the trans-Durand Pushtuns in unison with Kabul, at least through the nineteenth and early twentieth century.[19]

Though postwar arguments for self-determination formed the basis for the establishment of some states, they generally received little sympathy in the aftermath of the Munich agreements of 1938–1939, especially if directed at the territory of another state. More than one British commentator recommended that Afghanistan neither be permitted to annex her "Sudetenland" nor receive a "Danzig Corridor" to the sea. A few others compared Afghan demands to a hypothetical Mexican claim on the southwestern United States. Nearly all concluded that, despite ethnological considerations, Pakistan, like other nations of the twentieth century, could hardly be expected to revert its borders to those of the eighteenth.[20]

There were other weaknesses in the Afghan argument. The common inclusion of Baluchistan, whose inhabitants are not of the same ethnic stock as the Pushtuns, in definitions of greater Pushtunistan contradicted the principle of self-determination. This inconsistency also seemed proof that the Afghan arguments were but a cover for designs to secure permanent access to the Arabian Sea.[21] Afghanistan's ethnic milieu further undermined its position. Pushtunistan enjoyed no support among the non-Pushtuns of Afghanistan, who recognized that the incorporation of the NWFP would only leave them swamped politically, culturally, and economically. Furthermore, in arguing for frontiers defined on an ethnic basis, the Kabul government was arguing for its own partition between Iran, Pakistan, and the U.S.S.R.[22]

While elements of the Afghan argument were simply illogical, others were dangerous. The annexation of large numbers of Pushtun tribesmen was unlikely to increase the political or economic security of Afghanistan. Given the difficulties Afghanistan experienced with the tribes throughout the 1930s and more recently with the Safis, Shah Mahmud himself admitted that Afghanistan "would find it virtually impossible to absorb the turbulent mass of tribesmen on the British side of the Frontier." The sparsely populated, barren, landlocked region, heretofore dependent on India for subsidies, would constitute a steady drain on the Afghan economy. Afghanistan could neither control nor afford such an amalgamation.[23]

The Afghan demands also invited a Soviet response. Any claim they made on the tribes begged a Soviet counterclaim on Afghanistan's northern provinces, whose inhabitants were of the same ethnic stock as the citizens of the Central Asian Republics. The Afghan unwillingness to define their claims and their avowed support of an independent Pushtunistan rather than outright annexation seem calculated ploys taken in light of such fears. This fact did not escape British and Pakistani authorities, who repeatedly reminded Kabul of the Soviet danger while dismissing the entire Pushtunistan campaign.

Many came to believe that the Soviet threat would force Afghanistan to make amends with Pakistan out of sheer necessity.[24]

The danger of Soviet counterclaims leads one to question why the Afghans started the agitation. Lancaster thought the Afghans had begun their "suicidally stupid" policy on a belief that India would fall to anarchy and continued it in the hope that Pakistan would collapse. Territorial ambitions should not be discounted, since securing an outlet to the sea had been a goal of Afghan policy for generations, which Axis propaganda and a smattering of British proposals had buoyed. While ulterior motives perhaps influenced the Pushtunistan crisis, it seems likely that most Afghans also felt legitimate ethnic claims upon the area.[25]

Throughout independence discussions, Afghanistan publicly supported a united India. In the months immediately preceding partition, however, several press articles stated that the Sikhs, Baluch, Burmese, Bengalis, and others, along with the Muslims in general, would have the right to secession. There was also wide speculation that many princely states would declare independence. It only stood to reason that such rights would be granted to the quasi-independent Pushtuns, whose status more closely resembled the princes than the provinces. Tribal territory had never come under the administrative aegis of British India. The tribes had instead remained free to conduct internal affairs to their liking, as long as they did not menace the security of the Indus Valley or Afghanistan. The actual concession of partition, however, considered Congress and League attitudes only. From the Afghan perspective, freedom of choice was not uniformly applied. Consequently, many continued to question why the Pushtuns had been prohibited independence and demanded that Pushtunistan be formed into "an independent state with intimate relations with Afghanistan."[26]

It also seems of consequence that Hashim Khan and Wali Khan, long the elder statesmen of Afghanistan and champions of cooperation with the British, were out of the country through most of June 1947. Younger officials, desirous of rapid modernization and possessed of a strong anti-British bias, courted provocation. Yet even Hashim, when he returned, expressed concern that Britain had not consulted Afghanistan during partition discussions and voiced hopes for a beneficial settlement: "If an independent Pushtunistan cannot be set up, the Frontier Province should join Afghanistan. . . . Our neighbor will realize that our country, with its population and trade, needs an outlet to the sea, which is very essential. The British government knows . . . if the nations of the world desire peace and justice . . . It will be easy for us to get an outlet to the sea."[27] In that regard, Hashim conveyed the ambitions of virtually the entire Afghan nation. Such desires, coupled with ethnological concerns, in part balance the inconsistencies in the Afghan argument for Pushtunistan.[28]

Over time, the Afghans tempered their stance. Whether alerted to the weaknesses in their argument, disappointed by the lack of international support for the Pushtunistan campaign, or simply stymied by superior military force, the Afghan leadership resolved to negotiate. The public excitement generated by the Pushtunistan propaganda left Mahmud unable to simply drop the campaign without enduring a serious loss of face. Mahmud hoped for a way to circumvent this dilemma and would have appreciated having "someone else to pull the chestnut out of the fire."[29]

Mahmud requested British assistance to obtain a negotiated settlement. A few Britons acknowledged Afghan difficulty in disassociating from the issue and supported a mediation effort. General Geoffery Scoones, for example, admonished the Pakistanis for their inflexibility toward the Afghan claims. He thought that Afghanistan realized the danger that the tribes constituted to Pakistan and itself but claimed "Pakistan appears to realize neither." Britain, he argued, must make Pakistan face the issue, perhaps inducing a military alliance. Scoones's views apparently remained confined to a minority of officials. Though Afghanistan seemed willing to accept an agreement given face-saving concessions, since Pakistan was a Commonwealth member and Afghanistan was not, the British refused to facilitate discussion barring a request from Karachi. Pakistan, however, declared the tribes a purely internal matter of no concern to Afghanistan and voiced hostility to the very idea of discussion. Despite earlier support for joint British-Afghan-Pakistani discussions within JDC, Britain left the matter in abeyance, attempting only (and rather quietly) to persuade the Pakistanis to handle the situation with tolerance and tact.[30]

Though service representatives were to have negotiated future defense policy regarding Afghanistan within the JDC, the collapse of that organization left relations up to the individual states. Before partition, Indian authorities had delivered about 35 percent of the supplies promised in the Lancaster Plan to Afghanistan. Since India possessed the requisite stores, it was to continue the program, but shortly after independence, the Indian government, facing conflict with the Pakistanis, denied all knowledge of the scheme and claimed to have lost the records. When shown British copies of relevant documents, the Indians assumed a legalistic attitude, claiming the agreement no longer binding in the wake of partition. India had no sustained political desire to support the Afghans, whose calls for self-determination in Pushtunistan echoed those of the Pakistanis in Kashmir.[31] The Pushtunistan dispute precluded any possibility of Pakistan assuming the Indian responsibility, as the Pakistanis feared that the arms would fall into the hands of the frontier agitators. Furthermore, neither India nor Pakistan had spare equipment to provide. With their armies struggling to organize themselves after partition and battling one another in Kashmir, neither nation was prepared to supply equipment to the Afghans, especially at cut-rate prices.

Though Afghanistan continued to express desires for military collaboration and requested extensive development loans from the United Kingdom as well, Britain's war-ravaged economy forced the rejection of all but a few limited Afghan requests. Pushtunistan also precluded extensive Anglo-Afghan military cooperation, for as long as Pakistan remained a Commonwealth member, "Afghanistan must be aware that there is no hope of getting any military aid from Great Britain." Most importantly, once the break with India was finalized, the foci of British policy began to shift from the subcontinent, and Afghanistan became of but minimal importance to Britain. Given these circumstances, Britain did not press for continuation of the assistance program and eventually declared that it had "no further role to play in the Lancaster Plan." The plan's provisions remained unfulfilled.[32]

The Chiefs of Staff had earlier concluded that, in the absence of British aid, Afghanistan would likely turn to the United States for military assistance. Lancaster, however, felt the Americans could never exercise appropriate influence. The Chiefs similarly thought that given "erratic American policy" and general inexperience in Asia, Afghanistan would do well to stick to her "old friend."[33] Yet, with Pakistan and India weak and hostile and Afghanistan's "old friend" not capable of or particularly interested in providing for Afghanistan's defense, the United States remained as the only potential Western benefactor of Afghanistan.

NOTES

1. Record of Interview between Mountbatten and Ghandi, 9 July 1947, *ITOP,* XII/43, pp. 50–51.

2. Viceroy's Personal Report No. 3, 17 April 1947, *ITOP,* X/165, pp. 300–301; Viceroy's Personal Report No. 8, 5 June 1947, *ITOP,* XI/91, p. 163; Minutes of Viceroy's Fifth Miscellaneous Meeting, 21 April 1947, *ITOP,* X/190, p. 358; Record of Interview between Mountbatten and Liaquat Ali Khan, 11 April 1947, *ITOP,* X/126, p. 201; Minutes of Viceroy's Fourteenth Miscellaneous Meeting, 11 May 1947, *ITOP,* X/405, p. 766; Minutes of Viceroy's Seventh Miscellaneous Meeting, 23 April 1947, *ITOP,* X/203, p. 381.

3. Record of Interview between Mountbatten and Krishna Menon, 22 April 1947, *ITOP,* X/200, p. 373; Viceroy's Personal Report No. 5, 1 May 1947, *ITOP,* X/276, p. 545; see also Barton, *India's North-West Frontier,* p. 207. Barton proposed two separate armies, one imperial and the other dominion.

4. Liaquat to Mountbatten, 7 April 1947, *ITOP,* X/94, pp. 151–152; Minutes of the Viceroy's Seventh Miscellaneous Meeting, 23 April 1947, *ITOP,* X/203, p. 381; Record of Interview between Mountbatten and Auchenleck, 14 April 1947, *ITOP,* X/138, pp. 223–224; Cabinet, India and Burma Committee, *ITOP,* IX/480, pp. 849–850; Connell, *Auchenleck,* p. 873; Zeigler, *Mountbatten,* p. 389.

5. Viceroy's Personal Report No. 11, 4 July 1947, *ITOP,* XI/506, p. 893; Zeigler, *Mountbatten,* pp. 390, 465; Record of Interview between Mountbatten and Jinnah, 23 June 1947, *ITOP,* XI/311, p. 582; Partition Council Meeting, 30 June 1947, *ITOP,* XI/416, p. 757; Record of Interview between Mountbatten and Auchenleck, 14 April 1947, *ITOP,* X/138, pp. 223–224; Paper I.B.(47) 89, 27 May 1947, *ITOP,* X/547, pp. 1004–1007; Qureshi, *Anglo-Pakistan Relations,* pp. 74–76; Khan, *Story of Pakistan Army,* pp. 21–22. By 1947 Muslims comprised 29 percent of the army, down

from 37 percent in the prewar force. Officers were mixed throughout the army in every unit, irrespective of class or religion. There were no wholly Muslim units, though there were some in which the rank-and-file were exclusively Hindu. (There were no purely Hindu or Muslim units in either the navy or the air force or in ordnance, supply, or medical units, however.) Chiefs of Staff Committee, COS(47) 86th Meeting, 9 July 1947, *ITOP*, XII/41, p. 44.

6. Viceroy's Personal Report No. 9, 12 June 1947, *ITOP*, XI/162, p. 306; Mountbatten to Listowel, 12 June 1947, *ITOP*, XI/174, p. 320; Mountbatten to Listowel, 24 June 1947, *ITOP*, XI/335, p. 614.

7. Chiefs of Staff Committee, COS(47) 86th Meeting, 9 July 1947, *ITOP*, XII/41, pp. 45–49; Ismay to Mountbatten, 16 July 1947, *ITOP*, XII/143, p. 201fn; Meeting of the Provisional Joint Defense Council, 6 August 1947, *ITOP*, XII/352, pp. 546–547; Mountbatten to Listowel, 16 August 1947, *ITOP*, XII/488, pp. 742–743; Listowel to Attlee, 12 August 1947, *ITOP*, XII/443, p. 683.

8. Cabinet, India and Burma Committee, I.B.(47) 31st Meeting, 17 June 1947, *ITOP*, XI/244, p. 482; Listowel to Mountbatten, 18 June 1947, *ITOP*, XI/258, p. 501; Lieutenant General Hollis to Alexander, 25 June 1947, *ITOP*, XI/346, p. 647; Chiefs of Staff Committee, COS(47) 76th Meeting, 16 June 1947, *ITOP*, XI/221, pp. 432–434; Listowel to Mountbatten, 3 July 1947, *ITOP*, XI/487, pp. 871–872.

9. Meeting of Special Committee of the Indian Cabinet, 26 June 1947, *ITOP*, XI/354, pp. 654–655; Note by H.M. Patel, 27 June 1947, *ITOP*, XI/372, pp. 694–698; Partition Council Meeting, 30 June 1947, *ITOP*, XI/416, p. 759; Joint Defense Council Order, 11 August 1947, *ITOP*, XII/425, p. 657; Mountbatten to Listowel, 24 June 1947, *ITOP*, XI/335, p. 614; Zeigler, *Mountbatten*, pp. 378, 389–390. Mountbatten wrote the king: "It was in my mind, that its [JDC] scope might indeed expand to cover financial and economic matters also, and eventually External Affairs and Communications, which would mean a virtual accession of the Two Dominions to one another, on the same basis as the States" (quoted in Hodson, *Great Divide*, p. 535).

10. Ismay to Messervy, 11 August 1947, *ITOP*, XII/429, p. 664.

11. Connell, *Auchenleck*, pp. 912–915, 917, 920–922, 927, 930; Smith to Ismay, 3 July 1947, *ITOP*, XI/477, p. 851; Qureshi, *Anglo-Pakistan Relations*, p. 70.

12. Connell, *Auchenleck*, pp. 912–917, 920–922, 927–930; Khan, *Story of Pakistan Army*, pp. 35–37; Zeigler, *Mountbatten*, p. 464.

13. The adoption of the "Ten Year Rule," which specified that no great war need be expected until 1956, further limited any strategic discussion. See L/WS/1/987 and L/WS/1/988 generally; Pillai, *Political Triangle*, pp. 13, 17–18, 143; Asopa, *Military Alliance*, pp. 4–6; Darby, *British Defence Policy*, pp. 6, 9–10, 25–26, 38–39, 43, 76. The British did not conduct any major re-evaluation of strategic policy following partition. ("The removal of the hub did not lead to a reconsideration of the role of the spokes.") Defense policy remained largely reactive. The British remained obligated to several dependencies (Cyprus, Aden, Suez, Zanzibar, Hong Kong, Singapore, Bahrain, Mombasa, etc.), formerly required to protect India's maritime frontiers and facilitate trade. Some, such as Malaya, took on an economic importance of their own. Others maintained their former role, serving to safeguard and facilitate the flow of Middle Eastern oil. Safe passage through Suez and the Red Sea and the Straits of Molucca remained of importance, as Britain held sizable investments in major oil consortiums in Iran, Iraq, Kuwait, and other gulf states. Commanders responded to immediate

threats faced them with whatever limited resources were available, be it Malaya, Kenya, or the Persian Gulf.

14. Chiefs of Staff Committee, "Afghanistan—Strategic Importance," COS(47) 182(0), L/WS/1/986, ff. 141–148; COS 967/29/8/7, 29 August 1947, L/P&S/12/1821; see Wavell to Pethick-Lawrence, 26 February 1947, *ITOP,* IX/469, p. 820. Doubts were raised earlier that in cases like Afghanistan, "it may prove to be physically impossible [given Indian obtrusiveness] to give full effect to [Her Majesty's Government] policy as hitherto conceived." See Cabinet Paper C.P.(46)329, 30 August 1946, *ITOP,* VIII/228, p. 365.

15. Mohammed Ali, Minister of Foreign Affairs to Squire, 10 July 1947, R/12/178, ff. 70–81. He declared the area "exactly analogous to Burma" and claimed that denial of reunification was "like cutting a body apart and not expecting it to sob or cry." Military Attaché's Summary of Intelligence for the Week Ending 23 August 1947, L/P&S/12/1850.

16. Dupree, *AUFS,* 4/4, p.5; Fletcher, *Afghanistan,* p. 247; "Survey, Part III, The Indo-Afghan Frontier," L/P&S/12/1321. This official document claims the Durand agreement defined the border not as an international frontier but as "the limit of their respective spheres of influence." The 1921 treaty, however defined "the Indo-Afghan frontier as accepted by the Afghan Government." The Afghans retorted that the treaties signed in 1893 and 1905 did not mention the Durand Line as a "frontier" and those of 1921 and 1930 did not sanction British sovereignty over the tribesmen, who remained "protected persons," rather than citizens of the Empire.

17. The Anglo-Afghan Treaty of 1921 [n.s., n.d., late 1947?], R/12/178, ff. 217–218; Quddus, *Afghanistan and Pakistan,* p. 104; Qureshi, *Anglo-Pakistan Relations,* p. 197; Squire to Crichton, 19 April 1947, L/P&S/12/1811, ff. 187–188.

18. Stephens, *Pakistan,* pp. 48–49; Kaur, *Pak-Afghanistan Relations,* p. 46; "Survey, Part III, The Indo-Afghan Frontier," L/P&S/12/1321.

19. Barton, *India's North-West Frontier,* p. 1101; Sykes, "Afghanistan: Its History and Present Position in Asia," p. 17.

20. Government of India, External Affairs and Commonwealth Relations Department, to Secretary of State, 29 June 1947, *ITOP,* XI/395, p. 732 and 30 June 1947, *ITOP,* XI/431, p. 800; "Brief for UK Delegation to the United Nations; Afghan/Pakistan Relations" [n.s., n.d.; 1948?], L/P&S/12/1812, ff. 95–96; "Possibility of War between Pakistan and Afghanistan," 11 August 1949, J.I.C. (49)57, L/WS/1/1169, ff. 4–20; Report of Lecture Tour, 5 May–10 June 1952, MSS.EUR F.203/64 (Olaf Caroe Papers); "Proposal of the Royal Afghan Government, November, 1944," L/P&S/12/1811, ff. 262–286.

21. Government of India, External Affairs and Commonwealth Relations Department, to Secretary of State, 29 June 1947, *ITOP,* XI/395, pp. 730, 731fn, 732; Cabinet, India and Burma Committee, I.B.(47) 40th Meeting, 3 July 1947, *ITOP,* XI/493, p. 878; Note by the Government of India, External Affairs Department [n.d., March 1946?], *ITOP,* VII/15, pp. 30–32; "Survey of Anglo-Afghan Relations, Part II, 1919–1947," L/P&S/12/1321; Stephens, *Pakistan,* p. 218; Caroe, *Pathans,* pp. 435–436; Quddus, *Afghanistan and Pakistan,* p. 151; Kaur, *Pak-Afghanistan Relations,* pp. 45, 59, 196. The Afghan government never officially defined the extent of Pushtunistan or its future relationship with Kabul. Proposals advanced in newspapers, articles, and public speeches varied widely in both the territorial extent of Pushtunistan and its relations with Pakistan and Afghanistan. While some demanded an independent

state, others seemed concerned only with Pushtun autonomy, but all seemed willing to incorporate Pushtunistan into Afghanistan. Some writers included Baluchistan, and the NWFP, others just the NWFP, while still more sought only the tribal agencies. Only a few demanded the whole of Pakistan west of the Indus.

22. *ITOP,* I/256, fn 6; Government of India, External Affairs and Commonwealth Relations Department, to Secretary of State, 29 June 1947, *ITOP,* XI/395, pp. 730, 731fn; Cabinet, India and Burma Committee, I.B.(47) 40th Meeting, 3 July 1947, *ITOP,* XI/493, p. 878; Caroe, *Pathans,* p. 436. Dupree, "The Durand Line of 1893," in *Current Problems in Afghanistan,* pp. 88–89; Kaur, *Pak-Afghanistan Relations,* pp. 56, 60, 62, 197; Crichton to Lt. Col. R.R. Burnett, Secretary, External Affairs Department, GOI, 30 December 1945, L/P&S/12/1811, ff. 308–314; Griffiths, *Afghanistan,* pp. 75–76; Tabibi ("Aftermath Created by British Policy," p. 105) claims, via a roundabout analysis, that the Baluch language "belongs to the same group as Pushtu" and therefore considers the Baluch of Afghan origin. The Brahui, however, speak a Dravidian, not an Indo-European, language. The inhabitants of Chitral and Gilgit are not Pushtun, either. Military Attaché's Summary of Intelligence for the Week Ending 23 August 1947, L/P&S/12/1850; Squire to Bevin, 23 August 1947, R/12/178, f. 146. Much of Afghan society, including the peoples of the north, the economic community, and the majority of the tribes, sought friendly relations with Pakistan.

23. Squire to the External Affairs and Commonwealth Relations Department, 23 June 1947, *ITOP,* XI/309, p. 577. Squire believed the Afghans did not thoroughly appreciate the political, military, and economic ramifications of an independent Pushtunistan. The External Affairs Department voiced similar concerns earlier (Note by External Affairs Department, "The Tribes of the North-West and North-East Frontiers in a Future Constitution" [n.d.; March 1946?], *ITOP,* VII/15, pp. 30–32). See also Military Attaché in Kabul, Weekly Intelligence Summary, 26 April 1947, L/P&S/12/1849; Adamec, *Afghanistan's Foreign Relations,* p. 187. Tabibi takes the opposite view ("Aftermath Created by British Policy," pp. 110–111), claiming the agricultural and mineral resources of the area, coupled with the skills of the inhabitants and access to the sea, could make Pushtunistan economically independent of Pakistan.

24. Squire to Crichton, 19 April 1947, L/P&S/12/1811, ff. 187–188; Military Attaché in Kabul, Weekly Intelligence Summary, 26 April 1947, L/P&S/12/1849; Peshawar Weekly Intelligence Surveys, 5 July 1947, 12 July 1947, and 26 July 1947, L/P&S/12/3201; G.C. Whitterage to F.K. Roberts (Moscow), 2 October 1947, R/12/178, f. 193; Foreign Office, Delhi, to the Secretary of State for Foreign Affairs, London, R/12/178, ff. 35–37; *Times,* 3 July 1947, L/P&S/12/1811; *Daily Mail,* 4 July 1947, L/P&S/12/1811.

25. Peshawar Weekly Intelligence Surveys, 5 July 1947 and 9 August 1947, L/P&S/12/3201; Military Attaché's Summary of Intelligence for the Week Ending 13 June 1947, 4 July 1947, and 2 August 1947, L/P&S/12/1850. *Islah* published extracts of Barton's book throughout July and August. Stephens, *Pakistan,* p. 218. Caroe dismissed the agitation as "clumsily veiled Afghan irridenta" ("Review of Peter Mayne, *Narrow Smile,*" in *Time and Tide,* June 1955, MSS.EUR F.203/12; Olaf Caroe Papers). The Americans picked up on this in their refusal to negotiate in the 1950s. Foreign Office to Washington, 2 July 1947, L/P&S/12/1811, ff. 48–49. Squire to Bevin, 21 June 1947, R/12/178, f. 18; Foreign Office, Delhi, to the Secretary of State for Foreign Affairs, London, R/12/178, ff. 35–37. According to British sources, much Pushtunistan agitation came from the Departments of the Economy and Education,

headed by Abdul Majid and Najibullah Khan, respectively. Majid, ever the opportunist and apparently still desirous of the government's ruin, was in touch with Congress leaders and even considered enlisting Soviet support. "The Afghan dynasty is believed to be precariously balanced between the attacks of the Communists on the one hand and those of supporters of the family of ex-king Amanullah on the other, and to be attempting to save itself by concentrating attention on external rather than internal affairs" (Symonds, *Making of Pakistan,* p. 167); Dupree, *AUFS,* 4/4, p. 6.

26. *Reuters,* Bombay, 22 June 1947, L/P&S/12/1811, f. 98; Translation of *Anis,* 21 June 1947, L/P&S/12/1811, ff. 32–33; Military Attaché's Summary of Intelligence for the Week Ending 13 June 1947, L/P&S/12/1850; Griffiths, *Afghanistan,* p. 64; Fletcher, *Afghanistan,* p. 249; Translation of *Islah,* "Future of India and the Destinies of Afghans," R/12/178, 9 June 1947, ff. 10–17; Squire, "Afghanistan and Her Neighbors," p. 71.

27. Hashim Khan, as quoted in the *Statesman,* 22 June 1947. Hashim and Wali were in England.

28. Squire to the Secretary of State for Foreign Affairs, 1 July 1947, L/P&S/12/1811, f. 70; Squire to Bevin, 14 June 1947, L/P&S/12/1811, ff. 100–101; *Reuter,* Bombay, 22 June 1947, L/P&S/12/1811, f. 97; Military Attaché's Summary of Intelligence for the Week Ending 27 June 1947, L/P&S/12/1850; L/P&S/12/1850, 24 May 1947.

29. Military Attaché's (Kabul) Summary of Intelligence for the Fortnight Ending 18 July 1947, L/P&S/12/1849; Mahmud told Squire that Afghanistan wanted no territory, simply an agreement concerning the tribes to prevent unrest. Military Attaché's Summary of Intelligence for the Week Ending 5 September 1947, L/P&S/12/1850; Squire to Bevin, 12 May 1949 and 14 May 1949, FO 983/46; Fraser-Tytler, *Afghanistan,* p. 311. Fraser-Tytler wrote: "There are among the rulers in Kabul men who have recognized the Pushtunistan project for the chimera that it is, and would gladly find a way out of the quagmire into which they have fallen if they could do so without too great loss of face." Even most pro-Pakistani writers acknowledge the importance of the Pushtunistan issue to the Afghan ruling family. Those who sought to curtail the activities of the nationalists and improve relations with Pakistan risked their political ouster. See Kaur, *Pak-Afghanistan Relations,* pp. 55, 63, 199; Dupree, "Durand Agreement of 1893," pp. 91–92; Fraser-Tytler, *Afghanistan,* p. 327. "No Afghan government can entirely abandon the Pushtunistan ideal."

30. Cabinet, Decisions on Afghanistan, 9 December 1947, L/WS/1/1168, ff. 146–149; U.K. High Commissioner in Pakistan to Commonwealth Relations Office, 3 April 1949, L/WS/1/1168, f. 18; "Brief for UK Delegation to the United Nations; Afghan/Pakistan Relations" [n.s., n.d.; 1948?], L/P&S/12/1812, ff. 95–96; "Possibility of War between Pakistan and Afghanistan," 11 August 1949, J.I.C. (49)57, L/WS/1/1169, ff. 4–20; Interview with Shah Mahmud, by Squire (?) [n.s.], 13 November 1948, FO 983/12; Secretary of State for Foreign Affairs to the Kabul Embassy, 9 December 1947, R/12/178, ff. 213–214; U.K High Commissioner in Karachi to the C.R.O, 22 March 1949, FO 983/37; Squire, "Afghanistan and Her Neighbors," p. 71.

31. Squire to Bevin, 12 and 14 May 1949, FO 983/46. The Afghans entered negotiations with the Czech firm Skoda for weapons not delivered by the Lancaster Plan. Squire to the Foreign Office (reporting conversation with the Indian ambassador), 28 April 1951, FO 983/73.

32. Lancaster, "Annual Review—Afghan Army," 1 January 1948, L/P&S/12/1667, ff. 3–20; Chiefs of Staff Committee, "Afghanistan—Strategic Importance," COS(47) 182(0), L/WS/1/986, ff. 141–148; COS 967/29/8/7, 29 August 1947, L/P&S/12/ 1821; Lancaster, Report of Interview with War Minister Daud Khan and Chief of the General Staff Assadullah Khan, 10 June 1947, L/WS/1/986, ff. 149–156; Military Attaché's Summary of Intelligence for the Week Ending 24 October 1947, L/P&S/ 12/1850; "Survey of Anglo-Afghan Relations, Part II, 1919–1947," L/P&S/12/1321; "Possibility of War between Pakistan and Afghanistan," 11 August 1949, J.I.C (49)57, L/WS/1/1169, ff. 4–20; Gardener to the Secretary of State for Foreign Affairs [n.d.], FO 983/73; Bevin to Squire, 19 September 1946, L/P&S/12/1811, f. 244. The Afghan government indicated great distress upon the return of their officers from India. The Afghans wanted to keep their arms supply standardized, ease the replacement of arms, supplies, and training, and avoid the logistical problems they had experienced with a "Magpie" collection of arms in the prewar period.

33. Lancaster, "Annual Review—Afghan Army," 1 January 1948, L/P&S/12/1667, ff. 3–20; Lancaster, Report of Interview with War Minister Daud Khan and Chief of the General Staff Assadullah Khan, 10 June 1947, L/WS/1/986, ff. 149–156; Chiefs of Staff Committee, "Afghanistan—Strategic Importance," COS(47)182(0), L/WS/ 1/986, ff. 141–148; COS 967/29/8/7, 29 August 1947, L/P&S/12/1821.

10

THE TRUMAN ADMINISTRATION AND AMERICAN POLICY IN SOUTH ASIA

Throughout the partition discussions, British officers had considered the strategic implications of a divided India. Though nearly all resented the Congress, most opposed the idea of Pakistan categorically. Auchinleck, for example, doubted whether Pakistan would have the "necessary resources in raw materiel, industrial production, manpower, and above all the requisite space to enable it to become a base for warlike operations." A nation composed of two widely separated halves in northwest India and East Bengal, having only one major port, self-supporting only in cereals, and nearly devoid of industry, would be hard-pressed to protect the most vulnerable frontiers of the subcontinent. Pakistan would not have the support of India if it were created against the wishes of Congress. Division of the army would only increase costs while decreasing efficiency, and the entire economy of India, designed for a united state, would be undermined by partition. Even though Auchinleck assumed that Pakistan would dominate Kashmir, at least protecting its northern flank, he concluded that while "Hindustan . . . would be an efficient base for modern war . . . Pakistan can never be." Pakistan could never "provide the means by which the British Commonwealth can hope to influence or coerce an independent Hindustan and keep it free of hostile foreign influence." Auchinleck ultimately advised that "on a long term view the military position of Pakistan . . . [is] weak and its defense would cost as much as the defense of the whole of India and would therefore be a long term drain on our resources with little advantage to us. . . . If we desire to maintain our power . . . in the Indian Ocean area . . . we can do so only by keeping in being a United India which will be a willing member of that Commonwealth."[1]

In the event of partition, however, nothing precluded British acceptance of Pakistan as a dominion. While the Chiefs hoped that the successor states would pursue a common defense policy directed through a central command organization, in the event of a hostile division, they thought military assistance to Pakistan advisable to curtail tribal incursions, deter outside aggression, and "give a measure of confidence to Afghanistan." The dangers of supporting Pakistan against a hostile India seemed minimal, while ejecting willful members of the Commonwealth would eliminate access to all strategic facilities in the subcontinent and diminish Britain's reputation throughout the Muslim world. Montgomery, in particular, valued the bases, airfields, ports, and manpower of Pakistan and assumed that access would leave Britain "in a much stronger position to support the integrity of Afghanistan."[2]

During the years immediately following partition, the United States would, in part, move to replace British authority in the South Asian region. Though initially desirous of an accord with India, in time, Nehru's economic policies and adherence to a neutralist foreign policy would alienate Washington. Encouraged by Pakistani promises of military and economic cooperation and the advice of certain British "experts," the United States eventually courted Karachi. Like the British, the Americans saw no major disadvantages arising from such an understanding and thought access to Pakistani facilities and manpower of advantage in the containment effort. The alliance with Pakistan, however, neither "gave a measure of confidence to Afghanistan" nor left the United States "in a much stronger position to support the territorial integrity of Afghanistan." Instead, it led to the alienation of Afghanistan from the West.

As many British officials had predicted, partition left Pakistan a weak, divided state, at the apparent mercy of its larger neighbor. India had nearly five times the population of Pakistan, more industry, more than double the armed forces, most of the bases, and all the ordnance factories of the defunct Raj. West Pakistan's long, featureless frontier with India was exposed to aggression, while East Bengal was but an isolated, indefensible enclave. Jinnah's government faced war in Kashmir, continued communal violence in the Punjab, and a precarious economic situation worsened by the influx of over 6 million refugees.[3]

The Pakistani army, having received only part of the aid promised it in the partition agreement, was underequipped and disorganized. After the Great Mutiny of 1857, the British had kept the Indian army devoid of all-Muslim units. Thus, while purely Hindu, Sikh, and Gurkha regiments transferred intact to the Indian army, the Pakistanis had to reorganize their entire armed forces from scattered platoons and sections. India, pledged to divide common military assets according to Trivedi's agreement, used the Kashmir aggression to justify retention of hardware, further aggravating Pakistan's difficulties. According to a Pakistani general, the Indians remitted little but obsolete, perishable, or unwanted items such as gas masks, waterproofing equipment, boots "meant either for Ghurkas or West Africans," and a number of crates full of bricks.[4]

Though Congress accepted partition, it did so to speed the British withdrawal and avoid continued violence. Congress never accepted concession of Pakistan as a permanent solution to Muslim concerns in the subcontinent and continued to hope for reunification. While Indian leaders periodically expressed these sentiments, radical groups such as the Hindu Mahasaba advocated destruction and reabsorption of Pakistan. That many Westerners also supported eventual reunification only heightened Pakistani fears.[5]

In the face of Indian hostility, Pakistan's primary strategic objective became simple survival. Rather like France after 1871 (with Kashmir serving as Alsace-Lorraine), Pakistan would attempt to procure a strong ally who would shore up its economy, bolster its military, and protect it against India. Pakistan looked first to the United States.[6]

Prior to the 1920s, the United States maintained few contacts with the Middle East and South Asia. During the interwar period, desires arose within the business community to replace European oil firms operating in the Middle East, and by the end of World War II, American control of production had risen from 13 to 42 percent. Yet most Americans remained uninterested and uninformed about South Asia. As one former official put it, regional knowledge was often limited to "Lipton tea bags which had a map of Ceylon."[7]

Though President Harry S Truman's administration broke with traditional isolationist policies shortly after the end of the Second World War, its attention remained focused on the Soviet threat to Western Europe. A few officials periodically expressed concern with the containment of communism in South Asia or with maintaining limited economic interests in the area, while others sought to ensure the continued flow of Middle East oil through naval dominance in the Indian Ocean and control of the Persian Gulf. But with the Greeks facing an insurgency, the Turks under constant diplomatic pressure, and the Soviet Union consolidating its grip on Eastern Europe, American policymakers remained content to let the British have primary responsibility for Southwest Asia.[8]

In October 1947, less than two months after partition, Jinnah requested a 2-billion-dollar loan from the United States. The proposal sought American expertise to assist with resource exploitation, technical training, and industrial development. The plan also called for the United States to assume complete responsibility for providing equipment and training for the Pakistani armed forces and to assist in the modernization and maintenance of defense facilities. Pakistan promised complete alliance in return, couching their proposal in virulent anti-Communist rhetoric that would become a staple of their correspondence in future years.[9]

Jinnah's proposal proved unattractive to the Americans, whose strategic priorities remained focused on Europe. South Asia faced no immediate threat and commanded no high priority for the limited resources available. Furthermore, military and civilian authorities alike saw Pakistan incapable of promoting American global security interests. Washington proved unwilling to become the guarantor of any South Asian state, since "there was nothing to be gained by trying to make an ally of India or Pakistan or any other countries in the area." Indo-Pakistani hostility, coupled with the general dislocation that accompanied partition, left both states unable to assist the Western powers. Prior to a settlement of the Kashmir dispute, investments in the modernization of the Pakistani armed forces would only waste resources and heighten regional tensions. The United States not only rejected Jinnah's proposal but also imposed an arms embargo on Pakistan and India from March 1948 through March 1949. The Truman administration concentrated its few regional initiatives on promoting economic development, combating food shortages, and attempting to find impartial solutions to various border disputes.[10]

Thus rebuffed, Pakistan looked elsewhere for support. At an April 1949 Commonwealth conference, the member nations proved unwilling to offend India by supporting the Pakistani position on Kashmir and refused to underwrite the security of Pakistan. Pakistan saw little value in an organization that only offered protection against Afghanistan, whose army seemed inferior, or the Soviet Union, with whom Pakistan had no immediate quarrel. Convinced that India would always wield greater power within the Commonwealth, Pakistan turned its attention westward.[11]

The following year, League President Choudhry Khaliquzzaman toured the Middle East, pleading for the formation of an alliance or confederation of Muslim states. The Arab states, often citing Pakistan's inability to solve its problems with Muslim neighbor Afghanistan, showed little enthusiasm. Most were preoccupied with Palestine or other lingering problems of imperialism and saw a revived pan-Islamic movement providing no solution. Some saw the effort to form "Islamistan" as a Pakistani attempt to dominate other Muslim states. Following indications of disinterest, Pakistan abandoned the Islamistan concept.[12]

While seeking support elsewhere, Pakistan never abandoned thoughts of American assistance. Throughout the late 1940s and early 1950s, Pakistani leaders persistently endeavored to attract American interest, repeatedly indicating a desire to collaborate with Washington in economic and military matters. They stressed the incompatibility of Soviet-style communism and the Islamic way of life, vowing to fight to the death before allowing communism to permeate their society. Other officials praised American industrial achievements and expressed their willingness to open their economy to American investors. They appealed for technical assistance and capital investment, stressing the desirability of Pakistan's markets and opportunities for resource exploitation. Some industrial and banking concerns took interest, though the Truman administration remained noncommittal.[13]

Over time, the administration gradually became convinced of the need to assist other areas besides Western Europe. Pentagon and State Department officials began to re-examine Pakistan's potential role in future conflict. By 1949 the American Joint Chiefs of Staff still deemed the other nations of South Asia, including Afghanistan, of "little value to the United States," claiming their remoteness from the United States, their difficult terrain, and the lack of communications and other essential facilities required by modern combat forces would pose a difficult logistical problem if military operations by either Western or indigenous forces were to be supported in the South Asian area, particularly in the light of probable heavy commitments elsewhere.

The Joint Chiefs of Staff, however, thought the Karachi-Lahore area of Pakistan, under certain conditions, "might be required as a base for air operations against [the] central U.S.S.R. and as a staging area for forces engaged in [the] defense or recapture of Middle East oil areas." Pakistani bases could be utilized for ideological penetration and intelligence-gathering operations as well. The Joint Chiefs of Staff suggested the establishment of commercial arrangements, which would promote the development of base facilities and encourage leasing agreements. As the Communist victory in China, mounting insurrection in Indochina, and the outbreak of the Korean War further modified the administration's European fixation, Pakistan's willingness to support construction of an Islamic bloc would evoke even more sympathy in Washington, where ideas of Middle Eastern or South Asian alliances were gradually taking shape.[14]

The United States would likely have continued to ignore Pakistan had it not been for growing irritation with India and Nehru. Though American businessmen hoped India would provide investment opportunities, Nehru feared the induction of economic imperialism and discouraged the entrance of foreign capital. As a result, economic aid remained limited. Despite domestic policies that were fairly tough on the Communist party, many politicians and businessmen would eventually equate Nehru's socialist leanings with sympathy for communism.[15]

The Indian decision to recognize Communist China (December 30, 1949) aroused American ire. Though Pakistan also recognized Mao's regime only five days later and Britain followed two days after that, neither of those states proved ardent supporters of Beijing. Continued Indian support for Communist China following the outbreak of the Korean War in June 1950 would thoroughly anger Washington. Nehru hoped to localize the conflict, sought a negotiated settlement, and refused to dispatch Indian combat units to the war. Washington regarded Nehru's peace initiative as "unwarranted temerity" and appeasement and dismissed his attempts to work with Mao through the "five principles of peace" as naive, cowardly, and dangerous.[16]

Indian and American strategic policy simply did not correlate. Nehru believed that pressing domestic problems had to be solved before India could afford to increase military expenditures. Thus, he stressed a need for continued peace from a practical as well as an ideological perspective. Furthermore, Nehru considered local forces no serious deterrent. "The only real deterrent," he claimed, "is Russia's fear of war with the United States." Though Indian neutrality was similar to nineteenth-century American policy in its desire to avoid entangling alliances and global conflicts, it conflicted dramatically with the postwar American emphasis on collective security. Support for Pakistan would grow among the Americans as this discord became more pronounced.[17]

As relations with India plummeted, the United States sought favor with Pakistan, whose supposed defense potential attracted increased American attention. Pakistan possessed several modern airfields and potential airfield sites within range of the Soviet industrial heartland and Communist China. The Pentagon strongly desired access to these bases, which could also support ground operations from the Middle East to the Pacific Rim. In addition, since the Joint Chiefs opposed the commitment of American troops for Middle East defense, Pentagon and State Department planners alike began to consider the possibility of building up Pakistani ground forces for area operations.[18]

After the British conceded an inability to supply all of Pakistan's military needs, the United States had begun selling small quantities of equipment in June 1949. The Truman administration hoped such nominal assistance, delivered without any political commitment, would create a favorable climate in which to foster establishment of a regional alliance and help persuade the Pakistanis to grant the U.S. Air Force base access rights. The United States remained firm in demanding cash for these end items, allowed for similar purchases by India, and offered Pakistan no territorial or diplomatic guarantees.[19]

In the wake of continued difficulties in Egypt and Iran, American officials began to doubt Britain's ability to meet even limited area defense requirements and considered increased commitments to Southwest Asia. Discussion within the Pentagon, concurrent with British efforts to establish a Suez-based Middle East command, examined a possible American alliance with Turkey, Iran, and Pakistan.

South Asian experts within the State Department, however, continued to argue that successful defense of the subcontinent would require joint action by Pakistan, India, and Afghanistan. As long as the primary mission of the Pakistani army remained defense against India, Pakistan, they claimed, "could probably furnish few if any troops" for operations outside its borders. Since any alliance "would only be used by [Pakistan] in terms of their conflict with India" and a build-up would do little more than hamper economic growth, most regional officials actively opposed any bilateral alliance. Department officials still acknowledged that Pakistan would remain of potential value owing to "the strategically located airbases which it can provide" and concluded that "if relations between Pakistan and India can be improved, the military strength of Pakistan might become effective as a stabilizing factor in the Middle East." Its policy statement acknowledged that Pakistan was devoid of the "violent anti-western and deep-rooted neutrality that prevents India from cooperating fully with the United States and its allies" and concluded: "A strong Muslim bloc under the leadership of Pakistan, and friendly to the US, might afford a desirable balance of power in South Asia."[20]

Continued annoyance with Indian neutralism led increasing numbers of American officials to favor Pakistan. In January 1951, the National Security Council approved NSC 98/1, which sanctioned cooperative and independent approaches to Pakistan to encourage a regional alliance and secure base-access rights. A State Department policy statement of July 1, 1951, further argued that a strengthened Pakistani army could fulfill the traditional function of British-Indian troops in the area, assisting Iran and other Middle East countries against Russian aggression. The following year, the conclusions of a regional conference of diplomatic and consular officials recommended the inclusion of Pakistan in any regional program and urgent consideration of an increase in the provision of supplies to Pakistan's armed forces, "to ensure the availability of Pakistani ground forces on the western flank at the outset of war." American military planners came to a similar consensus. At a joint conference with British military officials in the Middle East, the participants agreed that they could not hold the oil-producing areas with the current supply of troops. A commitment of Pakistani troops might make a successful defense feasible. While assistance to Greece and Turkey retained top priority, the Joint Chiefs of Staff recommended that the United States should attempt to orient Pakistan toward Turkey and make every effort to expose the "fallacious basis of present foreign policy in India."[21]

Throughout independence discussions, British military and political officials had steadfastly opposed the creation of Pakistan, claiming it would constitute a severe strategic liability. Over time, however, a number of British "experts" advanced plans that favored Pakistan and proposed the veritable abandonment of India. Sir Olaf Caroe was paramount among them. Following his resignation from the North West Frontier Province (NWFP) in 1947, Caroe returned to England, where he eventually accepted an assignment writing for the *Round Table*. In a March 1949 article, he argued that the Soviet challenge to the West would not come in Europe but in the Middle East, where a power vacuum existed in the wake of the partition of India. Since control of the oil reserves remained essential to the West, Caroe argued, a Soviet attack against them had to be stopped. The article elicited praise from a number of Western dignitaries, prompting Caroe to expand it to a book. *Wells of Power*, which appeared in 1951, argued that British control of India had checked Russian ambitions toward Turkey, Iran, and Afghanistan. Now, independent India was unwilling and unable to defend Southwest Asia. British bases in Egypt and Iraq currently sufficed as a deterrent, but the Middle

East, Caroe argued, could only be secured through an accord with the Muslim states, underwritten by the Western powers.[22]

Caroe argued that Pakistan, "the largest, if not the most experienced, Muslim state," would prove a valuable member of any Middle Eastern alliance. Pakistan, he claimed, "lies well within the grouping of South-Western Asia, as seen from the air." Citing "Toynbee's theory of human gravitation, and the airman's eye," Caroe claimed Pakistan "vital to the reckoning" of the Persian Gulf area and supported its inclusion in Middle East defense plans. Many Americans would subsequently echo Caroe's citations of Pakistan's geographic importance, including "its seaport and airport at Karachi and its long coastline of Baluchistan, [which] stands at the mouth of the larger Gulf," and the Khyber Pass astride the historical invasion routes of India.[23]

Caroe praised Pakistan's two "priceless legacies" of "a government and administration based on Western liberal ideas . . . [and] membership in the Commonwealth of Nations." Pakistani nationalism, Caroe claimed, reared in British synthesis, was "real nationalism" that did not inflate minor events and saw global threats in a clearer light. He cited Muslim rejection of Congress philosophy as proof of their militant anti-communism. Pakistan's military doctrine, Caroe argued, echoed the British strategy in opposing all threats from the north.

While praising Pakistan, however, Caroe discounted or overlooked its weaknesses, ignored the historical interdependence of the subcontinent, and neglected logistical constraints in supporting its inclusion in Middle East defense plans. Though he noted how partition had disrupted the economy and left the army devoid of resources and acknowledged Pakistan's recurrent governmental difficulties, he expressed optimism that Pakistan would overcome these challenges. Given Western assistance, he argued, Pakistan could provide a credible deterrent and prove a valuable asset to the Western defense effort.[24]

From May 5 through June 10, 1952, Caroe toured the United States. He met with a variety of State Department personnel, congressmen, and army and air force officers and delivered a series of lectures at leading American universities. He also wrote newspaper articles and appeared on radio and television interviews. Throughout his tour, he stressed how the partition had altered the regional balance of power. He argued that the regional states must be shown that Western assistance was essential to their independence and enlisted in an area defense plan, which he described as the "Northern Screen." Caroe deemed Pakistan "essential to the concept." Caroe would later claim that John Foster Dulles obtained his "Northern Tier" idea from the Northern Screen and wrote that the Pakistanis "regard me as the inventor of the Baghdad Pact." While the extent of his influence on American strategic thought cannot be ascertained with complete certainty, the similarities of his arguments to those advanced by various American personnel are indeed striking.[25]

Caroe was not the epitome of British opinion, yet others echoed his sentiments. Sir Basil Liddell Hart also feared a sweeping Soviet armored advance toward Middle East oil. The North African campaign, he claimed, showed how rapidly modern forces could move across desert terrain thought impenetrable. Liddell Hart doubted whether the Iranian army, slowly being improved by the Americans, would fare any better than had the Yugoslavs and Greeks in 1941. Persian officers, he claimed, had admitted to him that the U.S.S.R. could overrun their nation within a week, barring the arrival of significant outside assistance. Naturally, he favored an increased regional deterrent. The Royal Institute of International Affairs published conclusions that recommended strengthening Pakistan and Turkey to improve the chances of a successful Middle Eastern defense.[26] Furthermore, Sir William Barton, former champion of Afghanistan and Pushtunistan, now claimed Pakistan economically and politically stable. Pakistan should, he argued, be entrusted with leading a Muslim belt that could, even with India actively assisting the enemy, serve as a springboard for offensive operations against the Soviet Union.[27]

Other British Foreign Office officials, however, remained skeptical of Pakistan's ability to assist in defense of the Middle East prior to a Kashmir settlement. They assumed Pakistan both incapable and unwilling to supply expeditionary forces, a fact supported at times by the Pakistanis themselves. Consequently, they saw little benefit originating from Pakistan's enlistment in an alliance, which would only increase commitments while alienating India.[28]

Meanwhile, following the October 16, 1951, assassination of Liaquat, real power in Pakistan had fallen into the hands of a number of politicians and military officers, including Foreign Minister Zafrullah Khan, Ambassador to Washington Mohammed Ali, Governor-General Ghulam Mohammed, Foreign Secretary Irkamullah, Defense Secretary Iskander Mirza, and Ayub, who favored aggressive pursuit of an alliance with the United States.[29] Irkamullah arrived in Washington less than a week after the assassination to "get as much military equipment as he could." He routinely stated that Pakistan would participate in any Middle East defense program and was ready to hear what the Americans planned for it. Pakistani interests in that area, he claimed, were so natural that the nation would relish such an assignment, provided its defenses could be built up to allow for such a role. Other Pakistani politicians and military officers repeatedly informed the Americans of their contempt for communism and their desire to contribute to regional defense programs.[30] Though increasingly incensed with Indian policy, the Truman administration remained unsupportive of a policy of partisan support for Pakistan.

In the waning months of the Truman administration's tenure, however, the State Department and the Joint Chiefs of Staff re-examined the threat posed by a conventional Soviet thrust toward the Suez Canal or Persian Gulf. British plans envisaged defense of an "Inner Ring," comprising a beachhead area southward along the coast from Aleppo to the Gulf of Aqaba. Such plans made no use of recently allied Turkish forces and abandoned as indefensible the Gulf oil reserves. As early as 1950, the British and American Chiefs of Staff had debated the benefits of an "Outer Ring" defense, running along the Taurus and Zagros Mountains to the Baluchistan coast. While the Outer Ring would cover the oil-producing areas, insufficient forces seemed to render implementation impossible. With priorities in Korea, Southeast Asia, and NATO unlikely to abate in the near future, the development of indigenous forces would be essential to any expanded area defense program.[31]

By mid-1952, General Omar Bradley, then chairman of the Joint Chiefs of Staff, still claimed that a successful defense of the Middle East "is not now too realistic" and saw the Inner Ring as the pragmatic option. While acknowledging these difficulties, several State Department officials argued that passivity would impart an impression that the United States did not care about the Middle East. Paul Nitze and Elbert Matthews were among those who advocated an approach that considered Middle Eastern defense "a 1956 problem rather than a current problem."[32]

In November 1952, the Joint Chiefs drafted a Middle Eastern defense plan based on holding the "Outer Ring." The envisioned defense line was over 1,780 miles long. The indigenous states could field but a fraction of the needed troops, and even given optimistic suppositions for British, Australian, and American assistance, barely half the overall requirements could be met. The Joint Chiefs recognized that the program was not feasible in the immediate future. Given an estimated Soviet strike force of twenty-four divisions, moving simultaneously with an invasion of Europe, General Lawton Collins thought "we could probably hold Suez, but there is no chance to hold the Persian Gulf." Bradley similarly concluded that, in the immediate future, "MEDO [Middle East Defense Organization] objectives will be largely political."[33]

With neither pressing strategic imperative nor strategic capability, the United States remained disinclined to alliance with Pakistan. Several State Department officials continued to oppose direct alliance with Pakistan, which "would only be used by them in context of their dispute with India."[34] Yet optimistic assumptions of future contributions led many officials to favor inclusion of Pakistan in regional defense arrangements. Increased worries surrounding the internal security of the regional nations would, in time, reinforce desires to strengthen defenses against conventional attack.[35] While the Truman administration had remained noncommittal in its policies toward Pakistan, the Eisenhower administration would not prove so timid.

NOTES

1. Note by Auchinleck, 11 May 1946, L/WS/1/1092, ff. 51–56; Note by Indian Cabinet Secretariat, Remarks by the Commander-in-Chief, 25 April 1947, *ITOP,* X/215, p. 423; see also Draft Statement by the Cabinet Mission and Wavell, undated, *ITOP,* VII/156, pp. 364–365; Statement by the Cabinet Mission and Wavell, 16 May

1946, *ITOP*, VII/303, pp. 583–586; Aziz, *Britain and Pakistan*, pp. 28–31; Moore, *Escape from Empire*, p. 352.

2. Chiefs of Staff Committee, Paper C.O.S.(47)134(0), 26 June 1947, *ITOP*, XI/362, p. 668; Chiefs of Staff Committee, Paper C.O.S/(47)59(0), 18 March 1947, *ITOP*, IX/544, p. 978; Chiefs of Staff Committee, C.O.S.(47) 62nd Meeting, 12 May 1947, *ITOP*, X/416, pp. 790–792, 792fn. Britain required strategic facilities in India, and no matter how few, "some were better than none."

3. Brown, *United States, India and Pakistan*, pp. 144–145, 150–153, 247, 252. Following a population influx of approximately 2 million, roughly one quarter of all Pakistanis were homeless. The flow of refugees continued well into the 1950s and only then gradually abated. Panikkar, *Problems of Indian Defense*, pp. 38–40; Asopa, *Military Alliance*, p. 49.

4. Khan, *Story of Pakistan Army*, pp. 39–40. He also concluded that "not all of this could have been the result of misconceived patriotism on the part of junior officers and clerks." Stephens, *Pakistan*, pp. 213–214; Burke, *Mainsprings*, p. 65; Sayeed, *Pakistan, the Formative Phase*, p. 299.

5. Khan, *Friends Not Masters*, pp. 115–116, 154. He quotes Kripalani: "Neither Congress nor the nation has given up its claims of a united India" and Patel: "Sooner or later, we shall again be united in common allegiance to our country." Callard, *Pakistan's Foreign Policy*, pp. 6–7, 14; Stephens, *Pakistan*, pp. 220–221; Maulana Azam exhorted: "The division is only of the map of the country and not in the hearts of the people, and I am sure it is going to be a short-lived partition." Asopa, *Military Alliance*, pp. 43–44; Hasan, "Pakistan's Threat Perception," *Pakistan-US Relations*, pp. 125–126; Burke, *Mainsprings*, pp. 57–58, 73; Singh, *U.S.-Pakistan and India*, pp. 32, 42fn; ; Brown, *United States, India and Pakistan*, pp. 148–150; Khan, *Story of Pakistan Army*, pp. 23, 153; Aziz, *Britain and Pakistan*, p. 44.

6. Callard, *Pakistan's Foreign Policy*, p. 1; Asopa, *Military Alliance*, pp. 41–43.

7. Joseph C. Satterthwaite, Truman Library Oral History Interviews, p. 36; Asopa, *Military Alliance*, pp. 12–14.

8. Fraser Wilkins, Truman Library Oral History Interviews, pp. 47–48; George McGhee, Truman Library Oral History Interviews, p. 62. Elbert Mathews, Truman Library Oral History Interviews, pp. 27–28. With the Indian and Pakistani armies organized and equipped along British lines, it also made logistical sense to leave the area a British responsibility. *FRUS*, 1949, VI, p. 10; see also Kaur, *Pak-Afghanistan Relations*, pp. 161–162; NSC 98/1, 5 January 1951, paragraph 11.

9. Venkataramani, *American Role in Pakistan*, pp. 2, 16, 18–19; McMahon, "United States Cold War Strategy," pp. 818–819; *FRUS*, 1949, VI, pp. 25–26.

10. Venkataramani, *American Role in Pakistan*, pp. 23, 26, 28–30, 51, 58–60, 68; "Estimated Probable Developments in the World Political Situation Up to 1957," JCS Joint Strategic Planning Committee, JSPC 814/3; CIA Report "India-Pakistan," SR-21, 16 September 1948, CIA Reports File, Truman Papers, Truman Library, Elbert G. Mathews, Truman Library Oral History Interviews, pp. 27–28; McMahon, "United States Cold War Strategy," p. 819. Throughout its tenure, the Truman administration saw famine and border disputes such as Kashmir as greater potential dangers to the subcontinent than communism.

11. Palmer, *South Asia and United States Policy*, p. 175; Muttam, *U.S., Pakistan, and India*, p. 7; Symonds, *Making of Pakistan*, p. 172; Burke, *Mainsprings*, p. 123.

12. Burke, *Mainsprings,* pp. 133–139; Asopa, *Military Alliance,* pp. 47–49; Qureshi, *Anglo-Pakistan Relations,* pp. 132, 167fn.

13. Elbert Mathews, Oral History Interviews, Truman Library, pp. 44–45. He states simply that the Pakistanis "were quite prepared to enter into an alliance; they would have loved it." Memorandum of Conversation by the Secretary of State, 17 November 1951, *FRUS,* 1951, VI, pp. 2227–2228; *FRUS* 1949, VI, p. 25; Jain, *US-Pak Relations,* p. 8; see *FRUS,* 1951, VI, pp. 1655–1663; CIA SR-21, "India-Pakistan," Intelligence File, Box 180, Truman Papers, Truman Library; Venkataramani, *American Role in Pakistan,* pp. 16, 24–25, 59, 82, 99, 187–188; Ram, *Super Powers,* pp. 38–39.

14. Memorandum by the Joint Chiefs of Staff, *FRUS,* 1949, VI, 24 March 1949, pp. 10, 17, 28–31; see also McMahon, "United States Cold War Strategy," pp. 818–822. Even before the outbreak of the Korean War, the Joint Chiefs had recommended the establishment of "one or two pacts" in the area, mentioning both India and Pakistan as possible adherents.

15. Venkataramani, *American Role in Pakistan,* pp. 4–5, 21, 47–48, 54; Ram, *Super Powers,* pp. 5, 13–14, 101; Mathews, Truman Library Oral History Interviews, pp. 34–36, 60–62; Henderson, Truman Library Oral History Interviews , pp. 178–179; Choudhury, *India, Pakistan, Bangladesh,* pp. 75–76. Nehru leaned toward the Hobson-Lenin interpretation of imperialism that viewed it as a necessary facet of capitalism, but he was not a Communist and on many occasions voiced disapproval of the Eastern Bloc. Brown (*United States and India and Pakistan,* pp. 259–260) provides three such examples: In the 1930s, he wrote: "I dislike dogmatism, and the treatment of Karl Marx's writings or any other books as revealed scripture which cannot be challenged." In the 1940s, he criticized the Communist party of India as "divorced from, and ignorant of, the national traditions that fill the minds of the people." On May 22, 1952, he claimed that India "would never pay the price that the Soviet Union and China have paid to achieve progress."

16. Venkataramani, *American Role in Pakistan,* p. 132; Ram, *Super Powers,* pp. 21, 34; Palmer, *South Asia and United States Policy,* pp. 14, 172; Kaul, *U.S.A. and the Hindustan Peninsula,* p. 33; Brown, *United States and India and Pakistan,* pp. 253–255, 273; Ram, *Super Powers,* pp. 69, 70fn. In August 1950, Nehru was described as "the hope of the future." One year later, he was denounced as "one of the greatest disappointments of the post-war era" or a "political Peter Pan," while some went as far as to claim that he had "gone over to the Communists." See also Acheson to a Joint Session of the House and Senate Foreign Affairs and Foreign Relations Committees, Acheson, "Building Collective Strength," p. 465.

17. Burke, *Mainsprings,* pp. 260–261; Palmer, *South Asia and United States Policy,* pp. 65–66, 95, 98, 104–106, 123, 166–167; Hovey, *United States Military Assistance,* pp. 100–101; Ahmad, "Pakistan-U.S. Interests in South Asia," p. 71. Perhaps still under Ghandian illusions of nonviolence, neither Nehru nor Defense Minister Krishna Menon paid great attention to strategic issues, until the Chinese attack in 1962 shocked them to action. Prior to 1962, India had few military journals or prominent theorists. Nehru apparently feared the military, big business, and the Mahasaba more than the Communists.

18. NSC 98/1, *FRUS* 1951, pp. 1783, 1791, 1798–1800; Hahn, "Containment and Egyptian Nationalism," pp. 28–29; Ahmad, "Pakistan-US Interests in South

Asia," p. 68; Venkataramani, *American Role in Pakistan,* pp. 21, 68, 82, 135–139, 157–158.

19. Warren, "Pakistan," pp. 1011–1012; Department of State Policy Statement, 3 April 1950, 790d.00/4–350; NSC 98/1, 5 January 1951, paragraphs 20, 25. Pakistan had signed a trade agreement with the Czechs and had purchased some arms from them, and the Soviets had extended them offers, which prompted department officials to conclude that "if some military aid is not forthcoming from us, it is clear that the GOP [government of Pakistan] must request the aid from other sources." Asopa, *Military Alliance,* p. 49; Venkataramani, *American Role in Pakistan,* pp. 52–53, 66–67, 104, 108–109, 121–122, 184–185, 194–197, 200–202. Some members of the administration thought arms provision would redress the disparity of Pakistan versus India and bring stability to the region.

20. Department of State Policy Statement, 3 April 1950, 790d.00/4–350; NSC 98/1, 5 January 1951, paragraph 14; Elbert Mathews, Truman Library Oral History Interviews, pp. 42–43; George McGhee, Truman Library Oral History Interviews, p. 62; Special Estimate SE-32, "Consequences of Communist Control over South Asia," 3 October 1952, *FRUS,* 1952–1954, IX, p. 1070; NIE-79, "Probable Developments in South Asia," 30 June 1953, *FRUS,* 1952–1954, IX, pp. 1082–1083; Venkataramani, *American Role in Pakistan,* pp. 70, 184–185.

21. Department of State Policy Statement, 3 April 1950, 790d.00/4–350; Agreed Conclusions and Recommendations, South Asian Regional Conference of US Diplomatic and Consular Officials, 6 February–2 March 1951, *FRUS,* 1951, VI, pp. 1664–1669. They stressed a similar offer should be made to India and did not favor outright support of the Pakistani position on Kashmir or Pushtunistan, favoring continued efforts to resolve both these matters through negotiations. Department of State Policy Statement, 1 July 1951, *FRUS,* 1951, VI, pp. 2208, 2215; McMahon, "United States Cold War Policy," pp. 822–824. As of October 1951, American objectives in South Asia included removing the danger of regional conflict through settlement of the Kashmir conflict and reducing the disparity of Pakistan's armed forces with India's, securing access rights to Pakistani air bases and the availability of Pakistani ground forces for use in the Middle East, and encouraging Pakistan to form a regional alliance with other Middle Eastern Muslim states. Special Estimate SE-32, "Consequences of Communist Control over South Asia," 3 October 1952, *FRUS,* 1952–1954, XI, p. 1070.

22. Caroe, "Persian Gulf—A Romance," Caroe, *New York Herald Tribune,* 28 June 1952, MSS.EUR F.203/64 (Olaf Caroe Papers); Extract from an Unfinished Autobiography by Sir Olaf Caroe, in conjunction with P.L. Mehta, MSS.EUR F.203/77.

23. Caroe, *Wells of Power,* pp. xvii, 180–183. See, e.g., Secretary of State to Certain Diplomatic Missions, 13 November 1952, *FRUS,* 1952–1954, IX, p. 316. Acheson argues that Pakistan would be useful not only for manpower but also as a base in which to stockpile supplies. Acheson claimed, "Pakistan potentially has valuable contribution to make to Middle East defense. It occupies strategic position great importance to control of Persian gulf [sic]."

24. Caroe, *Wells of Power,* pp. 189–192; Caroe, Lecture to the Royal Institute of International Affairs, 4 February 1948, MSS.EUR F.203/4 (Olaf Caroe Papers). He all but dismissed internal difficulties, once claiming that "the mirage of self-government is far more attractive than the prospects of economic improvement. . . . The masses are accustomed to poverty, and will listen to their own political leaders

rather than foreigners who offer them opulence with a political string attached." See MSS.EUR F.203/17 (Olaf Caroe Papers). In June 1951, Liaquat wrote to Caroe, thanking him for the reference to Pakistan in *Wells of Power.* Extract from an unfinished autobiography by Sir Olaf Caroe, MSS.EUR F.203/78 (Olaf Caroe Papers); see also Caroe, *Pathans,* pp. xiv–xv, and Caroe, Lecture to the Pakistan Society, 20 March 1980, MSS.EUR F.203/6 (Olaf Caroe Papers). "I have an immense esteem for Pakistan itself . . . particularly for my Pathan friends."

25. Report of Lecture Tour, 5 May–10 June 1952, MSS.EUR F.203.64 (Olaf Caroe Papers). With the Iranian oil crisis at its peak, many of Caroe's speeches were devoted to it. He praised Truman's determination toward Soviet incursions in Iran in 1946 and hoped the United States would continue to support that nation, without letting Iran escape "the written word" of their oil contracts. See also Dulles to the Embassy in Afghanistan, 20 February 1953, *FRUS,* 1952–1954, XI, pp. 1465–1466. Caroe occasionally included Afghanistan in his "Northern Screen" plan.

26. Royal Institute of International Affairs, *Defense in the Cold War,* p. 39. Deterrence would remain based on Strategic Air Command bombing. Liddell Hart, "Can We Defend the Middle East?" pp. 33–35; see also Memorandum from Major A.E.G. Davy, "The Strategic and Political Importance of Pakistan in Event of War with the Soviet Union," 845.00/5–2948.

27. Barton, "Pakistan's Claim to Kashmir," pp. 279–308. A 1954 article by A.L. Ratcliffe ("Strategic Situation in the Middle East," pp. 95–100) forewarned of Soviet mechanized forces overrunning local opposition and reaching Baghdad and the Persian Gulf within three days. India, the "spokesman for the colored race," would be of no value, given her misunderstanding of communism's true nature. Pakistan, with her well-trained and dependable army, could, together with Turkey, provide assistance to thwart Soviet aggression.

28. McMahon, "United States Cold War Policy," pp. 824–827.

29. Saiyid Akbar, an exiled Afghan national and frontier agitator, assassinated Liaquat. There is little evidence that would implicate Afghanistan, India, or the Soviet Union in the assassination, and suggestions of British complicity or CIA activity, occasionally advanced by regional authors, fail from lack of motive. The most plausible explanation involves an in-country conspiracy of disgruntled officials desirous of a more vigorous pursuit of an alliance with the West. Venkataramani, *American Role in Pakistan,* pp. 140–141, 158–162, 171, 177–179, 191–192; Akhtar, *Political Conspiracies in Pakistan,* p. 8; Khan, *Friends Not Masters,* pp. 21–22, 38–40, 177; Callard, *Pakistan's Foreign Policy,* p. 24; Palmer, *South Asia and United States Policy,* p. 29; Choudhury, *India, Pakistan, Bangladesh,* p. 78; Symonds, *Making of Pakistan,* pp. 126, 129.

30. Memorandum of Conversation with Ikramullah, 18 October 1951, *FRUS,* 1951, pp. 2220–2221; Memorandum of Conversation with Irkamullah, 22 October 1951, *FRUS,* 1951, pp. 2225–2226; Memorandum of Conversation with Foreign Minister Zafrullah Khan, *FRUS,* 1951, pp. 2227–2228. Ayub arrived later to make a similar plea, expressing desire to join a Middle East Command and contribute forces to the defense of the region. General Shadhi Hamid visited Washington in March 1952 and returned convinced that some sort of military aid program would commence; Choudhury, *India, Pakistan, Bangladesh,* pp. 80–81.

31. Memorandum by the Acting Regional Planning Advisor, Bureau of Near Eastern, South Asian, and African Affairs (Hoskins), to the Assistant Secretary of State for

Near Eastern, South Asian, and African Affairs (Byroade), 7 April 1952, *FRUS,* 1952–1954, IX, p. 204; *FRUS,* 1952–1954, 25 July 1952, p. 266; Secretary of State to the Secretary of Defense (Lovett), 28 May 1952, *FRUS,* 1952–1954, p. 233; Department of State Minutes of State—Joint Chiefs of Staff Meeting, 18 June 1952, *FRUS,* 1952–1954, p. 240. Scattered crises in Egypt, Iran, Palestine, and Kashmir had prompted piecemeal reappraisals of policy, but American military planners had "always considered the British responsible for the defense of the Middle East" JCS 1844/126, 2 July 1952; JCS 1844/156, 14 April 1954; NSC 73/4, 25 August 1950; Kirk to Acheson, *FRUS,* 1950, I, pp. 367–369.

32. JCS 1887/4, 19 October 1950; JCS/1887/50, 16 June 1952; JCS/1887/73, 13 October 1953; Department of State Minutes of State—Joint Chiefs of Staff Meeting, 18 June 1952, *FRUS,* 1952–1954, IX, pp. 238–242, 246; *FRUS,* 1952–1954, 28 November 1952, pp. 324–325; see also Acheson to the Secretary of Defense (Lovett), 28 May 1952, *FRUS,* 1952–1954, pp. 233–234.

33. Department of State, Minutes of State—Joint Chiefs of Staff Meeting, 28 November 1952, *FRUS,* 1952–1954, IX, pp. 320–326. By comparison, the front in Korea was some 150 miles long, that in Western Europe during World War II roughly 300, while German lines from Leningrad to the Caucasus were roughly double, or about 3,600 miles long. The whole plan in retrospect seems so logistically ludicrous as to be almost inconceivable. Collins further noted how there was but one railroad on the Outer Ring and, practically speaking, only one road as well.

34. Memorandum of Conversation, McGhee with Ikramullah, former Foreign Secretary of Pakistan, 18 October 1951, *FRUS,* 1951, VI, p. 2219. George McGhee found it difficult "to give much consideration to supplying arms to a country which did not have a problem of internal security or was not in need of protection from outside aggression." Department of State Policy Statement, 3 April 1950, *FRUS,* 1950, V, pp. 1490–1499; Report to NSC by the Secretaries of State and Defense and the Director of the Mutual Security Program on Reexamination of US Programs for National Security, 19 January 1953, Documents of the National Security Council; Elbert Mathews (Truman Library Oral History Interviews, pp. 42–43) claims: "I always opposed that, because any aid to Pakistan would only be used by them in context of their dispute with India. We would not get anything out of the alliance in terms of anti-communism." McGhee, "Tasks," pp. 892–894; Fraser Wilkins, Truman Library Oral History Interview, p. 77; Evan Wilson, Truman Library Oral History Interview, pp. 68–69, 76–77; McMahon, "United States Cold War Policy," pp. 829–830; Venkataramani, *American Role in Pakistan,* pp. 123–125, 156–157, 166–167, 200–202; Ram, *Super Powers,* pp. 35–37; Bowles, "Fresh Look at Free Asia," pp. 55–58; Bowles, *Ambassador's Report,* p. 243.

35. McMahon, "United States Cold War Policy," pp. 824–830. Other officials expressed apprehension that if more aid were not forthcoming, Pakistan would turn to Moscow, a threat that Karachi officials would often fortify. *FRUS,* 1952–1954, IX, pp. 222–226.

11

THE EISENHOWER ADMINISTRATION'S DEFENSE PROGRAM AND THE DECISION FOR ALLIANCE WITH PAKISTAN

The Eisenhower administration came to power amidst war in Korea, increasing French difficulties in Indochina, and several other scattered insurrections across Asia. Thought communist inspired and supported, these wars seemed harbingers of an even bigger showdown. Yet Eisenhower campaigned to end the Korean conflict, avoid further foreign entanglements, reduce taxes, and balance the budget. His strategic dilemma, thus, was how to maintain a strong military without incurring undue cost.[1]

The Eisenhower defense strategy sought to take maximum advantage of American technological superiority as a deterrent. The threat of massive retaliation from the American nuclear arsenal would discourage major Soviet offensives. The American army, meanwhile, would be reduced in strength to allow for lower defense budgets. Allied ground forces, gradually built up along the periphery of the Sino-Soviet bloc and supported by American naval and air forces, would be relied upon to serve as tripwires and prevent any more Koreas. The build-up of indigenous forces would cost less and would attract fewer foreign and domestic objections than would the stationing of substantial numbers of Western troops abroad.[2]

The traditions of Pakistan's army, a legacy of British rule and continued Commonwealth connections, and outward support for democracy and private enterprise would appeal to the Eisenhower administration. With American nuclear capacity still dependent on manned bombers, Pakistan's air bases continued to attract the attention of the air force as well. During the late 1940s, the United States, by virtue of its atomic monopoly and air superiority, held a tremendous strategic advantage over the U.S.S.R. The dawn of Soviet nuclear capabilities, expansion of the Soviet air force, and maintenance of substantial numbers of ground forces threatened that advantage. For massive retaliation to deter aggression, the ring of bases around the perimeter would have to be dispersed so as to reduce vulnerability to enemy attack as well as to changing political conditions in the host countries. By 1953 the air force strongly desired the acquisition of base facilities in the area between the Arabian Peninsula and Indian subcontinent. Suitably located bases would fill a large gap between existing facilities and ease transit in both wartime and peace.[3]

The Pakistani army also intrigued administration officials. The British-Indian army had contained a disproportionate number of troops from certain societal elements, such as the Rajputs, Gurkhas, Sikhs, Punjabis, and Pushtuns, who, in contrast to the supposedly docile Hindus, had acquired an aura of military superiority in the minds of their British commanders and society at large. Pakistani officials perpetuated the myth of "martial races" after partition, convincing some Pentagon and State Department officials that their army, composed mostly of men from the latter two groups, would be of great value in future wars. The all-volunteer army staged elaborate parade ground drills, which impressed numerous visiting officials. The Pakistani army also retained its close relationship with the British. Many Pakistani officers, most of whom were career men from long-standing military families, were educated in Britain. Given these predilections, the Eisenhower administration moved quickly to expand Truman's initiatives regarding Pakistan.[4]

With the Suez situation deadlocked and Britain's position in Iran worsening daily, Eisenhower's Secretary of State, John Foster Dulles, embarked on a tour of the Middle East and South Asia in May 1953. Initially advised that visits to "Cairo, Karachi and New Delhi" would be useful, Dulles eventually added nine other Middle Eastern capitals to his itinerary. The embassy staff in Tehran and other department officials advised against a visit to Iran, claiming it would only aggravate the stubborn Prime Minister Mohammed Mossadeq and impart nothing constructive to the situation there. There is no evidence that anyone even suggested visiting Afghanistan.[5]

During his visit to Cairo, Dulles listened to the Egyptian prime minister express dissatisfaction with the British while insisting on full, independent control of Suez base facilities. The visit to Egypt further convinced the already doubtful Dulles that hostility toward Israel and lingering resentment of the colonial powers distracted most Arab states from the Soviet threat and precluded the formation of a Suez-based defense system. At the same time, fears of Anglo-Egyptian conflict increased Dulles's desire to secure access to alternative regional bases.[6]

Dulles returned from his fact-finding mission desirous of an arrangement among the "Northern Tier" states of Turkey, Pakistan, Iran, and Iraq. Owing to geographic proximity, those nations were more aware of the Soviet menace, had historically opposed Russian and Soviet territorial ambitions, and consequently remained more attuned to potential alliances. They also seemed well positioned to protect the Middle East and Persian Gulf area as a whole. Dulles envisioned other states, including Syria, Lebanon, Jordan, Saudi Arabia, Egypt, Libya, and even Afghanistan eventually adhering to varying degrees, but most of those states would be unable to make any immediate contribution to the area beyond maintaining internal stability and open lines of communication. Assistance to Pakistan, however, seemed of immediate tangible value.[7]

Dulles visited Pakistan on May 23 and 24, 1953, and later claimed to have observed greater displays of support for American policy and experienced a more genuine feeling of friendship than in any other country. Instead of having to sell his views, his hosts ardently wooed the secretary. Dulles returned, convinced that the "strong spiritual faith and martial spirit of Pakistani people would make them a dependable bulwark against communism." He was impressed by the morale, training, discipline, and appearance of the armed forces and their leaders. Parade ground drills of the Khyber Rifles and other famed regiments convinced the secretary that they would be tremendous assets to free world defense. He also toured the air bases in the country, noting their strategic position near China and the Soviet Union, on the flanks of Iran and the Middle East, and guarding the historical invasion routes to India. He left, convinced that Pakistan's leaders recognized the Soviet threat and had the "moral courage to do [their] part in resisting communism." He believed Pakistan would cooperate with any Middle Eastern defense plan and felt that Pakistan could, with assistance, constitute a stabilizing force in the region. He saw no reason for the United States to await formal defense arrangements before providing military assistance to Pakistan.[8]

Throughout the months following Dulles's return, Defense and State Department officials considered the advantages and risks of a Northern Tier arrangement. NSC 155/1, the product of these discussions, encouraged the formation of a bilateral agreement between Pakistan and Turkey, from which a more extensive defense organization could be erected. In the meantime, the United States would provide limited assistance to the indigenous forces of certain countries, notably Syria, Turkey, Pakistan, Iran, and Iraq, to increase confidence in the West, improve political stability, and maintain pro-Western regimes. The administration eventually hoped to bring those countries into a defense organization designed to "influence the political organization, increase the internal stability, and strengthen the defense of the area," while ensuring access to regional resources, strategic positions, and communications centers.[9]

A series of events during the latter half of 1953 made the establishment of a pact more likely. From August 17 to 20, 1953, "spontaneous demonstrations" (now commonly assumed to have been CIA instigated and supported) led to the ouster of Mossadeq and brought Shah Reza Pahlavi to power in Iran. Anxiety over the oil crises abated. The shah's interest in strengthening his army and domestic position, Iraq's continued cooperation with the British, Turkey's firm anti-Soviet stance, and "the insistently expressed desire of Pakistani leaders for closer military ties with us" convinced both the Joint Chiefs and doubters within the State Department of the desirability of a four-power Northern Tier pact.[10]

Throughout the months following Dulles's tour, the Pakistani leadership expressed desires to enter Western-sponsored defense arrangements. Pakistan often asserted itself the most dependable of all allies, voicing determination to make any sacrifices necessary to stop the communist menace wherever and whenever encountered. In pursuing this super-loyal strategy, the Pakistanis expressed desires to join a Pacific alliance, a Middle Eastern pact, and other groupings that would tighten their bonds to the West, with little apparent regard for the political or military practicability of membership.[11]

The Pakistanis proved adept both at emphasizing the red threat and stressing a potential bulwark role while concealing their primary concern with India. Governor-General Ghulam Mohammed promised American aid would not be used against India and even voiced willingness to sign an agreement promising aid to India in the event of an attack against it. Other officials routinely echoed this pledge, promising resistance to the Sino-Soviet threat that could prevent India from going communist. Prime Minister Mohammed Ali promised to make expeditionary forces available, should support for Iran or Iraq be required. Ayub, who was the most effusive, outlandish, and ultimately successful lobbyist, mentioned threats from China, the U.S.S.R., and a communist India when requesting arms assistance. At times, he spoke of a Sino-Soviet pincer move through the Himalayas and Afghanistan that, in the absence of aid, would "catch Pakistan in its grip and crack it like a walnut." At the same time, he emphasized Pakistan manpower assets and air bases, effectively arguing that his seven or eight divisions could halt several threatening developments. Ayub added that American economic assistance would strengthen Pakistan to the point that Nehru would be forced to approach Washington to achieve a Kashmir settlement and ultimately "would frighten India out of her passiveness." Ayub reiterated opposition to neutralism often, adding that Pakistan would fight communism whether it received American assistance or not.[12]

The Pakistanis proved equally adept at obfuscating their multitude of internal difficulties. Ghulam and Ayub routinely blamed domestic disturbances on communist agitators, which found a receptive audience among American officials. The Pakistanis also maintained an image of democracy despite totalitarian behavior. Pakistan's government had remained an extension of the viceregal system, with power vested in the governor-general, who could suspend constitutional processes and overrule the cabinet and legislature, in what one critic has called a "constitutional dictatorship." Further sanctions for governor's rule in the provinces permitted mass arrests of communists in disturbed areas. Allegedly for emergency use only, successive governments proved eager to dispense with constitutional formalities on the pretext of threats to law and order. Mirza proved especially adept at preserving a sem-blance of democracy, claiming, for example, that his nation needed "the American system with modifications to suit the special conditions prevalent in Pakistan," which another critic defined as a "presidential system with a toothless legislature and without inconvenient elections."[13]

Though a variety of official correspondence illustrated Pakistan's ethnic, social, and physical divisiveness, growing economic strains, lack of natural resources and industry, and constitutional difficulties, such literature appar-ently made little impact on American officials, who persistently dismissed Pakistan's problems as "democratic growing pains" while lauding its open-ness to investors and overestimating its development and strategic potential. Most remained convinced that the Pakistani people supported the prime min-ister and his efforts to solve the nagging problems of provincialism, religious extremism, and "colleagues who are not sympathetic to his aims." Horace Hildreth, the American ambassador to Pakistan, summed up the prevailing optimism, when he stated: "In spite of East Bengal, provincialism, constitu-tional difficulties, Muslim League incompetence, political immaturity, and vexing international problems, the Embassy believes that political stability can be maintained by the present ruling group."[14] The United States would soon enlist Pakistan at the very time it was entering its worst period of internal difficulties.

By October 1953, the Eisenhower administration had decided in principle to extend grants of military aid to Pakistan and entered into secret negotia-tions with Karachi. Assistance seemed likely to lead to the establishment of Pakistani expeditionary forces and would discourage neutralism, pave the way for the acquisition of base rights, strengthen the existing administration, and mitigate the danger of communist aggression or internal disintegration. That November, however, a series of articles appeared in several major newspapers, including the *New York Times,* which spoke of alliance as a *fait accompli.* This evoked criticism from Nehru and the Soviet Union, which curtailed American options and effectively guaranteed the pact. It is now clear that Pakistani authorities had informed American reporters of impending alliance through a "campaign of deliberate leaks," apparently to put pressure on the United States to sanctify the arrangement.[15]

In the light of the publicity, Ghulam argued that an aid denial to Pakistan "would be like taking a poor girl for a walk and then walking out on her, leaving her only with a bad name." Other Pakistani officials followed suit, convincing several Americans that rejection would damage the government, to the benefit of reactionary elements and the leftist opposition, and would also force the abandonment of any plans to make Pakistan a regional defensive bulwark. Most importantly, abandonment of Pakistan would seem appease-ment of the Soviet Union and India and would strengthen proponents of neutralism throughout Asia. Other nations would assume the United States would back down in moments of crisis. Potential political repercussions prompted consensus among administration officials, who agreed with Dulles that a "failure to follow through after recent publicity and statements by Nehru would dissolution [sic] Pakistanis and give Nehru good reason to think that we dance to his tune." Furthermore, "In the state of the world today, it did not seem good policy to rebuke those who unite as we do and who can contribute to the security of the Free World on which our security depends."[16]

Vice-President Richard M. Nixon visited both Pakistan and India (and Afghanistan) in December 1953. Though given a rousing welcome in Pakistan, his reception in India was less than enthusiastic. Not surprisingly, upon his return, Nixon argued before the National Security Council that Pakistan's firm opposition to communism mandated aid. He further argued that the time had come to assail neutralism. Pakistan, Nixon claimed, would become a "counterweight to the confirmed neutralism of Jawaharlal Nehru's India" that would help seal the Soviet Union behind a "military crescent" of pro-Western powers. The National Security Council gave him a standing ovation after his speech and thereafter agreed to give aid to Pakistan, claiming one advantage "should be a weakening of neutralist sentiment and a strengthening of the hands of those who favor alignment with the West." More than one commentator has claimed that Nixon tipped the scales to Pakistan's favor.[17]

Other department officials shared Nixon's frustration with Nehru, who seemed to be playing East against West for economic and political advantage while attempting to stop communism with incantations. Dulles resented India's unwillingness to carry its share of the burden and would eventually decry neutralism as an obsolete conception that, except under unusual circumstances, was "immoral and short-sighted." Dulles further thought Pakistan willing to compromise on the problem of Kashmir, while Nehru seemed content to invoke "factual amnesia" to advantage. He saw little hope in India ever agreeing to a compromise solution, a belief that in part would scrap earlier preconditions on a Kashmir settlement as requisite to extensive assistance with Pakistan.[18]

While the Joint Chiefs were all but certain that India and Afghanistan would react unfavorably to the inclusion of Pakistan in U.S. defense plans and for a time considered indirect aid to Pakistan through Turkey, the National Security Council decided on direct aid largely owing to their interpretation that Indian opposition would not be a costly or permanent liability. While conceding that India might seek some accord with the U.S.S.R., resentment seemed likely to be of short duration and would not cause any major change in policy. Dulles believed "we can ride out the storm without fatal effects on U.S.-Indian relations" and thought India might even join the alliance later. Pakistani officials also believed Indian opposition would "blow over in three or four months." A denial of aid to Pakistan, on the other hand, promised few benefits. India would likely remain uncooperative on Kashmir and other regional issues and would be encouraged to try pressure tactics again. While the Eisenhower administration feared Soviet countermeasures, perhaps including political pressure on Iran or Afghanistan, it seemed unlikely that the U.S.S.R. would "undertake major retaliatory actions such as invasion of either of these states."[19]

On February 19, 1954, Pakistan and Turkey announced their imminent alliance. Pakistan thereupon requested arms assistance from the United States, and Eisenhower informed Karachi of his readiness to provide military aid in context of the Pakistan-Turkish accord, as expected, on February 25. The Turkish-Pakistani agreement provided for general consultation and cooperation in military planning but avoided implications of a mutual defense guarantee that might have extended the NATO commitments. The Pakistanis would join SEATO in September and the Baghdad Pact one year later.[20]

There remained, however, little tangible justification for the pact. NIE 54–30 clearly stated that the agreement would produce no "significant reduction of the area's military vulnerability." Its primary effects would be "political and psychological rather than military." It would foster greater awareness of the communist threat, encourage cooperation on area defense planning and other matters, alleviate opposition to base access agreements, and "strengthen the position of Western-oriented elements in participating countries." In response to British inquiries as to the overt military value of the Turkish-Pakistani agreement, State Department officials could only reply that it would make adherence of Iran and Iraq easier to secure and coordinate.[21]

Throughout 1955 and 1956, serious doubts would surface regularly among Eisenhower administration personnel concerning the wisdom of large-scale, long-term assistance to Pakistan. A variety of government literature assailed Pakistan's commitment to Middle East defense, claiming its adherence to the Baghdad Pact and SEATO motivated by fear of India and disputes with Afghanistan, while raising doubts as to assistance Pakistan could provide for defense of the Middle East against Soviet aggression. One such report dismissed the Pakistani government as "not likely to tackle the country's pressing economic, social and political problems with vigor, since the group is so largely preoccupied with constant political maneuvering and since most effective solutions—land reform or greater voice for East Pakistanis in national affairs—would basically undermine their position of dominance. . . . Meanwhile intrigue and corruption are corroding the administrative machinery and encouraging disillusionment with constitutional government and democratic processes in general."[22]

By 1958 the State Department's Office of Intelligence Research had concluded that Pakistan's military expenditures were designed neither to protect the country from a Soviet or Chinese attack, "for which Pakistani resources will never be sufficient," nor to maintain internal security, "for which the present military establishment is excessive." In addition, "Pakistan's limited resources are inadequate either to sustain the burden of its military build-up or, after the build-up period, to bear both the military maintenance costs and the needs of economic growth. There is only the slightest prospect that in the early post build-up period Pakistan could, unaided, support even one of these programs."[23]

With the advent of satellite surveillance technologies, modern bombers and ballistic missiles rendered even Pakistan's bases of limited use, the United States began to phase out the commitment to Pakistan. Though the 1958 revolution in Iraq would frighten Washington into making renewed promises to Karachi, the revival would prove temporary. Outlays to Pakistan had all but ceased by 1961. The final break came in the autumn of 1962, following the provision of American military assistance to India in the wake of Chinese aggression.

In 1954, however, few American diplomats, politicians, or military officers had opposed alliance with Pakistan. The vast majority of State and Defense department personnel had thought it a good idea to encourage Pakistan and other regional powers to collaborate. Chester Bowles, the former ambassador to India, was among the few opponents of alliance. He claimed simple mathematics rendered it foolish to alienate 360 million Indians for the sake of 80 million Pakistanis and further warned that Afghanistan and India would be driven to embrace the U.S.S.R.. He wrote Dulles: "I believe we will isolate Pakistan, draw the Soviet Union certainly into Afghanistan and probably into India, eliminate the possibility of Pakistani-Indian or Pakistan-Afghan rapprochement, further jeopardize the outlook for the Indian five-year plan, increase the dangerous wave of anti-Americanism throughout India and other South Asian countries, open up explosive new opportunities for the Soviet Union, gravely weaken the hopes for stable democratic government in India, and add nothing whatsoever to our military strength in this area."[24]

Earlier, Bowles had argued that arms aid to Pakistan would "almost certainly result in acceptance of military aid and economic assistance from the Soviet Union," which would foster increased penetration of the Afghan state.[25] Bowles thus claimed that the Soviet Union would come to dominate Afghanistan, leaving Pakistan equally at their mercy. One of Dulles's first acts as secretary, however, had been to replace Bowles, and the former ambassador's opinions carried little weight or authority.

When the proposal came before the Congress, Senator William Fulbright voiced disapproval of what he deemed an "unfortunate mistake" that would exacerbate regional tensions and increase the threat of war. Congressman Emmanuel Cellar of New York was among the few representatives who shared similar concerns. These criticisms, however, were dwarfed by the support of a large delegation, headed by Senator William Knowland (who had been wooed in Pakistan himself), that favored the initiative. In general, Congress raised few objections to a plan that seemed consistent with overall containment policy.[26]

As the administration realized that India would regard the agreement with

Pakistan as an affront, Eisenhower tried to allay Indian fears, minimize political repercussions, and avoid creating an impression that the United States had abandoned India for the sake of Pakistan. He repeatedly informed Nehru that Mutual Security Legislation prohibited use of American hardware except for internal security or self-defense. This rendered little comfort to Indian Defense Minister Krishna Menon, who explained: "We cannot believe that guns that fire in only one direction have been made." The president also indicated that the United States would offer Nehru a similar agreement to that given Pakistan, but the Indians never expressed interest.[27]

No similar terms, or even expressions of reassurance, were ever offered Afghanistan. A few officials warned Dulles that any agreement with Pakistan should be prefaced by an agreement that at least guaranteed transit facilities to Kabul (or established similar facilities through Iran). Yet most American officials attached no strategic importance to Afghanistan and remained indifferent to its fate. Indeed, during the whole course of the debate over supplying arms to Pakistan, American officials, even within the Kabul Embassy, routinely dismissed Afghan concerns as inconsequential to the global containment effort. That attitude colored the entire course of American policy toward Afghanistan in the postwar period. Whereas the British had always attached strategic importance to Afghanistan, if only as adjunct to Indian defense, the United States had launched its regional initiatives primarily to support defense of the Middle East. They did not consider protection of the subcontinent a high priority. This factor, coupled with then-prevalent emphasis on conventional operations, meant that despite Afghanistan's historical hostility to the Soviet Union, its size, terrain, and reputation for guerrilla warfare, and its geographic position protecting Pakistan and Iran, the United States would see no reason to court or even appease the Afghans. Instead, their recruitment of Pakistan into the Western alliance system, coupled with the still-unsolved Pushtunistan controversy, would preclude arrangements with Afghanistan and eventually drove that nation to seek an alternative agreement with the Soviet Union.

NOTES

1. Kinnard, *President Eisenhower*, pp. 4, 10, 13, 124, 127; Eisenhower, *Mandate for Change*, p. 97.

2. Kinnard, *President Eisenhower*, pp. 8–10, 33, 123, 126, 135. The "logical role of our allies along the periphery of the Iron Curtain, therefore, would be to provide for their own local security, especially ground forces, while the US, centrally located and strong in productive powers, provided mobile reserve forces of all arms, with emphasis on sea and air contingents." Eisenhower, *Mandate for Change*, p. 447.

3. *Rand Report*, pp. xi, xx, 40, 184. By the end of its term, the Eisenhower administration would acquire base rights in the United Kingdom, Morocco, Canada, Greenland, Iceland, Japan, Spain, Portugal, Libya, Egypt, Lebanon, Saudi Arabia,

Algeria, Tunisia, Turkey, Cyprus, Greece, Italy, Iran, Iraq, Ceylon, and eventually Pakistan.

4. Even during the presidential campaign, the Republicans voiced support for strengthening ties with Pakistan. Tahir-Kheli, *United States and Pakistan,* p. 2; Choudhury, *India, Pakistan, Bangladesh,* pp. 80–81. Major-General George Olmsted, director of the Office of Military Assistance, was a strong advocate of closer military ties with Pakistan. He described the Pakistanis as "the fighting element in the old Indian Army." He added, "Anything we could do to intensify their determination to fight the Soviet was desirable." He later noted the Pakistan's airfields would offer a safe haven for U.S. planes returning from missions against the U.S.S.R. Mowrer, "New Frontiers for Freedom," p. 36. He was impressed by the army's "indomitable spirit and fine military tradition." Palmer, *South Asia and United States Policy,* pp. 99, 107, 114.

5. Editorial Note, *FRUS,* 1952–1954, IX, p. 1; Dulles, "Report on the Near East," pp. 831–833. This notes how it was impossible to visit Iran but does not mention Afghanistan. Loy Henderson, Eisenhower Library, Oral History Interviews, pp. 10–11. Dulles visited Egypt, Israel, Jordan, Syria, Lebanon, Iraq, Saudi Arabia, India, Pakistan, Turkey, Greece, and Libya.

6. Memorandum of Conversation, Prepared in the Embassy in Cairo, 11 May 1953, *FRUS,* 1952–1954, IX, pp. 10–11, 13–15; Ambassador in Egypt (Cafferty) to the Department of State, 13 May 1953, *FRUS,* 1952–1954, p. 25; Memorandum of Conversation Prepared in the Embassy in Syria, 16 May 1953, *FRUS,* 1952–1954, pp. 60–61. The tour convinced Dulles that "MEDO is a future rather than immediate possibility." Dulles, "Report on the Near East," p. 835.

7. Memorandum of Discussion at the 147th Meeting of the National Security Council, 1 June 1953, *FRUS,* 1952–1954, IX, pp. 385–386; Secretary of State to Certain Diplomatic Missions, 30 July 1953, *FRUS,* 1952–1954, pp. 406–407; see also Paper Approved by the Chiefs of Mission Conference at Istanbul, May 11–14, 1954, "Conference Conclusions on Regional Security in the Middle East," *FRUS,* 1952–1954, IX, pp. 508–509; Paper Approved by the Chiefs of Mission Conference at Istanbul, May 11–14, 1954, "Conference Statement on Middle East Defense Commenting on OIR Contribution to NIE 54–30," *FRUS,* 1952–1954, IX, pp. 511–512.

8. Secretary of State to the Department of State, 26 May 1953, *FRUS,* 1952–1954, IX, p. 147; Memorandum of Conversation by the Counselor in Pakistan (MacArthur), 24 May 1953, *FRUS,* 1952–1954, pp. 135–136; Dulles to the House Committee on Agriculture, 83rd Congress, 2nd Session, "Wheat Aid to Pakistan," quoted in Ram, *Super Powers,* p. 106. "One of my clearest impressions was that of the outstanding and sincere friendship which the leaders of Pakistan felt for the United States. I was greatly impressed by their understanding of world problems. . . . They will resist the menace of Communism as their strength permits." See also Memorandum of Conversation by Lieutenant Colonel Stephen J. Meade, 23 May 1953, *FRUS,* 1952–1954, IX, pp. 132–133; Choudhury, *India, Pakistan, Bangladesh,* p. 83; Venkataramani, *American Role in Pakistan,* pp. 203–204; *Department of State Bulletin,* 22 June 1953, pp. 890–891; "A Real Ally in South Asia," *US News & World Report,* November 13, 1953, 44–46. Dulles was impressed by the "lancers that had to be 6 (feet) 2 (inches) sat there on great big horses, were out of this world." The *US News* reporter was similarly impressed by these "warrior people . . . mainly six footers . . . tall, rugged eaters of meat and wheat."

9. Statement of Policy by the National Security Council, NSC 155/1, "United States Objectives and Policies with Respect to the Near East," 14 July 1953, *FRUS*, 1952–1954, IX, pp. 400–403; National Intelligence Estimate, NIE 54–30, 22 June 1954, *FRUS*, 1952–1954, IX, p. 518; McMahon, "United States Cold War Policy," p. 832. The administration acknowledged that prospects of economic and military assistance would be powerful inducements to potential alliance members and that their willingness to join would depend on the extent of the offers.

10. Deputy Assistant Secretary of State for Near Eastern, South Asian, and African Affairs (Jernegan) to the Assistant Secretary of Defense (Nash), 15 October 1953, *FRUS*, 1952–1954, IX, pp. 425–426; Memorandum by the Joint Chiefs of Staff to the Secretary of Defense (Wilson), 14 November 1953, *FRUS*, 1952–1954, p. 1431. Though Iran still appeared too weak to join a pact, the Chiefs deemed an agreement between any two powers a significant step toward the establishment of a comprehensive Middle East pact.

11. Singh, *U.S.-Pakistan and India*, pp. 28, 46, 46fn.

12. Memorandum of Conversation, by Lieutenant Colonel Stephen J. Meade, 23 May 1953, *FRUS*, 1952–1954, IX, p. 134; Memorandum by the Assistant Secretary of State for Near Eastern, South Asian, and African Affairs (Byroade) to the Assistant Secretary of Defense (Nash), 15 October 1953, *FRUS*, 1952–1954, pp. 421–422. Ayub forecast Soviet forces overwhelming the Middle East and pressing on into Africa, while the Chinese routed ill-prepared Indian troops. Ambassador in Turkey (Warren) to the Department of State, 17 September 1953, *FRUS*, 1952–1954, XI, p. 418; Ambassador in Turkey (Warren) to the Department of State, 15 June 1954, *FRUS*, 1952–1954, IX, p. 514; Memorandum of Conversation, Prepared in the Embassy in Pakistan, 23 May 1953, *FRUS*, 1952–1954, pp. 122, 124; "Assessment of Soviet Threat to Pakistan and the Armed Forces Required to Meet This Threat," 790D.5/6–453; Khan, *Raiders in Kashmir*, pp. 160–162.

13. Chargé in Pakistan (Emmerson) to the Department of State, 29 May 1954, *FRUS*, 1952–1954, XI, p. 1846; Memorandum of Conversation by the Officer in Charge of Economic Affairs, Office of South Asian Affairs (Fluker), 22 June 1954, *FRUS*, 1952–1954, pp. 1849–1850; Hildreth to the Department of State, 10 July 1954, *FRUS*, 1952–1954, p. 1852; Venkataramani, *American Role in Pakistan*, pp. 74–79, 142–143, 287; (American officials became convinced that such "vigorous and imaginative" men as Mirza could save Bengal from communism through the postponement of democratic processes. Sayeed, *Pakistan, the Formative Phase*, pp. 242, 258–259, 282, 300. An embryonic communist party had developed within Pakistan, secured limited support, and staged scattered demonstrations. By late 1948, the Pakistan government embarked on a drive to crush internal communist activity. They continued such activities well into the 1950s. There is no reason to believe, however, that the party ever attracted more than minimal support or ever posed a serious threat to the government. See Progress Report on NSC 5701, 24 July 1957, paragraph B13a, and Memorandum of Conversation by Byroade, 25 March 1953, *FRUS*, 1952–1954, XI, p. 1825.

14. Hildreth to the Department of State, 10 July 1954, *FRUS*, 1952–1954, XI, p. 1853. Hildreth also noted "a widening gap between the financial capability of the Government and its essential requirements for minimum consumer demands." He presented no evidence to support his optimistic conclusions. Memorandum of Conversation, Prepared in the Embassy in Pakistan, May 23, 1953, *FRUS*, 1952–1954,

IX, p. 125; Acting Secretary of State to the Embassy in Pakistan, 4 December 1953, *FRUS*, 1952–1954, XI, p. 1831. The American emphasis on the prime minister, who was little more than a figurehead, itself casts doubts on analysis of the political situation in Pakistan. See Hildreth to the Department of State, 10 July 1954, *FRUS*, 1952–1954, XI, p. 1853; Stephens, *Pakistan*, p. 220; Venkataramani, *American Role in Pakistan*, pp. 228–232; Callard, *Pakistan's Foreign Policy*, pp. 8–9; Hayes, *Impact of US Policy*, p. 27.

15. McMahon, "United States Cold War Policy," pp. 833–835.

16. Jernegan, "The Middle East," pp. 445–446; Memorandum of Conversation by the Assistant Secretary of State for Near Eastern, South Asian, and African Affairs (Byroade), 14 January 1954, *FRUS*, 1952–1954, IX, p. 453; Editorial Note, *FRUS*, 1952–1954, p. 467; Under Secretary of State (Smith) to the Secretary of Defense (Wilson), 12 November 1953, *FRUS*, 1952–1954, p. 429; Ambassador in Pakistan (Hildreth) to the Department of State, 26 January 1954, *FRUS*, 1952–1954, p. 469; Special Estimate SE-55, "The Probable Repercussions of a US Decision to Grant or Deny Military Aid to Pakistan," 15 January 1954, *FRUS*, 1952–1954, XI, pp. 1840–1844; Hildreth to the Department of State, 1 December 1953, *FRUS*, 1952–1954, p. 1830; Memorandum of Conversation by Hildreth, 7 December 1953, *FRUS*, 1952–1954 p. 1832; Hildreth to the Department of State, 8 December 1953, *FRUS*, 1952–1954, p. 1834.

17. Meetings of the NSC, 16 and 23 December, Whitman File, Eisenhower Library; Memorandum by the Assistant Secretary of State for Near Eastern, South Asian, and African Affairs (Byroade) to the Acting Secretary of State, 1 March 1954, *FRUS*, 1952–1954, XI, pp. 1118–1119; Singh, *U.S.-Pakistan and India*, pp. 30–31; De-Toldano, *Nixon*, p. 164; Choudhury, *India, Pakistan, Bangladesh*, p. 86; Muttam, *U.S., Pakistan and India*, pp. 12, 41fn; McMahon, "United States Cold War Policy," p. 837; Ma'arof, *Afghanistan in World Politics*, p. 87; Dulles, "Cost of Peace," p. 999; 18 June 1956. Neutrality "pretends that a nation can best gain safety for itself by being indifferent to the fate of others."

18. Memorandum of Conversation, by Lieutenant Colonel Stephen J. Meade, 23 May 1953, *FRUS*, 1952–1954, IX, p. 133; Memorandum of Conversation, Prepared in the Embassy in Pakistan, 23 May 1953, *FRUS*, 1952–1954, pp. 122, 127–129; Secretary of State to the Department of State, 26 May 1953, *FRUS*, 1952–1954, p. 147; Memorandum of Conversation by Hildreth, 7 December 1953, *FRUS*, 1952–1954, XI, p. 1832; Hildreth to the Department of State, 8 December 1953, *FRUS*, 1952–1954, p. 1834; Singh, *U.S.-Pakistan and India*, p. 32; Muttam, *U.S., Pakistan and India*, p. 34; Venkataramani, *American Role in Pakistan*, pp. 199, 226; Palmer, *South Asia and United States Policy*, pp. 15–16; Kaul, *U.S.A. and the Hindustan Peninsula*, p. 22. Eisenhower likewise considered Nehru a nuisance. Radford thought any country willing to sign an alliance was deserving of support, but those who were content to "shilly-shally,—well, to hell with them."

19. Special Estimate SE-55, "The Probable Repercussions of a US Decision to Grant or Deny Military Aid to Pakistan," 15 January 1954, *FRUS*, 1952–1954, XI, pp. 1840, 1843–1845; National Intelligence Estimate NIE 54-30, 22 June 1954, *FRUS*, 1952–1954, IX, p. 520; Memorandum by the Joint Chiefs of Staff to the Secretary of Defense (Wilson), 14 November 1953, *FRUS*, 1952–1954, IX, p. 431.

Those statements contradict others that worry about Afghan vulnerability such as: Ambassador in India (Bowles) to the Department of State, 20 November 1952, *FRUS*, 1952–1954, p. 318. Bowles had similar concerns seventeen months earlier, adding that Iran and Afghanistan might resent being unable to participate in such an organization. Progress Report, NSC 5409, 25 February 1955, paragraph C34; Dulles to Senator H. Alexander Smith, 26 February 1954; NSC 5409, 19 February 1954, paragraph 8, NIE-79, "Probable Developments in South Asia," 30 June 1953, *FRUS*, 1952–1954, XI, p. 1087; Memorandum of Conversation by Hildreth, 7 December 1953, *FRUS*, 1952–1954, XI, p. 1832; Hildreth to the Department of State, 8 December 1953, *FRUS*, 1952–1954, pp. 1833, 1835; U.S. House of Representatives, 93/1, Committee for Foreign Affairs, Sub-Committee on the Near East and South Asia, Hearings, p. 671; Memorandum of Conversation, by the Secretary of State, 21 May 1953, *FRUS*, 1952–1954, IX, pp. 115–116; Memorandum of Conversation, by the Secretary of State, 22 May 1953, *FRUS*, 1952–1954, IX, p. 120; Ambassador in India (Allen) to the Department of State, 21 May 1953, *FRUS*, 1952–1954, p. 114.

20. Secretary of State to the Embassy in Lebanon, 20 March 1954, *FRUS*, 1952–1954, IX, p. 489; Secretary of State to the Embassy in Turkey, 16 January 1954, *FRUS*, 1952–1954, pp. 455, 455fn; Acting Secretary of State (Smith) to the Embassy in Iran, 13 February 1954, *FRUS*, 1952–1954, IX, p. 483. Pakistani and American dignitaries signed the Mutual Security Agreement on May 19.

21. National Intelligence Estimate NIE 54–30, 22 June 1954, *FRUS*, 1952–1954, IX, p. 519; Acting Secretary of State (Smith) to the Embassy in Pakistan, 16 April 1954, *FRUS*, 1952–1954, IX, p. 495; Memorandum of Conversation by the Deputy Assistant Secretary of State for Near Eastern, South Asian, and African Affairs (Jernegan), 6 January 1954, *FRUS*, 1952–1954, IX, pp. 444–445; Deputy Assistant Secretary of State for Near Eastern, South Asian, and African Affairs (Jernegan) to the Assistant Secretary of Defense (Nash), 15 October 1953, *FRUS*, 1952–1954, IX, p. 426.

22. Department of State, Office of Intelligence Research, Intelligence Report No. 7459, "Prospects and Problems of Pakistan's Ruling Group," 8 March 1957.

23. Ibid., "Pakistan's Current Economic Situation and Prospects," 15 May 1958, quoted in Venkataramani, *American Role in Pakistan*, pp. 390–391; see also U.S. Senate, Committee on Foreign Relations, "Review of Foreign Policy," Hearings, 85th Congress, 3rd Session, 1958, p. 617; NSC 5617, 7 December 1956, paragraphs 11 and 66; Progress Report, NSC 5701, 16 July 1958, paragraph A5; Harrison, "Case History of a Mistake," pt. 2, p. 5.

24. Quoted in McMahon, "United States Cold War Policy," p. 839.

25. Quoted in Harrison, "Case History of a Mistake," pt. 1, pp. 6–7.

26. *Congressional Record*, 100, p. 2481; House, Committee on Foreign Affairs, Report, Mutual Security Act of 1954, p. 33; Senate, Committee on Foreign Relations, Report, Mutual Security Act of 1954, p. 35, both 83rd Congress, 2nd Session; Venkataramani, *American Role in Pakistan*, pp. 243–245; Ram, *Super Powers*, pp. 89–90, 110; Palmer, *South Asia and United States Policy*, pp. 29, 31; Choudhury, *India, Pakistan, Bangladesh*, p. 86.

27. Venkataramani, *American Role in Pakistan*, pp. 240, 301; Memorandum of Conversation by the Deputy Assistant Secretary of State for Near Eastern, South Asian,

and African Affairs (Jernegan), 6 January 1954, *FRUS,* 1952–1954, IX, pp. 445–446; *FRUS,* 1952–1954, XI, 1838–9; Special Estimate SE-55, "The Probable Repercussions of a US Decision to Grant or Deny Military Aid to Pakistan," 15 January 1954, *FRUS,* 1952–1954, XI, pp. 1840–1841; Memorandum of Conversation by the Secretary of State, 5 January 1954, *FRUS,* 1952–1954, XI, pp. 1438–1439; Kaul, *U.S.A. and Hindustan Peninsula,* p. 46.

12

THE TRUMAN ADMINISTRATION AND AFGHANISTAN: THE HELMAND VALLEY PROJECT, PUSHTUNISTAN, AND MILITARY AID

Following independence in 1919, Afghanistan established diplomatic relations with several nations. Some states, notably France, Germany, and Japan, soon became involved in educational, economic, and cultural projects in Afghanistan. Relations with the United States, however, remained virtually non-existent. Though Afghan emissaries suggested diplomatic recognition and economic cooperation as early as 1921, President Warren Harding dismissed commercial opportunities in Afghanistan and reserved diplomatic relations for "further consideration."[1] Throughout the decade, subsequent Afghan efforts met a similar fate. Though "Afghan representatives in foreign capitals continually approached our diplomatic representatives and endeavored . . . to obtain American representation in Washington," Harding and Calvin Coolidge shunned friendly Afghan gestures, often in rather brusque fashion.[2]

American political disinterest stemmed in part from interpretations of Afghan society then prevalent within the State Department as well as from the isolationism of the times. Few American diplomats had any firsthand knowledge of Afghanistan. Given a diet of popular British literature and a smattering of erratic travelogues, most saw the Afghans as treacherous savages and decried an exchange of ambassadors as wasteful and potentially dangerous. Wallace Smith Murray, the chief of the State Department's Division of Near Eastern Affairs, exemplified these attitudes when he spoke before Congress on the issue of diplomatic relations with Afghanistan in 1930. Murray claimed:

Afghanistan is doubtless the most fanatic, hostile country in the world today. . . . There is no pretense of according Christians equal rights with Moslems. There are no banks in Afghanistan . . . [It] is necessary to make payments by sending caravans of gold and silver hundreds of miles through robber-infested territory. . . . [The Afghans] detest taxation and military service and welcome chaos and confusion which enables them to do . . . as they see fit on helpless communities and passing caravans. . . . No foreign lives in the country can be protected and no foreign interests guaranteed.[3]

Murray's comments were certainly exaggerated and at times wildly incorrect, though, coming as they did in the wake of Amanullah's overthrow and Bacha-I-Saqao's brief interlude, they are, to a certain extent, understandable. There is little doubt, however, that such opinions delayed American recognition of Afghanistan. William Phillips, the acting secretary of state when the United States finally recognized Afghanistan in August 1934, confirmed that the delay stemmed in part from "the primitive condition of the country, the lack of . . . guarantees for the safety of foreigners," and "the absence of any important interests."[4]

Phillips also summarized the reasons for Franklin Roosevelt's change in American policy as follows: "From many sources I am informed that the establishment of diplomatic relations with the U.S. is earnestly desired by government officials in Afghanistan, who feel that recognition by this country would be of inestimable moral assistance in their endeavors properly to bring Afghanistan into the family of nations. Since the government of Afghanistan is recognized by all of the great powers and since the present regime appears to be a stable one, I can see no reason why we should withhold recognition of that country."[5]

William H. Hornybrook became the first American minister assigned to Afghanistan on May 4, 1935, but relations changed little.[6] Though Hashim Khan desired American economic assistance and attempted to lure American businesses to Afghanistan, nearly every company solicited rejected their offers. The global economic situation of the 1930s coupled with the limited market, lack of skilled workers, landlocked location, and the primitive transportation network in Afghanistan combined to discourage investors. In November 1936, for example, the Afghan government offered the Inland Exploration Company a seventy-five-year concession for the exploration of oil reserves in five provinces. The company, however, abandoned the project less than one year after its commencement, even before completion of the preliminary geological survey, citing prohibitive costs arising from the inaccessibility of the deposits and the poor transportation network. The company also expressed concern regarding the vulnerability of the oil fields to the Soviet Union. The deaths of two company leaders interested in the concessions, as well as discoveries of more easily accessible oil elsewhere, sealed the fate of the project. It was a stunning blow to the Afghan government, especially as the Americans had given up so easily when other nations had sought to gain such concessions. Afghan-American contacts remained limited to a few scholarly and business endeavors.[7]

Efforts to expand diplomatic operations in Kabul and Washington likewise failed. During the Inland negotiations, Afghan officials and oil consortium executives proposed the establishment of legations in each capital. Murray remained adamantly opposed to such, however, claiming, "American interests in Afghanistan would hardly warrant the great expense that would be incurred in establishing any appropriate form of diplomatic representation in Kabul."[8] He had further reservations about protection for an eventual American diplomatic mission in Afghanistan. Afghanistan is a country, Murray wrote, "in which turbulent disorders in the past have been not uncommon. . . . It should be borne in mind . . . the almost non-existent system of justice, in the Western sense of the word, in Afghanistan, foreigners enjoy there no capitulatory rights and are subject to Afghan laws and justice." He provided two examples, one Italian and one German, "in which the governments were powerless to accord them adequate protection." In view of this, Murray urged the government "to refrain from establishing diplomatic and consular representation in Afghanistan." He argued to defer to the British, who had vital political interests there and were accustomed to the culture.[9]

Afghan-American contacts increased dramatically during the Second World War. In June 1941, the American minister to Iran visited Afghanistan and recommended the immediate establishment of a permanent American mission in Kabul. He reported as follows:

The Afghans have a sincere and a deep-rooted desire, in the absence of a friend or neighbor to whom they can turn, to have a disinterested third power friend to assist and advise them, and they have always hoped that the U.S. would be willing to fill such a role. . . . The U.S. should accept the hand of friendship offered it by this small and independent nation. . . . This is an opportunity which should not be missed of establishing ourselves solidly in a strategic position in Asia. . . . Our interests in Afghanistan should increase, since negotiations are now under way to bring a number of American teachers and technical advisers, and many more are contemplated if all goes well.[10]

Shortly thereafter, the Roosevelt administration sanctioned resident diplomatic representation in Afghanistan.[11]

In July 1942, Cornelius Van H. Engert arrived as the first American minister to Afghanistan, with secret orders to lay groundwork for the establishment of an alternate lend-lease route to the Soviet Union and China. Plans called for the construction of a road through the Khyber and across the Hindu Kush. The British argued against the proposal for a number of reasons, including official government neutrality, unpredictable tribal behavior, and the limited amounts of aid that could be delivered given the effort required. Whether their points, Soviet objections, or the success of the other lend-lease routes dissuaded the Americans is not clear, but the plan was never implemented. Nor was Engert's suggestion to bolster Afghan morale by stationing a token force of U.S. bombers in Afghanistan.[12]

Engert clearly saw short- and long-term political advantages in providing continued assistance to Afghanistan. Not only would such aid assist the pro-Allied government, but furthermore, "by encouraging Afghanistan . . . to establish friendly commercial relations with the U.S. we would be preparing the ground for close ties with the United Nations not only at this date but after the war. . . . If we permit the Afghans to buy a few urgently needed supplies for their minimum legitimate requirements and if we give them a little shipping space for her Persian lamb the government would hail us as a true friend who had helped to free the country from the economic domination of the Axis."[13] Afghanistan's supply requirements, Engert continued, were not large, and American provisions would be a "small premium to insure against an annoying distraction while the war is still in progress and a focus of Muslim disaffection in the postwar period."[14]

Engert's duties eventually evolved into finding ways to provide civilian supplies to Afghanistan and shipping for exporting *karakul* hides and skins.[15] His ability to circumvent wartime restrictions and procure needed goods earned the United States much gratitude. The arrival of gasoline, textiles, tea, sugar, other essentials, along with industrial supplies and equipment not only helped prevent the average Afghan from falling to privation but also increased the strength and prestige of the government. By the end of the war, the Afghans were, according to Lancaster, "praising everything American."[16]

Engert commented often on the willingness of the Afghans to cooperate with the West. This stemmed from fears of the Soviet Union, which derived from Afghan experiences with the cynicism of Imperial Russian and Soviet diplomacy. Engert astutely concluded that "fear of Russia has dominated Afghan policy far more than fear of Britain and the British today are much less unpopular than the Soviets." Though some Afghan leaders felt that the damage incurred by Russia during the war would weaken it for some time, others became increasingly nervous as Soviet postwar territorial designs became evident. Engert ultimately concluded that "the Afghans are convinced that when the war is over Russia will demand substantial territorial concessions of her neighbors and that neither the US nor Great Britain will be able to stop her."[17] "The highest officials felt quite sincerely that . . . Afghanistan's only hope of escaping communism and of maintaining her independence lies in close friendship with Great Britain and the United States." "From the Afghan point of view," Engert concluded, "the US would be the ideal powerful friend to whom to cling."[18]

Engert clearly understood the politics of aid to Afghanistan. He was firmly convinced "that our present policy is laying a firm foundation for cordial postwar relations between the United States and Afghanistan in the general political sphere, as well as in economic and commercial fields." But if the results were to be lasting, Engert realized that generous policies must continue through the postwar period. He continued to call for support for "this small country, with [its] important geographic position and influence as an independent Islamic state.[19] He added, "With a view to further consolidate our gains it is essential to continue our present policy during the war period and subsequent period of reconstruction . . . I request the department of State, Washington and the future policy makers to take into consideration the fact that Afghanistan, besides being an important Muslim country, is also strategically important for the United States' policy in the Middle East." His correspondence sadly concludes with a prophetic fear that Afghanistan would be forgotten.[20]

In the immediate postwar period, Afghanistan looked to the United States for development and military assistance. The economic and military might of the United States, together with an apparent lack of colonial ambitions in Southwest Asia, made Washington, in Afghan eyes, an ideal counterweight to potential Soviet encroachment. Such sentiment created an opportunity for the establishment of economic and political links that could have permanently bound Afghanistan and the West. Throughout the late 1940s and 1950s, Afghan leaders repeatedly expressed desires for closer economic and military cooperation with the United States. American policies, however, inadvertently pushed Afghanistan toward rapprochement with the U.S.S.R.

By the end of the war, Afghanistan had accumulated a 20-million-dollar foreign exchange surplus, mostly from the sale of *karakul* skins and wool. In 1946 the Afghan regime allocated more than 17 million dollars to an agricultural development plan in the Helmand and Arghandab River Valleys. They hired the Morrison-Knudson Company of Boise, Idaho, to construct two dams and a series of canals and to train Afghan workers in maintenance and supply functions. The Helmand Valley Project, as this enterprise came to be known, hoped to revert the desolate southwest of Afghanistan into the granary it had been before the Mongol conquest.[21]

The plan was wildly overambitious. The engineering obstacles, formidable in themselves, were compounded by the difficulties of recruiting and training illiterate peasants in modern agricultural techniques, all in a largely untamed region, hundreds of miles from the center of government administration. Neither the Afghan government nor the American firm fully appreciated the administrative complexities inherent in the project.[22]

Within a few years, the original funds were exhausted, yet nearly all the construction work remained unfinished. Pakistan, in retaliation for Pushtunistan agitation, "bureaucratically hindered" the passage of supplies bound for Afghanistan. Strict allocations of admittedly limited transport allowed the Pakistanis to compound their exorbitant freight rates with high demurrage charges and effectively drain the Afghan treasury. Afghanistan's foreign exchange surplus disappeared into the hands of Morrison-Knudson and Pakistani "entrepreneurs."[23]

In 1949 Abdul Majid Zabuli, minister of the national economy, went to Washington with a 118-million-dollar comprehensive aid plan involving several distinct development projects. After considerable bureaucratic delays, the

Export-Import Bank approved a 21-million-dollar loan for use solely in conjunction with the Helmand Valley Project. Zabuli recommended refusing the loan. His superiors, while disappointed with the single loan and its high interest rate, wanted to establish close relations with the United States and saw no advantage in refusing acceptance.[24]

The project continued to encounter a multitude of problems. Land reclamation is difficult even with experienced farmers and modern technology, but Afghanistan possessed neither. Afghan plows were little more than "iron-pointed sticks . . . pulled by slow moving oxen." The farmers broadcast the seeds by hand. They did not practice effective crop rotation, and weed control was limited to an occasional assault with bare hands or a sickle. That same saw-toothed sickle, modeled upon "the flint sickle of Neolithic peoples living 12,000 years ago," was used to harvest.[25]

Technological deficiencies were in many ways less serious than social issues. The Afghan government had hoped to settle nomadic peoples on project lands, thereby easing tensions between those tribes and sedentary populations. The failure of these plans owed predominantly to lack of interest on the part of the nomads themselves. Few showed much enthusiasm or capability for adopting new technologies or lifestyles. In contrast to common stereotypes, most anthropologists and sociologists agree that nomadic peoples tend to be content with their lifestyle and are seldom interested in abandoning their wandering. This proved true in relatively poor Afghanistan, where nomads were often among the richer elements in society.[26]

When the failure of the nomadic experiment became evident, Afghan authorities began bringing in other settlers. The new arrivals, Turkish or Persian speakers from the Oxus Plain, often clashed with the established groups, who resented nomads and northerners alike. Entire villages, organized along tribal lines, kept to themselves, rejecting thought of regional cooperation. Scattered incidents of violence punctuated the general disharmony.[27]

Geological and geographical difficulties exacerbated the human problems. The target region was quite distant from the country's administrative and population centers. Communications were painfully slow, and initially there were no roads over which to bring in supplies or export the produce. The dams held more water than could be effectively used, and there were no local markets for their electricity. Weeds quickly infested the canals, and silt clogged the dam feeders. Understaffed Afghan maintenance crews, who possessed but "two flat-bed trucks, one jeep station-wagon and one universal jeep, and an assortment of hand tools," could not maintain free channels. The soil itself, rarely abetted by rain, scorched by high summer temperatures, and almost devoid of plant nutrients owing to centuries of abuse and neglect, offered little potential to sustain even limited quantities of crops.[28]

The worst tactical obstacle was not discovered until well after the project commenced. Over one third of the target lands were contaminated with salts and alkaline agents, which directly interfere with the germination and growth of most crops. While such soils can be reclaimed, the processes involved are expensive and time consuming. Given the poor drainage of the region, which threatened to exacerbate costs, and the financial constraints of the Afghan government, such reclamation was unfeasible.[29]

Afghanistan also suffered from an absence of central financial planning. The establishment of a Helmand Valley Authority in 1952, with Cabinet status accorded its president, eased the problems somewhat, but even then the organization was not authorized for nor capable of providing credit to the settlers. Afghanistan's banks remained aloof from the project through 1956, advancing "no credit which directly benefits agriculture in the Helmand Valley."[30]

The American bureaucracy, lacking the comprehensive foreign assistance agencies it has since developed, also contributed to the confusion. Misunderstandings arose between Morrison-Knudson, the Export-Import Bank, and the Afghan government as well as between the headquarters and field representatives of the company. For example, though the loan was approved in November 1949, delays postponed the receipt of disbursements until March 1951. In the interim, the bank eliminated incentive bonuses previously awarded the company, and Morrison-Knudson in turn curtailed the pace of the project.[31]

In refusing to finance any industrial projects, the Export-Import Bank ultimately crippled Afghan supporters of private enterprise. According to Afghan development plans, private investment in textiles, cement, and power development was to receive some 6 million dollars' worth of assistance. Increased competition and lessened global demand for *karakul*, however, caused government income to plummet. With continued American assistance dependent on matching contributions from Kabul, the growth of indigenous industries fell off rapidly. Private investors thus became critical of the Helmand Valley Project, and the United States found itself supporting statists against those who favored free trade.[32]

Assistance to fledgling cottage industries would have gained favorable recognition for the United States, while giving the Afghans experience in planning, organization, and administration. Yet bank decisions remained governed by standard fiscal policy, which made little reference to the political consequences of such action. While the bank justified its position, citing concern with local food supply, other sources claim Morrison-Knudson used its considerable political influence to secure its own profits. Instead of improving relations, the exclusive support given the company created the impression among many leading Afghans that the U.S. government was concerned only with ensuring the profits of American businesses.[33]

Like the bank, Morrison-Knudson was guided more by profit motive than any desire for harmonious political relations with Afghanistan. Though company technicians occasionally raised doubts concerning the ability of the government of Afghanistan to carry out some of the required work, they "never advised against a construction project to which they were assigned, resulting in some malinvestments from a technological point of view." The company also failed to introduce its employees to Afghan traditions and did not establish contacts among those Afghans who could have assisted in the implementation of the project. To neutral observers, company technicians and administrators often seemed as bewildered by their environment as by the challenges of the project itself. Many flaunted their high salaries and standards of living, while a few engaged in alcohol-induced philandering that inflamed Afghan sensibilities. Others simply isolated themselves behind the high walls of the company compound, a veritable "America-in-Asia." Few remained in Afghanistan long enough to establish lasting partnerships.[34]

The Helmand Valley Project lasted well into the 1970s, consuming vast quantities of Afghan and American money, without producing many tangible results. Both sides at times considered abandoning the project, blaming the other for its failure. Both instead sent more capital chasing the initial investment, while other sectors of the Afghan economy languished. The project's failure played no small role in the eventual Afghan decision to accept large quantities of Soviet aid.[35]

The Truman administration experienced a similar lack of success in attempting to resolve the Pushtunistan dispute. Officially Afghanistan welcomed the new state of Pakistan. The intensity of Pushtunistan propaganda abated through the fall of 1947, though it never ceased entirely. In November, the Afghan government sent Najibullah Khan to Pakistan for a series of talks. Though initially cordial, the talks failed to achieve a compromise. Upon his return to Kabul, Najibullah made a speech demanding that Pakistan designate the tribal areas a "sovereign province" and grant a "free Afghan import zone" in Karachi, if not an actual land corridor through Baluchistan. A virtual trade war ensued. Afghanistan subsequently voted against Pakistani admittance to the United Nations but later withdrew the negative vote, formally recognized Pakistan in early 1948, and sent Wali Khan to Karachi as ambassador.[36]

In early 1949, the frontier ministry cracked down on Pushtunistan agitation and arrested over 350 frontier leaders. Ghaffar Khan, who had repeatedly labeled the Pakistan government an irreligious British puppet, was sent with his son, Wali, to spend five more years in prison in Baluchistan. His arrest, however, increased the popularity of the Pushtunistan idea and fueled renewed disturbances.[37]

Following Ghaffar Khan's arrest, Afghanistan recalled its ambassador and abandoned negotiations in favor of a propaganda campaign in support of a free Pushtunistan. In July, a *Loya Jirgah* formally abrogated the Durand Line agreement and declared all treaties with the British null and void. The following month, a tribal *jirgah* passed the "Tirah Bagh" resolution, which declared an independent Pushtunistan with the *faqir* of Ipi as its president.

Border incidents continued to increase into 1950, prompting Pakistan to implement a de facto blockade of Afghanistan.[38]

The blockade brought construction in the Helmand Valley to a standstill, prompting an American mediation effort. On November 6, 1950, Ely Palmer, then U.S. ambassador to Afghanistan, proposed a meeting of Pakistani and Afghan officials. Palmer presented a list of four general guidelines for the meeting, which stated no more than that both sides should approach the talks without a set agenda. The Afghans accepted the proposal immediately, but after a five-month delay, "the Pakistanis gave us [the U.S.] a flat rejection and were extremely resentful of what they considered to be our gratuitous intervention."[39] Pakistan clearly regarded any negotiations as mere encouragement for Afghan agitation and expected the United States simply to acknowledge the Durand Line as an international frontier, as the British had previously done.

Following the rejection, Afghanistan again withdrew its ambassador from Pakistan. Despite economic hardships that accompanied continued hostility, the Afghan regime, fearing that abandonment of the Pushtunistan issue would result in a serious loss of face, refused to re-establish diplomatic relations until Pakistan accepted Palmer's "November proposal." They continued to argue that American pressure on Pakistan would force that nation to agree to a face-saving solution acceptable to both sides.[40]

Following Palmer's retirement, the chargé d'affaires in Kabul, John Evarts Horner, informed Afghan Minister of Foreign Affairs Mohammed Ali that the United States considered the November plan a "dead issue." Horner derided the Pushtunistan argument, citing economic and political inviability, the lack of ethnic consistency in the Afghan position, and the danger of Soviet counterclaims on northern Afghanistan. Yet Horner still thought the United States should attempt to solve the problem. He believed the Afghans sincerely desired a way out of the conflict and feared that the Soviets might attempt to exploit disenchanted elements if Pushtunistan were simply shelved. He thought a face-saving solution possible, given Pakistani assurance of continued cultural autonomy. He suggested the formation of a joint commission on tribal welfare, stressing how American financial assistance would increase the attraction of a binational body devoted to development.[41]

Officials within the State Department's Office of South Asian Affairs similarly deemed the Afghan position unreasonable but eschewed the idea of renewed negotiations. Fearful of being "stuck in the middle again," they deemed it inadvisable to broach the matter with Pakistan. The United States repeatedly pressured Afghanistan to reopen diplomatic relations with Pakistan as a sign of sincere desire for rapprochement, implying that they should completely drop their Pushtunistan demands.[42]

The Afghans attempted bilateral negotiation but ran afoul of Pakistani obduracy. In what might have been a favorable turn, former Prime Minister Hashim Khan "accepted an invitation extended by [Pakistan] to stop in Karachi for discussions." Yet, upon his arrival, no officials met him. The foreign minister was at the United Nations, the prime minister was in London, and the governor-general had gone to Lahore. Though some Americans criticized such "dilatory tactics," most echoed the new ambassador to Afghanistan, Angus Ward, who, despite these efforts, saw no indication of genuine Afghan interest in a settlement and little advantage in American involvement.[43]

Some American officials even tried to disarm the issue by putting Pakistan on the offensive. Donald Kennedy, the director of the Office of South Asian Affairs, suggested to the Pakistani ambassador to the United States that his government draft a text that read: "Pakistan is agreeable to discussing with Afghanistan through diplomatic channels the welfare of the Pushtu-speaking people on both sides of the frontier." Henry Byroade passed on similar ideas to other Pakistani officials. Pakistan did not immediately follow through on this idea but issued a similar version in 1953. Curiously, when the Afghans surprisingly agreed to include all Pushtuns in a proposed plebiscite, the State Department, while still critical of the "apparent contradictions" of the Afghan position, suddenly found the approach filled with "inherent dangers," including the possibility of an unfavorable outcome for Pakistan.[44]

In August 1952, the Soviet chargé d'affaires issued the Kabul regime a *demarche* against the use of French technicians (under U.N. auspices) on oil-drilling operations in north Afghanistan. It read in part: "Oil exploration and exploitation in areas of Afghanistan bordering on the Soviet Union, by foreign firms and specialists belonging to the aggressive North Atlantic bloc . . . might endanger the frontiers of the USSR and might do damage to the good neighborly relations existing between the USSR and Afghanistan."[45]

The *demarche* left the Afghan government on the horns of a dilemma. North Afghanistan harbored the bulk of the country's resources, and to leave it to Soviet whims would invite economic stagnation and political risks. Even Najibullah Khan, Afghan ambassador to India and heretofore one of the most vocal champions of Pushtunistan, saw coming to terms with Pakistan as an escape and thought this possible with "a little assistance from the US." Some Americans, including Ambassador to India Chester Bowles, also thought the Soviet action presented an opportunity to ease Afghan relations with Pakistan. Horner agreed that some "workable and face-saving compromise, if combined with assurances of Pak[istani] moral or military support," would have a good chance of solving the problem and avoid the tantamount surrender of north Afghanistan. He added: "US positive pressure on Pakistan . . . could well result in an acceptable solution."[46]

After consultation with British officials, however, Secretary of State Dean Acheson concluded that "when considered in historical perspective," the *demarche* "does not pose any substantially new political problem" or forecast any immediate threat to Afghanistan. He felt the Afghans were simply using it "for what it was worth," in an effort to achieve increased economic and military assistance and to obtain Western pressure for a Pushtunistan settlement. He cited Afghanistan's refusal to send an ambassador to Karachi as an indication of Kabul's lack of concern and sincerity. Deeming Afghan fears exaggerated, he suggested continuing U.N. operations unabated.[47]

Horner's blunt reply countered Acheson's notion that the Afghans were attempting to capitalize on the *demarche*. He noted that the Afghans had already delivered a firm negative response to the Soviets before informing the American embassy and had so far requested only economic and moral support. He went on to blast the State Department, claiming it "seriously underestimates . . . [the] potentialities [of] Sov[iet] pressure on this country, and utterly neglects regional aspects." Delivering Acheson's negative messages, Horner argued, would alienate pro-American elements, strengthen the position of those who wish to accommodate the Soviets, and "cause Afghans of all persuasions to think that we regard this country of negligible importance to our effort to stem [the] flood of Sov[iet] aggression." Such would constitute a "serious blow to US policy objectives in this area."[48]

Department officials in Washington remained unconvinced of the seriousness of the immediate crisis, continued to argue that the Afghans were using the *demarche* for their own benefit, and made no change in policy. They ruled out increased assistance as unproductive and impossible anyway, given present appropriations. There would be no change in American policy in the wake of the *demarche*. The Afghans felt obliged to suspend drilling operations and bar all nationals of NATO countries from the northern provinces. Prospecting would not resume until 1957, when Daoud would grant the Soviets drilling and exploitation rights.[49]

The Truman administration demonstrated similar disinterest in supplying the Afghan armed forces. Afghan officials had requested American military assistance as early as 1942, when the foreign minister suggested to the American military attaché that, as the Japanese were about to overrun India, the United States should supply lend-lease weapons to Afghanistan. He claimed Afghanistan "would make any return which America would require of her." He added that postwar Afghanistan, if left unarmed, "would be at the mercy of the Russians, the indigenous government of India being no effective counterpoise to inevitable Russian designs on the integrity of Afghanistan."[50]

That same year, an Office of Strategic Services survey team concluded a report on Afghanistan. While the survey noted that Afghanistan had a favorable attitude toward the West and acknowledged the stamina of the populace and their skill at guerrilla warfare, they concluded that the Afghans were "poor material for a disciplined army." Afghanistan also had few strategic resources to offer the United States. There were no railroads or asphalt roads, and her airports were "little more than cleared fields." There were no major industries, few skilled laborers, and no minerals of vital importance. The government, the survey concluded, was as ineffectual as it had been in the nineteenth century. It governed people infested with trachoma, intestinal ailments, and an assortment of other vile diseases, from a capital with excrement-laden water flowing through the streets.[51]

After consultation with British officials, the United States declined to offer military hardware to Afghanistan and similarly rejected subsequent Afghan solicitations. Though the American legation favored a joint Anglo-American guarantee of Afghan independence and the military attaché encouraged discussion of supply of Afghanistan's postwar military needs, Afghanistan's apparent lack of strategic value prompted dismissal of these ideas. Similar conclusions would preclude closer relations between the United States and Afghanistan throughout the 1950s.[52]

During his trip to Washington, Zabuli requested political, economic, cultural, educational, technical, and military assistance. Zabuli stressed that "Afghanistan urgently wants US arms to maintain internal security . . . [and] to make a positive contribution in the event there is war with the Soviets." He promised a delaying action in the Hindu Kush, which would assist Western forces in Pakistan and India.[53] "For such purposes, no large amount of expensive equipment is required. Compared with assistance the US had extended on a world wide scale," Zabuli continued, "Afghanistan's requirements are microscopic." When war came, "Afghanistan would of course be overrun and occupied," but the Russians would be unable to pacify the country. "Afghanistan could and would pursue guerilla tactics for an infinite period." Zabuli also indicated "that a regional pact among Turkey, Iran, Afghanistan and Pakistan was a reasonable possibility. If US assistance were extended to include the countries in this arc, it would cost relatively little now to create a Muslim cordon which would be a considerable factor in any future struggle with Soviet Russia." [54] The American response was noncommittal.

Certain officials within the Truman administration noted Afghanistan's strategic importance and argued for measures to protect it from Soviet encroachment. Officials at the Kabul Embassy recommended arms sales to Afghanistan "to exclude Soviet influence, cement Afghan-American friendship, maintain internal security and promote settlement of differences with Pakistan."[55] The American army attaché in Kabul favored similar measures. Though he duly noted that the Afghan army was ill equipped and the troops suffered from a lack of education, he nonetheless recommended that the United States strive to make the army an effective guerrilla force, by supplying it with field telephones, bazookas, mortars, scout cars, and similar second-line equipment not required in Korea or Europe. The attaché suggested that such supplies, coupled with an economic assistance program, "might be made a conduit for dropping the Pushtunistan propaganda." Even Lancaster, in the wake of his plan's collapse, suggested the Americans supply vehicles, signal and engineering equipment, and "possibly a few planes."[56]

Most American officials, however, opposed extensive military involvement in Afghanistan. In general, the State Department regarded Afghanistan as politically unstable, militarily weak, devoid of economic potential, and of little global importance. The National Security Council concluded that with defense emphasis still on the rebuilding of Western Europe, arms aid to Afghanistan was not essential. They considered a Soviet invasion of Afghanistan unlikely, arguing that nation's meager resources would not be worth the effort of attack. Furthermore, the National Security Council had "little doubt that Afghanistan could be conquered regardless of its will to resist." Given urgent defense needs elsewhere and the Afghan attitude on Pushtunistan, Afghanistan's priority for arms and equipment remained very low indeed.[57]

Thus, while an arms sale was approved in 1951, the agreement contained so many catches as to render it inoperative. The United States required the Afghans to pay full price for all equipment, and in cash, which was impossible since most of their foreign exchange was tied up in the Helmand Valley Project. Furthermore, the United States left the Afghans to arrange transit through Pakistan. Even if Kabul had produced the needed funds, the Pakistanis would never have assisted in such a venture for fear that the weapons would fall into the hands of the tribes. The Americans did not even agree to provide training, and, as if to add insult to injury, the telegram that authorized the sale chastised the Afghan position on Pushtunistan as ill conceived and destabilizing to the entire area. The Afghan leadership regarded the American offer as a "political refusal." The Americans met subsequent requests for grant aid, or at least liberal credit terms, with the response that no weapons were available owing to other global commitments and would involve special obligations and necessary authorization by Congress.[58]

While the Afghan government admitted that a Soviet thrust in their direction was unlikely and conceded that they could not halt a determined Soviet attack, they still argued that Afghanistan should at least "be in a position to put down any internal uprisings financed or aided by the Soviets."[59] The Afghans continued to request arms assistance, and while discussions of a Middle East Defense Organization (MEDO) circulated, Afghan officials and newspapers indicated interested in alliance membership. In response to Soviet denunciations of the proposed agreement, Deputy Foreign Minister Mohammed Aziz stated that since MEDO would be a defensive arrangement, his government would not be barred from membership owing to the 1931 treaty of nonaggression with the U.S.S.R. Such suggestions prompted Horner to confide to British Ambassador W.B.J. Ledwidge his fears that Afghanistan would request MEDO membership in expectation of an Anglo-American guarantee of its northern border. While Horner saw Pakistan as a valuable addition to MEDO, Afghanistan, subject to Soviet pressure, seemed only a liability. Ledwidge agreed that the "interests of Middle East defense would at present be better served by maintaining Afghanistan as an island of neutrality than by seeking to enlist her on our side." He believed that fear of Russian pressure would likely keep Afghanistan aloof, and if not, Afghanistan still could not join without agreeing to a frontier settlement. But while there seemed no logic in inviting Afghanistan to join MEDO, Ledwidge still saw reason to make some sort of provision for Afghanistan. He dismissed the American notion that Afghanistan was "worse than useless," claiming them formidable opponents on their own ground—"witness our experiences." He believed the Afghan army and tribes could tie up two to six divisions in a guerrilla war, harass supply lines, and deny the Soviets use of any bases within Afghanistan. But while Ledwidge supported actions that would demonstrate that the "Western powers [were] not completely forgetful of the existence of Afghanistan," he thought potential Afghan objections "not of significant consequence" as to interfere with "so important an aim as securing the adhesion of Pakistan to MEDO." Ward would subsequently concur that Afghan concerns could be readily dismissed and American policy would "be best served by inclusion [of] Pakistan into MEDO nonetheless." Not only would Pakistan prove a valuable ally, Ward argued, but the Afghans would be forced to abandon their Pushtunistan plans.[60]

The Truman administration left office with the Helmand Valley Project on the road to ruin. Though hardly the singular failing of Washington, the project's continued difficulties still damaged relations. The administration also did little to diminish the Pushtunistan problem. Finally, American policymakers indicated profound disinterest in the Afghan military and indirectly in the strategic interests of Afghanistan. Assistance could have improved internal security and strengthened bilateral relations, but views of Afghanistan as worthless and insignificant precluded cooperation. The Afghans would soon find a similar lack of interest within the Eisenhower administration, which the latter's courting of Pakistan would only exacerbate.[61]

NOTES

1. Harding to King Amanullah, 29 July 1921, *FRUS*, 1921, vol.1, p. 261. Wali Khan was the emissary.

2. Secretary of State (Hughes) to Harding, 18 and 21 July 1921 *FRUS*, 1921, vol. 1, pp. 258–260; Secretary of State to Engert (Ambassador in Iran), 25 August 1921, p. 262; Nadir Khan to Merrick (Ambassador in France), 30 October 1925, *FRUS*, 1926, vol.1, pp. 557–558; Dawes (Ambassador to London) to Secretary of State, 15 April 1931, *FRUS*, 1931, vol. 1, p. 825; Memorandum by Wallace Murray, July 27, 1937, *FRUS*, pp. 607–609. For one example, when Amanullah visited Europe in 1928, he hoped to visit the United States. American officials declined his visit, greatly insulting the king. See Poullada, *Kingdom of Afghanistan,* pp. 46–48.

3. Quoted in Poullada, "Afghanistan and the United States," p. 179; Adamec, *Afghanistan's Foreign Affairs,* pp. 235–236, 302fn. Poullada described Murray as "an adroit and influential bureaucrat who had never been near Afghanistan but had accumulated a vast store of misinformation and bias concerning that country." For examples of earlier American contacts with Afghanistan, see Poullada, *Kingdom of Afghanistan,* pp. 9–20. See also Sir Maurice Peterson ("Conversation with Mr. Wallace Murray Regarding the Middle East," 11 April 1944, L/P&S/12/4626) as a demon-

stration of Murray's prejudice and tendency toward overgeneralizations. The British nonetheless tended to like Murray, as he agreed to formulate Middle East policy in almost complete agreement with them.

4. Acting Secretary of State to Roosevelt, 21 August 1934, *FRUS*, vol. 2, 1934, pp. 747–750. For its part, the American military thought occupation of Afghanistan of direct concern to the U.K. and Russia only. See Report of Committee No. 7, Military Geography Conference, 30 September 1930, G-3 Course No. 15, U.S. Army Military History Institute, pp. 373–377.

5. Acting Secretary of State to FDR, 21 August 1934.

6. Haggling over the details of the friendship treaty delayed the actual signing of the agreement until March 26, 1936. Strauss (Ambassador to France) to the Secretary of State, 26 March 1936, *FRUS*, vol. III, p. 7.

7. Chargé in Iran (Engert) to Secretary of State, 21 June 1938, *FRUS*, p. 756; Murray to Dreyfus (Ambassador in Tehran), 28 January 1941, *FRUS*, vol. III, pp. 255–258; Murray to the Under Secretary of State (Welles), 21 October 1937, *FRUS*, pp. 611–613; Fox, *Travels in Afghanistan*, pp. xvi–xviii. Fox was a geologist on the project.

8. Memo by Chief of Division of Near Eastern Affairs (Murray), 22 June 1937, *FRUS*, pp. 605–606.

9. Memo by Murray, 27 July 1937, Ibid., pp. 607–609.

10. Dreyfus to the Secretary of State, 27 June 1941, *FRUS*, 1941, vol. III, pp. 258–259. He further noted that Afghanistan had never been a European colony, which left no banks, oil companies, or other foreign influences present to manipulate the economy and arouse popular dissent.

11. Ibid., pp. 259–263; Wilber, *Afghanistan*, p. 174.

12. Engert to Secretary of State, 7 August 1942, *FRUS*, p. 54. The Legation opened June 6, 1942. Engert arrived in July. Engert had visited Afghanistan in 1922, and composed "the authoritative handbook on that country."

13. Engert to Secretary of State, 27 January 1943, *FRUS*, 1943, vol. IV, pp. 20–21.

14. Ibid., 25 August 1944, *FRUS*, 1944, vol. V, pp. 48–50.

15. Ibid., 5 August 1943, *FRUS*, 1942, vol. IV, pp. 53–54; Thyes to Secretary of State, 6 June 1942, *FRUS*, 1942, vol. IV, p. 50; Secretary of State to US Representative in India (Phillips) 28 January 1943, and Phillips to Secretary of State, 16 January 1943, vol. I, pp. 616–618; Assistant Chief of the Division of Defense Materials (Livingston Merchant) to the Second Secretary of the British Embassy (Dent), 16 November 1942, *FRUS*, vol. IV, pp. 58–59.

16. See file L/P&S/12/4621, generally; see also Poullada, "Afghanistan and the United States," p. 181, citing an interview with Engert; Memorandum of Conversation by Richard S. Leach of the Division of South Asian Affairs, 8 December 1948, *FRUS*, V, 1948, pp. 492–493; *Afghanistan Today*, 14–17 August 1946, L/P&S/12/1582, ff. 11–14; Weekly Intelligence Report, Military Attaché in Kabul, 2 August 1946, 6 September 1946, 9 November 1946, and 29 November 1946, L/P&S/12/1849. The Afghan government even scheduled an exhibition baseball game and declared it would ban the production of opium (Ma'aroof, *Afghanistan*, p. 102).

17. Engert to Secretary of State, 29 April 1943, *FRUS*, 1943, vol. IV, pp. 22–23; 16 August 1942, *FRUS*, 1942, vol. IV, pp. 54–57.

18. Engert to Secretary of State, 6 November 1943, *FRUS*, 1943, vol. IV, pp. 31–32; 16 May 1943, *FRUS*, 1943, vol. IV, p. 25; , 22 November 1943, *FRUS*, 1943,

vol. IV, pp. 32–34. "Afghanistan is ready to exercise a stabilizing influence in Central Asia and on the northwest frontier of India provided only that she can be reasonably certain that she will not be ground between the upper and nether millstones of rival powers struggling for supremacy."

19. Ibid., 11 November 1944, pp. 53–54.

20. Ibid., vol. 1, pp. 54–63.

21. Tudor Engineering Company, *Report on Development of the Helmand Valley* (Washington, D.C., 1956), pp. 16–17, 49 (*Tudor Report*); Newell, *Politics of Afghanistan*, p. 120; Franck, *Afghanistan between East and West*, pp. 3, 36; Griffiths, *Afghanistan*, p. 129; Collins, *Soviet Invasion of Afghanistan*, p. 18.

22. Newell, *Politics of Afghanistan*, pp. 120–121; Dupree, *Afghanistan*, p. 483; *Tudor Report*, p. 25; Fletcher, *Afghanistan*, pp. 243, 309fn. Fletcher believes the idea probably originated with Afghan engineering students who returned from the U.S.A. impressed with the success of the Tennessee Valley Authority.

23. Dupree, *Afghanistan*, pp. 433–484; Memorandum by the Deputy Assistant Secretary of State for Near Eastern, South Asian, and African Affairs to the Acting Deputy Under Secretary of State, 5 November 1954, *FRUS*, 1952–1954, XI, p. 1429. Border closures hit Afghanistan especially hard, as a large percentage of its revenue came from customs duties. Memorandum of Discussion between Abdul Majid and Mr. F.H. Nixon, 12–13 November 1937, L/P&S/12/1727, ff. 47–49; Military Attaché in Kabul, Weekly Intelligence Summary, 26 April 1947 and 17 May 1947, L/P&S/12/1849; Memorandum of Conversation, Leach with Abdul Hal Aziz of the Afghan Economic Mission, 11 February 1949, *FRUS*, 1949, pp. 1777–1778; Razamani, *Northern Tier*, pp. 125–126. Shipments of petroleum products were delayed, technically because Afghan trucks did not meet Pakistani regulations. For 20 million dollars, Afghanistan has gotten only "one short road, one diversion dam and one incomplete canal." Criticism of Morrison-Knudson and of the United States in general became widespread.

24. Memorandum of Conversation, Leach with Abdul Hal Aziz of the Afghan Economic Mission, 11 February 1949, *FRUS*, 1949, pp. 1777–1778. Zabuli submitted his report to the Export-Import Bank on March 21, 1949, and a formal application August 15. The loan was approved November 23 (p. 1779fn). Fraser-Tytler to the Foreign Office, 27 November 1937, L/P&S/12/1683, ff. 22–23; Wilber, *Afghanistan*, pp. 145–146; see L/P&S/12/1747 generally; Franck, *Afghanistan between East and West*, pp. 38–40. Franck questions whether the plan was realistically assessed. Poullada, "Afghanistan and the United States," pp. 181–182. Poullada calls it balanced and integrated and claims the bank did not fully appreciate it, development plans not yet being the style.

25. *Tudor Report*, pp. 40–42, 44, 105.

26. Fletcher, *Afghanistan*, p. 284; Griffiths, *Afghanistan*, pp. 91–93; Dupree, *Afghanistan*, pp. 502–504. Nomads have always tended to avoid contact with government authorities, fearing taxation and conscription. According to Dupree, some were brought in only through military force. He rightly questions why no one remembered similar failed efforts by Iran in the 1930s or the Soviets in Central Asia.

27. *Tudor Report*, pp. 90, 93, 105; Griffiths, *Afghanistan*, pp. 127–133. Griffiths further argues that the illiterate and ill-disciplined Afghan peasants, plagued with a "fatalistic satisfaction with the status quo" and trapped in a subsistence economy that

discouraged savings, did not really put forth the effort to improve their lot. Their unfamiliarity with modern equipment, plus their relatively small land holdings, discouraged purchase and use of heavy equipment, and much of what was sent went to waste.

28. *Tudor Report,* pp. 27–28, 32, 43, 75, 93, 98, 115, 126, 130; Memorandum of Discussion at the 228th meeting of the National Security Council, 9 December 1954, *FRUS,* 1952–1954, XI, p. 1150; Dupree, *Afghanistan,* pp. 484, 502, 504.

29. Fletcher, *Afghanistan,* p. 268; *Tudor Report,* pp. 27–29, 32–35.

30. *Tudor Report,* pp. 112–113, 117.

31. Dupree, *Afghanistan,* pp. 483–484; Franck, *Afghanistan between East and West,* pp. 40–41, 46–47. Morrison-Knudson again curtailed activity owing to shortages of funds in late 1953.

32. National Intelligence Estimate NIE-53–54, "Outlook for Afghanistan," 19 October 1954, *FRUS,* 1952–1954, XI, pp. 1488–1490; Memorandum by N.H. Kirk of the Investment and Development Staff to the Chief of the Investment and Development Staff (Ross), 11 August 1953, *FRUS,* 1952–1954, XI, p. 1467; see also Griffiths, *Afghanistan,* p. 136; Franck, *Afghanistan between East and West,* p. 48.

33. Franck, *Afghanistan between East and West,* pp. 49–51, 73–74; Memorandum of Conversation by the Acting Officer in Charge of Pakistan-Afghanistan Affairs (Thatcher), 8 October 1954, *FRUS,* 1952–1954, XI, p. 1422; Poullada, "Afghanistan and the United States," p. 182; Memorandum by N.H. Kirk of the Investment and Development Staff to the Chief of the Investment and Development Staff (Ross), 11 August 1953, *FRUS,* 1952–1954, XI, pp. 1368–1370. The bank remained of the attitude that as long as the Afghan government was willing to borrow, grant aid was "a somewhat incongruous possibility."

34. Grey to Squire, 5 July 1948, FO 983/13; Squire to Bevin, 24 May 1947, L/P&S/12/1801, ff. 22–25; Lancaster, Weekly Intelligence Report, 2 August 1946 and 9 November 1946, L/P&S/12/1849; Memorandum by N.H. Kirk of the Investment and Development Staff to the Chief of the Investment and Development Staff (Ross), 11 August 1953, *FRUS,* 1952–1954, XI, p. 1368. Morrison-Knudson admittedly had difficulty finding quality employees who were willing to work in Afghanistan. Fletcher, *Afghanistan,* p. 263; Toynbee, *Between Oxus and Jumna,* pp. 67–8; Griffiths, *Afghanistan,* pp. 142–143; Franck, *Afghanistan between East and West,* pp. 38, 50, 71–72; Dupree, *Afghanistan,* pp. 500–501. Dupree claims that when he asked employees who would prepare villagers for the influx of water, responses ranged from "Who cares?" to "That is the business of the Afghan government."

35. Memorandum by N.H. Kirk of the Investment and Development Staff to the Chief of the Investment and Development Staff (Ross), 11 August 1953, *FRUS,* 1952–1954, XI, pp. 1368–1370. "There was considerable danger that the Helmand Valley project would fail completely because of the inability of the Afghans to solve institutional and human problems." Assistant Director of the Export Import Bank (Arey) to the Secretary of the National Advisory Council on International Monetary and Financial Problems (Glendenning), Ibid., 19 April 1954, pp. 1472–1473. Ward favored continuing the project, warning the "failure of the project . . . would be a severe blow to American prestige . . . in this part of the world." Squire to Grey, 2 November 1948, L/P&S/12/1678, f. 4; Extract from a letter by Squire, recipient unknown, 10 April 1947, L/P&S/12/1811, f. 189. Morrison-Knudson "did not want to

scrap the whole scheme and admit past mistakes but it would be greater folly to go on with it." Squire noted many Afghans also desired to terminate the contract but did not do so fearing a loss of future funding.

36. Squire to Bevin, 3 April 1948, FO 983/3; Translation of *Islah,* 12 October 1947, R/12/178, ff. 183–185; Squire to Bevin, 29 November 1947, R/12/178, ff. 206–207; Squire to Bevin, 10 January 1948, L/P&S/12/1812, f. 58; Telegram from the Commonwealth Relations Office, 17 January 1948, L/P&S/12/1812, f. 74; Military Attaché's Summary of Intelligence for the Weeks Ending 23 August 1947, 15 November 1947, and 13 December 1947, L/P&S/12/1850. Squire claimed that Pakistan was willing to concede three points to Afghanistan, including recognition of the "separate identity of [North West Frontier]," renaming the province, and a free zone in Karachi (the latter was conceded by the government of India many years previously). Qureshi, *Anglo-Pakistan Relations,* p. 192; Fraser-Tytler, *Afghanistan,* p. 308; Quddus, *Afghanistan and Pakistan,* p. 100 ; Adamec, *Afghanistan's Foreign Affairs,* p. 264; Kaur, *Pak-Afghanistan Relations,* p. 70fn). British authorities, meanwhile, continued to refuse Afghan requests for Pushtunistan mediation.

37. Sayeed, *Pakistan, the Formative Phase,* pp. 244–245, 273–274; Fletcher, *Afghanistan,* p. 254; Symonds, *Making of Pakistan,* p. 123; Tabibi, "Aftermath Created by British Policy," pp. 106–108; Dupree, *Afghanistan,* p. 492; Schofield, *Every Rock,* p. 249; Indian Council of World Affairs, *Defense and Security,* p. 92; Dupree, "Durand Agreement of 1893," *Current Problems in Afghanistan,* p. 87. Reported executions of other Pushtun nationalists further aroused frontier sentiments.

38. "Possibility of War between Pakistan and Afghanistan," 11 August 1949, J.I.C. (49)57, L/WS/1/1169, ff. 4–20; Griffiths, *Afghanistan,* p. 65; Tabibi, "Aftermath Created by British Policy," p. 73; Dupree, *Afghanistan,* pp. 491–493; Fletcher, *Afghanistan,* p. 256. In June, Pakistani planes mistakenly bombed the village of Moghulgai on the Afghan side of the border. Though Pakistan blamed pilot error and offered compensation, the Afghans rejected the recompense, noting with some justification that the explanation was an interesting commentary on Pakistani relations with its citizens.

39. Memorandum of Conversation by the Deputy Assistant Secretary of State for Near Eastern, South Asian, and African Affairs (Jernegan), *FRUS,* 1952–1954, XI, p. 1380; *FRUS,* 1950, V, 1457; *FRUS,* 1951, VI, pp. 1938–1942; *FRUS,* 1951, VI, p. 1959; *FRUS,* VI, 1962–1963, 1983; Caroe, *Pathans,* p. 465. Palmer had been appointed ambassador in late 1948 (*Department of State Bulletin,* December 12, 1948). Earlier Washington had suggested the formation of a joint Afghan-Pakistani commission to sort out mutual differences.

40. Horner to the Department of State, 7 July 1952, *FRUS,* 1952–1954, XI, p. 1367; Memorandum of Conversation by the Acting Secretary of State, *FRUS,* 1952–1954, 24 October 1952, pp. 1377–1378; Ambassador in Afghanistan (Ward) to the Department of State, 13 November 1952, *FRUS,* 1952–1954, pp. 1380–1382; Horner to the Department of State, Foreign Service Dispatch #400, 789.00/6–1951.

41. Memorandum of Conversation by Horner, 2 January 1952, *FRUS,* 1952–1954, XI, p. 1366; Memorandum, by Horner, 31 May 1951, 789.00/5–3151; Horner to the Department of State, 9 September 1952, *FRUS,* 1952–1954, XI, p. 1449; Horner to the Department of State, 7 July 1952, 9 September 1952, *FRUS,* 1952–1954, XI, pp. 1367–1368; Horner to the Department of State, 16 September 1952, *FRUS,* 1952–1954, XI, p. 1452.

42. Memorandum by Jernegan to the Under Secretary of State (Bruce), 4 November 1952, *FRUS,* 1952–1954, XI, p. 1380; Director of the Office of South Asian Affairs (Kennedy) to the Ambassador in Turkey (McGhee), 7 January 1953, *FRUS,* 1952–1954, XI, p. 1386; Secretary of State to the Embassy in India, 6 October 1952, *FRUS,* 1952–1954, XI, p. 1375. According to Fletcher (*Afghanistan,* p. 256), the United States suggested the offices of Egypt or Turkey.

43. Memorandum of Conversation by Horner, 7 July 1952, *FRUS,* 1952–1954, XI, p. 1366; Memorandum of Conversation by Byroade, 12 February 1953, *FRUS,* 1952–1954, XI, p. 1390; Ambassador in Afghanistan (Ward) to the Department of State, 14 February 1953, *FRUS,* 1952–1954, XI, p. 1491. The Afghans also requested Saudi support to no avail. Even Acheson admitted the Pakistanis were being intransigent. Zabuli and Naim were among those who participated in fruitless discussion with Pakistani officials.

44. Memorandum of Conversation by the Director of the Office of South Asian Affairs (Kennedy), 5 December 1952, *FRUS,* 1952–1954, pp. 1383–1384; Memorandum of Conversation by the Counselor of the Embassy in Pakistan (Emerson), 5 October 1954, *FRUS,* 1952–1954, p. 1418.

45. Cited in Horner to the Department of State, 9 September 1942, *FRUS,* 1952–1954, XI, p. 1447. Shpedko invoked article two of the Soviet-Afghan treaty, gave the Afghan ambassador in Moscow a "tongue-lashing," and demanded that such actions cease or revert to Soviet control.

46. Memorandum of Conversation by the First Secretary of the Embassy in India (Leach), 31 August 1952, *FRUS,* 1952–1954, pp. 1371–1372; Bowles to the Department of State, 1 October 1952, *FRUS,* 1952–1954, p. 1373; Memorandum by Byroade to the Under Secretary of State (Bruce), 10 October 1952, *FRUS,* 1952–1954, p. 1459; Horner to the Department of State, 9 September 1952, *FRUS,* 1952–1954, pp. 1448–1450. Afghan Minister Mohammed Aziz described the incident as the most serious in recent Afghan history. He noted that Afghanistan "considered the US her really true friend" and counted on her help.

47. Acheson to the Embassy in Afghanistan, 12 September 1952, p. 1450, and 29 September 1952, *FRUS,* XI, 1952–1954, pp. 1454–1455.

48. Horner to the Department of State, 2 October 1952, *FRUS,* 1952–1954, XI, pp. 1456–1458; Byroade to the Under Secretary of State (Bruce), 10 October 1952, *FRUS,* 1952–1954, XI, p. 1460. See also Horner to the Department of State, 9 September 1952, *FRUS,* 1952–1954, XI, p. 1449, and 23 September 1952, p. 1453. Horner continued to argue for a "more powerful counterweight than moral support." He now favored U.S.-assisted Pushtunistan negotiations, noting how a complete retreat from an "admittedly unreasonable stand" would cause a dangerous loss of prestige for the Kabul government. Horner also warned of power falling into the hands of those "who will weigh honeyed Soviet promises of aid with the relatively negligible assistance received to date from the UN and ourselves." Curiously he claimed concurrence in his views with the British ambassador. Even Nehru voiced concern over the Soviet *demarche* and urged a strong response. See J.G. Tahourdin, Foreign Office, to Lingeman, Kabul, 28 November 1952, FO 983/87.

49. Byroade to the Under Secretary of State (Bruce), 10 October 1952, *FRUS,* 1952–1954, XI, pp. 1459–1461; Amstutz, *Afghanistan,* pp. 27, 258. Memorandum of Telephone Conversation by the Secretary of State, 24 December 1952, *FRUS,* 1952–1954, XI, pp. 1464, 1464fn. By December, Acheson, aware that all Western-

sponsored economic activity in northern Afghanistan had ceased, supported granting an Afghan request for assistance in reducing a wheat shortage. In January 1953, Truman authorized a credit of 1.5 million dollars for about 10,000 tons of wheat, at 2.5 percent interest, repayable over thirty-five years. Even Ward would later concede some genuine fear in the *demarche*.

50. Wylie to the Viceroy and the Secretary of State for Foreign Affairs (Report of Conversation), 6 March 1942, R/12/169, ff. 7–10.

51. "Strategic Survey—Afghanistan," Prepared by the Near East Section, Division of Special Information, OSS, 8 August, 1942; Donovan Papers, Box 16A, U.S. Army Military History Institute. The Office of Strategic Services team considered Afghanistan "probably the most fanatically Mohammedan country left in the world today," but thought the significance of the Saadabad Pact "lies in the alignment and sentiments expressed."

52. Sir Maurice Peterson, "Report of Conversation with Mr. Wallace Murray Regarding the Middle East," 11 April 1944, L/P&S/12/4626, ff. 4–16; Squire to Eden, 19 May 1944, L/P&S/12/1789, ff. 26–27; Squire to Eden, L/P&S/12/1789, 23 October 1943, ff. 63–64. British opinion also helped sway the Americans from these options.

53. Memo of Conversation by Richard S. Leach, Division of South Asian Affairs, 19 November 1948, *FRUS*, 1948, V, pp. 491–492.

54. Memorandum of Conversation, by Richard Leach, 8 December 1948, *FRUS*, pp. 492–494.

55. Poullada, "Afghanistan and the United States," p. 186; *FRUS*, 1952–1954, XI, p. 1417fn; Hearings, 82nd Congress, 1st Session, Committee on Foreign Affairs, Mutual Security Program, Washington, 1951, p. 996. George McGhee, assistant secretary for Near Eastern, South Asian, and African affairs, agreed that "a certain amount of arms were essential." Grey to Squire, 5 July 1948, FO 983/13.

56. Airgram A-2, Kabul to Department of State, 789.5-MAP/9–2250, containing "Summary of Conversation with the Chief of Staff, Afghan Army," by the American military attaché in Kabul (Colonel Alan F. S. MacKenzie), 15 February 1949, 890h.20/7–2048. The attaché noted how the prompt American response in Korea had stimulated Afghan belief in the United States and argued that doing nothing would lead to bitter disillusionment. He also noted that the British would not sell arms to the Afghans. Dreyfus to Secretary of State, 789.56/1–450. "The embassy has already expressed its opinion that the US should assist Afghanistan to the extent necessary to guarantee internal security . . . in combination with other justifiable and well-selected means . . . our arms policy could make some contribution toward the betterment of Afghan-Pakistan relations." Horner to the Department of State, 23 September 1952, *FRUS*, XI, 1952–1954, pp. 1453–1454. Horner proposed the U.S.A. assist Afghanistan in acquiring medium transport aircraft, which would strengthen the regime against internal subversion and tribal uprisings, without alarming either the Soviets or the Pakistanis. Such aircraft could also serve the civilian economy. Lancaster's remarks are contained in Palmer to Department of State, 890H.24/9–2448. The collapse of the Lancaster plan is noted in 890H.24/3–348.

57. NSC 98/1, *FRUS*, 1949, VI, pp. 6–7; Department of State Policy Statement, 21 February 1951, *FRUS*, 1951, VI, pp. 2006, 2011; Acheson to the Embassy in Afghanistan, 11 October 1952, *FRUS*, 1952–1954, XI, p. 1462; Horner to the Department of State, Foreign Service Dispatch No. 218, 789.00/12–2951; 18; Foreign

Office (J.D. Murray) to Gardener (British Ambassador in Kabul following Squire), 18 January 1951 (citing talks with George McGhee), FO 983/73.

58. Poullada, "Afghanistan and the United States," pp. 186–187. Daoud, then minister of war, was miffed by the effective rejection. Merrill to the Department of State, Telegram No. 279, 789.5/12–851; State Department to Kabul Embassy, 789.5/11–2751; Memorandum of Conversation with Mohammed Aziz, Charge d'Affairs of the Afghan Embassy, 789.5/12–1351; State Department to Kabul Embassy, 789.5/9–651; Memoradum for the President from Secretary Acheson, 789.13/4–2351; Department of State to Kabul Embassy, 890H.24/8–1249..

59. Horner to the Department of State, 16 September 1952, FRUS, 1952–1954, XI, p. 1452 (Ali was speaking).

60. Foreign Office (J.N.O. Curle) to Kabul (W.B.J. Ledwidge) 7 April 1953, FO 983/103; Ledwidge to J. Dalton Murray (High Commissioner, Karachi), February 1953, FO 983/103; Ledwidge (Kabul) to the Southeast Asian Department, Foreign Office, 6 March 1953, FO 983/103; Ledwidge, Minutes, 18 December 1952, FO 983/90. On the same sheet are written comments, of unknown origin, which note recent Afghan requests for arms and advice, their abandonment of neutrality, and desire to become a "second Turkey." Some recent unwillingness to cooperate was blamed on the "slow and unforthcoming response" to the *demarche*. Dulles to the Embassy in Afghanistan, 20 February 1953, FRUS, 1952–1954, XI, pp. 1465–1466; Ward to the Department of State, 17 February 1953, FRUS, 1952–1954, XI, pp. 1392–1392; Ward to the Department of State, 21 July 1953, FRUS, 1952–1954, XI, p. 1398.

61. FRUS, 1952–1954, XI, p. 1386fn2; Khan, *Story of Pakistan Army,* pp. 132–133. Between December 7 and 10, 1952, several attacks were launched by Afridi tribesmen. The Pakistani air force replied with a series of bombings, which hardened the Afghan attitude.

13

THE EISENHOWER ADMINISTRATION, AFGHANISTAN, AND THE ALLIANCES

In May 1946, Shah Mahmud replaced Hashim as prime minister of Afghanistan. Unlike his predecessor, he strove to open the government. In 1949 Mahmud altered Hashim's policy regarding elections to the National Assembly. Rather than suggesting candidates, he left selection entirely to the people. Beginning that June, however, some fifty progressive members of the assembly openly attacked Mahmud's political, economic, and social policies. Political dissent, which focused on the failures of the Helmand Valley Project, the Pushtunistan stalemate, and the military weakness of the country, increased steadily during the next three years and eventually led the king to replace Mahmud with Mohammed Daoud on September 6, 1953. Daoud appointed his brother, Naim Khan, as deputy prime minister and minister of foreign affairs, and for nearly ten years, together they controlled the government.

A first cousin and military college classmate of the king, Daoud had moved through the ranks of the army, attaining the position of minister of war, despite Mahmud's objections, in 1946. Over time, however, Daoud had acquired a reputation for brashness, arrogance, and truculence toward subordinates and political opponents alike. Daoud had been among those who had met with Axis agents during the war, and he made no secret of his desire to secure Afghanistan an outlet to the sea at Pakistan's expense. Though he favored neither the Western nor the Eastern bloc, Daoud was willing to work with both to achieve his ends. That willingness, his expansionist, authoritarian leanings, and his general reputation would eventually prompt some Western officials to declare Daoud a socialist or even a Communist.[1]

By the mid-1950s, the Afghan economy remained at the mercy of its neighbors. Afghanistan's limited transportation network further restricted development. The national literacy rate was below 10 percent and the estimated per-capita average income was but fifty dollars per year. Most Afghans engaged in subsistence agriculture, and the economy remained predominantly barter based. Agricultural production had experienced but minimal increases in recent years, and the few Afghan industries were operating well below capacity. Afghanistan was easily the most underdeveloped country in the region.[2]

The younger generation of the Afghan leadership, many of whom had been educated in Western countries, considered rapid modernization essential. Unlike his predecessors, Daoud could ill afford to pursue minimal development schemes. Through strong control of the executive branch, Daoud planned a massive socioeconomic reform program, in which private enterprise would be curtailed in favor of state-controlled development. Believing that social progress and economic growth could not be achieved at the same time as political reforms, he decided that democracy would be deferred until economic advancement and improvements in standards of living had been achieved. The example of Amanullah, along with instances of tribal violence, convinced Daoud that he could not implement his plans without a modern military. As minister of war, Daoud himself had overseen the suppression of the Safi revolt in 1947 and, shortly after his assumption of power, had commanded government forces in renewed clashes with the Mangals. Like his predecessor, Daoud would seek American military assistance.[3]

Daoud assumed power only a few months before speculation on a Pakistani-American military aid agreement appeared in the world press. He voiced strong opposition to the bilateral agreement, fearing it would heighten Pakistani intransigence on Pushtunistan and give the Soviets a pretext with which to pressure Afghanistan into a similar arrangement. In contrast, however, Daoud welcomed the Turkish-Pakistani agreement and indicated possible Afghan adherence to a regional alliance, claiming, "If all countries of the Middle East agreed to join such a defense arrangement, Afghanistan could not remain in isolation."[4]

Many previous manuscripts, written in the 1960s or later, claim Dulles wanted to enlist Afghanistan in a pact, but Daoud, beholden to neutrality, never considered joining a Western alliance and rejected his urgings. Others have claimed that Afghanistan failed to qualify for aid under Mutual Security Legislation.[5] There is, however, no evidence to substantiate a claim that the administration ever offered Daoud the chance to sign a mutual defense agreement. On the contrary, when citing constraints on potential member states, the National Security Council noted India's nonalignment policy, Nepal's dependence on India, and Ceylon's rubber trade with Communist China but discounted Afghanistan as "vulnerable to Soviet economic and military pressure."[6] Afghanistan did not avoid the alliances owing to popular inclinations, obstinacy, or established policy. Rather, the United States and Pakistan, deeming Afghanistan a greater liability than asset, remained reluctant to endure any obligation to Afghanistan and did not desire its participation. Their reluctance, rather than any Afghan predilection, left the Kabul regime ineligible to become a partner of the West.

Afghan criticism of the Pakistan-United States accord does not prove that Afghanistan would not have joined a Western pact. Historically, Afghanistan had remained neutral, preferring independence to existence as a British or Russian vassal. The Afghans did not, however, oppose strengthening the Southwest Asian area as a whole through an alliance of neighboring Muslim states. In fact, they had joined such an alliance in 1937, the ill-fated, oft-forgotten Saadabad Pact.[7]

Afghanistan continued to express support for and interest in collective defense ideas through 1955. In February 1953, for example, the Afghan ambassador to the United Nations (later to the United States) Mohammed Ludin told a CBS interviewer that Afghanistan was "fully committed to the idea of collective security. Afghanistan has always been ready to defend her freedom and independence and the inviolability of her soil against invasion."[8] Vice-President Richard Nixon, who visited Afghanistan that December, clearly reported the Afghan attitude to the National Security Council, stating: "I feel that Afghanistan will stand up to the communists. I discussed the Pakistan aid program with the Prime Minister and the King, who suggested it would be a good idea if Pakistan, Afghanistan, Iraq, Iran and Turkey entered into something like an 'Atlantic alliance,' with aid going to these countries as a group instead of individually where they might be a threat to each other. The Pakistanis had the opposite view."[9]

A National Intelligence Estimate concurred that Afghanistan "has not opposed US efforts to strengthen the area as a whole" and had expressed interest in receiving military aid. Some Afghan leaders, the estimate continued, regarding American power as a replacement for the departed British, "would like to join in a defense pact with other states of the area if it had US backing and US arms aid were involved."[10]

Certain Afghan leaders periodically indicated interest in American arms assistance. Some military officers demonstrated considerable enthusiasm. Potential adherence would have depended on specifics of the agreement. Had accord included a guarantee of Afghanistan's borders against Soviet aggression, substantial assistance at reasonable rates, and perhaps a resolution of the Pushtunistan dispute, Afghan adherence does not seem unlikely. Then again, if the terms of the arrangement were not worth the risk of Soviet response, the Afghans need not have agreed.[11]

The Afghans certainly agreed with the United States on the necessity to contain the Soviet Union. Since 1929 the ruling dynasty had restricted Soviet activities within Afghanistan, banned all Communist and Communist-affiliated parties, and persecuted known sympathizers. The government rejected most Soviet aid offers and discouraged cultural contacts with the

U.S.S.R. They kept Soviet diplomats under constant surveillance and even prohibited Communist embassies from distributing materials in any language native to Afghanistan, thereby insulating the population from propaganda.[12]

A few State Department and Pentagon personnel suggested the inclusion of Afghanistan in a Northern Tier alliance. The deputy director of the Office of South Asian Affairs, Joseph H. Smith, suggested that it the Soviets were allowed to extend their power into Afghanistan, the whole of South Asia would be jeopardized. At the same time, he thought "Afghan fighting forces . . . might be very effective in immobilizing Soviet troops through guerilla warfare." Smith noted a growing belief among Afghans that the United States had discarded them in recommending that American military and political authorities conduct an appraisal of the significance of Afghanistan. If its loss was judged sufficiently detrimental to U.S. interests, "we should extend military assistance to Afghanistan."[13]

At a May 1954 conference, the Chiefs of Mission similarly recommended that the "US make special efforts to bring about a clear association between Afghanistan and the members of the Northern Tier." Afghan desires for military assistance, they argued, should be used to encourage it to stand up to Soviet pressures and to promote collaboration on regional defense. They recommended a study on the possibility of using an extension of military and economic aid to ameliorate the Pushtunistan dispute.[14]

While the British had seen Afghanistan as a vital link in the system of buffer states that surrounded and protected India, most Americans of the 1950s thought Afghanistan of questionable political loyalty and of limited value to the global economy, the defense of the region, and the worldwide containment effort. Its army seemed lackluster, incapable of offensive action, and of no potential assistance to other regional powers. While perhaps "capable of maintaining internal security . . . [the Afghan army] would quickly disintegrate as an organized force against outside aggression." Afghanistan had no ports, and her air bases were few in number, primitive, distant from sources of supply, difficult to access, subject to extreme weather, and vulnerable to Soviet countermeasures.[15]

On the other hand, the Soviet Union appeared capable of taking over Afghanistan at will. As always, no amount of arms shipments could strengthen Afghanistan to the point where it could, in a conventional sense, successfully resist invasion. Having no strike force in the vicinity, the United States could not have offered significant help to Afghanistan short of nuclear options. Convinced that extensive involvement in Afghanistan would merely provide the Soviets with a pretext for action while overburdening the Afghan budget, the National Security Council concluded that the "adherence of Afghanistan to a Middle East defense system at this stage in the system's development would result in a worsening of the position of Afghanistan and a weakening of the system itself." The administration remained "unwilling to commit itself to the defense of Afghanistan" and rejected military assistance owing to Soviet threats to "the independence of Afghanistan and perhaps the security of its neighbors as well." In event of aggression, they "preferred to meet the Russians on the subcontinent."[16]

Owing to Afghanistan's exposed position, the administration considered it incapable of joining any pact "despite any Afghan desire to participate in regional defense." Soviet protests over development activities in the Helmand Valley and the *demarche* against United Nations-sponsored projects in the northern provinces seemed to illustrate Afghan vulnerability to the Soviet Union. A National Intelligence Estimate further concluded that the Soviet-Afghan treaty of 1931 forbade Afghan enlistment in a Western alliance as it bound Afghanistan to refrain from acts prejudicial to the interests of the U.S.S.R. While the estimate conceded that the Afghans would display passing interest in Western-sponsored military assistance programs and propose arms aid at varying intervals, it assumed that they would never accept alliance membership "since the Afghans most certainly recognize that any foreseeable arrangement, even with the firmest US backing, could scarcely offer Afghanistan realistic protection against Soviet attack." As continued controversy surrounding Pushtunistan made cooperation with Pakistan difficult, the administration presumed Afghanistan would "remain committed to a policy of passive neutrality in view of its extreme vulnerability to Soviet military and economic pressure" and ultimately dismissed Afghan expressions of interest as propaganda ploys, claiming the Kabul government recognized the illogic of pact membership.[17]

Aversion to Afghan membership extended to Pakistan. As long as the Pushtunistan controversy lingered, Americans and Pakistanis alike feared that a strong Afghanistan would be more likely to offer support to tribal uprisings than improve its defenses opposite the Soviet Union. Yet throughout Daoud's tenure, Afghan officials continued to request American assistance to attain a Pushtunistan settlement. Most implied contentment with face-saving measures and expressed a readiness to make substantial concessions. Some even proposed a customs union and a defensive agreement with the Pakistanis. Ludin typified a common Afghan belief "that upon a word from [the US] Pakistan would be willing to consider some dignified and reasonable settlement of the Pushtun question."[18]

A few American officials argued for aid for bilateral economic projects as part of a "step by step development of closer economic relations." Jernegan, for example, suggested a free port in Karachi and joint distribution of hydroelectric power generated from the Helmand Valley and Warsak Dam Projects. A National Security Council staff study reached similar conclusions. While offers of assistance might have promoted a settlement, securing access to Afghanistan's meager resources seemed hardly worth the effort of mediation. Though other officials noted that Pakistan had abused Afghan efforts to achieve a compromise, the State Department continued to leave the problem to bilateral solution.[19]

Throughout the period, Pakistani rhetoric vilified the Kabul regime and obfuscated its stance on a variety of issues. This propaganda undermined Afghan dealings with the United States and, together with traditional impressions of Afghanistan, would lead American policymakers to exaggerate Afghan failings while they overlooked or dismissed Pakistan's problems. Despite Karachi's constant implementation of governor's rule, American officials would ultimately assert that democracy in Pakistan was well ahead of primitive, feudal, polyglot Afghanistan. Others, ignoring the situation in Bengal and elsewhere in Punjabi-dominated Pakistan, characterized Afghanistan's "reactionary regime" as sitting atop a powder keg of unrest among minorities, business interests, and the intelligentsia. Some even believed Pakistani exhortations that claimed "socially medieval" Afghanistan would soon disintegrate into "traditional anarchy."[20]

Most American officials dismissed the Afghan argument for Pushtunistan as either a contrivance designed to divert internal dissent or an irredentist plot to secure an outlet to the sea. Few acknowledged Afghan ethnic ties to the area or legitimate economic grievances and concerns. Many berated Afghanistan as a treacherous state out to undermine Pakistan. Ward, for example, dismissed the "extremely weak" Afghan position as fostered by dreams of expansion and designed to preserve tribal anarchy. He recommended that the United States postpone negotiations until "a more propitious time." Though Dulles offered assistance for bilateral negotiations, this was a useless gesture in the face of Pakistani intransigence. In strengthening Pakistan, meanwhile, the United States virtually eliminated any possibility of that nation ever agreeing to a settlement and destroyed Afghan confidence in American impartiality.[21]

Some American officials acknowledged that leading Afghans favored the West, distrusted the U.S.S.R., and desired to forestall Soviet domination but, owing to geographic proximity, could not simply ignore Moscow. While conceding the Afghans' inability to disregard the Soviet attitude, few demonstrated any sympathy for their position but condemned her "habitual policy of playing off Russia and the West" and, since Afghanistan historically had balanced British and Russian influence, assumed the Kabul regime would likely "continue with its fundamental policy of attempting to play off the great powers to Afghanistan's advantage." When Afghan emissaries threatened to turn to Moscow, administration officials castigated their disloyal, fence-sitting policies. Meanwhile, the Pakistanis received plaudits for their stated desires to oppose communism, despite the fact that they often tempered their pledges with threats to turn north if no aid were forthcoming.[22]

American bias against Afghanistan extended to relations with Iran. The ever-shifting course of the Helmand River perpetuated border disputes between those two nations, which the United States attempted to mediate. Between 1948 and 1951, the Helmand River Delta Commission examined the problem. Afghanistan accepted the report of the arbitration commission in 1952. Iran, however, rejected the report and refused to resume negotiations until late 1954. Despite noting this and traditional "Iranian contempt for Afghan culture," a CIA report concluded that Afghanistan would prove intransigent and provoke increased tension in the area.[23]

Afghanistan indeed had its share of internal problems. Inefficiency, ethnic strife, and tribal violence plagued its government, its army remained poorly equipped and ill disciplined, and the economy was chronically underdeveloped. Yet Afghanistan, however, still had comparatively fewer internal crises than did Pakistan, likely owing to greater regional autonomy and relative economic parity. Furthermore, no amount of aid to Iraq, Iran, or Pakistan could have enabled those countries to do more than annoy an advancing Soviet army for some time to come. Afghanistan, however, seemed devoid of potential worth as well.

The view of Afghanistan as troublesome and valueless did not extend to all American allies. The Turkish ambassador to Washington expressed his country's belief that Afghanistan "occupied an important geographic position from the point of the security of the Middle East" and called for the pact members to endeavor to secure Afghan participation. Treaty arrangements, he claimed, would keep Afghanistan friendly and prevent "impulsive action which might allow expansion of Russian authority." Though cautioned of potential Soviet reaction, the ambassador dismissed that as unlikely, and while he admitted that Pushtunistan would have to be resolved, he felt that possible through third-party negotiation.[24]

While the State Department indicated appreciation of Turkish considerations and claimed awareness of Afghanistan's strategic dilemma, they continued to stress Afghan vulnerability and lack of value. It remained "questionable that benefits which might flow to Afghanistan under [a] possible program of US military aid would be sufficient to compensate for [the] difficulties and risks involved." Though the department did not wish to "cold-shoulder" the Afghans and planned to approve a wheat loan and a second loan for the Helmand Valley Project, they still considered it unwise to encourage Afghan expectations of military aid. Acting Secretary of State Smith surmised that: "If Turkey proposes [an] agreement with Afghanistan similar to one with Pakistan, this might prove embarrassing to [the] US at this time since we expect to use [the] Pakistan-Turkey agreement as [a] framework for Pakistani military aid. Because of this [I/we] believe it would be better if Turkey would make any agreement called for of different character."[25]

Other American officials noted that congressional approval for aid to Afghanistan would take a long time to obtain, claimed that budgetary constraints would limit available support, and asserted repeatedly that no amount of aid could provide total security for Afghanistan. Though the administration did not rule out future Afghan adherence or some sort of interim agreement, they insisted that it would "be better for Afghanistan to allow this system to gather strength before joining it." Though the Turks still voiced hope that the United States would send some assistance to Afghanistan, they did not press the issue.[26]

Though increasingly disillusioned with the United States following the commencement of the aid program to Pakistan, Afghan officials continued to request military aid on a bilateral basis, without specific reference to the regional pacts, throughout 1954 and 1955. In September 1954, Ludin, claiming his nation willing to risk Soviet reaction, indicated Afghan interest in purchasing small arms and ammunition. He suggested using the Turks as a conduit to provide Afghanistan's military needs, averting Soviet (and Pakistani) hostility. A few weeks later, Naim reiterated Afghanistan's need for arms and trained officers, arguing "the safety of Afghanistan is . . . the safety of the whole Indian subcontinent." In October, the American Embassy staff in Kabul recommended consideration of military aid to Afghanistan, through Pakistan, "to encourage a settlement of the Pushtunistan issue."[27]

That December, Dulles informed Ludin that the United States would not supply Afghanistan as such assistance "would create problems not offset by the strength it would create." The department agreed to reconsider extending military assistance only "upon improved Afghan relations with Pakistan and Iran" but refused to assist in procurement of either and continued to discourage alliance membership. Dulles further aroused Afghan ire by disclosing details of their negotiations to the Pakistanis.[28]

At the same time, the Eisenhower administration rejected suggestions of increased economic aid for Afghanistan. The Afghan government had complained of the small amount of Western assistance it received long before its neighbors signed pacts with the United States. The Afghans were further offended by the rigid repayment terms that accompanied their loans, which even American officials would subsequently label "excessively conservative." By 1954 most Afghans and some Americans agreed that the Helmand Valley Project had swallowed funds without producing any tangible benefits. With the project floundering, the Export-Import Bank executed a new contract with the Afghan government on June 21. The loan, however, was but half of what the Afghans had requested, and neither the interest rate (4.5 percent) nor the amortization period (eighteen years, with but a four-year grace period) pleased the Kabul regime. Since Afghanistan had never defaulted on a financial obligation, the government considered the terms insults to their integrity and indicative of American perceptions of Afghanistan's lack of importance. Yet when the Afghans criticized the aid program or complained of procedures regarding the Helmand Valley Project, American officials assailed them as impatient or unable to understand the workings of a modern bureaucracy.[29]

That same June, the officer in charge of economic affairs in the Office of South Asian Affairs completed an examination of the Afghan economy, which acknowledged the Afghan government's disappointment with its share of aid. Noting the split in the hierarchy between statists and supporters of private enterprise, he suggested giving the Afghans better loan terms as a means to encourage increased contacts with Pakistan. He forewarned of Afghan acceptance of Soviet assistance, in suggesting that the National Security Council consider American regional military and political interests in deciding whether or not the United States should increase or decrease its commitment to Afghanistan.[30]

On December 9, 1954, the National Security Council debated plans to increase economic aid to Afghanistan by 30 million dollars per year. Nixon, impressed by the hospitable welcome he received during his visit to Kabul, thought additional economic aid might have great benefit. The president at first indicated potential support, stating: "If the Afghans really wished to be on the side of the free world rather than merely to play off the Soviet Union and the US to their own advantage, then we might be willing to take a chance with increased assistance."

Dulles, however, did not support the plan. His brother Allen, the director of the Central Intelligence Agency, concurred, cautioning that aid programs be implemented in a subtle manner, perhaps through a third government or private organizations, as "the Soviets were inclined to look on Afghanistan much as the United States did on Guatemala" (the United States had recently subverted the government of that nation). He further admonished Afghanistan for its recent recognition of Communist China, disregarding Pakistan's existent relations, and the fact that Afghanistan had offered the diplomatic exchange in mid-January 1950 and Beijing had taken five years to respond. Following the Dulles brothers' denunciation of Afghanistan as both vulnerable and politically unreliable, the National Security Council concluded that increased aid would only heighten Soviet suspicions and "do little to facilitate an understanding between Afghanistan and Pakistan." Ludin was subsequently informed that no funds were available, and the American Embassy in Kabul was instructed to offer similar explanations to the Afghan government.[31]

Given the moral overtones of the Eisenhower administration's defense policy, had the secretary of state understood the Afghan attitude toward the Soviet Union and the Western alliances, it follows that an aid program might have received consideration. Instead, Dulles remained suspicious of Kabul. Within his near-dualistic view of world politics, the Afghans, owing to disputes with Pakistan and occasional appeasement of the U.S.S.R., seemed neither stalwart nor valuable supporters of the West. Though Afghanistan's freedom depended on walking a tightrope between appeasement and provocation, Dulles proved more receptive to the Pakistanis. His suspicions might have been alleviated had he included Afghanistan on his multination tour of May and June 1953. Instead, his failure to visit Kabul reinforced suspicions of partiality toward Pakistan and left the regime feeling that Afghanistan would remain a negligible factor in U.S. policy considerations.[32]

Part of the blame for the negative impression of Afghanistan must rest with the Afghans themselves. They were reluctant to abandon traditional government policies of secrecy, which limited information flow. Even after such restrictions were lifted, they failed to create organizations to espouse their cause in the United States. Since missionary activities had been banned in Afghanistan throughout the nineteenth and twentieth centuries and economic contacts remained limited, few Americans ever had a chance to acquire intimate knowledge of the country. Dependence on German and French educators, meanwhile, had left Afghanistan relatively bereft of individuals with knowledge of English, much less American culture or politics. This placed the nation at a disadvantage, especially opposite the Pakistanis, who had learned proper techniques of influencing English speakers through years of Muslim League agitation.[33]

Afghanistan received no support from those British "experts" who vociferously praised Pakistan. Caroe had few positive words for Afghanistan. He made sharp distinctions between the "Pathans" of India and the "Afghans" of Afghanistan, dismissing Afghanistan as "not really a Pathan state at all." Pushtunistan, he wrote, was born of irredentist sentiment, which had been dormant during British rule. While he conceded Afghan interest in alliances, he dismissed the Saadabad Pact as a "shadowy concept," devoid of the administrative machinery necessary to achieve even its own "limited aspirations." Weak in industrial output, agricultural production, and modern communications, Afghanistan, he concluded, "possesses scarcely any military value within itself." Even Barton, heretofore champion of the Afghan cause, had by 1953 dismissed the Pushtunistan campaign as ill founded. He thought Afghanistan would have to come to terms with Pakistan, for only with Pakistani support could Afghanistan stand up to the Soviet threat. Otherwise, "Afghanistan is militarily helpless; attacked from the West and North she would rapidly collapse."[34]

Afghanistan was also profoundly unlucky to have had Angus Ward as the American ambassador during the critical period from 1952 to 1956. Pakistan had ensured alliance with the United States by procuring support of a number of influential American officials. Ward was among the most ardent Pakophiles. Ward had served time in a Maoist prison camp, emerging a hard-line anti-Communist. Buoyed by allegations from Pakistani authorities and Afghan dissidents, he dismissed Daoud as a Communist. Together with his CIA station chief, whom Leon Poullada described as a "free-wheeling, hard-drinking, pistol-packing adventurer who fancied himself Lawrence of Afghanistan," they plotted to destabilize Daoud's regime, apparently without the knowledge or approval of Washington.[35]

While in office, Ward did nothing to endear the Afghans to the administration. Though earlier State Department reports had indicated "no evidence of the existence of a Communist party in Afghanistan" and had dismissed the number of sympathizers as inconsequential, Ward nonetheless reported, "The embassy assumes that there is a certain amount of communist activity throughout the country, which is clandestine and unknown to the embassy." He gave no reason as to why he would make such a statement so contradictory to the actual situation. While receptive to Pakistani exhortations, Ward blasted the Afghan government for continuing to vilify the Karachi government "in a manner probably unequalled in malignancy anywhere in the non-Communist world." When the Afghans reported threatening Soviet actions, Ward dismissed the reports as efforts to procure American assistance. He persistently blamed Afghan food shortages on smuggling and scorned a request for American armaments as "an attempt to verify the prices of the Czech mission." Had Ward portrayed Afghanistan in an accurate light, the moralistic Dulles might well have been persuaded to include it in Western defense plans. Instead, he likely ensured that Afghanistan would not receive a fair hearing in Washington.[36]

Despite often expressed desires to obtain arms assistance, Ward did not believe Afghanistan would risk joining any defense arrangement, and though he acknowledged that Daoud would be upset by Pakistani participation, he "did not feel that [the US] need be deterred by an adverse Afghan reaction" and argued that the United States should proceed with the alliance regardless of Afghan objections. Indeed, virtually every American official involved thought the Afghan attitude could be ignored, and all agreed that they must "avoid giving the impression that the United States favors including Afghanistan in a regional pact." Thus, while the administration attempted to mollify Indian opinion in the wake of the alliance with Pakistan, they made no similar offers to Afghanistan. The administration fell back on the hope that by avoiding indication of interest in Afghanistan, the Soviets would likewise leave it alone. There seemed few incentives for increased Soviet involvement, and a direct Soviet attack seemed even more unlikely, as even a successful invasion offered few strategic advantages yet entailed considerable economic and political liabilities. A few American officials even seemed to desire such aggression to cement other Muslim states and Asian neutrals to the West.[37]

The Afghan leadership similarly considered a Soviet attack unlikely and hoped that world opinion and Afghanistan's lack of value would serve as a deterrent, but still sought to purchase arms to increase that deterrent and enforce government reform. They acknowledged that the U.S.S.R. might react to such aid with a move into northern Afghanistan but realized that a possibility of invasion existed regardless of extension of military aid or alliance membership. That the United States proved willing to confront threats of similar aggression against the other equally exposed northern tier states irked the Afghans considerably.[38]

Passive American policy coupled with large-scale assistance to Pakistan and later to Iran left Afghanistan in an economic and political vacuum and convinced the Afghan leadership that the United States would remain partial to its neighbors. Daoud could not idly watch while Iran and Pakistan modernized. Though he warned that continued neglect amidst the still unresolved

Pushtunistan crisis would force him to seek accommodation with the Soviet Union, the Americans dismissed those threats as mere bluffs. Dulles, for example, found it "difficult [to] believe [that] Afghanistan, with its familiarity with [the] USSR and its reputation as [a] freedom-loving nation, would commit political suicide over a dispute with a friendly Moslem neighbor."[39]

Afghanistan, however, had already begun to seek economic assistance from the Soviet Union. During the 1950 blockade, the Mahmud government signed a four-year barter-trade agreement with the U.S.S.R., the first such agreement since the 1930s. The U.S.S.R. agreed to supply Afghanistan petroleum products, sugar, textiles, machinery, and transport equipment in exchange for Afghan cotton, minerals, furs, fruits and nuts, on favorable terms. Beginning in 1954, Daoud accepted Soviet offers to complete small-scale economic projects. The first project commenced in January and involved construction of two 20,000-ton capacity grain elevators, a flour mill, and an attached bakery. In July, construction of four gasoline storage tanks, one each at Kabul, Mazir-i-Sharif, Herat, and Kilift, provided Afghanistan a measure of security against another Pakistan blockade. In August, the U.S.S.R. provided the financing and training necessary for Afghan workers to pave the streets of Kabul. Related housing projects and utilities development further improved general comfort. The Czechs also provided a 5-million-dollar loan for construction of a cement plant, which, owing to high cost of foreign imports, brought the Afghan government sizable savings. The Eastern bloc endeavors, unlike similar American ventures, were completed with a minimum of delay and in a cost-effective manner, caused few aggravations for Afghan authorities, and brought immediate, positive benefits to the population.[40]

Daoud never came to trust the Soviet Union, but the success of these limited projects, coupled with continued rejections from the West, encouraged expanded contacts. After the United States and Pakistan became pact partners, Daoud faced a choice between continued economic stagnation, military impotence, and political frustration or rapprochement with the Soviet Union. Daoud chose the latter option, hoping he could control the inherent dangers. While he has been berated for exposing his country to Soviet invasion by allowing for the establishment of a fifth column in the military, one fails to see where he had any other viable alternative.

NOTES

1. Lancaster, Weekly Intelligence Survey, 10 May 1946 and 6 September 1946, L/P&S/12/1849; Squire to Eden, 24 December 1943, L/P&S/12/1678, f. 10; see also R/12/145. British authorities had derided Daoud's behavior well before he assumed positions of significance and would continue to do so. Hashim had groomed Naim as his successor. Squire was not alone in thinking Naim "would be preferable to his more forceful but tactless and unpopular elder brother Daoud." Naim and his brother dif-

fered over the Pushtunistan issue, where Naim sought reconciliation with Pakistan, and he opposed the extent of involvement with the Soviet Union. Still Daoud placed great confidence and trust in his "younger, more cultivated brother." Ward to Department of State, 789.13/9–853; Foreign Service Dispatch #190, Ward to Department of State, 789.00(W)/11–2454. Wilber, *Afghanistan*, pp. 23, 147–149; Newell, *Politics of Afghanistan*, pp. 65–66; Dupree, *Afghanistan*, p. 495; Franck, *Afghanistan between East and West*, p. 5; Reardon ("Modernization and Reform, the Contemporary Endeavor," in Grassmuck, Adamec, and Irwin, eds, *Afghanistan: Some New Approaches*, pp. 153–154, 163–164; Bhaneja, *Afghanistan*, p. 24; Dupree and Albert, *Afghanistan in the 1970's*, p. 11; Arnold, *Afghanistan*, pp. 33, 47–48.

2. Franck, *Afghanistan between East and West*, pp. vi, xiii, 2; Griffiths, *Afghanistan*, pp. 105, 134–135, 139, 154–155; Hyman, *Afghanistan under Soviet Domination*, pp. 13–14, 23–24; Dupree and Albert, *Afghanistan in the 1970's*, p. 6. High infant mortality rates and childhood disease killed half of all Afghan children before they reached the age of five, which, together with a paucity of medical facilities and staff and the continued practice of Pushtunwali, kept average life expectancy at roughly forty years. Part of the health problem stemmed from taking drinking water from the same open ditches used for laundry and for the deposit of human waste.

3. Lascelles to Eden, 17 April 1954, FO 983/107; Kabul to Southeast Asian Department [n.s.], 6 February 1954, FO 983/107; Dupree, *AUFS*, 3/3, pp. 2–3. Daoud himself told Dupree: "Afghanistan is a backward country. We accept this. We know that we must do something about it or die as a nation." Fletcher, *Afghanistan*, p. 259; Ramazani, *Northern Tier*, p. 108; Fraser-Tytler, *Afghanistan*, pp. 316–317; Wilber, *Afghanistan*, p. 23; Newell, *Politics of Afghanistan*, p. 66. Newell claims this decision to limit political progress was a conscious choice of Daoud's.

4. The *Statesman*, (Edinburgh), 3 April 1954, as quoted in Quddus, *Afghanistan and Pakistan*, pp. 106–107; *New York Times*, 23 December 1953, as quoted in Kaur, *Pak-Afghanistan Relations*, pp. 166, 188fn. Daoud described U.S. aid to Pakistan as a "grave danger to the security and peace of Afghanistan," but he claimed the Turkish-Pakistan accord was "likely to lead to better understanding and improvement of economic conditions for all." During discussions on the establishment of MEDO, Naim had expressed concern with potential Pakistani participation. Were Pakistan to be enlisted, Afghanistan would be left isolated between the alliance and the U.S.S.R. Declaring third-party negotiation over Pushtunistan essential, he foresaw Pakistani intransigence forcing Afghanistan toward Moscow. See Ward to the Department of State, 17 February 1953, *FRUS*, 1952–1954, XI, pp. 1392–1393; Memorandum of Conversation by Jernegan, 19 February 1953, *FRUS*, 1952–1954, XI, p. 1395; Ward to the Department of State, 11 June 1952, *FRUS*, 1952–1954, XI, p. 1395; Dulles to the Embassy in Afghanistan, 20 February 1953, *FRUS*, 1952–1954, XI, pp. 1465–1466; Sulzberger, *Long Row of Candles*, p. 770. Eisenhower thought Afghan opposition to the Pakistani-American accord understandable.

5. Franck (*Afghanistan*, p. 44) and Dupree (*AUFS*, 1/3, p. 16) both claim Afghan requests were refused for failing to sign the Mutual Security Legislation. Dupree (*Afghanistan*, pp. 508–511) claims Daoud used its rejection to justify to its people the acceptance of Soviet military assistance. Adamec, *Afghanistan's Foreign Relations*, p. 263. Wolpert (*Roots of Confrontation*, p. 160) claims Dulles "tried to get Daoud to join the Baghdad Pact in 1955, but Afghanistan refused all of Washington's overtures to ally itself with the Free World's struggle against communist expansion," being in-

terested only in procuring arms for use against Pakistan. Kaur (*Pak-Afghanistan Relations*, p. 165) also claims that the United States failed to persuade the Afghans to join the alliance system, as does Quddus (*Afghanistan and Pakistan*, pp. 106–107). Hyman (*Afghanistan under Soviet Domination*, pp. 28–29) claims Afghanistan "was determined to keep a position of non-alignment or neutrality in its relations with the superpowers, rejecting the idea that it should join its neighbors Iran and Pakistan in membership in the Baghdad Pact." The only previous work to generally support the view argued within can be found in Reardon ("Modernization and Reform, the Contemporary Endeavor," p. 156).

6. Memorandum by the Acting Secretary of State (Bruce) to the Executive Secretary of the National Security Council (Lay), Progress Report on NSC 98/1, "The Position of the United States with Respect to South Asia, 19 August 1952, *FRUS*, 1952–1954, XI, pp. 1060, 1060fn; Draft Statement of Policy Proposed by the National Security Council, NSC-5409, 19 February 1954, *FRUS*, 1952–1954, XI, p. 1090.

7. The Saadabad Pact would seem to have suited Dulles's and the Joint Chiefs' predilections for an organization more loosely organized and less binding than NATO, in which neither the United States nor any other Western power would entail binding commitments. Such an arrangement would also have been less likely to prompt a Soviet reaction. The provisions of the pact emphasized collaborative efforts against subversion, the only immediate benefit of the Baghdad Pact, and the charter contained provisions for the establishment of a permanent council and secretariat, with annual meetings, that could have facilitated further military, cultural, and economic collaboration. While one can wonder what sort of entente might have developed had the United States attempted to revitalize this agreement, there is no evidence to indicate that any Eisenhower administration official considered the potential benefits of the Saadabad Pact or even acknowledged its existence. See Secretary of State to the Embassy in Turkey, 24 December 1953, *FRUS*, 1951–954, XI, p. 1836; Asopa, *Military Alliance*, p. 34; Gregorian, *Emergence of Modern Afghanistan*, pp. 376–377; Wilber, "Contemporary Society and Politics in Afghanistan," *Current Problems in Afghanistan*, p. 22; Dupree, *Afghanistan*, p. 479.

8. Ludin, CBS Interview, 4 February 1953, transcript in FO 983/103.

9. Eisenhower Papers, Whitman File, Discussion at the 177th meeting of the National Security Council, 23 December 1953, Eisenhower Library; see also Dupree, *AUFS*, 4/6, pp. 2fn, 3. Nixon's trip to Afghanistan coincided with a newspaper strike in New York; thus, the nation's leading international newspapers made no report of it. Other papers paid little attention to the vice president's visit.

10. National Intelligence Estimate NIE-53–54, "Outlook for Afghanistan," 19 October 1954, *FRUS*, 1952–1954, p. 1494; see also Memorandum by the Officer in Charge of Pakistan-Afghanistan Affairs (Thatcher), 8 October 1954, *FRUS*, 1952–1954, p. 1422; Telegram, United States Representative at the United Nations (Lodge) to the Department of State, 12 October 1954, *FRUS*, 1952–1954, p. 1423; Memorandum by the Assistant Secretary of State for Near Eastern, South Asian, and African Affairs (Byroade), 27 July 1954, *FRUS*, 1952–1954, p. 1479; Airgram A-62, Ward to Department of State, 789.00/4–654.

11. Memorandum by the Deputy Director, Office of South Asian Affairs (Smith), to Donald Kennedy of the Bureau of Near Eastern, South Asian, and African Affairs, 23 June 1954, *FRUS*, 1952–1954, p. 1475; Dupree, *Afghanistan*, pp. 510–511; Poul-

lada, "Search for National Unity," in Dupree and Albert, eds., *Afghanistan in the 1970's*, p. 44. Poullada claims that Mahmud and Daoud could have had arms aid had they not insisted on a guarantee of their borders. Other evidence does not support those conclusions.

12. Byroade to the Under Secretary of State (Bruce), 10 October 1952, *FRUS*, 1952–1954, XI, pp. 1459–1461; Memorandum of Telephone Conversation by the Secretary of State, 24 December 1952, *FRUS*, 1952–1954, XI, pp. 1464, 1464fn. Both documents note the lack of Communist organizations or of any other leaders or groups that constituted any more than a long-range threat to Afghanistan. See also: Chargé in Afghanistan (Horner) to the Department of State, 16 September 1952, *FRUS*, 1952–1954, XI, p. 1452. Hyman (*Afghanistan under Soviet Domination*, p. 97) claims "Kummunist" is understood as the Pashto "*kum*" (God), and the Persian "*nist*" (without), i.e., without God or godless. Arnold, *Afghanistan*, p. 48; Fletcher, *Afghanistan*, pp. 261–262, 281; Alpert, "Afghanistan, a Perspective," in Dupree and Albert, eds., *Afghanistan in the 1970's*, p. 258; Mowrer, "New Frontiers for Freedom," p. 38; Dupree, *Afghanistan*, pp. 511–516..

13. Memorandum by the Deputy Director, Office of South Asian Affairs (Smith), to Donald Kennedy of the Bureau of Near Eastern, South Asian, and African Affairs, 23 June 1954, *FRUS*, 1952–1954, XI, pp. 1474–1475. Echoing the Forward Policy advocates, Smith wrote: "The natural frontier of Pakistan for defense purposes is the Hindu Kush. If we do not move before the Soviets do, we may find them on the Durand Line, which would be less possible to defend." For earlier suggestions, see Agreed Conclusions and Recommendations, South Asian Regional Conference of United States Diplomatic and Consular Officials, 2 March 1951, *FRUS*, 1951, VI, p. 1666; Memorandum of Conversation, 8 December 1948, *FRUS*, 1948, V, p. 493; see also National Security Council Staff Study, NSC 5409, *FRUS*, 1952–1954, XI, pp. 1099–1101.

14. Paper Approved by the Chiefs of Mission Conference at Istanbul, May 11–14, 1954, "Conference Statement on Regional Security in the Middle East," *FRUS*, 1952–1954, IX, p. 507.

15. National Intelligence Estimate NIE 53–54, "Outlook for Afghanistan," 19 October 1954, *FRUS*, 1952–1954, XI, p. 1482. This attitude persisted through the 1970s, evidenced by U.S. Embassy in Kabul, "Policy Review, US Strategy for the 1970's," pt. 1, Annex: "For the United States, Afghanistan has at present limited direct interest: it is not an important trading partner; it is not an access route for US trade with others; it is not presently as far as it is known a source of oil or scarce strategic metals nor does it appear likely that it will become so; there are no treaty ties or defense commitments; and Afghanistan does not provide us with significant defense, intelligence, or scientific facilities. United States policy has long recognized these facts" (quoted in Collins, *Soviet Invasion of Afghanistan*, p. 19; Hammond, *Red Flag over Afghanistan*, p. 26; and Bradsher, *Afghanistan and the Soviet Union*, p. 51).

16. NSC 5409, paragraph 58; Draft Statement of Policy Proposed by the National Security Council, NSC 5409, 19 February 1954, *FRUS*, 1952–1954, XI, p. 1095; Memorandum by the Executive Secretary (Lay) to the National Security Council, 14 December 1954, enclosure, "Staff Study on Afghanistan," *FRUS*, 1952–1954, XI, pp. 1153, 1157–1158; National Intelligence Estimate NIE-53–54, "Outlook for Afghanistan," 19 October 1954, *FRUS*, 1952–1954, XI, p. 1491; Acting Memorandum of Discussion at the 228th Meeting of the National Security Council, 9 December

1954, *FRUS,* 1952–1954, XI, p. 1157; Acting Secretary of State (Hoover) to the Embassy in Afghanistan, 16 December 1954, *FRUS,* 1952–1954, XI, p. 1497; Memorandum of Conversation by the Acting Officer in Charge of Pakistan-Afghanistan Affairs (Thatcher), 13 December 1954, *FRUS,* 1952–1954, XI, p. 1435; Secretary of State (Smith) to the Embassy in Turkey, 26 January 1954, *FRUS,* 1952–54, IX, pp. 465–466; see also Franck, *Afghanistan between East and West,* p. 12; Newell, *Politics of Afghanistan,* p. 124.

17. National Intelligence Estimate NIE-53–54, "Outlook for Afghanistan," 19 October 1954, *FRUS,* 1952–1954, XI, p. 1482–1483, 1491, 1494–1495; see also Secretary of State (Dulles) to the Embassy in Afghanistan, 20 February 1953, *FRUS,* 1952–1954, XI, p. 1465; National Intelligence Estimate NIE-79, "Probable Developments in South Asia," 30 June 1953, *FRUS,* 1952–1954, XI, p. 1074, which similarly concurred that "Afghanistan's proximity to the USSR, its remoteness from centers of Western strength, its military weakness, and its growing reliance on the USSR for trade and loans with technical assistance make it highly vulnerable to Soviet pressures." See also Paper Approved by the Chiefs of Mission Conference at Istanbul, May 11–14, 1954, "Conference Statement on Middle East Defense Commenting on OIR Contribution to NIE 54–30," *FRUS,* 1952–1954, IX, p. 512.

18. Progress Report, NSC 5409, 25 February 1955, paragraph C53; CA-3379, Kabul to Department of State, 789.00/11–2254; Ward to the Department of State, 21 July 1953, *FRUS,* XI, 1952–1954, p. 1401; Consul General at Bombay (Turner) to the Department of State, 10 February 1954, *FRUS,* XI, 1952–1954, p. 1411; Ward to the Department of State, 25 December 1954, *FRUS,* XI, 1952–1954, p. 1441; R.A. Conner, Military Attaché in Kabul to the Under Secretary of State, War Office, 19 February 1953, FO 983/103; Squire, "Recent Progress in Afghanistan," p. 17.

19. Memorandum of Conversation by the Acting Officer in Charge of Pakistan-Afghanistan Affairs (Thatcher), 8 October 1954, *FRUS,* 1952–1954, XI, pp. 1420–1421; Memorandum by the Deputy Assistant Secretary of State for Near Eastern, South Asian, and African Affairs (Jernegan) to the Acting Deputy Under Secretary of State, 5 November 1954, *FRUS,* XI, 1952–1954, p. 1429; Memorandum of Conversation by the Acting Officer in Charge of Pakistan-Afghanistan Affairs (Thatcher), 13 December 1954, *FRUS,* XI, 1952–1954, p. 1436; Memorandum by the Executive Secretary (Lay) to the National Security Council, 14 December 1954, enclosing "Staff Study on Afghanistan," *FRUS,* XI, 1952–1954, pp. 1156–1157.

20. Pakistan disseminated anti-Afghan propaganda from its inception in 1947. Typical accusations labeled Afghanistan "a third-rate backward country . . . groveling under a medieval form of government . . . [and] trying to oppress educated, prosperous, progressive Frontier Pathans." The Kabulis were the "Italians of Central Asia, with too much bravado but very little of guts." *Civil and Military Gazette,* 19 October 1947, L/P&S/12/1812, f. 133; *Khyber Mail,* 24 October 1947, L/P&S/12/1812, f. 133. Memorandum by the Executive Secretary (Lay) to the National Security Council, 14 December 1954, enclosing "Staff Study on Afghanistan," *FRUS,* 1952–1954, XI, pp. 1154fn, 1155; Horner to the Department of State, 9 September 1952, *FRUS,* 1952–1954, XI, p. 1449; National Intelligence Estimate NIE-53–54, "Outlook for Afghanistan," 19 October 1954, *FRUS,* 1952–1954, XI, pp. 1482–1486. Afghanistan is a primitive tribal kingdom with a heterogeneous population. "The various groups have little in common beyond adherence to Islam." Personal loyalties devolve on the tribe or family group rather than the nation. National consciousness and spirit are

lacking. Non-Pushtun ethnic groups "have been forced to accept a second-class status within the state." Horner to the Department of State, Foreign Service Dispatch No. 218, 789.00/12–2951; Horner to the Department of State, Foreign Service Dispatch No. 317, 789.00/3–352; Horner to the Department of State, Foreign Service Dispatch No. 81, 789.00/10–2352; Stephens, *Pakistan*, p. 218; see also NSC 5409, 19 February 1954, paragraph 5; Horner to the Department of State, 2 January 1952, *FRUS, 1952–1954*, XI, p. 1365; Memorandum of Conversation by Kennedy, 26 November 1952, *FRUS, 1952–1954*, XI, p. 1383; Memorandum of Conversation by Thatcher, 20 October 1954, *FRUS, 1952–54*, XI, p. 1425; Fletcher, *Afghanistan*, p. 256; Fraser-Tytler, *Afghanistan*, p. 321; Newell and Newell, *Struggle for Afghanistan*, p. 41; Kaur, *Pak-Afghanistan Relations*, p. 165.

21. NSC 5409, 19 February 1954, *FRUS, 1952–1954*, XI, p. 1095; Ward to the Department of State, 21 July 1953, *FRUS, 1952–1954*, XI, pp. 1398–1401; Ward to the Department of State, 15 December 1953, FRUS, 1952–1954, XI, p. 1407; Embassy Dispatch to the Department of State, 689.90D/10–1251; Memorandum of Conversation by the Acting Officers in Charge of Pakistan-Afghanistan Affairs (Thatcher), 28 December 1954, *FRUS, 1952–1954*, XI, p. 1443; Dulles to the Embassy in Afghanistan, 15 June 1953, *FRUS, 1952–1954*, XI, p. 1397; *FRUS, 1952–1954*, XI, p. 1412fn; *FRUS, 1952–1954*, XI, p. 1493. Hildreth, for example, saw Pakistan "willing to cooperate in solving tribal problems . . . [having] facilitated Afghan trade within the limits of its transportation system . . . and would welcome closer ties if the Pushtunistan irritant could be removed." Squire, "Recent Progress in Afghanistan," pp. 17–18; Poullada, "Afghanistan and the United States," pp. 188–189; Dupree, *AUFS*, 4/6, p. 10. During his visit to Kabul, Nixon assailed Daoud on Pushtunistan in a "patronizing, dogmatic and offensive" style, before repeating these views to appreciative Pakistani audiences.

22. National Intelligence Estimate, NIE-53-54, "Outlook for Afghanistan," 19 October 1954, *FRUS, 1952–1954*, XI, pp. 1483–1484, 1493–1494; Memorandum of Conversation by the Secretary of State, 12 June 1952, pp. 1820–1821; Memorandum of Conversation by Byroade, 28 January 1953, pp. 1824–1825; Memorandum of Conversation, Prepared in the Embassy in Pakistan, May 23, 1953, *FRUS, 1952–1954*, IX, p. 125; Venkataramani, *American Role in Pakistan*, p. 229. Perhaps the best example of sabotage occurred in the fall of 1954, when Naim visited Karachi and broached the subject of a possible confederation of Afghanistan and Pakistan with American authorities. His proposals impressed the American U.N. Representative Henry Cabot Lodge as "bold and statesmanlike" and of value to the West. Radford similarly thought the idea a good one, and even the president indicated interest in a "possibility of Pakistan and Afghanistan drawing together." However, on April 11, the *New York Times* published an article on the proposed Pak-Afghan merger. Publication forced the Afghan government to deny any such a suggestion to appease India and the U.S.S.R. Zafrullah Khan told American Embassy officials that the Afghan Minister Atiq Rafiq had leaked the story. Colonel Shah, the Pakistani ambassador in Kabul, later claimed that Atiq was reprimanded upon his return. The correspondent, however, later admitted that he had received his information from the Pakistanis. Memorandum of Conversation by the Acting Officer in Charge of Pakistan-Afghanistan Affairs (Thatcher), 18 September 1954, *FRUS, 1952–1954*, XI, pp. 1416–1417; Memorandum of Conversation by the Counselor in the Embassy in Pakistan (Emerson), *FRUS, 1952–1954*, XI, p. 1418; Memorandum of Conversation by Thatcher, 22 December

1954, *FRUS*, 1952–1954, XI, p. 1440; Memorandum of Conversation by the Acting Officer in Charge of Pakistan-Afghanistan Affairs (Thatcher), 8 October 1954, *FRUS*, 1952–1954, XI, pp. 1420–1421; United States Representative at the United Nations (Lodge) to the Department of State, 12 October 1954, *FRUS*, 1952–1954, XI, pp. 1423–1424; Lodge to the Department of State, 8 November 1954, *FRUS*, 1952–1954, XI, pp.1424–1426; Memorandum of Discussion at the 228th Meeting of the National Security Council, 9 December 1954, *FRUS*, 1952–1954, XI, p. 1148.

23. *FRUS*, 1952–1954, XI, fn4; National Intelligence Estimate NIE-53–54, "Outlook for Afghanistan," 19 October 1954, *FRUS*, 1952–1954, XI, p. 1495.

24. Memorandum of Conversation by the Officer in Charge of Turkish Affairs (Wright), 9 January 1954, *FRUS*, 1952–1954, IX, p. 448; *FRUS*, 1952–1954, XI, p. 449fn. Naim had indicated a desire to have the Turks act as a go-between in order to acquire U.S. military aid, and Ankara supported the idea. Ambassador in Turkey (Warren) to the Department of State, *FRUS*, 1952–1954, XI, p. 459.

25. Acting Secretary of State (Smith) to the Embassy in Turkey, 26 January 1954, *FRUS*, 1952–1954, IX, pp. 465–466. He did add that "Turkey might wish consider adding to its approach suggestion it willing consider expanded training program for Afghan military personnel in Turkey [sic]."

26. Memorandum of Conversation by the Deputy Director of the Office of Greek, Turkish, and Iranian Affairs (Baxter), 29 January 1954, *FRUS*, 1952–1954, IX, p. 478; Memorandum of Conversation by the Acting Officer in Charge of Pakistan-Afghanistan Relations (Thatcher), 8 October 1954, *FRUS*, 1952–1954, XI, p. 1422; *FRUS*, 1952–1954, XI, 28 December 1954, p. 1442. Byroade commented that "U.S. military assistance to these countries should make clear to the Russians that they could not take the area without a general war." This concept, for an organization to command the respect of the U.S.S.R., was often repeated. Memorandum of Conversation by the Acting Officer in Charge of Pakistan-Afghanistan Relations (Metcalf), 27 July 1954, *FRUS*, 1952–1954, XI, p. 1480; National Intelligence Estimate, NIE-53–54, "Outlook for Afghanistan," 19 October 1954, *FRUS*, 1952–1954, XI, p. 1481; Secretary of State to the Embassy in Turkey, 24 December 1953, *FRUS*, 1952–1954, IX, p. 440. Dulles concurred that an aid agreement with Afghanistan would create problems not offset by advantages. He ultimately concluded: "We do not believe time has yet come for inclusion [of] Iran or Afghanistan in such an arrangement." Memorandum by the Joint Chiefs of Staff to the Secretary of Defense (Wilson), 14 November 1953, *FRUS*, 1952–1954, XI, p. 431.

27. *FRUS*, 1952–1954, XI, p. 1470fn; *FRUS*, 1952–1954, XI, p. 1417fn; Memorandum of Conversation by the Acting Officer in Charge of Pakistan-Afghanistan Affairs (Thatcher), 15 September 1954, *FRUS*, 1952–1954, XI, pp. 1414–1415; *FRUS*, 1952–1954, XI, 8 October 1954, p. 1421; *FRUS*, 1952–1954, XI, 29 October 1954, p. 1427; Memorandum by the Assistant Secretary of State for Near Eastern, South Asian, and African Affairs (Byroade) to the Secretary of State, 27 July 1954, *FRUS*, 1952–1954, XI, p. 1479; National Intelligence Estimate NIE-53–54, "Outlook for Afghanistan," 19 October 1954, *FRUS*, 1952–1954, XI, p. 1495; Memoradum of Conversation, "US Military Assistance for Afghanistan." 789.5-MSP/7–854; Memoradum of Conversation, "US Attitude in Event of Afghan Request for US Military Assistance," 789.5-MSP/1–1554; Dupree, *Afghanistan*, pp. 508–511.

28. Acting Secretary of State (Hoover) to the Embassy in Afghanistan, 16 Decem-

ber 1954, *FRUS*, 1952–1954, XI, p. 1437; Poullada, "Afghanistan and the United States," p. 187.

29. Memorandum by N.H. Kirk of the Investment and Development Staff to the Chief of the Investment and Development Staff (Ross), 11 August 1953, *FRUS*, 1952–54, XI, p. 1469; Assistant Director of the Export-Import Bank (Arey) to the Secretary of the National Advisory Council on International Monetary and Financial Problems (Glendenning), 19 April 1954, *FRUS*, 1952–1954, XI, p. 1473. The original 1949 Helmand Valley loan had a six-year grace period and nine-year repayment schedule. Memorandum by the Acting Executive Officer of the Operations Coordinating Board (Morgan) to the Executive Secretary of the National Security Council (Lay), 29 July 1954, "Progress Report on NSC 5409, *FRUS*, 1952–1954, XI, pp. 1140–1141; Franck, *Afghanistan between East and West*, pp. 42, 50. Assorted bureaucratic differences delayed commencement of new work until renewed Pushtunistan agitation again halted shipment of equipment intended for the project from May through November (Fletcher, *Afghanistan*, pp. 266–267). While India, Pakistan and Iran all received over 100 million dollars in technical assistance, Afghanistan received barely 6 million. Pakistan received 93 Department of State Educational Exchange Program grants in 1954; Afghanistan received only 4. Pakistan, India, and Ceylon had Fulbright programs; Afghanistan did not.

30. Memorandum by the Officer in Charge of Economic Affairs, Office of South Asian Affairs (Fluker), to the Deputy Director of That Office, 25 June 1954, *FRUS*, 1952–1954, XI, pp. 1476–1478.

31. Memorandum of Conversation at the 228th Meeting of the National Security Council, 9 December 1954, *FRUS*, 1952–1954, XI, pp. 1148–1150; Acting Secretary of State (Hoover) to the Embassy in Afghanistan, 16 December 1954, pp. 1497–1498; Vertzberger, "China and Afghanistan," pp. 1–2.

32. Memorandum of Conversation by the Acting Officer in Charge of Pakistan-Afghanistan Affairs (Thatcher), 15 September 1954, *FRUS*, 1952–1954, XI, p. 1416. While in India, Dulles met with Afghan ambassador Najibullah Khan. The Afghans requested the meeting, fearing Dulles would get a distorted view of the Pushtunistan controversy by spending two days in Karachi. No memorandum of the conversation has been found in the Department of State files.

33. Wilber, "Contemporary Society and Politics in Afghanistan," in *Princeton University Conference* pp. 19, 23; Newell, "Foreign Relations," in Dupree and Albert, eds., *Afghanistan in the 1970's*, p. 85; Gregorian, *Emergence of Modern Afghanistan*, pp. 69, 151, 336–337, 355, 491fn.

34. Caroe, *Wells of Power*, pp. 16, 33, 188. Later he admitted that "the Afghan government had been pressing for easier access to the sea" for some time. Extract from an unfinished autobiography by Sir Olaf Caroe, MSS.EUR F.203/78 (Olaf Caroe Papers); Caroe, *Pathans*, pp. xiv–xv; Caroe to Sir J. Colville, 22 May 1947, *ITOP*, X/512, p. 944. Later, Caroe's *Pathans* took a more moderate stance, but it came too late to influence alliance diplomacy. Barton, "Afghans and Middle East Defense," p. 15; see also Ratcliffe, "Strategic Situation," pp. 95–100. Acheson, interestingly, rejected the Saadabad Pact as "not sufficiently binding to meet the present needs." The director of the Office of South Asian affairs likewise concluded that "we are not in favor of direct US efforts to revive this agreement." Acheson to Tehran Embassy, Airgram-184, 790d.5/11-2850; Office Memo, Mathews to McGhee, 790d.00/5–

31–51. There is little evidence that would suggest that any Eisenhower administration personnel ever considered reviving the agreement.

35. Poullada, "Afghanistan and the United States," pp. 180–181, 184; Fletcher, *Afghanistan,* p. 264. Ward succeeded in making himself the most unpopular foreign representative in Afghanistan, surpassing even his Soviet counterpart.

36. Memorandum by the Acting Executive Officer of the Operations Coordinating Board (Morgan) to the Executive Secretary of the National Security Council (Lay), 29 July 1954, "Progress Report on NSC 5409, *FRUS,* 1952–1954, XI, p. 1144; Ward to Dulles, Airgram A-75, 789.00/5/2554; Ward to Department of State, FSD No. 134, *789.00/12–353;* Ward to Department of State, FSD No. 193, 789.00(W)/12–353; Ward to Department of State, 789.00(W)/10–754; "Significant Developments Affecting U.S. Security," 15 October 1954, Eisenhower Papers, Whitman File, Eisenhower Library. Franck (*Afghanistan between East and West,* pp. 10, 72) reported simply that there is "no open or clandestine communist propaganda in Afghanistan." Ward even suggested that few Afghans had even heard of Marxism or were too dumb to understand it. *FRUS,* 1952–1954, XI, p. 1383. He also suggested putting a Ferris wheel in Kabul to counteract Soviet prestige gained by their supply of buses. National Intelligence Estimate, NIE-53–54, "Outlook for Afghanistan," 19 October 1954, *FRUS,* 1952–1954, XI, p. 1490. Ward was probably influenced by Mahmud, who had earlier told him: "Whereas no Commies in country 15 years ago such not case today and young people are falling away from Orthodox Religion and many turning to Communism [sic]." See Ward to the Department of State, 13 November 1952, *FRUS,* 1952–1954, XI, p. 1382. Some of Ward's predecessors also reported perceived Communist activity. Merrill thought the "Awakened Youth" organization Communist inspired (FSD No. 389, 789.00/4–752). Another (unsigned) report from the Kabul embassy to the Secretary of State cited student demonstrations and communist efforts to infiltrate the Afghan army (789.00/6–1551). Horner, however, thought the threat of communist subversion slight. (Telegram No. 459, Horner to Department of State, 789.52/9–552.)

37. Memorandum of Conversation by the Deputy Assistant Secretary of State for Near Eastern, South Asian, and African Affairs (Jernegan), 6 January 1954, *FRUS,* 195221954, IX, p. 446; Memorandum of Conversation by the Officer in Charge of Turkish Affairs (Wright), 9 January 1954, *FRUS,* 1952–1954, XI, p. 447; Deputy Assistant Secretary of State for Near Eastern, South Asian, and African Affairs (Jernegan) to the Ambassador in Iran (Henderson), 19 November 1953, *FRUS,* 1952–1954, p. 433; Special Estimate SE-55, "The Probable Repercussions of a US Decision to Grant or Deny Military Aid to Pakistan," 15 January 1954, *FRUS,* 1952–1954, XI, p. 1841.

38. National Intelligence Estimate, NIE-53–54, "Outlook for Afghanistan," 19 October 1954, *FRUS,* 1952–1954, XI, pp. 1482–1483, 1492; NSC-5409, "United States Policy toward South Asia," *FRUS,* 1952–1954, XI, p. 1114; U.S. Department of State, Bureau of Near Eastern Affairs, "Long-Term Commitment to Afghanistan's Economic Development Program," quoted in Collins, *Soviet Invasion of Afghanistan,* p. 20. Though "Afghanistan could offer only insignificant resistance to Soviet attack . . . aggression would serve to draw the South Asian states together and toward an alignment with the West." Fletcher, *Afghanistan,* pp. 257–258, 261, 310fn; Newell, "Foreign Relations," in Dupree and Albert, eds., *Afghanistan in the 1970's,* p. 85. Soviet "forbearance probably stems from the realization that the benefits . . . would

be outweighed by the costs of pacification and international resentment, especially among other Muslim countries." Poullada, "Afghanistan and the United States," p. 183.

39. Memorandum of Conversation with Mohammed Daoud, by James Spain, 789.13/10–2754; Daoud repeatedly "asked why Afghanistan was being left out, why she was being ignored in plans for regional security." Ambassador in Afghanistan to the Department of State, 3 December 1953, *FRUS*, 1952–1954, XI, p. 1406; Dupree, *AUFS*, 4/6, p.3.

40. National Intelligence Estimate NIE-53–54, *FRUS*, 1952–1954, XI, pp. 1488–1490; Ward to the Department of State, FSD No. 251, 789.00(W)/1–2854; Ward to the Department of State, FSD No. 352, 789.00(W)4–2954; Kaur, *Pak-Afghanistan Relations*, p. 173; Dupree, *AUFS*, 4/3, p. 16, and 4/4, p. 9; Giradet, *Afghanistan*, p. 94; Griffiths, *Afghanistan*, p. 143; Fraser-Tytler, *Afghanistan*, pp. 321–322; Newell, *Politics of Afghanistan*, p. 127; Franck, *Afghanistan between East and West*, pp. 32, 55–56, 59–60, 64–65, 73–74; Dupree, *Afghanistan*, pp. 493–494, 507; Fletcher, *Afghanistan*, p. 285; Arnold, *Afghanistan*, pp. 30–35. O'Ballance, "Afghanistan," p. 229. At one time or another, the Afghans had requested American support for road building, mineral exploitation, a cement plant, a bakery, oil-refining facilities, and a "new Kabul." Export-Import Bank, for example, twice rejected the Kabul street-paving project as economically insignificant, and while Morrison-Knudson submitted cost estimates for the construction of a cement plant, the Afghans rejected them as too expensive. The Afghans also requested American assistance to build an alternate route through Iran to the sea. The United States rejected the plans as economically impractical but would later agree to construct a highway from Herat to the Iranian border and supported improved Afghan-Iranian contacts through the 1960s to the late 1970s.

14

MOHAMMED DAOUD, THE SOVIET-AFGHAN AGREEMENTS, AND THE ROAD TO WAR, 1955–1979

On November 20, 1954, in response to the League's crushing defeat in elections in East Bengal, Pakistani Prime Minister Mohammed Ali announced a plan for the amalgamation of all West Pakistan into one administrative unit. Designed to offset the greater population of Bengal and perpetuate Punjabi leadership, the "One Unit Plan" also promised to curtail Pushtun autonomy. Daoud decried the plan an as abrogation of Jinnah's promise that the frontier would never be merged with the Punjab and issued public statements that reaffirmed his commitment to Pushtunistan. Daoud's actions did not deter the Pakistani Cabinet from approving the One-Unit Plan in March 1955.[1]

Following a public condemnation of the act by the Afghan Cabinet and a fiery speech by Daoud, a Kabuli mob, composed mostly of students, attacked the Pakistani Embassy, roughed up some staff members, and burned their flag. The "Flag Incident" eventually brought the two nations to the brink of war. The following day, Pakistani mobs attacked Afghan consulates in Peshawar and Quetta. Soon thereafter, Pakistan imposed another border closure and withdrew its ambassador. Afghanistan mobilized its army. Scattered border incidents occurred throughout the summer and early fall.[2]

Negotiations conducted by Prince Musiad Din Abdur Rahman of Saudi Arabia and a youthful Egyptian colonel, Anwar Sadat, produced a settlement. The Afghan army demobilized in late July, and both flags were rehoisted in public ceremonies in September. Pakistan, however, implemented the One Unit Plan in October. Afghanistan recalled its ambassador, and Pakistan followed suit. In November, Daoud summoned a Loya Jirgah, which declared that Afghanistan would never recognize the North West Frontier Province as an integral part of Pakistan and sanctioned any move necessary to redress the balance of power lost when the United States had agreed to ship arms to Karachi.[3]

By late 1955, disappointment surrounding the Helmand Valley Project and persistent American rejection of Afghan requests for increased economic, military, and political support had alienated the Kabul regime. Aid programs to Pakistan and Iran undermined American excuses that global commitments, strained finances, or requisite congressional approval precluded similar assistance to Afghanistan. Meanwhile, the supply of economic aid and military hardware to Pakistan hardened that nation's Pushtunistan stance. Daoud, tired of Afghanistan's economic vulnerability and Pakistani exploitation thereof and possessed of an army unable to maintain internal security or challenge Pakistan, was forced to look elsewhere for support. His knowledge of Ward's intrigues, coupled with painfully evident American insinuations on his country's lack of importance, left Daoud open to Faustian options.

In December, Soviet General Secretary Nikita Khrushchev and Premier Nikolai Bulganin visited Kabul, where they offered Daoud economic and military assistance. Daoud, confident that he could contain the dangers inherent in such an agreement and convinced that inactivity could prove even more dangerous, accepted the Soviet offer. Signed in January 1956, the agreement provided Afghanistan with over 100 million dollars' worth of economic assistance. The aid package included credits for construction of hydroelectric plants, industrial complexes, storage facilities, three major irrigation projects, two modern airports near Kabul, and a north-south highway from Kabul through the Hindu Kush to the Oxus. The total value of the Soviet offer more than doubled all foreign assistance previously granted Afghanistan. Its terms were also lucrative, with an eight-year amortization period, 2 percent interest, and a thirty-year, barter-based repayment plan.[4]

Increased Soviet economic activity heightened dependency on Moscow and posed serious dangers to Afghanistan's independence. More critically, the Afghan military soon became dependent upon the U.S.S.R. for training and equipment. After signing the economic agreement, Daoud made one final request to the United States for military hardware. Washington again declined. In August 1956, facing confrontation with Pakistan and sanctioned by the Loya Jirgah to acquire arms aid from any source, Daoud announced an agreement with the Soviet Union to provide military aid to Afghanistan.[5]

Between 1955 and 1972, the U.S.S.R. would supply nearly half a billion dollars' worth of military aid to Afghanistan. Soviet assistance amounted to approximately 95 percent of the total supplied to Kabul during that period. The Afghans received a variety of equipment including MiG-17 fighters, IL-28 light bombers, T-34 tanks, howitzers, and armored personnel carriers. The majority of arms shipments consisted of second- and third-line equipment, affordable yet superior to the weapons of the general population, which served adequately for internal security. The terms of repayment allowed the

Afghans to pay less than half the cost of the items and again allowed for barter exchange rather than strict monetary transactions.[6]

The modernization of the armed forces reduced the tribal threat against the government and supplied Daoud with the force needed to guarantee stability in the wake of social and economic reforms. Daoud often used the army to enforce government policy, and on more than one occasion, it responded successfully to rural uprisings and protests within cities. Particularly illustrative examples occurred in Qandahar in 1959 and 1960, when the Afghan army suppressed riots that followed government efforts to increase taxation, enforce conscription, and abolish *purdah.*

Strengthening the military further contributed to domestic growth. Throughout the 1950s, and 1960s, the army was asked to supervise and execute various development programs including construction of roads, dams, and airports. The Afghan military, privy to the nation's best educational opportunities, became the national repository for engineering, communications, electronics, and medical technologies. Even the limited training afforded the enlisted men gave them an educational background superior to the average Afghan. Yet, while Daoud had mitigated some threats and fostered growth, in so doing, he had increased his nation's dependency upon and vulnerability toward the Soviet Union.[7]

The possession of modern military hardware brought with it a dependency on the U.S.S.R. for training, spare parts, ammunition, and replacement items that left Afghanistan susceptible to the termination of contacts and effectively limited its political options, even in the absence of formal treaty arrangements. Khrushchev certainly recognized this and may have deliberately oversupplied Afghanistan to ensure domination. Furthermore, the construction of highways, bridges (the tonnage capacity of which conveniently corresponded to the weight of the heaviest Soviet tanks), port facilities on the Oxus, airports, and satellite communications centers facilitated access to the Afghan interior. Soviet instructors also assumed near total responsibility for training Afghan officers, creating opportunities for subversion within the government's most important enforcing instrument.[8]

Soviet assistance to Afghanistan would eventually pave the way for invasion of that country. In the late 1950s, however, Daoud's bargain seemed born of genius. The acceptance of the Soviet offer prompted the United States, heretofore uninterested in Afghanistan, to implement a sizable assistance program of its own. Hoping to limit Soviet influence and preserve Afghan independence, the Eisenhower administration financed several economic plans, some of which it had rejected earlier. Private American investment in Afghanistan also increased. Through the next decade, Soviet and American engineers built a variety of civic, industrial, hydroelectric, mining, agricultural, health, education, and communications facilities across Afghanistan, to the delight of Daoud's regime. Throughout the late 1950s and 1960s, Afghanistan remained the only country in the world where the U.S.A. and the U.S.S.R. cooperated, at times even collaborated, in development programs.[9]

In economic competition, however, the Soviet Union possessed many advantages over the West. First and foremost, Soviet goods were simply less expensive. Though Western goods were of higher quality, most Soviet items served an equal purpose in relatively poor Afghanistan. Similarly, Afghan produce, much of which was disdained in the West, proved acceptable on the Soviet market. Geographic proximity and a nationalized transportation system further allowed the Soviet Union to pay the Afghans higher prices for their goods while offering long-term, low-interest loans tied in to barter agreements. Soviet advisors and technicians also cost less to employ, lived in simple quarters, and behaved in less conspicuous manners than their American counterparts. Finally, Soviet freedom from democratic processes allowed them to fashion policy with comparative speed and administrative efficiency.[10]

The Americans, on the other hand, remained handicapped by their standard of living, which often precluded integration with the Afghan population, and by basic business instincts, which focused too narrowly on the immediate economic ramifications of policy. American programs continued to neglect the private sector, took too long to mature, and remained less noticeable and thus less influential than Soviet ventures. The most notable new American project, the construction of Qandahar International Airport, became another example of bureaucratic slowness that so irritated the Afghans. Military considerations played a key role in the Qandahar project, though whether it was designed to prevent the Soviets from establishing the Afghan national airline, to augment Afghan internal security, or for use as a base by bombers crossing the North Pole remains unclear. Funds were approved in 1956, the contract signed in 1957, construction began in 1958, and the airport finally opened in 1962. By the time the project was finally completed, the evolution of jet aircraft rendered the airport unnecessary for stopovers. Thereafter, it sat all but useless, until the Soviet air force began using it for operations against the *mujahidin* in the 1980s.

In the Helmand Valley, yields remained lower than when the project began. Even American efforts to influence the educational system produced less than desired results. While thousands of Afghans received their education in the United States and many returned with superior knowledge and favorable impressions, the increasingly critical atmosphere on American college campuses throughout the 1960s, however, turned some Afghans against the United States, other Western powers, and their own government. Hafizullah Amin, the most obvious example, actually obtained his affection for Marxism while attending Columbia University and the University of Wisconsin.[11]

In addition to economic efforts, by 1959 the United States had acknowledged the potential threat that Soviet predominance in the Afghan armed forces entailed and strove to "encourage Afghanistan to minimize its reliance upon the Communist bloc for military training and equipment, and to look

to the US and other free world sources for military training and assistance."
By 1965, 147 Afghan officers (61 army and 86 air force) had been trained
in the United States. The American programs provided technical training to
the Afghans and also fostered inducement of civic responsibility, proper civil-
military relations, support for economic growth, and the value of democracy
in general. The entire assistance program for Afghanistan, however,
amounted to only 3.3 million dollars, almost all of which went to transportation and per diem costs. Virtually all heavy equipment, including all aircraft,
continued to be provided by the Soviet Union. Furthermore, those officers
who trained in the United States constituted only a tiny fraction of the Afghan
establishment. Consequently, the impact of the American program remained
limited.[12]

Though Daoud was aware of past history of Soviet actions in Eastern Europe (he once told a concerned American correspondent: "Does anyone think
we have not heard of Czechoslovakia?") and their postwar attempt to establish a client state in north Iran, Daoud believed that he could prevent subversion in the officer corps and maintain the independence of Afghanistan.
He hoped his country, like Finland, could make use of Soviet assistance without sacrificing its sovereignty. Given his personal ties to the army, widespread
police activity, a lack of class antagonism, and the absence of a Communist
party in Afghanistan, the dangers of subversion had to seem remote and
worth the risk.

Daoud implemented extensive precautionary measures to avoid possible
infiltration of the military, most of which continued during the subsequent
constitutional experiment. He increased the size of the West German-trained
police force and had them monitor the actions of Soviet officers and technicians and the activities of domestic organizations with progressive or leftist
leanings. Daoud rotated Soviet technicians frequently and rarely renewed
their contracts upon termination of designated projects. Daoud also tried to
keep the army and air force insulated from political ideology. He continued
a time-honored practice of discharging officers who expressed political opinions and prohibited all members of the armed forces from seeking public
office. As a precaution against a potential coup, he appointed members of
the traditional ruling elite, including personal friends or family members, to
the highest ranks. Units were stationed away from their home regions, where
they remained less likely to sympathize with any regional rebellion. Most
notably, Daoud treated Soviet-trained officers and civilians with suspicion and
assigned them to less sensitive, often rudimentary posts.[13]

Throughout the 1960s, the Soviet Union continued to assist Afghanistan,
building motor repair facilities, fruit canneries, and a glass factory while assuming responsibility for oil and natural gas exploration. The Soviets emphasized these and other advantages that Afghanistan received through
cooperation and disseminated no ideological or anti-religious propaganda.
Given that and stringent security measures, most Afghans seem to have re-

mained complacent, perhaps noting one of their own proverbs: "When you ride a good horse, who cares in what country it was born." Yet, as an on-scene observer would note, "nothing was to preclude, with the passage of time, the development of a Soviet-oriented fifth column of some magnitude."[14]

Daoud eventually proved his own undoing through vigorous pursuit of Pushtunistan. In 1961, following a series of border incidents, Pakistan again blocked economic traffic to and from Afghanistan, thoroughly disrupting the Afghan economy for the third time in a dozen years. The losses incurred during the two-year blockade prompted Zahir Shah to request Daoud's resignation, which he obtained in March 1963.[15]

In October 1964, the king approved a new constitution. It contained elements typical of Western democracies, including the separation of powers, secret ballot elections, the right to trial, and freedom of the press. It established a bicameral legislature, consisting of the Meshrano Jirgah (House of Elders), one third of whose 84 members were appointed by the king, and the rest elected, and the Wolesi Jirgah (House of the People) with 215 elected members. The constitution, however, contained critical deficiencies that rendered responsible government difficult, if not impossible, to establish.

Had the constitution legalized political parties (traditionally outlawed in Afghanistan), the prime minister and his Cabinet could have orchestrated policy in expectation of legislative support. Instead, the executive and legislative branches remained at loggerheads. Though the Afghan ministers were often well educated and experienced in government, the legislature proved "inflexible and intemperate," especially from 1969 to 1973. The representatives showed little cohesion or self-discipline in opposing almost all executive initiatives. In the 1969–1970 session, for example, only one minor measure passed. Lower-level administration likewise remained slow, inept, and plagued with corruption.[16]

During the one-year interim between the formation of the constitution and its taking effect, two leading Afghan radicals, Nur Mohammed Taraki and Babrak Karmal, secretly founded the People's Democratic Party of Afghanistan (PDPA). Its rank-and-file consisted predominantly of military officers, civil servants, teachers, students, and recent graduates. Some analysts claim party membership further included "rootless radicals" and a "sizable criminal element."[17] Following the 1965 elections, Karmal packed the Wolesi Jirgah chamber gallery with student supporters who disrupted the proceedings through incessant chants of slogans. Three were killed and scores wounded in an ensuing riot. The Cabinet resigned following a no-confidence vote obtained in the wake of the violence. Babrak had thus established a precedent that would leave Afghanistan bereft of consistency in the executive branch as well. Four Cabinets would be voted out in the next ten years.[18]

Afghanistan's lack of experience with democratic traditions on the national level proved another damning obstacle facing the constitutional experiment.

Earlier kings had promulgated constitutions that established parliaments, but those bodies were little more than consultative chambers supporting a near-absolute monarchy. While local *jirgahs* practiced democracy in the villages, peasants and nomads traditionally avoided unnecessary contact with central government officials. Many feared the new elections as but a government ploy to obtain tax lists or conscripts. Consequently, public enthusiasm for the new government remained limited. Government failure to prevent or adequately avenge PDPA-incited violence alienated many who did participate. While some rural leaders eventually formed a fundamentalist opposition, attracted thousands of adherents, and directly challenged the PDPA in Kabul street demonstrations, they withheld support for a constitution whose provisions allowed the PDPA to function in an irreligious, disruptive, and cowardly fashion.[19]

Rural indifference also allowed for the over-representation of the Afghan intelligentsia (especially those resident in Kabul) in the government. Since the 1950s, improvements in the educational system had produced an expanding educated elite, of which over 90 percent were employed in the public sector. While the competitive assistance programs fueled the Afghan economy, ample employment existed for new graduates. By the late 1960s, however, both the United States and the Soviet Union began to curtail their aid programs to Afghanistan. The increasingly stagnant economy left most educated Afghans without positions or with traditional work assignments ill suited to their qualifications. The surplus graduates, frustrated by the slow rate of reform and the perceived nepotism of the traditional elite, proved bountiful receptacles for radical ideologues.[20]

Continued government incompetence only aggravated popular grievances. Through 1970 and 1971, drought and famine caused the deaths of an estimated 100,000 people and devastated herds and flocks. Government inefficiency during the crisis, buffeted by numerous allegations of scandal, undermined the legitimacy of the regime. Though support for the PDPA had declined when their activities turned increasingly violent and disruptive and the party had split in 1967 along personal and ethnic lines (with Taraki heading the Khalq [Masses] faction and Karmal the Parcham [Banner] group), popular resentment fueled a resurgence of support for opposition groups.[21]

Radical groups found the armed forces a fertile field in which to recruit. Professional training, coupled with intimate involvement with the civilian economy, politicized officers and enlisted men alike. In many ways the most modern social institution in Afghanistan, the army could not remain aloof from politics. Throughout the constitutional period, various Cabinets called upon the army to keep order between the political factions, which it did effectively while its loyalty remained with the royal family. The institution of democracy, however, as well as frustrations with the existing system undermined loyalty to the king. Similar phenomena have occurred in many Third World nations, where military elites often serve as key elements in modernization. In states where the civilian government remained strong and stable, the military rarely challenged the authority of the political authorities. The unstable political situation in Afghanistan, however, led several officers to consider direct alternatives. Since the Afghan armed forces constituted one of the few channels of upward mobility in the nation, exposure to foreign technologies aggravated existing grievances and prompted demands for rapid and extensive changes. As a result of their contacts with Soviet instructors, many officers and enlisted men came to support radical leftist groups, which were demanding sweeping changes to Afghanistan's existing socioeconomic structure.[22]

The Soviets required all Afghan officers to take courses in "dialectical and historical materialism and in the history of the international communist movement." Still, many Afghan officers who experienced training in the U.S.S.R. came home intense nationalists, owing to Russian racism and Communist disrespect for Islam. Soviet ideology attracted but a small minority of the trainees, but by 1973, perhaps as many as 600 supported the PDPA and its radical program. By that time, many such officers had reached positions of importance as majors or colonels, in command of key army and air force units and installations. While the regime continued to closely supervise the appointments and activities of its generals, those high-ranking officers, detached from the troops and committed to, if not implicated by, government policy, had little to risk through revolution. The colonels and majors, however, resented the incompetence of the government and their "superannuated and inefficient senior officers."[23]

A final constitutional flaw provided incentive to destroy the democratic experiment. Article 24 prohibited members of the royal family, including the king's uncles and first cousins, from holding office in the government. Designed to insulate the king from criticism and bar Daoud from politics, Article 24 ensured that the former prime minister became disaffected. Left with no channel for legal opposition, on July 17, 1973, the sixty-four-year-old Daoud, with the support of several young officers and troops, overthrew the monarchy in a virtually bloodless coup. Daoud proclaimed himself president of an Islamic Afghan Republic and appointed eight known PDPA (Parchami) members, former members, or sympathizers to Cabinet positions.[24]

Though he initially pursued policies in line with socialism and increased his nation's dependence on the Soviet Union, Daoud subsequently tried to distance himself from the U.S.S.R. and the PDPA. By 1976 Daoud had removed all Parchamis from his Cabinet and had lowered the number of in-country Soviet advisors from 1,000 to 200. He cleverly dispatched the Parchami rank-and-file into the countryside, ostensibly as part of a grass-roots modernization program, knowing that the rural Afghans would not cooperate. Most Parchamis quickly became disillusioned with the ignorance and obstinacy of the people and resigned. Daoud also diversified Afghan sources of economic assistance, seeking funds from the United States, West Germany,

China, India, Saudi Arabia, and, most notably, Iran. In July 1974, the shah promised Daoud a 2-billion-dollar loan, more aid than the entirety of Soviet and American assistance provided since 1953. Yet Daoud's government remained plagued by inefficiency, lethargy, and corruption.[25]

By the late 1970s, Daoud had banned all parties besides his own and forced all opposition groups underground. Right-wing Islamist groups responded with a series of violent acts in Kabul, including several abortive coup attempts. Amidst the chaos, the PDPA reunited, almost certainly at Soviet urging. On April 17, 1978, Mir Akbar Khyber, a prominent Parchami, was assassinated. His funeral sparked a massive multifactioned anti-government protest. The regime responded with arrests of several top PDPA leaders, whom Daoud apparently planned to execute. Yet Daoud left many lesser officials at large, including Taraki's chief lieutenant Hafizullah Amin, who, though confined to house arrest, nonetheless received an endless string of visitors as he planned for a coup. Daoud also left several military officers loyal to the PDPA at their stations.[26]

On the morning of April 27, those disaffected, Soviet-trained officers, either sympathizers or members of the PDPA, launched their forces against the government. Major Mohammed Aslam Watanjar led an armored assault against the presidential palace, repeating a role he had performed in 1973, while another attack against the Ministry of Defense disrupted the regime's ability to coordinate a response. Meanwhile, Colonel Mohammed Qader, generally regarded as the mastermind of the coup, led air strikes against Daoud's forces that tilted the balance in favor of the insurgents. Some units bitterly contested the city. The bulk of Daoud's 2,000-man presidential guard was killed in battle for the palace. Most units in the armed forces, however, took no part in the fighting.[27]

The civilian population showed greater indifference. Louis Dupree, who witnessed the episode, noted how "despite the danger, people queued up for buses—even in the firefight zone! Taxis honked for tanks to move over, and wove in and out as the fighting continued. At some corners, traffic policemen motioned for the tanks to pull over to the curb. The tanks ignored the gestures, and rumbled on to their objectives."[28]

While such widespread popular apathy, also apparent in 1973, had historical roots, Daoud had done little to foster public support. Like the constitutional experiment, his republic never proved attractive to the average Afghan. Repressive policies instead aroused widespread dissent. The majority of dissenters, however, supported fundamentalist groups. Daoud directed intelligence efforts and retaliatory measures against them, while dismissing the PDPA as inconsequential.

After a brief interim, the military officers relinquished power to the PDPA. With Taraki as president and Amin in charge of internal security, the Khalqis quickly purged the Parchamis. They sent Babrak and other prominent officials into virtual exile as ambassadors and imprisoned or executed less notable members. Throughout their tenure, the Khalqis routinely imprisoned or executed perceived political or ideological opponents, including many members of the intelligentsia.[29]

Once consolidated in power, the Khalqi government, in a manner tragically similar to the earlier reforms of Amanullah, drove the people to rebellion through attempted implementation of economic and social reforms, most of which conflicted with Islam or Afghan tradition. The greatest failure involved land reform. PDPA attempts to relieve the alleged "land hunger" of the peasants eventually resulted in huge grain deficits. In canceling tenant debts, abolishing usury, and limiting the amount of land ownership, the Khalqis "struck at the heart of the reciprocal rights and obligations around which rural life in Afghanistan is organized." They deprived Afghan peasants of any credit system and effectively prohibited them from farming. Furthermore, the average peasant considered land confiscation *khiyanat* (treachery) contrary to both the laws of Islam and national codes of behavior.[30]

Another government decree granted equal social, economic, civil, and political rights to women, mandated their compulsory education, all but eliminated dowries, set a minimum marital age, and prohibited arranged marriages. Though impossible to enforce, this assault on patriarchy provoked widespread resentment among men and women alike. Perhaps most foolishly, Taraki changed the national flag from the traditional black-red-green pattern to an all-red flag, which closely resembled those of the Soviet Central Asian Republics. He later ordered virtually everything in Kabul painted red, including pigeons released at the flag-unveiling ceremony. Taraki's obvious subservience to the Soviet Union, his direct affronts to Islam, Afghan culture, and national pride, and increased government repression spawned nationwide resistance.[31] Popular resentment to PDPA rule exploded in a mass public uprising in Herat in March 1979. The Heratis killed some fifty Soviet advisors and their families and several hundred PDPA officials, soldiers, and sympathizers. Government troops eventually shelled the city into submission, killing thousands in the process. By most accounts, the incident had a dramatic effect on the Soviets, who began planning for invasion shortly afterward.[32]

The Soviets sought political solutions first. The Soviet ambassador to Afghanistan, with Taraki and Babrak's connivance, attempted to assassinate Amin and make him a scapegoat for the regime's failings. Amin, tipped off to the plan, came to a prearranged meeting armed, and Taraki was fatally wounded instead. Amin assumed power in September. Continued repression, economic collapse, and the anti-Islamic, pro-Soviet reputation of the PDPA left him without support. The insurgency spread to the majority of Afghanistan's provinces, some of which fell under complete control of *mujahidin* forces. Mutinies among government troops became commonplace. Some units defected en masse, taking their equipment with them, while others attempted coups of their own.[33]

That December, Soviet forces invaded Afghanistan. Soviet officers, ostensibly in Afghanistan to provide training, proved invaluable in assisting the invasion. Some successfully duped Afghan officers into removing ammunition supplies and vehicle batteries, allegedly for inventory and winterization. With the government forces disarmed, Soviet airborne troops secured key posts within Kabul. Most Kabulis, including the PDPA leaders, ignored the increased air activity, thinking it but a massive resupply effort. Amin's bodyguard resisted the Soviet attack, but the assault forces overwhelmed them and killed Amin during the fighting. Meanwhile, Soviet armored forces moved rapidly down Afghanistan's main highways and established themselves in all major cities. The Soviets suffered fewer than 300 casualties in the entire operation. In the next ten years, however, they would lose thousands.[34]

The road to war in Afghanistan was certainly a complicated one. Constitutional failings and general incompetence amidst the PDPA-inspired violence ordained the failure of the democratic experiment. PDPA machinations and Daoud's tactical errors contributed to the collapse of his Islamic Republic. Perhaps most importantly, the passive indifference of both the civilian population and the majority of the units of the armed forces facilitated both Daoud's 1973 coup and the PDPA's 1978 takeover. The Khalqi's neglect of Amanullah's precedents led to near-instantaneous failure, which in turn prompted the Soviet invasion.

Daoud's decision to accept Soviet military assistance, however, must remain the point from whence invasion became a realistic possibility, as it fostered infiltration of radicals into the armed forces. Daoud himself had always realized that Soviet actions were motivated by self-interest, but he reasoned that they would not risk attack, as "the country would be an economic liability to the USSR: to control it would be difficult and costly; and, most important, any such aggression would have disastrous repercussions among the neutralist nations in Asia and Africa."[35] Another Afghan writer would voice similar conclusions as late as 1968: "Looking at the Soviet intentions in Afghanistan one could reasonably rule out a direct Soviet invasion of Afghanistan. In addition to the fact that the Afghans would defend themselves directly and through guerilla war, the Soviet Union would lose the confidence of other neutral nations. She would suffer from world popular pressures and about 300 million Moslems of Asia and the Middle East would turn against her."[36]

There are certainly elements of logic in these arguments, which not only Afghans, but Americans as well, would voice. The threat of guerrilla war and adverse world reaction did constitute deterrents to Soviet aggression. In time, however, precedents of successful proxy activity in Angola, Ethiopia, and South Yemen and global distraction with the hostage crisis in Iran apparently led the Soviets to discount unfavorable world reaction. At the same time, the Soviets, like many Western powers before them, underestimated guerrilla potential.[37] Soviet control over the Afghan military also rendered tactical advantages, which likely gave further encouragement to invasion. Given that Soviet involvement had also created opportunities for subversion, which ultimately led to the ouster of two governments, one must be left to wonder whether similar Western measures, coupled with the aforementioned deterrents, might well have rendered invasion all but impossible.

NOTES

1. Daoud, "Statement," p. 26; Memorandum of Conversation by the Acting Officer in Charge of Pakistan-Afghanistan Affairs (Thatcher), 22 December 1954, *FRUS, 1952–1954*, XI, p. 1439; *FRUS, 1952–1954*, XI, p. 1434fn; Kaur, *Pak-Afghanistan Relations*, pp. 79–82. Ghaffar Khan led protests against the act and was once again arrested and banned from the frontier. Sahib curiously supported the scheme from within the Cabinet.

2. Kaur, *Pak-Afghanistan Relations*, pp. 86–92; Reardon, "Modernization and Reform," p. 157; Fraser-Tytler, *Afghanistan*, p. 321; Newell, *Politics of Afghanistan*, p. 68; Dupree, *AUFS*, 1/4, p. 1. The Afghans claimed the Pakistani mob in Peshawar threatened their consul with a pistol and made off with the treasury and other valuables. Pakistan claimed the Afghans incited the mob by throwing furniture on them from inside the consulate.

3. Dupree, *Afghanistan*, p. 538; Quddus, *Afghanistan and Pakistan*, pp. 78–79; Franck, *Afghanistan between East and West*, p. 12; Arnold, *Afghanistan*, p. 35; Wilber, *Afghanistan*, p. 143; Progress Report, NSC 5409, 25 February 1955; Progress Report, NSC 5409, 24 August 1955; Poullada, "Afghanistan and the United States," p. 189. The progress reports admit the Afghans asked for Pushtunistan assistance in 1955 but that the United States saw no way to help them. Poullada claims the United States, having lost influence in Afghanistan and remaining unwilling to pressure Pakistan, could do little but "wring its hands."

4. Dupree, *AUFS*, 4/4, p. 7; Arnold, *Afghanistan*, pp. 31, 36–38; Bradcher, *Afghanistan and the Soviet Union*, pp. 19–20; Franck, *Afghanistan between East and West*, pp. vii, xiii, 21, 32, 57–58; Kamrany, *Peaceful Competition*, p. 62. The treaty included an extension of the 1931 treaty of neutrality and nonaggression and voiced support for Pushtunistan. The Soviets also built a 100-bed hospital and provided fifteen buses to Kabul, ostensibly as gifts.

5. Sutton and Kemp, *Arms to Developing Countries*, pp. 5–7; Reardon, "Modernization and Reform," pp. 157–158, 164–165; Rubenstein, "Afghanistan and the Great Powers," p. 67; Poullada, "Search for National Unity," p. 43.

6. Collins, *Soviet Invasion of Afghanistan*, p. 23; Reardon, "Modernization and Reform, " p. 159; O'Ballance, "Afghanistan," pp. 227–228; Sutton and Kemp, *Arms to Developing Countries*, p. 6; Franck, *Afghanistan between East and West*, p. 57; Bradcher, *Afghanistan and the Soviet Union*, p. 28.

7. Smith, *Area Handbook for Afghanistan*, pp. 379, 395–397; Khalizad, *Security of Southwest Asia*, p. 74; Griffiths, *Afghanistan*, pp. 119, 160–161; Bhaneja, *Afghanistan*, pp. 45–46; Ziring, *Iran, Turkey and Afghanistan*, p. 52; Reardon, "Modernization and Reform, " pp. 162, 195–197; O'Ballance, "Afghanistan," p. 231; Poullada, "Search for National Unity," p. 44. He claims simply: "It is incontestible that the creation of a modern military establishment enabled Daoud Khan to make his writ run throughout the land, probably for the first time in Afghan history."

8. Smith, *Area Handbook for Afghanistan*, pp. 375–381, 395–397. "The almost

total dependence of the military on Soviet logistical support appears to give the Soviets a large measure of control over Afghan military operations." Dupree, *AUFS*, 4/4, p. 14; Wakman, *Afghanistan*, p. 56; Griffiths, *Afghanistan*, pp. 146–147; Amstutz, *Afghanistan*, pp. 22, 256–257.

9. Poullada, "Afghanistan and the United States," pp. 184–185; Schofield, *Every Rock*, p. 266; see also Dupree, *AUFS*, 4/9, "American Private Enterprise in Afghanistan"; U.S. Senate, 88th Congress, 1st Session, Committee on Foreign Relations, "Hearing on Foreign Assistance Act of 1963," pp. 154–159. For example, the Americans supplied electrical and communications equipment for the Soviet-built airport at Kabul. Progress Report, NSC 5409, 30 March 1956, paragraphs A9, A13. For other examples see "US Will Help Transport Afghan Pilgrims to Mecca (*Department of State Bulletin*, 2 July 1956, p. 25) or "US to Assist Afghanistan to Rebuild Habibya College (*Department of State Bulletin*, 3 December 1956, p. 886).

10. Franck, *Afghanistan between East and West*, pp. vii, 26–28, 32–34, 70, 78; Toynbee, *Between Oxus and Jumna*, pp. 186–187; Giradet, *Afghanistan*, pp. 94–95; Newell, *Politics of Afghanistan*, pp. 128–129; Griffiths, *Afghanistan*, pp. 137, 151–154.

11. Dupree, *Afghanistan*, pp. 513–514; Franck, *Afghanistan between East and West*, pp. 28, 46, 51, 68, 74, 82; Razamani, *Northern Tier*, p. 128; Toynbee, *From Oxus to Jumna*, pp. 188–189; Fletcher, *Afghanistan*, pp. 271–272; Arnold, *Afghanistan*, p. 101; Amstutz, *Afghanistan*, pp. 32–34; Hangen, "Afghanistan," pp. 61–72.

12. U.S. Strike Command, "Military Assistance Program—Afghanistan," DD-ISA-MAP-A3-P14, U.S. Army Military History Institute; Hovey, *United States Military Assistance*, pp. 47–48, 178–180; NSC 5617, 7 December 1956, paragraph 77; Progress Report, NSC 5701, 22 January 1958, Annex A; Progress Report on NSC 5701, 16 July 1958, Annex A; Progress Report, NSC 5701, 18 March 1959, paragraph 29a; see also Giradet, *Afghanistan*, p. 93; Hyman, *Afghanistan under Soviet Domination*, p. 29. By 1979, 10,000 officers and enlisted men, fully 10 percent of the entire establishment, had been trained in the U.S.S.R., whereas only a few hundred had trained in Western bloc nations. Besides the United States, small numbers of Afghan officers trained in Britian, India, and Turkey.

13. Dupree, *AUFS*, 4/4, p. 3; Fletcher, *Afghanistan*, p. 261; Wilber, *Afghanistan*, p. 149; Franck, *Afghanistan between East and West*, pp. 34, 61–63; Griffiths, *Afghanistan*, p. 147; Bhaneja, *Political Modernization*, pp. 42–48; Giradet, *Afghanistan*, pp. 91–92, 117; U.S. Department of State, Bureau of Near Eastern Affairs, "Long-Term Commitment to Afghanistan's Economic Development Program," p. 11; Arnold, *Afghanistan*, pp. 40–41; Hangen, "Afghanistan," pp. 63–67. Daoud resisted Soviet efforts to impose their Tables of Equipment and Organization upon the Afghan army and eventually replaced Russian communications equipment with American. See also Military Attaché's Summary of Intelligence for the Week Ending 4 July 1947, L/P&S/ 12/1850.

14. Progress Report on NSC 5701, 22 January 1958, Annex B; Franck, *Afghanistan between East and West*, pp. vi, 10, 62; Hyman, *Afghanistan under Soviet Domination*, p. 34; Amstutz, *Afghanistan*, p. 23.

15. Arnold, *Afghanistan*, pp. 42–45; Kaur, *Pak-Afghanistan Relations*, p. 121. Daoud's arrogance and irreligious behavior may have contributed to his demise. His reforms certainly put him at odds with tribal leaders and the religious establishment.

Bhaneja, *Afghanistan*, p. 24; Reardon, "Modernization and Reform, " p. 167. Daoud could perhaps have resisted, but he had lost the loyalty of the army. Wali Khan, Daoud's uncle, rival, and hero of the civil war of 1929, secured the support of officers thought to be Daoud loyalists.

16. Dupree, *AUFS*, 12/6, p. 12; Kakar, *Fall of Afghan Monarchy*, p. 213; Poullada, "Search for National Unity," pp. 46–48; Arnold, *Afghanistan*, p. 46; Griffiths, *Afghanistan*, pp. 117–118, 162–163, 169–172; Bhaneja, *Afghanistan*, pp. 28fn, 30, 35, 35fn, 39, 51–53; Ziring, *Iran, Turkey and Afghanistan*, pp. 54, 91–92; Collins, *Soviet Invasion of Afghanistan*, p. 27; Hyman, *Afghanistan under Soviet Domination*, pp. 53, 62. The legislature passed a Political Parties Act in 1968, but it remained "with the King" for five years. He never signed the legislation. Griffiths blames the failure of the constitutional attempt on the king, who was "well-mannered, but more interested in culture, history, and open-air sports than the practice of government and exercise of power." Most rural leaders, as skeptical of the new Parliament as their constituents, did not run for election in 1965 or 1967. Once the legislature demonstrated real authority, however, they carried the election of 1969. By 1973 half the legislature was illiterate.

17. Collins, *Soviet Invasion of Afghanistan*, pp. 28, 41–42; Hyman, *Afghanistan under Soviet Domination*, pp. 55–58, 63, 70; Giradet, *Afghanistan*, pp. 98–102, 111; Arnold, *Afghanistan*, pp. 52–54.

18. Dupree, *AUFS*, 10/4 (p. 7) and 12/7 (pp. 2–3); Schofield, *Every Rock*, pp. 266–267; Griffiths, *Afghanistan*, pp. 92, 168–170, 168fn, 173–174; Wolpert, *Roots of Confrontation*, pp. 162–166; Bhaneja, *Afghanistan*, pp. 28–29.

19. Payind, "Soviet-Afghan Relations," pp. 114–115. The assassinations of historian Mohammed Ali and an anti-Soviet newspaper editor were among the incidents that dissuaded conservative elements from support of the constitution. Hyman, *Afghanistan under Soviet Domination*, pp. 9–11, 47, 54, 114. In an average election (1964–1973), only 15 percent of the population voted, including just 5 to 10 percent in some major towns and cities and less than 2 percent in rural areas. Even in Kabul, less than half eligible voters participated. Dupree, *AUFS*, 4/6 (p. 4), 9/4 (pp. 14–15), and 10/4 (p. 2); Dupree, "Afghanistan, Problems of a Peasant-Tribal Society," pp. 3, 8; Griffiths, *Afghanistan*, pp. 166, 170–171, 176–179; Bhaneja, *Afghanistan*, pp. 32–35, 40.

20. Wilber, *Afghanistan*, pp. 146–149; Giradet, *Afghanistan*, pp. 96–100; Dupree, "Afghanistan, Problems of a Peasant-Tribal Society," pp. 4, 10–11; Reardon, "Political Modernization," pp. 166–167, 171, 195; Dupree, *AUFS*, 4/3, p. 23; Hyman, *Afghanistan under Soviet Domination*, pp. 51–52, 61; Arnold, *Afghanistan*, p. 101; Bhaneja, *Afghanistan*, pp. 5, 36fn; Newell, *Politics of Afghanistan*, pp. 119–120, 144. Soviet assistance fell from 44.7 million in 1967–1968 to 30.5 million in 1968–1969 to 28.4 million in 1969–1970. American assistance for the same period fell from 12.7 to 4.8 to 1.4 million dollars.

21. Hyman, *Afghanistan under Soviet Domination*, pp. 34, 55–58, 63, 70, 128; Collins, *Soviet Invasion of Afghanistan*, pp. 28–29, 41–42; Arnold, *Afghanistan*, pp. 52–54; Quddus, *Afghanistan and Pakistan*, p. 133; Giradet, *Afghanistan*, p. 100; Ziring, *Iran, Turkey and Afghanistan*, p. 92. The American Embassy attempted to relieve the famine, providing 200,000 tons of wheat.

22. Daalder, *Role of the Military*, pp. 12–13, 16–20; Hyman, *Afghanistan under Soviet Domination*, pp. 30, 52; Khalizad, *Security of Southwest Asia*, p. 75; Bhanaja,

Afghanistan, pp. 44–45; Newell, *Politics of Afghanistan,* p. 73; Reardon, "Modernization and Reform," pp. 195–197.

23. Daalder, *Role of the Military,* p. 14; Bhaneja, *Afghanistan,* pp. 42–43; Griffiths, *Afghanistan,* pp. 147–148; Hyman, *Afghanistan under Soviet Domination,* p. 29; Amstutz, *Afghanistan,* p. 181.

24. Dupree, *AUFS,* 4/4, p. 7; Arnold, *Afghanistan,* pp. 45–46, 55–59; Quddus, *Pakistan and Afghanistan,* p. 124; Hyman, *Afghanistan under Soviet Domination,* pp. 64–66. The only casualties were a tank commander who swerved to avoid a bus and drowned in the Kabul River and seven policemen who did not recognize the rebels. Griffiths, *Afghanistan,* pp. 162–179. The king and the royal family were in Italy at the time. Griffiths suspects that Zahir made a deal with Daoud. Daoud received such assistance from the Parchamis that Dupree called them "Daoud's own Communist Party." Dupree, "Afghanistan under Khalq, *Problems of Communism,* July-August 1979, p. 38; see also *AUFS,* 18/8.

25. Arnold, *Afghanistan,* pp. 58, 61, 63–64. Arnold has insinuated that the leftist ministers of finance and commerce sabotaged the Iranian aid program. Collins, *Soviet Invasion of Afghanistan,* p. 38. Barely 10 percent of the loan was delivered, owing to internal problems in Iran and the festering Helmand dispute. Giradet, *Afghanistan,* p. 101; Griffiths, *Afghanistan,* p. 181. Perhaps inspired by the emergence of Bangladesh at the end of the 1971 war, Daoud initially pursued the old Pushtunistan policy toward Pakistan. Afghanistan supported the National Awami Party of Abdul Wali Khan, son of Abdur Ghaffar Khan, which from 1973 to 1975 committed a spate of terrorist acts across the North West Frontier Province and Baluchistan. Given his desire for third-party aid, Daoud soon adopted a more conciliatory policy. See Miller, *Khyber,* pp. 371–372.

26. Griffiths, *Afghanistan,* p. 182; Collins, *Soviet Invasion of Afghanistan,* pp. 48–49, 52; Hyman, *Afghanistan under Soviet Domination,* pp. 66–67, 76, 175; Arnold, *Afghanistan,* pp. 65–66; Payind, "Soviet-Afghan Relations," p. 117.

27. Dupree, *AUFS,* 4/4 (p. 13), 4/5 (pp. 5, 14), and 4/6 (pp. 6–13). Dupree states simply, "The side with the fewer foul-ups won." It was "more a monument to the disorganization, poor leadership of Daoud than skill, cunning, or foreign support of undoers." The PDPA forces executed those few taken prisoner along with Daoud and some thirty members of the royal family. The Soviet Union apparently knew of the coup and gave their approval, but actual Soviet participation was minimal. Amstutz, *Afghanistan,* pp. 391–392, 395. Both Qader and Watanjar provided critical assistance to Daoud in the 1973 coup. Though Daoud later assigned them to insignificant positions (placing Qader in charge of the military slaughterhouse), he subsequently reinstated them to important posts. Both had been trained in the U.S.S.R. and would eventually achieve high rank in the PDPA regime. Arnold, *Afghanistan,* pp. 62–63, 69–73. Griffiths, *Afghanistan,* pp. 182–183, 186.

28. Dupree, *AUFS,* 4/5, p. 8; see also Collins, *Soviet Invasion of Afghanistan,* pp. 50–52; Hyman, *Afghanistan under Soviet Domination,* pp. 75–76.

29. Bradsher, *Afghanistan and the Soviet Union,* pp. 78–80; Arnold, *Afghanistan,* pp. 74–76; Griffiths, *Afghanistan,* pp. 184–185; Giradet, *Afghanistan,* p. 104; Hyman, *Afghanistan under Soviet Domination,* pp. 82–83, 92, 108, 114; Payind, "Soviet-Afghan Relations," p. 119.

30. Amstutz, *Afghanistan,* pp. 238–239, 315–317; Giradet, *Afghanistan,* p. 111–113; Hyman, *Afghanistan under Soviet Domination,* pp. 86–92. Most Afghan

landlord-peasant relationships were cooperative. Many peasants respected or even loved their landlords, who in turn took paternalistic interest in their tenants. Indeed, later resistance groups at times consisted of former tenants under command of their landlord.

31. Collins, *Soviet Invasion of Afghanistan,* pp. 86–88; Hyman, *Afghanistan under Soviet Domination,* pp. 112–118; Arnold, *Afghanistan,* pp. 77–80; Griffiths, *Afghanistan,* pp. 183–184; Schofield, *Every Rock,* pp. 281–282. Taraki also reinstated *begari* (a form of public labor similar to the French *corvèe*), prompting further outrage.

32. Collins, *Soviet Invasion of Afghanistan,* p. 59; Schofield, *Every Rock,* p. 282; Giradet, *Afghanistan,* pp. 115–116; Griffiths, *Afghanistan,* pp. 185–186; Hyman, *Afghanistan under Soviet Domination,* pp. 100–101, 159. The Heratis reportedly flayed some alive and beheaded or otherwise dismembered others and then carried the mutilated bodies through the streets on pikes.

33. Amstutz, *Afghanistan,* pp. 41–43, 53–55; Bradsher, *Afghanistan,* pp. 163–164; Griffiths, *Afghanistan,* pp. 187–188; Hyman, *Afghanistan under Soviet Domination,* pp. 152–158; Arnold, *Afghanistan,* pp. 80–82, 86–91, 95–100; Payind, "Soviet-Afghan Relations," pp. 119–120.

34. Arnold, *Afghanistan,* pp. 94–95; Giradet, *Afghanistan,* pp. 12–13; Collins, *Soviet Invasion of Afghanistan,* p. 78; Hyman, *Afghanistan under Soviet Domination,* pp. 156, 159, 165, 168–169; Amstutz, *Afghanistan,* p. 48; Hammond, *Red Flag over Afghanistan,* p. 99; Payind, "Soviet-Afghan Relations," p. 120. There were nearly 10,000 Soviet officers and troops within Afghanistan before the invasion actually began.

35. Daoud quoted in Fletcher, *Afghanistan,* p. 261.

36. Nake Kamrany quoted in Griffiths, *Afghanistan,* p. 157.

37. Bradsher, *Afghanistan and the Soviet Union,* pp. 142–147.

15

SUMMARY AND CONCLUSIONS

Twice in the nineteenth century, British forces invaded Afghanistan in an effort to reduce that land to subservience. In 1839 they drove out a ruler who had repeatedly expressed a desire to ally with London. Two years later, vengeful Afghans destroyed a retreating force almost to a man, and the exiled amir returned to his throne. After a brief mid-century lull, a second invasion similarly failed to incorporate Afghanistan within the Empire. The wars left a legacy of mutual hatred and distrust that, coupled with British occupation of Pushtun-populated districts along the Northwest Frontier, led to recurring conflict and rendered extensive cooperation impossible. The two wars served only to force the British to acknowledge the fighting ability of the Afghans and to forgo further invasions.

Fears of Russia, which systematically absorbed several Central Asian *khanates* and seized territory claimed by Afghanistan, mitigated Afghan loathing of the British and encouraged accommodating policy. From 1880 on, British India provided subsidies to Afghanistan that allowed that nation's rulers to consolidate authority and effect limited modernization. Such aid, especially the provision of military hardware, rendered the British a measure of influence at Kabul. Anglo-Afghan relations thus remained relatively stable, if not particularly cordial.

Turn-of-the-century Afghanistan resembled an Indian princely state, nominally allied to Britain and robbed of an independent foreign policy, though free of British garrisons. Abdur Rahman raised a dependable national army that proved essential to his efforts to restore central authority. He and his son Habibullah maintained Afghan autonomy, but prohibited extensive modernization programs, fearing foreign influences and infrastructure development that might facilitate an invasion. Afghanistan remained lamentably backward, even compared with its immediate neighbors. Meanwhile, the Northwest Frontier of India became the celebrated trouble spot of the British Empire. British attempts to police the populace encountered sustained resistance, to which Afghanistan's rulers sporadically offered verbal encouragement and material support. Interminable uprisings overshadowed occasional accord between Afghan and British-Indian political authorities. In the Western media, Afghanistan itself remained synonymous for a land of anarchy and barbarism.

The Anglo-Russian alliance of the First World War limited Afghan policy options and practically forced Habibullah to seek closer relations with Britain. The interlude of peace, however, ended in 1919 with Habibullah's assassination and Amanullah's assumption of power. Like his fellow modernists, Amanullah was fervently anti-British. He destroyed the old buffer state relationship, courted Soviet favor, and offered militant support to the border tribes and pan-Islamic movements, bringing Anglo-Afghan relations to their nadir. Though Amanullah in time grew suspicious of his northern neighbor, expanded contacts with other nations, and eventually adopted a more conciliatory policy toward Britain, possibilities for extensive cooperation between Kabul, London, and Delhi remained severely restricted.

Amanullah proved his own undoing when he attempted to transform his premodern kingdom into a progressive, westernized state almost overnight. In assailing national traditions and several tenets of Islam, Amanullah managed to alienate virtually everyone in the country. His army, which had suffered from the termination of the British subsidy and a lack of attention to its needs, simply disintegrated. By early 1929, rebel forces had driven Amanullah into exile. His failures left a lasting impression on those who would succeed him. Amanullah's downfall also heralded new opportunities for British influence in Afghanistan.

The year of civil war that accompanied Amanullah's ouster and the brief reign of Bacha-i-Saqao left Afghanistan weak and in dire need of foreign support. No longer fearful of British invasion, yet wary of potential Soviet threats to Afghan independence, Nadir Shah established a more cooperative policy with British India. In exchange for continued assistance, Nadir provided no overt support to the trans-Durand Pushtuns. Though Nadir's "Anglophile" policy fueled domestic opposition and circuitously led to his assassination, his brother and successor, Hashim Khan, proved even more anti-Soviet and hence more inclined to cooperate with British and Indian authorities. Bilateral relations steadily improved, though frontier violence throughout the decade overshadowed the rapprochement.

Britain's reluctance or inability to offer more extensive assistance and the inherent attractiveness of working with a distant third party led Hashim to establish educational, economic, and military contacts with Nazi Germany. Though the Afghan-German agreements strained relations with Britain during the early years of the Second World War, as Allied victory became imminent, Anglo-Afghan relations improved steadily. By the end of the war, despite the misunderstandings and setbacks of the previous century, Britain and Afghanistan had reached a common understanding on a variety of issues. Most notably, through the "Lancaster Plan," the British agreed to provide equipment and training for the Afghan military. During its limited tenure, the Afghans routinely expressed satisfaction with the plan and other existing arrangements and hopes for expanded contacts in the future.

The rise of the Indian nationalist movement, however, led to the demise of British hegemony in South Asia. Throughout the independence debates, British authorities sought to preserve as much of the old strategic position as possible. Though civil disorder and Jinnah's persistence eventually led Mountbatten to concede partition, he still thought it possible to preserve the strategic status quo through retention of both successor states in the Commonwealth. Given hope (or delusion) that partition would not alter strategic policy, British planners assumed Afghanistan would continue its role as a buffer state. They deemed India's frontier inviolable and repeatedly declared the retention of the North West Frontier Province (NWFP) within the successor states vital to the security of the region.

Within the NWFP several political quirks had left the Congress-allied *Khudai Khidmatgaran* governing a predominantly Muslim province. Mountbatten realized that the frontier could not be left to such a government without risk of catastrophe. He persuaded Nehru and Jinnah to rest the fate of the province on a referendum, limiting the options to union with Pakistan or India. The British, Congress, and League agreed to remove provincial secession options from the final partition plan. Consequently, when Afghanistan and the *Khudai Khidmatgaran* argued for expansion of the existing referendum options to include union of the NWFP with Afghanistan or creation of an independent "Pushtunistan," British authorities dismissed them outright. While a few officials acknowledged recent Afghan cooperation, saw a need for continued joint action, and supported immediate discussions with the Afghans, Nehru, Jinnah, and Mountbatten agreed to leave the details of future relations with Afghanistan to subsequent negotiations. With Pakistan and India both committed to the Commonwealth, the British assumed they would pursue time-honored frontier policies and fully expected cooperation with Afghanistan to continue.

Despite efforts to ensure the maintenance of previous strategic policies, the plethora of differences that made partition inevitable likewise precluded continuation of the strategic status quo. Once India and Pakistan achieved independence, Afghanistan became of minimal value to Britain. Weakened by war and soon divested of political and military responsibility for the area, Britain was no longer able or even particularly interested in assisting Afghanistan. The successor states, meanwhile, emerged from the partition weak and poised against the other. Disputes over Kashmir, the partitions of Bengal and the Punjab, the division of military and industrial assets, and the communal atrocities left Pakistan and India more inclined to battle one another than forge a common defense policy. The Joint Defense Council, entrusted with the task of defining future relations with Afghanistan, disbanded only a few weeks after partition. The economic and political disruption that accompanied partition also ensured that neither Pakistan nor India would have much to spare Afghanistan, even in the absence of political hindrances. India, technically responsible for the continuation of the Lancaster Plan, showed little desire to assist the Muslim Afghans, whose calls for self-determination on the frontier echoed those of Pakistan in Kashmir. Continual controversy over the fate of the NWFP, meanwhile, precluded close relations between Afghanistan and Pakistan.

Following partition, the Kabul authorities, supported by the *Khudai Khidmatgaran* and a variety of frontier luminaries, argued for an independent Pushtun state. Pakistan steadfastly refused to consider proposals that hinted at further dismemberment and dismissed Afghan claims as thinly disguised irredentism. The Pakistanis claimed all rights to the area as legitimate heirs of the British, citing the results of the plebiscite in which 99 percent of the voters had opted for incorporation into Pakistan. The opposition continued to challenge the validity of the vote, claiming that the limited electorate and the lack of suitable options rendered it invalid. Protest would last in some form for decades, poisoning relations between the two states and playing a prominent role in the eventual alienation of Afghanistan from the West.

Throughout the ensuing period, Afghanistan, searching for a replacement for the departed British, courted the United States. Though the Afghan government repeatedly expressed desires for an intimate partnership with Washington, both the Truman and the Eisenhower administrations proved disinterested. Southwest Asia never attracted more than occasional concern from the Washington hierarchy. Afghanistan, which seemed of no immediate or potential value, attracted even less attention. According to one embassy chief, the United States showed "absolutely no interest" in Afghanistan and demonstrated "[neither] recognition of its central position [nor any] apparent knowledge of historical precedents which affected British-Russian relations."[1]

The Truman administration did offer limited support to an agricultural development program in the Helmand Valley, embassy officials briefly tried to mediate the Pushtunistan controversy, and at one time Pentagon officials even approved Afghan purchases of military hardware. The Helmand Valley Project, however, proved a dismal failure, the stipulations of the military aid agreement rendered purchase impractical, and Pushtunistan negotiations were aborted in the face of Pakistani intransigence. Plagued by a series of errors, oversights, and misunderstandings, Afghan-American relations would gradually wane, until the American alliance with Pakistan undermined Afghan faith in the United States almost entirely.

Though courted by Pakistan from its inception, the United States initially saw no reason to justify alliance with that nation. Over the next half dozen years, however, American impressions of Pakistan changed. In marked contrast to their Indian counterparts, Pakistan politicians scoffed at neutralism, trumpeted their martial tradition, and routinely swore unflinching loyalty to the Western bloc. The recommendations of several avowed British experts helped further convince the American bureaucracy that Pakistan would be a beneficial addition to the containment program. Increasingly desirous of access to Pakistani manpower and air bases, the United States courted favor through increased provision of military and economic assistance. The Truman administration stopped short of binding agreements with Karachi, but the Pakistanis continued to exploit Washington's preoccupation with communism, skillfully manipulating American sentiments until they all but forced the Eisenhower administration to offer Pakistan membership in the Western-sponsored pacts.

Afghanistan never seemed of corresponding value. Its lack of modern base facilities, limited resources, and inability to field proficient conventional forces seemed to render it of little consequence to the containment effort. Afghanistan's geographic position also left it vulnerable to Soviet encroachment. Though the Afghans detested communism, showed no objection to ideas of collective security, and might have joined a Western-sponsored alliance of Muslim states given suitable preconditions, Eisenhower's administration, considering Afghanistan more burden than asset, thought it best to leave the nation outside their area of responsibility.

Like the British before, the United States had several legitimate reasons not to offer Afghanistan alliance membership. But while the British never considered Afghanistan of intrinsic value and regarded its armed forces as of little worth off the barracks square, they did not dismiss Afghanistan out of hand. They recognized, even in the twentieth century, that the Afghans would resist a Soviet invasion as a nation. To that end, prior to 1947, they provided suitable assistance to the Afghan army, knowing that such would increase Afghanistan's deterrent and secure for Britain a degree of political leverage in Kabul, without drastic cost or unpalatable commitments. Whether Afghanistan would have joined an alliance is a subjective question. Alliances aside, the United States could have supplied the Afghan armed forces, perhaps via a third party such as Turkey. The provision of second-line equipment, taken from surplus stocks left over from World War II, and provided at suitable prices, would have increased Afghanistan's deterrent and internal security, fostered economic development, and strengthened bilateral relations and need not have entailed binding commitments. Such assistance would also have prevented the U.S.S.R. from securing similar advantages. The Americans, however, never shared Britain's concern with Afghanistan and in the climate of the Cold War did not consider similar military arrangements.

Creative policy could perhaps have resolved the Pushtunistan dispute, pro-

moted Pakistani-Afghan cooperation, and allowed for greater American contacts with Afghanistan. Given fears of India, which had led the Karachi regime
to prostrate itself to Washington, Pakistan should have been malleable to
agreement with Kabul, especially if accord brought with it economic aid.
Pakistan might have succored Afghanistan through a grant of free port facilities at Karachi or cooperative construction of a new port in Baluchistan.
Such endeavors, which the British had proposed before the war, could have
given Afghanistan a way out of the dispute without a loss of prestige. Pakistan
also would have benefited from a neighborly agreement designed to foster
the development of communications, transit, and trade. Without agreement,
the only beneficiaries were frontier agitators, who consumed the funds of
both nations in competitive subsidies.

There is no evidence to suggest that Pakistan ever offered Afghanistan any
comprehensive settlement or face-saving escape from the Pushtunistan en-
tanglement. Nor did the Americans press the issue. Though a few embassy
officials and Washington bureaucrats occasionally advanced proposals to effect limited cooperation, without any compelling inducement, bilateral cooperation schemes never reached fruition. The majority of American leaders,
meanwhile, remained unconvinced of Afghanistan's value and largely indifferent to its fate, rejecting mediation proposals as not worth the risk of upsetting the Pakistanis. The Eisenhower administration chose to avoid the
issue, quietly pushed the Afghans to drop it, and refused to pressure Karachi.
They would ultimately dismiss the Afghan position entirely.[2]

British policy toward Afghanistan had its share of failings. The importance
of India and the continual activity along the frontier, however, served as a
magnet that attracted ambitious civil servants and army officers to the area.
As a result, the NWFP would mold the elite of the Indian Civil Service, and
some of the finest officers and men in the British army. Since most military
and civil officials assigned to the frontier served there for extended periods
of time, they familiarized themselves with the local customs and language.
Many became true regional experts, who served Britain well as Anglo-Afghan
relations improved through the century. Cognizant of both the strengths and
the weaknesses of Afghanistan, they tolerated certain idiosyncrasies in bilateral relations, confident that Afghanistan would, if confronted, stand up to
the Russians.[3]

The United States, on the other hand, having traditionally left South Asia
to Britain, emerged from World War II all but devoid of anyone who could
be called a regional expert. There were notable exceptions who demonstrated
both considerable knowledge and professionalism, of whom Cornelius van
Engert is the most obvious example. Yet more often than not, the State
Department placed individuals in Kabul despite a lack of knowledge about
Afghan languages, politics, religion, and culture. According to Leon Poullada, an economic official on Ward's embassy staff, even senior diplomats

assigned to Afghanistan "had little knowledge of the country and could hardly mumble more than a few words of bazaar Farsi."[4]

With most of Africa not yet independent, Southeast Asia active militarily, and Latin America at least closer to home, one can reasonably assume that most American diplomats ranked Afghanistan near the bottom of their assignment selection lists. In direct contrast to their British predecessors, there is little evidence to suggest the Americans sent to Kabul were enthusiastic. Most who did arrive left within eighteen months, in accordance with a department rotation policy that classified Afghanistan as a hardship post. Thus, while their British and Soviet counterparts often remained in country for extended periods, most American officials departed just as they began to acquire sufficient knowledge of Afghanistan. Curiously, Pakistan experienced similar problems. Pakistani officials in Afghanistan "expressed annoyance that the people with 'big names' in Pakistan wanted assignments in Western countries and were reluctant to go to Afghanistan in spite of its greater importance to Pakistan."[5]

While one can criticize American policy as short-sighted, unfair, and at times simply ignorant, those who argued against providing support to Afghanistan did have valid concerns. While limited assistance might have strengthened regional defense capabilities, the inclusion of Afghanistan in an area alliance would have done little but increase American commitments in an area in which the United States lacked any appropriate counterforce. The problem with American policy was not so much neglect of Afghanistan, but partisan support of Pakistan. Such support not only left Afghanistan in a political, military, and economic vacuum, from which an accord with the Soviet Union seemed the only escape, it also made very little strategic sense.

When considering the future defense of the Middle East, the experiences of the Second World War heavily influenced American planners. They expected future wars to be dominated by conventional operations, in which opposing armies, corps, and divisions would engage one another across relatively well-defined lines, striving for geographic objectives. When applied to the Middle East, however, conventional plans ran afoul of the distances involved, the economic weakness of the local powers, and political and religious differences. Plans that envisioned Turkish, Iranian, Pakistani, Jordanian, Iraqi, and Commonwealth forces, supported by British and American air and naval units, holding an 1,800-mile-long front against a Soviet incursion seem ludicrous, especially considering the alternating mountain and desert terrain and the limitations of the regional transportation system.

This ill-advised emphasis on conventional operations nonetheless helped ordain the dismissal of Afghanistan as inconsequential. It also encouraged alliance with Pakistan. At times, American planners foresaw Pakistani forces serving in an expeditionary role similar to those performed by the British-Indian army. Throughout discussions on a potential alliance, for example, the Joint Chiefs of Staff hoped Pakistan could provide support in the event of a

Soviet attack on Iran. The likelihood of such an offensive was remote, but had it transpired, there are several reasons to doubt the Pakistani commitment. It seems unlikely that the predominantly Sunni Pakistanis would ever risk Soviet retaliatory measures in order to save their Shi'a neighbors, especially if such support entailed weakening their defenses vis-à-vis India. It is even harder to believe that Pakistani ground forces could traverse hundreds of miles across a near-trackless plateau before Iranian resistance collapsed. It would have taken them weeks simply to mobilize their forces and transport them across the wasteland, regardless of Soviet countermeasures. Even if the Pakistanis possessed the moral resolve and overcame the logistical barriers and likely interdiction, there is no reason to believe that a few divisions would have contributed decisively to the conflict. Indeed, in 1955 and for several years to come, such unlikely aggression would not be deterred through regional pacts, but through selective use of nuclear weapons. The Pakistani armed forces could at best dissuade Indian aggression, maintain internal security, and perhaps resist a limited Soviet thrust in their own immediate area. Even certain Pakistan officials admitted that their army could do little more than serve as a tripwire and combat subversives.[6]

As a result of economic weakness and continued dissension with its neighbors, Pakistan never provided the United States substantial assistance in the Cold War. Though the air force would stage intelligence operations from Pakistan for a few years (the "U-2 incident" of 1960, for example, began at a field near Peshawar), the advent of satellite technology soon rendered access to the airfields of minimal value.[7] The augmentation of Pakistani forces, meanwhile, did little to reduce the likelihood of brushfire wars in the region. There were no Communist proxies in the area, and Afghanistan, with perhaps one seventh the population of Pakistan, was no serious threat itself. American planners acknowledged that India, in possession of the most valuable two thirds of Kashmir, had little incentive to risk war against Pakistan. According to the conclusions of a General Staff study, Pakistan's leaders also seemed "convinced of the folly of attacking India's superior forces."[8] Those opinions, however, changed when Pakistan acquired new hardware. The arrangement with Pakistan did not resolve the problems of the subcontinent, but fostered an arms race that forced both Pakistan and India to divert funds from the civilian sector and ultimately led to two wars between them, financed in large part by American funds. The only immediate benefit of the accord was that it gave the Pakistani government a better chance of maintaining internal stability, the value of which can be debated in terms of political, moral, and economic cost.

Though the pacts aimed in part to discourage neutralist sentiment, they actually allowed India and other Asian states to obtain increased amounts of aid from both the Western and the Eastern blocs, without committing to either. In the wake of American initiatives, the U.S.S.R. offered assistance to India and a host of other nations, all of which bore grudges against an

American-supported neighbor. India improved its relations with the Soviet bloc without becoming subservient to it, still retained hegemony in South Asia, and maintained satisfactory relations with the United States, without a serious compromise of neutrality.

Though the Pak-American alliance fostered increased Indian involvement with the Soviet Union it did not irrevocably damage Indo-American relations. Even during the height of Nehru's pique, Indo-Soviet economic contacts remained limited, and no major change in Indian foreign policy transpired. American economic commitments to India gradually grew throughout the ensuing years, until, in the aftermath of the Chinese attack on India in 1962, the Kennedy administration provided extensive assistance. Ironically, such aid stipulated that the weapons would never be used against Pakistan. Later Indo-American estrangement owed more to subsequent policy, beginning with Nixon's "opening" of China and his tilt during the Indo-Pakistani war of 1971, than to events of the 1950s. The alliance with Pakistan was not, as some have argued, a catastrophe from which American diplomacy could not recover.[9] The same cannot be said for Afghanistan, for which the alliance had disastrous consequences.

Though the Afghans warned that a Pak-American alliance would force them to court improved relations with the U.S.S.R., the United States did not consider Afghan objections of great significance. Many officials actually felt the alliance would force Afghanistan to come to terms on Pushtunistan. Dulles, for example, considered an Afghan rapprochement with the U.S.S.R. unrealistic, believed the Afghan threats mere bluffs, and thought he could threaten them in kind. This persistent belief that Afghanistan would make amends with Pakistan out of sheer necessity, however, disregarded Afghan pride, ignored previous Soviet-Afghan trade agreements, and failed to consider Afghanistan's lack of other options.[10]

In time, the failed economic enterprises, aborted diplomatic initiatives, and persistent rejections of requests for military assistance destroyed Afghan faith in the United States. At the same time, economic aid to Pakistan and Iran left Afghanistan in a trough of depression. While American officials bemoaned an unavailability of funds, cited requisite congressional approval, and warned the Afghans of their feeble deterrent against possible Soviet countermeasures, none of those issues stopped the United States from supplying economic and military assistance to the other regional states. That the United States was sufficiently concerned with the security of Afghanistan's neighbors to risk Soviet retaliation, but did not extend that concern to Kabul, seems to have irritated the Afghans most of all.[11]

Without assistance from a major power, Afghanistan faced a continuum in an economic, political, and military vacuum between the Soviet Union and the Western pacts. Afghanistan could not remain inactive while its neighbors were modernizing. Denied access to the Western alliances and their accompanying economic assistance, Daoud faced a choice of stagnation or bargaining with the Soviet Union. Convinced that Pakistan would always retain a greater priority with the United States, he opted for the latter. Considering his alternatives, his choice seems neither surprising nor condemnable.

In the late 1950s Daoud's bargain seemed borne of genius. The acceptance of the Soviet offer prompted the heretofore uninterested United States to implement a sizeable assistance program of its own. Throughout the ensuing decade, Soviet and American engineers competed, and occasionally even collaborated, in building a variety of civic, industrial, agricultural, and communications facilities across Afghanistan. The Afghan military, however, became dependent upon the U.S.S.R. for training and equipment. While modernization of the armed forces allowed Daoud to implement various reforms, Daoud had also increased his nation's vulnerability to Soviet encroachment.

American officials would later admit that their military initiatives along the northern tier, coupled with neglect of Afghanistan, had facilitated Soviet involvement in that nation. A Western military commitment might have prevented Afghanistan's recent misfortune. Then again, a more rational Afghan constitution, greater participation in national politics, better tactics on Daoud's part, and other potentialities could also have forestalled the People's Democratic Party of Afghanistan (PDPA) takeover. One should not blame the United States for the Soviet-Afghan war. That responsibility remains with the Soviet Union and their PDPA allies.

In the aftermath of invasion, several manuscripts appeared which analyzed the Soviet decision to attack. Some commentators deemed the assault part of a long-term plan of conquest, in which Afghanistan, long considered the gateway to the Indian Ocean, would be subjugated and then used as a stepping-stone to other geographic objectives. Some observers forecast a dual-pronged invasion of Iran in which Soviet troops would drive to the Shatt-al-Arab and the Straits of Hormuz. Others predicted increased Soviet support for Baluch and Pushtun separatists, that would undermine Pakistan's unstable regime, paving the way for a joint Indo-Soviet invasion aimed at final dismemberment of Pakistan. India would thereupon annex Sind, West Punjab, and Azad Kashmir; the Northwest Frontier Province (NWFP) would be incorporated into Afghanistan, and the Soviets would establish a puppet People's Republic of Baluchistan, securing a long-desired warm-water port on the Indian Ocean.[12]

In the wake of the collapse of the Soviet Union, such dire predictions now seem as ludicrous as those of nineteenth-century British prognosticators who foretold of the tsar's armies overrunning India. The Soviet Union, like all would-be conquerors before them, proved unable to enforce its will upon the Afghan population. The Russians were worn down in a difficult struggle with tenacious enemies who proved far more stalwart than the assorted experts, or most of the world, expected. The war became a quagmire, often labeled the Soviet Vietnam.[13]

The Soviet invasion of Afghanistan was no disaster for Western policy.

While Soviet troops remained in Afghanistan, the U.S.S.R. suffered severe foreign policy repercussions. The vast majority of Third World nations, especially the Islamic states, routinely condemned Soviet aggression through passage of United Nations resolutions. The war also gave impetus to independence movements in the Caucasus and the Central Asian Republics. Though direct expenditures were not extravagant, when combined with the loss of access to Western grain, technology, and other items, the war imposed a steady drain on the already-suffering Soviet economy. Frustration with the war also fueled a growing Soviet dissident movement that increasingly counted veterans of the campaign among its most ardent members. The Afghan war taxed the Soviet economy and Soviet prestige, reemphasized domestic failings, and gave it only "thousands of mothers who lost sons, thousands of cripples, thousands of torn-up lives." Mikhail Gorbachev eventually chose to disengage, securing a UN-brokered withdrawal as part of his efforts to improve relations with the west. Ultimately, the war in Afghanistan played a substantial role in speeding the collapse of the Soviet Union.[14]

While one could argue that the war ultimately proved beneficial, it came at a terrible cost for the Afghan people. Given that most of them would have preferred Western aid to intimate relations with the U.S.S.R., one feels a strong degree of sympathy for the nation. A few deliveries of obsolete weaponry (that the British had promised and the Soviets later provided) might well have prevented all of Afghanistan's misfortune and need not have involved costly, permanent, or politically dangerous commitments. A combination of disinterest in and disdain for Afghanistan, however, effectively abandoned that nation to its fate.

Disinterest has remained a bane of Afghanistan in modern times, and will likely remain a threat in the near future. During the Soviet War, perhaps as many as two million Afghans died, millions more were wounded, and over half of the nation became refugees. Despite widespread documentation of atrocities and the magnitude of the human tragedy, Afghanistan rarely attracted much attention. Reports from the Afghan conflict stemmed primarily from a handful of journalists, who, despite risking their lives to gather information, often found their stories relegated to low-priority status. The Western press all but ignored the war, indeed they came to label any news item thought of no interest to the public as "an Afghanistan." The Afghan conflict generated few candle-lit rallies or benefit concerts. Even most humanitarian organizations, with but a handful of notable exceptions, tended to ignore the conflict.[15] When the war ended, Afghanistan disappeared from public view.

The withdrawal of the Soviet forces did not bring peace to Afghanistan. While other nations celebrated the end of the Cold War, Afghanistan degenerated into chaos, amidst the factional fighting of *mujahidin* leaders. The PDPA renamed itself the Homeland (Watan) Party, embraced Islam and a market economy, forged alliances with some of the northern peoples (notably Uzbek general Rashid Dostam), and, with the financial support of India,

Russia, and some Central Asian states, held out against the resistance. When the government finally collapsed, Kabul fell not to the Pakistan-based Pushtun groups, but to Tajik forces headed by Ahmed Shah Massoud. The civil war that followed was, on the surface, a clash between the Pushtuns and the northern peoples of Afghanistan. With a variety of independent commanders and neighboring states stoking the fires, however, the conflict came to resemble the Thirty Years' War in both its chaotic nature and widespread destruction. Afghanistan in the last decade of the twentieth century looked reminiscent of Afghanistan in the first decade of the eighteenth, with various warlords and brigands maneuvering amidst another kaleidoscope of intrigue, extortion, and slaughter.

The Taliban stepped into this vacuum. The movement arose at Pakistani schools (*madrassahs*) along the Northwest Frontier. Led by village mullah Mohammed Omar, the Taliban vowed to end the factionalism and restore law and order. They gained initial popularity by cracking down on some of the worst excesses of renegade warlords and promising to end the drug trade. Though all but universally despised today, this was not the case earlier, when even some Washington diplomats expressed hopes that they might bring stability to Afghanistan. Some saw the Taliban as a useful counter to Iranian fundamentalism, others hoped a stable regime could ensure the flow of oil from the Central Asian republics, while still more equated them with born-again Christians, who would wipe out "drugs and thugs."[16]

During 1994 and 1995 sizable portions of the Pushtun population saw the Taliban as potential saviors against both warlords and non-Pushtuns. Though woefully ignorant on many levels, the Taliban were not entirely removed from Afghan culture. Calls for justice and preference for harsh punishments of criminals resembled the policies of Dost Mohammed and Abdur Rahman Khan. Even their hostility toward women bears similarity to opponents of Amanullah and the PDPA, who centered their critiques of modernist reforms against the gender-based policies of those regimes.

The newest Mad Mullah and his followers conquered more territory than any previous frontier agitator. Taliban lashkars first entered Qandahar in 1994. Then, aided by the ever-shifting Dostam, the Taliban captured Herat in 1995. After a siege of almost a year, they prized Kabul from Massoud's forces in 1996. As Taliban conquests increased, so did the ensuing carnage. When their forces entered Mazar-I-Sharif in 1997 they slaughtered much of the non-Pushtun population. Ultimately, the surviving opposition forces coalesced into a loose confederation officially called The United National Islamic Front for the Salvation of Afghanistan, but more commonly referred to as the "Northern Alliance" (as the only parts of the country which they held were in the north). This mishmash of groups and individuals included many former enemies, including Dostam, Massoud, and Pushtun reactionary Gulbuddin Hekmatyar.

In time, Taliban policies rendered them anathema to the majority of Afghans and most of civilization. Mullah Omar proved a Pushtun rendition of Bacha-i-Saqao, made altogether worse by his warped interpretations of Islam. The Taliban, quite simply, "did not recognize the very idea of culture."[17] Within the nation, they enacted puritanical policies that essentially outlawed entertainment, prohibiting everything from music to movies, from watching television to playing soccer. Their intolerance of dissent proved more deadly. While most graphically demonstrated by the destruction of the Bamiyan Buddahs, their policies also fostered murders of aid workers, foreign diplomats, ethnic minorities, and any who dared oppose their policies.

Of all the loathsome Taliban qualities, their policies against women invoked the most international abhorrence. Harsh dress codes were enacted for both sexes (men had to grow beards and wear their pants above the ankle), but women caught uncovered in public were subject to vicious punishments. The Taliban prohibited females from attending school or working outside the home, even if they had no other source of income. They essentially condemned many female-headed households to starvation, while decimating the ranks of the medical and education professions. Feminist groups worldwide spearheaded lobbying efforts that forced many nations to take stands against the Taliban leadership. By 1999 the Taliban controlled 90 percent of Afghanistan but were recognized by only three nations: Pakistan, Saudi Arabia, and the United Arab Emirates.

Afghanistan under the Taliban was also a refuge for Islamic extremists. The Soviet war had attracted sizable numbers of such radicals. Most notably, Osama bin Laden spearheaded efforts to recruit, train, and assist the *mujahidin*. The Saudi-born millionaire not only financed the war effort, but allegedly fought in several engagements, acquiring a reputation for personal bravery that in part explains lingering support for him. The Soviet War also afforded his Al Qaeda organization cover under which it grew into a global entity. Following the defeat of the Soviet Union, bin Laden turned his anger against the United States and the west in general. Though he left Afghanistan shortly after Soviet forces did, he returned in 1996. Whether motivated by traditional hospitality, similar doctrines, or ulterior motives, Mullah Omar welcomed him as "one of our own."[18]

Bin Laden would prove a costly guest for the Taliban. Blamed for masterminding the September 11, 2001, attacks on New York and Washington, bin Laden was a primary target of an American attack on Afghanistan. Hoping to eliminate Afghanistan as a den for terrorists and a base for Al Qaeda operations, American and Northern Alliance forces drove the Taliban from power by late 2001. Hundreds of Taliban and Al Qaeda supporters were killed, but others, perhaps including bin Laden and Mullah Omar, found haven along or across the Pakistani border. From there, they have persisted in launching attacks against the occupation forces and successor government.

In the aftermath of the September 11th attacks, some pundits issued calls to bomb Afghanistan back to the stone age. Sadly, in many respects, it was already there. A quarter century of warfare has left the nation devastated. The Soviet invasion and ensuing civil war demolished Afghan cities, ruined fledgling industries, exploited natural resources, left the countryside mine-infested and otherwise contaminated, and decimated herds and flocks. One can measure Afghanistan's disadvantages in terms of shortages (jobs, health care, caloric intake, average life expectancy, safe water, intelligentsia) or surpluses (infant mortality, illiteracy, amputees, poverty, drug trafficking, war widows).[19] Either way, it is apparent that the people of Afghanistan face exacting difficulties in attempting to reconstruct their nation. The nation's inherent divisions only exacerbate the challenges.

President George W. Bush has repeatedly declared his desire to help Afghanistan recover. Initially he called for a "Marshall Plan" for Afghanistan. Recently, he proposed a $1 billion aid package designed to bolster Hamid Karzai's regime and counter charges that the United States has lost interest in the wake of the assault on Iraq. The President has signed legislation authorizing road building and education projects, the provision of medical care for Afghan women and children, even the transportation of Afghan pilgrims to Mecca.[20]

The sincerity and depth of the commitment, as well as the progress to date, remain open to speculation. Some reports note the return of Afghan refugees, the opening of new businesses, the stability of the Afghan currency, and ongoing construction projects, such as American efforts to rebuild the Kabul-Qandahar-Herat road. Yet other news sources and aid organizations have criticized the Bush administration for limited efforts to date and lack of success in certain areas, particularly in rural Afghanistan. The failure to reduce opium production (currently 15 times higher than what it was in 1979) is one oft-noted example. Complaints have surfaced regarding the Kabul-Qandahar-Herat road that are eerily similar to those voiced against the Helmand Valley Project: the pace of construction is slow, the company is overcharging, Afghan opinions and advice are all but ignored, and so on. The road remains impassable in many sections. In conclusion, some progress is being made, but reconstruction is not going as quickly or smoothly as some had hoped.

One hopes the Bush administration is sincere in its proclamations regarding Afghanistan. Given, however, that the needs of Afghanistan would seem far greater than those of Iraq, one cannot but be concerned that the latter is receiving a dramatically disproportionate amount of aid. Diversification of aid donors would help. In the past, unilateral assistance has risked termination of the projects (as with the Germans during World War II), aroused suspicions of government subservience, or left the government vulnerable to foreign influence. Such problems can be mitigated given a multi-national approach, perhaps including the United Nations and other international organizations.

Afghanistan's reconstruction must be multi-dimensional, to include education, transportation, agriculture, and industry. It must be spread among the various peoples of Afghanistan. The reconstruction must also, unlike Amanullah's schemes or the PDPA programs, take into account existing social norms. Without real security, however, there can be neither effective administration nor sustained development. As Lancaster realized, and the Soviet Union exploited, the Afghan national army has and will continue to play a vital role in the maintenance of the Afghan state. Efforts are underway to build a national police force and a new national army. Expected to eventually number 70,000, such an army could check factionalism and help ensure growth. To date, however, only a few thousand troops have been trained.

With a reliable army, Abdur Rahman brought assorted warlords under control. With a reliable army, Mohammed Daoud implemented a wide variety of development projects. Without genuine security, Afghanistan stands little chance to emerge as a democratic, moderate, unified state. At present, security remains fragile. While training the new army, the United States has provided funds to regional militia leaders who assisted in ousting the Taliban. These warlords vary a great deal in their personalities, politics, competence, and respect for central authority. The worst of the lot can be readily compared to the self-serving looters, killers, extortionists, and drug smugglers who ransacked the nation in the 1990s. Even those commonly regarded as among the more noble and competent at times ignore the Kabul regime. For example, the customs money that militia forces collect technically belongs to the central government. That government, however, receives only a fraction of its rightful due.

Approximately 10,000 American troops remain in Afghanistan today. They have at times intervened in squabbles between warlords and the government, or between the warlords themselves. Such employment, however, is generally to be avoided, as it carries with it not only the risk of casualties, but the possibility of undermining the nascent democracy. Dependence on foreign troops has traditionally been a lightning rod in Afghanistan, and foreign subservience still invites the *watan ferosh* label that befell Shah Shuja and others. Karzai, who seldom leaves the presidential compound and does so only with American bodyguards, already has become a target of Taliban remnants and some fundamentalist warlords, who accuse him of being a puppet of the Americans.

Afghanistan is struggling to form a working government. On paper, a draft constitution is making progress. Finding the right balance between local tradition and modern values is proving a challenge, yet there are reasons to be positive. Karzai is widely viewed as a stabilizing force, who has tried to promote national unity. He is not a strongman in the mold of Nadir Shah, but like his predecessor, Karzai seems the best hope of the available alternatives.

Most Afghans seem grateful for having been liberated from the sterile repression and close-minded policies of the Taliban. Like Muslims everywhere, most support the notion of democracy. Unlike many other Islamic nations, Afghanistan has tried democracy before. While the previous attempt had its failings, it can provide lessons for the future. If the warlords can be convinced to give up their fiefs and work with the government, and the flow of aid increases, Afghanistan does have a chance at stability. Disaffection with the slow pace of recovery, warlord corruption, and increasing violence, however, threaten to make future elections irrelevant.

American policy traditionally has favored the Pakistani agenda. It did so during the alliance of the 1950s, during the Soviet-Afghan War, and in the aftermath, each time with dire consequences. During the Soviet War, the open border with Pakistan provided the *mujahidin* and their families an essential sanctuary. Pakistan publicly denied assisting the resistance (to avoid Soviet reprisals), but in fact they footed much of the bill to support the refugees. Given the costs involved, one can perhaps understand why Pakistan authorities at times pilfered some of the aid shipments intended for the Afghans.[21]

What is harder to understand is why the Pakistanis funneled the bulk of the foreign aid to the most reactionary of *mujahidin* groups, the Hezb-i-Islami of Gulbuddin Hekmatyar. Perhaps it was sheer inertia, as Pakistan had supported conservative resistance against Daoud's republic since 1973. Perhaps Pakistani intelligence believed that the Pan-Islamist Hekmatyar would be less likely to revive Pushtunistan agitation. Most likely, the Pakistanis held a belief that Hekmatyar's forces were more effective than the other groups. American authorities did not object to Pakistani policy, despite the fact that Hekmatyar espoused vehemently anti-American rhetoric.[22]

Hekmatyar's alleged battlefield prowess was largely fictitious. He never took part in important operations, took credit for battles he did not win, and fought more against fellow *mujahidin* than the communists. Yet because he received a greater share of the aid, he attracted more followers than the moderate *mujahidin* leaders. Had Hekmatyar ever come to power, he would have been little improvement over the Taliban. He proved a persistent destabilizing influence in postwar Afghanistan. Recently he urged suicide attacks against American forces and is now believed to be cooperating with Taliban remnants and Al Qaeda.[23]

Pakistani mistakes did not stop with Hekmatyar. Pakistan essentially served as midwife to the Taliban, fostering the group's existence and helping bring the radical regime to power. Pakistan continued to support them long after every other nation, even Saudi Arabia, had condemned their atrocities. Apparently Pakistani intelligence believed that it could use the Taliban, but Mullah Omar proved nobody's puppet. In time, the policy backfired, as the Taliban encouraged extremist elements along the frontier to agitate against the Karachi regime, causing Pakistan no small degree of difficulty. Remnants remain a threat in parts of Pakistan today.[24]

The United States has not been well served in letting Pakistan manipulate its regional policy. In the future, American policies should compel cooperation rather than favor one state over the other. Both Afghanistan and Pakistan have interest in the border region, and neither stands to benefit as long as it remains a haven for terrorists. Pakistan can help Afghanistan recover, and its own economy could benefit from Afghan reconstruction. Discord will only increase costs, delay progress, and play into the hands of those who want reconstruction to fail.

The road to recovery in Afghanistan will be expensive and arduous. Ignoring Afghanistan, however, is not a realistic option. Such policy has failed twice: in the early 1950s, and again in the early 1990s. Having invested millions of dollars in helping the *mujahidin,* the United States promptly ceased aid to Afghanistan in the summer of 1991. After walking away from Afghanistan, however, it was not long until the United States faced "dead diplomats, destroyed embassies, bombs in New York, and cheap heroin on its streets."[25] Another withdrawal would eventually produce more of the same.

Staying in Afghanistan brings with it recurrent risks. Both British invasions, one should remember, were initially successful, but approximately two years later in both cases, disaster followed. While a repeat of the 1841 debacle seems most unlikely, carelessness and inattention, particularly amidst distractions elsewhere in the world, could produce a tragedy similar to the embassy slaughter in the Second Anglo-Afghan War or perhaps even a reprise of Maiwand Pass. Leaving the job unfinished, however, incurs more risks, including a possible resurgence of extremists bent on reverting Afghanistan to a medieval terrorist state.

As early as 1924, Cornelius H. Van Engert wrote: "If, therefore, the United States should enter the field as a politically absolutely disinterested Power, we should not only be able to reap the material benefits which the confidence of the people would confer upon our position, but we could effectively lend our moral support in favor of law and order by encouraging those elements which are trying to prevent chaos in a part of the world that harbors the seeds of future wars." He went on to argue for American efforts to develop Afghanistan's natural resources, mineral wealth, agriculture, power, and transportation infrastructure. He encouraged scholarship on the nation as well, to include archaeology, history, geology, and biology. He also warned against sending missionaries.[26] One can argue that the United States should have taken Engert's advice then. Perhaps if it does today, this long-suffering land will finally find a lasting peace.

NOTES

1. John Evarts Horner, quoted in Giradet, *Afghanistan,* p. 92.

2. Memorandum by the Executive Secretary (Lay) to the National Security Council, 14 December 1954, Enclosing "Staff Study on Afghanistan," *FRUS,* 1952–1954, XI, pp. 1154–1157; Ward to the Department of State, 13 November 1952, *FRUS,* p. 1382; Memorandum of Conversation by the Director of the Office of South Asian Affairs (Kennedy), 26 November 1952, *FRUS,* p. 1385; Memorandum of Conver-

sation by the Acting Officer in Charge of Pakistan-Afghanistan Affairs (Thatcher), 8 October 1954, *FRUS,* pp. 1420–1421; Memorandum by the Deputy Assistant Secretary of State for Near Eastern, South Asian, and African Affairs (Jernegan) to the Acting Deputy Under Secretary of State, 5 November 1954, *FRUS,* p. 1429; Memorandum of Conversation by the Acting Officer in Charge of Pakistan-Afghanistan Affairs (Thatcher), 13 December 1954, *FRUS,* p. 1436; Memorandum of Conversation by Thatcher, 22 December 1954, *FRUS,* p. 1441; Memorandum of Conversation by Thatcher, 28 December 1954, *FRUS,* p. 1445; Horner to the Department of State, 9 September 1952, *FRUS,* p. 1448. Cheema, "Threat Perception by Pakistan," *US-Pakistan Relations,* p.115; Qureshi, *Anglo-Pakistan Relations* (quoting Zafrullah Khan), p. 200: "We were not worried much about Afghanistan. We thought they could not do much." Though Amanullah was no longer a threat (by 1949 he had tendered his submission to the government), other oppositionists were still willing to invoke his name in effort to overthrow Daoud. See R.A. Conner, Military Attaché in Kabul to the Under Secretary of State, War Office, 19 February 1953, FO 983/103; Squire, "Recent Progress in Afghanistan," p. 17.

3. Many giants of British history, Nicholson, Edwardes, Taylor, Mackeson, Warburton, Deane, Roos-Keppel, Pears, Curzon, Kitchener, O'Connor, Auchenleck, and even Churchill, served on the frontier at one time. Barton would conclude in 1939 that "so long as Britain can send such men to India she need not despair of her Empire." Barton, *India's North West Frontier,* pp. 89, 111–112, 190; Schofield, *Every Rock,* pp. 90, 157, 167; Miller, *Khyber,* pp. 106–110, 129, 287. For the twenty-seven-year period from 1922 to 1949, the British sent five ministers to Afghanistan, including Humphreys (1922–1929), Maconachie (1929–1935), Fraser-Tytler (1935–1941), Wylie (1941–1943), and Squire (1943–1949). The United States sent five ambassadors to Afghanistan during the nine-year period from 1947 to 1956. Only one remained for more than two years, and that was Angus Ward (1952–1956).

4. Poullada, "Afghanistan and the United States," pp. 182–183; Foreign Office to the Government of India, 31 Mat 1943, L/P&S/12/1931A, f34; Neville Butler to Wylie, 24 April 1942, L/P&S/12/1931A, f. 69; C.O. Baxter to Squire, 27 February 1945, L/P&S/12/1931A, f. 11. Engert, the first American ambassador, was as popular with the British as he was with the Afghans. A devout Anglophile, Engert worked to provide common necessities to British prisoners of war interned in Turkey during World War I. He sent his son to Harrow, even insisting on his remaining there throughout the duration of the Blitz. British officials also regarded Ely Palmer highly, and Horner, as chargé d'affaires, advanced several potentially productive proposals. See Memorandum of Conversation by the Acting Officer in Charge of Pakistan-Afghanistan Affairs (Thatcher), 29 October 1954, *FRUS,* 1952–1954, XI, p. 1427, wherein Byroade commented that Dulles's "heavy load of other duties had made it impossible for him to give thoughtful and careful attention" to regional problems. Byroade later commented that Dulles was "ignorant on [the] subject of the Middle East."

5. *FRUS,* 1952–1954, p. 1431.

6. Burke, *Pakistan's Foreign Policy,* p. 252; Campbell, *Defense of the Middle East,* pp. 192–193, 242; Mowrer, "New Frontiers of Freedom," p. 36.

7. NSC 5617 and NSC 5701; Hovey, *United States Military Assistance,* p. 100. Hovey noted how the Americans constructed cold meat storage facilities, which, given that Islamic laws require consumption of meat shortly after killing the animal, could

only have been intended for Western use. See also Ram, *Super Powers*, p. 109; Tahir-Kheli, *United States and Pakistan*, pp. 3–7; Qureshi, *Anglo-Pakistan Relations*, p. 135; Khalid, "India as a Factor in Pakistan-US Relations," in *Pakistan-US Relations*, pp. 44–46; Venkataramani, *American Role in Pakistan*, pp. 224, 227, 332–337.

8. "Comparative Military Capabilities of India and Pakistan—16 March 1953," Intelligence Staff Study, Department of the Army, DA-G2 IRP 7692, General Staff (G-2), US Army Military History Institute, Carlisle. Stephens, *Pakistan*, pp. 218–219. He claims the Afghan forces were so ill equipped, poorly led, and undisciplined that "Kabul might have been captured by [Pakistani] militia and Frontier Corps alone." See also CIA NIE-41, "Probable Developments in the Kashmir Dispute during 1951," Draft Statement of Policy as Proposed by the National Security Council, *FRUS*, 1952–1954, XI, pp. 1082–1084; Campbell, *Defense of the Middle East*, p. 177.

9. Kaul, *U.S.A. and the Hindustan Peninsula*, pp. 23–26, 30–31, 146–147; Palmer, *South Asia and United States Policy*, pp. 5, 19, 25; Ram, *Super Powers*, pp. 89, 112.

10. Memorandum of Conversation by the Acting Officer in Charge of Pakistan-Afghanistan Relations (Metcalf), 5 January 1954, *FRUS*, 1952–1954, XI, p. 1410; Memorandum of Conversation by the Acting Officer in Charge of Pakistan-Afghanistan Relations (Thatcher), 22 December 1954, *FRUS*, 1952–1954, XI, p. 1440;

11. National Intelligence Estimate NIE-79, "Probable Developments in South Asia," 30 June 1953, 1952–1954, FRUS, XI, p. 1088; Poullada, "Afghanistan and the United States," pp. 183, 189.

12. Amstutz, *Afghanistan*, pp. 339–341, 353, 356. The Soviets showed particular interest in Afghan government files relating to Pushtunistan, including original maps of the Durand Line, perhaps indicative of future designs on Pakistan. Bradsher, *Afghanistan, and the Soviet Union*, pp. 240–255; Griffiths, *Afghanistan*, pp. 202–205; Arnold, *Afghanistan*, pp. 124, 127, 132, 137. Caroe, "The Strategic After-Effects of India's Partition," p. 131. He called it "the most terrible and threatening strategic problem to arise since the end of the Second World War."

13. Griffiths, *Afghanistan*, pp. 191–192, 213–214; Giradet, *Afghanistan*, pp. 47, 53, 66, 84, 137, 143–144, 237; Hyman, *Afghanistan Under Soviet Domination*, pp. 147–148, 182–185; Amstutz, *Afghanistan*, pp. 79, 183–189, 307–309; Hammond, *Red Flag Over Afghanistan*, p. 160; Tamarov, *Soviet Vietnam*, p. 114, Lohbeck, *Holy War*, p. 88.

14. Giradet, *Afghanistan*, pp. 41, 46–47, 77, 222–223; Griffiths, *Afghanistan*, pp. 198–199, 206–207; Collins, *The Soviet Invasion of Afghanistan*, pp. 81, 86–89, 139, 149; Amstutz, *Afghanistan*, pp. 169, 177–178, 330. Rather like the United States, the Soviet high command spent most of its time considering conventional war in Central Europe, devoting little attention to counterinsurgency tactics in the countryside, and paid the price accordingly. Tamarov, *Soviet Vietnam*, pp. 7, 164, 172; Sarin and Dvorestky, *The Afghan Syndrome*, pp. 146–148; Arnold, *Afghanistan*, pp. 115, 125–126, 132; Rubin, *Search for Peace*, pp. 69–78.

15. Amstutz, *Afghanistan*, pp. 158–159, 264–269, 273, 276–277, 306–309, 312; Hyman, *Afghanistan Under Soviet Domination*, pp. 96, 108–111, 118–120, 148–150, 181–185, 240fn. PDPA officials imprisoned entire families, placing them in overcrowded, filthy cells, devoid of sanitary devices. Children were tortured and killed before their parents' eyes. Prisoners were bound hand and foot, hung upside down,

deprived of sleep and/or food, had their nails torn from their fingers and toes, were subject to electric shocks, sexually molested, blinded, or dismembered. Some victims were buried alive, beaten to death with sticks, or drowned in prison cess pools. While some accounts are no doubt exaggerated, a variety of human rights organizations confirmed reports of the use of tortures barbaric by any standard. Thousands of Afghans, including a disproportionately large percentage of the intelligentsia, were simply murdered. Khalizad, *The Security of Southwest Asia,* pp. 76–77. Giradet, *Afghanistan,* pp. 121–123, 238–240; Lohbeck, *Holy War,* pp. 67–68, 94–95; Hammond, *Red Flag Over Afghanistan,* p. 223. Writing in 1984, Hammond posed an interesting question: "[W]here are the Jane Fondas, the Joan Baezs . . . the Hemingways writing novels about the struggle for freedom . . . the young idealists willing to fight and die on the side of the poor, oppressed peasants?"

16. Rashid, *Taliban,* pp. 32, 166, 176–177.

17. Rashid, *Taliban,* p. 115.

18. Reeve, *New Jackals,* pp. 195, 203; Rashid, *Taliban,* pp. 129, 137–140.

19. Arnold, *Afghanistan,* pp. 120–121. Lohbeck, *Holy War,* p. 241; Rashid, Taliban, p. 107; Giradet, *Afghanistan,* pp. 152–154, 160.

20. "Remarks by the President at the Signing Ceremony for the Afghan Women and Children Relief Act of 2001," December 12, 2001. Washington: Office of the Press Secretary.

21. Arnold, *Afghanistan,* p. 118; Schofield, *Every Rock,* p. 302; Giradet, *Afghanistan,* pp. 206–207; Hammond, *Red Flag over Afghanistan,* p. 156; Lohbeck, *Holy War,* p. 190.

22. Lohbeck, *Holy War,* pp. 9, 12, 172. During Operation Desert Storm, Hekmatyar lent no support to the Allied cause. Other moderate *mujahidin* not only aided the allies, but received commendations for their assistance.

23. Lohbeck, Holy War, pp. 76, 126, 165, 171.

24. Khalizad, *The Security of Southwest Asia,* p. 145; Rashid, *Taliban,* p. 185.

25. Rashid, *Taliban,* p. 209.

26. Cornelius H. Van Engert, "A Report on Afghanistan" pp. 148–150 (quote 150).

BIBLIOGRAPHY

PRIMARY SOURCES

Documents

India Office Library, London

George Cunningham Papers
Olaf Caroe Papers
Records of the Afghanistan Consulate (R/12)
Records of the Military Department (L/MIL)
Records of the Political and Secret Department (L/P&S)
Records of the Private Office (L/PO)
Records of the Public and Judicial Department (L/P&J)
Records of the War Staff (L/WS)

Public Record Office, Kew

Cabinet Office (CAB)
Commonwealth Relations Office (CRO)
Foreign Office (FO)
War Office (WO)

National Archives, Washington, D.C.

Department of State (DOS)
Joint Chiefs of Staff (JCS)
National Security Council (NSC)

U.S. Congress, Reports

House Committee on Foreign Affairs. Hearings, Mutual Security Act Extension, 83rd
     Congress, 1st Session, 1953.

House Reports. Miscellaneous Papers on Public Bills, 84th Congress, 1st Session, Volume 2, "Report of the Survey Mission to the Far East, South Asia, and the Middle East," 1955.

House Reports. Miscellaneous Papers on Public Bills, 84th Congress, 2nd Session, Volume 2, "Report of the Survey Mission to the Middle East, South and Southeast Asia and the Western Pacific," 1956.

Executive Sessions of the Senate Foreign Relations Committee, together with Joint Sessions of the Senate Armed Services Committee, 85th Congress, 1st Session, Volume 9, "Informal Meeting with Chester Bowles, March 26, 1957."

House Committee of Foreign Affairs, Subcommittee on Asian and Pacific Affairs, 96th Congress, 1st Session. "Crisis in the Subcontinent—Afghanistan and Pakistan," May 15 and September 26, 1979.

House Committee on Foreign Affairs, Subcommittee on Europe and the Middle East, 101st Congress, 2nd Session. "US Policy toward Afghanistan," March 7, 1990.

Published Collections of Documents

Ahmad, Jamil-ud-Din, ed. *Some Recent Speeches and Writings of Mr. Jinnah*. Lahore: Ashraf. Vol. I, 5th ed., 1952; Vol. II, 2nd ed., 1952.

Dar, Saeeduddin Ahmad, ed. *Selected Documents on Pakistan's Relations with Afghanistan, 1947–1985*. Islamabad: National Institute of Pakistan Studies, Quad-i-Azam University, 1986.

Dmytryshyn, Basil, and Coc, Frederick. *The Soviet Union and the Middle East: A Documentary Record of Afghanistan, Iran and Turkey, 1917–1985*. Princeton, NJ: Kingston Press, 1987.

Gwyer, M., and Appadorai, A., eds. *Speeches and Documents on the Indian Constitution, 1921–47*. Bombay: Oxford, 1957.

Hasan, K. Sarwar, ed. *Documents on the Foreign Relations of Pakistan: The Transfer of Power*. Karachi: Pakistan Institute for International Affairs, 1966.

Hurewitz, J.C. *Diplomacy in the Middle and Near East: A Documentary Record, 1914–1956*. Princeton, NJ: D. Van Nostrand, 1956.

Mansergh, Nicholas, ed. *Constitutional Relations between Britain and India: The Transfer of Power, 1942–1947*. London: HMSO. Vols. I–XII (noted within as *ITOP*).

U.S. Department of State. *Foreign Relations of the United States*. Washington, D.C.: U.S. Government Printing Office, 1921–1954. Vols. I–XI (noted within as *FRUS*).

Watson, Robert J. *History of the Joint Chiefs of Staff: The JCS and National Policy, 1949–1953*. Washington, D.C.: U.S. Government Printing Office, 1986.

American Universities—Field Staff Reports (AUFS)

Talbot, Phillips. "Pakistan's Pakhtuns: New Policies on the Northwest Frontier." 1 (December 10, 1956).

Dupree, Louis. "An Informal Talk with Prime Minister Daud." 3 (September 13, 1959).

———. "Afghanistan's Big Gamble, Part I, Historical Background of Afghan-Russian Relations." 4 (April 29, 1960).

————."Afghanistan's Big Gamble, Part II, The Economic and Strategic Aspects of Soviet Aid." 4 (May 2, 1960).

————. "Afghanistan's Big Gamble, Part III, Economic Competition in Afghanistan." 4 (May 9, 1960).

————. "The Mountains Go to Mohammed Zahir: Observations on Afghanistan's Reactions to Visits from Nixon, Bulganin-Khrushchev, Eisenhower and Khrushchev." 4 (May 20, 1960).

————. "A Note on Afghanistan." 4 (August 1960).

————. "Constitutional Developments and Cultural Change, Part III, The 1964 Afghan Constitution" 9 (1965).

————. "Afghanistan: 1966, Comments on a Compartively Calm State of Affairs with Reference to the Turbulence of Late 1965." 10 (1966).

————. "Afghanistan: 1968, Part III: Problems of a Free Press." 12 (1968).

————. "Afghanistan: 1968, Part IV: Strikes and Demonstrations." 12 (1968).

————. "Sports and Games in Afghanistan." 14 (1970).

Harry S Truman Library, Oral History Interviews (all by Richard D. McKinzie)

John M. Cabot, Consul General, Shanghai, 1948–1949; Ambassador to Pakistan, 1952–1953. July 18, 1973.

Loy W. Henderson. Director, Near Eastern and African Affairs, 1945–1948; Ambassador to India, 1948–1951; Ambassador to Iran, 1951–1955. June 14 and July 5, 1973.

Elbert G. Mathews. Second Secretary, Kabul, 1944–1946; Consul, Calcutta, 1946–1947; Assistant Chief, Division of South Asian Affairs, 1947–1948; Chief, 1948–1950; Director, Office of South Asian Affairs, 1950–1951. June 13, 1975.

George C. McGhee. Coordinator for Aid to Greece and Turkey, 1947; Special Assistant to the Secretary of State, 1947–1949; Assistant Secretary for Near Eastern, South Asian, and African Affairs, 1949–1951. June 11, 1975.

Joseph C. Satterthwaite. Assistant Chief, Division of Near Eastern Affairs, 1945–1946; Special Assistant to the Director, Office of Near Eastern and African Affairs, and Acting Chief, Division of Research for the Near East and Africa, 1946–1947; Deputy Director, 1947–1948; Director, 1948–1949; Ambassador to Ceylon, 1949–1953. November 13, 1972.

Fraser Wilkins. Foreign Service Officer, Serving in Canada, Iran, Morocco, Palestine, and India, 1940–1955; Director, Near East Affairs, 1955–1957. June 20, 1975.

Evan M. Wilson. Assistant Chief of the Division of Near Eastern Affairs, 1946–1947; Second Secretary and Vice-Consul, later First Secretary and Consul, Tehran, Iran, 1947–1949. July 18, 1975.

Dwight D. Eisenhower Library Oral History Transcripts

Loy Henderson. Ambassador to Iran, 1951–1955. By Don North. December 14, 1970.

General Lyman L. Lemnitzer. Commander-in-Chief of European Command, Far East Command, U.N. Command; later Chairman of the Joint Chiefs of Staff. By David C. Berliner. November 21, 1972.

Miscellaneous Documents

Angus Ward as Ambassador to Afghanistan, OF 3409, Truman Library.

Benz, John S., and Holmgreen, E.N. *The Helmand Valley: An Overall View.* Prepared for the AID Mission to Afghanistan, 1962.

CIA Report "India-Pakistan," SR-21, 16 September 1948. NSC-CIA Intelligence Memos, Truman Library.

Department of the Army. Assistant Chief of Staff G2, Intelligence Staff Study, "Intelligence Estimate of the Defensive Capabilities of Southeast Asia Pact Nations," DA-62-IRP-8844. U.S. Army Military History Institute.

Engert, Cornelius Van H. A Report on Afghanistan, Washington, D.C.: U.S. Government Printing Office, 1924. (Center for Afghanistan Studies, University of Nebraska-Omaha.)

General Staff Branch, Army Headquarters India. "The Third Afghan War, 1919: Official Record." Calcutta: Government of India, 1926. (Center for Afghanistan Studies, University of Nebraska-Omaha.)

Kavalsky, B.G., Borthwick, J., Haddad, W., Imam, H., Kundu, A., Meerman, J., Remy, C., and Taylor, S. *Afghanistan: The Journey to Economic Development.* World Bank Document Report No. 1777a-AF, Vols. 1 and 11.

Pell, Senator Clairborne. "Stalemate in Afghanistan, Democracy in Pakistan." A Report to the Committee of Foreign Relations, U.S. Senate. Washington, D.C.: U.S. Government Printing Office, 1990.

Poullada, Leon. "The Pushtun Role in the Afghan Political System." Occasional Paper #1, The Afghanistan Council of the Asia Society, 1970. (Center for Afghanistan Studies, University of Nebraska-Omaha.)

Tudor Engineering Company. *Report of Development of Helmand Valley, Afghanistan.* Washington, D.C.,1956 (noted within as *Tudor Report*).

U.S. Department of State. *Pocket Guide to Afghanistan.* Publication 2660. Washington, D.C.: Department of State, 1946.

———. Office of Intelligence Research. "Afghanistan and Middle East Defense," December 1955, Intelligence Brief 1845, SD-OIR-IB-1845. U.S. Army Military History Institute.

U.S. Department of State, "Chemical Warfare in South Asia and Afghanistan." Special Report 98. Washington, D.C.: Department of State, March, 1982.

U.S. Department of State, "Chemical Warfare in South Asia and Afghanistan, an Update." Special Report 104. Washington, D.C.: Department of State, November, 1982.

U.S. Department of State, "Afghanistan: Seven Years of Occupation." Special Report 155. Washington, D.C.: Department of State, December 1986.

U.S. Strike Command. "Military Assistance Program—Afghanistan," DD-ISA-MAP-A3-P14. U.S. Army Military History Institute.

Wohlstetter, A.J., Hoffman, F.S., Lutz, R.J., and Rowen, H.S. *Selection and Use of*

Strategic Air Bases. Rand Report R-266. Prepared for the U.S. Air Force, April 1954.

SECONDARY SOURCES

Books

Abul Khair, M. *United States Foreign Policy in the Indo-Pakistan Subcontinent, 1939–1947.* Dacca: Asiatic Society of Pakistan, 1968.

Acheson, Dean. *Present at the Creation: My Years in the State Department.* New York: W.W. Norton, 1969.

Adamec, Ludwig W. *Afghanistan's Foreign Affairs to the Mid-Twentieth Century: Relations with the USSR, Germany and Britain.* Tucson: Arizona University Press, 1974.

Adams, Sherman. *Firsthand Report: The Story of the Eisenhower Administration.* New York: Harper, 1961.

Ahmad, Nafis. *The Basis of Pakistan.* Calcutta: Thacker Spink, 1947.

———. *The Survival of Afghanistan: The Two Imperial Giants Held at Bay in the 19th Century.* Lahore: Peoples, 1973.

———. *The Survival of Afghanistan 1747–1979: A Diplomatic History.* Lahore: Institute of Islamic Culture, 1990.

Akhtar, Jamma Das. *Political Conspiracies in Pakistan: Liaquat Ali's Murder to Ayub Khan's Exit.* Delhi: Punjabi Pustak Bhandar, 1969.

Ali, Mohammed. *Afghanistan: The Mohammedzai Period.* Lahore: Punjab Educational Press, 1959.

———. *Manners and Customs of the Afghans.* Lahore: Punjab Educational Press, 1958.

Aliano, Richard A. *American Defense Policy from Eisenhower to Kennedy.* Athens: Ohio University Press, 1975.

Ambrose, Stephen E. *The Rise to Globalism: American Foreign Policy, 1938–1980.* New York: Penguin Books, 1981.

Amstutz, Bruce. *Afghanistan: The First Five Years of Soviet Occupation.* Washington, D.C.: National Defense University Press, 1986.

Andrews, C.F. *The Challenge of the Northwest Frontier: A Contribution to World Peace.* London: Allen & Unwin, 1937.

Anwar, Raja. *The Tragedy of Afghanistan.* London: Verso, 1989.

Armstrong, Lt. Col. Dewitt C. "The Changing Strategy of British Bases." Unpublished PhD dissertation, Princeton University, 1960.

Arnold, Anthony. *Afghanistan: The Soviet Invasion in Perspective.* Stanford: Hoover Institution Press, 1985.

———. *The Fateful Pebble: Afghanistan's Role in the Fall of the Soviet Empire.* Novato, CA: Presidio, 1993.

Asopa, Sheel K. *Military Alliance and Regional Cooperation in West Asia.* Meerut, India: Meerakshi Prakashan, 1971.

Attlee, Clement R. *Empire into Commonwealth.* New York: Oxford, 1961.

Avery, Peter. *Modern Iran.* New York: Praeger, 1965.

Azam, Maulana Abul Kalam. *India Wins Freedom.* New York: Longmans, Green, 1960.

Aziz, K.K. *Britain and Pakistan: A Study of British Attitude towards the East Pakistan Crisis of 1971.* Islamabad: University of Islamabad Press, 1974.

Baddeley, John F. *The Russian Conquest of the Caucasus.* London: Longmans, Green, 1908.

Banerji, Arun Kumar. *India and Britain, 1947–1968.* Calcutta: Minerva Associates, 1977.

Barnds, William J. *India, Pakistan and the Great Powers.* New York, Praeger: 1972.

Barnett, Correlli. *The Collapse of British Power.* Atlantic Highlands, NJ: Humanities Press International, 1986.

Barton, Sir William. *India's North-West Frontier.* London: Murray, 1939.

———. *India's Fateful Hour.* London: Murray, 1942.

Beal, John Robinson. *John Foster Dulles: A Biography.* New York: Harper, 1957.

Bell, Marjorie Jewett, ed. *An American Engineer in Afghanistan, from the letters and notes of A.C. Jewett.* Minneapolis, MN: University of Minnesota Press, 1948.

Bellew, H.W. *Afghanistan and the Afghans.* Lahore: Sange-Meel, 1979.

Bhaneja, Balwant. *Afghanistan: Political Modernization of a Mountain Kingdom.* New Delhi: Spectra, 1973.

Bhatia, H.S., ed. *Military History of British India.* Delhi: Deep & Deep, 1977.

Bidwell, Robin Leonard. *The British Empire and Successor States, 1900–1972.* London: F. Kass, 1974.

Bilgrami, Ashgar. *Afghanistan and British India, 1793–1907.* New Delhi: Sterling, 1972.

Birdwood, Lord. *A Continent Decides.* London: Robert Hale, 1953.

Bowles, Chester. *Ambassador's Report.* New York: Harper & Row, 1954.

Bradcher, Henry S. *Afghanistan and the Soviet Union.* Durham, NC: Duke University Press, 1983.

Brecher, Michael. *The Struggle for Kashmir.* London: Oxford University Press, 1953.

———. *Nehru: A Political Biography.* London: Oxford University Press, 1959.

Brines, Russell. *The Indo-Pakistani War.* New York: Praeger, 1968.

Brown, Seyom. *The Faces of Power: Consistency and Change in United States Foreign Policy from Truman to Johnson.* New York: Columbia University Press, 1968.

Brown, William Norman. *The United States and India and Pakistan.* Cambridge, MA: Harvard University Press, 1953.

Bullard, Sir Reader. *Britain and the Middle East.* London: Hutchinson, 1964.

Burke, S.M. *Pakistan's Foreign Policy: An Historical Analysis.* London: Oxford University Press, 1973.

———. *Mainsprings of Indian and Pakistani Foreign Policy.* Minneapolis: University of Minnesota Press, 1974.

Burnes, Sir Alexander. *Cabool: Being a Personal Narrative.* London: Murray, 1842.

Callard, Keith B. *Pakistan's Foreign Policy: An Interpretation.* New York: Institute of Pakistan Relations, 1959.

Campbell, John C. *Defense of the Middle East: Problems of American Policy.* New York: Harper for the Council of Foreign Relations, 1960.

Campbell-Johnson, Alan. *Mission with Mountbatten.* New York: Dutton, 1951.

Capitanchik, David B. *The Eisenhower Presidency and American Foreign Policy.* London: Routledge and Kegan Paul, 1969.

Caroe, Olaf. *Wells of Power: The Oilfields of South-Western Asia.* London: Macmillan, 1951.

———. *The Pathans, 550* B.C.–A.D. *1957*. New York: St. Martin's Press, 1958.

Carrington. C.E. *The Liquidation of the British Empire*. London: Harrap, 1961.

Chakravarty, Suhash. *From Khyber to Oxus*. New Delhi: Orient Longman, 1976.

Chaliand, Gerard. *Report from Afghanistan*. New York: Penguin Books, 1981.

Chand, Attar. *India, Pakistan and Afghanistan: A Study of Freedom Struggle and Abdul Ghaffar Khan*. New Delhi: Commonwealth, 1989.

Chaudhri, Mohammed Ahsan. *Pakistan and the Regional Pacts*. Karachi: East Publications, 1958.

———. *Pakistan and Great Powers*. Karachi: Council for Pakistan Studies, 1970.

Choudhury, G.W. *Foreign Policy of Pakistan*. New York: Praeger, 1958.

———. *India, Pakistan, Bangladesh, and the Major Powers*. New York: Free Press, 1975.

Churchill, Rogers Platt. *The Anglo-Russian Convention of 1907*. Cedar Rapids, IA: Torch Press, 1939.

Churchill, Sir Winston. *My Early Life*. New York: Scribner, 1930.

———. *The Story of the Malakand Field Force: An Episode of Frontier War*. London: Longmans and Green, 1898.

Cohen, Stephen. *The Pakistan Army*. Berkeley: University of California Press, 1984.

Collins, Joseph J. *The Soviet Invasion of Afghanistan: A Study of the Use of Force in Soviet Foreign Policy*. Lexington, MA: Lexington Books, 1986.

Connell, John. *Auchinleck: A Biography of Field Marshal Sir Claude Auchenleck*. London: Cassell 1959.

Coupland, Sir Reginald. *The Cripps Mission*. Oxford: Oxford University Press, 1942.

Cross, Colin. *The Fall of the British Empire*. London: Hodder & Stoughton, 1968.

Curzon, G.N. *Persia and the Persian Question*. London: Longmans Green, 1892.

Daalder, H. *The Role of the Military in the Emerging Countries*. S'Gravenhage, the Netherlands: Mouton & Co., 1962.

Daley, Tad. *Afghanistan and Gorbachev's Global Foreign Policy*. Santa Monica: Rand/UCLA Center for Soviet Studies, 1989.

Daoud, Zemaray. *L'État monarchique dans la formation sociale afghane*. Berne: Peter Lang, 1982.

Darby, Philip. *British Defence Policy East of Suez, 1947–1968*. London: Oxford, 1973.

Das, Manmath Nath. *Partition and Independence of India*. New Delhi: Vikas, 1982.

DeToldano, Ralph. *Nixon*. New York: Henry Holt, 1956.

Donaldson, Robert H. *Soviet Policy toward India: Ideology and Strategy*. Cambridge, MA: Harvard University Press, 1974.

Dupree, Louis. *Afghanistan*. Princeton, NJ: Princeton University Press, 1973.

——— and Albert, Linette, eds. *Afghanistan in the 1970's*. New York: Praeger, 1974.

Dutt, D. Som. *The Defense of India's Northern Borders*. London: Institute for Strategic Studies, 1966.

Eberhard, Wolfram, ed. *Settlement and Social Change in Asia*. Hong Kong: Hong Kong University Press, 1967.

Edwardes, Michael. *The Last Years of British India*. London: Cassell, 1963.

———. *Playing the Great Game*. London: Hamish Hamilton, 1975.

Eisenhower, Dwight D. *Mandate for Change: The White House Years, 1953–1956*. New York: Doubleday, 1963.

Elliot, Jason. *An Unexpected Light: Travels in Afghanistan*. New York: Picador, 1999.

Elliott, Major-General J.G. *The Frontier, 1939–1947: The Story of the North-West Frontier of India.* London: Cassell, 1968.

Elphinstone, Montstuart. *An Account of the Kingdom of Caubul.* Karachi: Oxford, 1972.

Farr, Grant M., and Merriam, John G., eds. *Afghan Resistance: The Politics of Survival.* Boulder, CO: Westview Press, 1987.

Fitzsimmons, M.A. *The Foreign Policy of the British Labour Government, 1945–51.* South Bend, IN: University of Notre Dame Press, 1953.

Fletcher, Arnold. *Afghanistan: Highway of Conquest.* Ithaca, NY: Cornell University Press, 1965.

Fox, E.F. *Travels in Afghanistan, 1937–1938.* New York: Macmillan, 1943.

Franck, Peter G. *Afghanistan between East and West.* Washington, D.C.: National Planning Association, 1959.

Fraser-Tytler, Sir Walter Kerr. *Afghanistan: A Study of Political Developments in Central and Southern Asia.* London: Oxford University Press, 1967.

Freedman, Robert. *Moscow and the Middle East.* Cambridge: Cambridge University Press, 1991.

Fry, Maxwell. *The Afghan Economy: Money, Finance, and the Critical Constraints to Economic Development.* Leiden: Brill, 1974.

Gaddis, John Lewis. *Strategies of Containment.* New York: Oxford University Press, 1982.

Ganguly, Sumit. *The Origins of War in South Asia: Indo-Pakistani Conflicts since 1947.* Boulder, CO: Westview Press, 1986.

Ganjoo, Satish. *Soviet-Afghan Relations.* Delhi: Akashdeep, 1990.

Gankovsky, Y.V., ed. *A History of Afghanistan.* Moscow: Progress Publishers, 1985.

Gaury, Gerald de, and Winstone, H.V.F., eds. *The Road to Kabul.* London: Quartet Books, 1981.

Ghaus, Abdul Samad. *The Fall of Afghanistan: An Insider's Account.* Washington, D.C.: Brassey, 1988.

Gilani, Ijaz. *The Four R's of Afghanistan: A Study of Pak-Afghan Relations and Their Impact on Foreign Policy Attitudes in Pakistan.* Islamabad: Pakistan Institute of Public Opinion, 1985.

Giradet, Eduard. *Afghanistan: The Soviet War.* London: Croon Helm, 1985.

Goldman, Eric F. *The Crucial Decade: America, 1945–1955.* New York: Alfred A. Knopf, 1959.

Goold-Adams, Richard. *The Time of Power: A Reappraisal of John Foster Dulles.* New York: Appleton-Century-Crofts, 1962.

Grassmuck, G., Adamec, L., and Irwin, F., eds. *Afghanistan: Some New Approaches.* Ann Arbor: University of Michigan Press, 1969.

Grau, Lester W., ed. *The Bear Went Over the Mountain.* Bath: Bookcraft, Ltd., 1998.

Gregorian, Varton. *The Emergence of Modern Afghanistan: Politics of Reform and Modernization.* Palo Alto, CA: Stanford University Press, 1969.

Griffiths, John C. *Afghanistan, Key to a Continent.* London: Andre Deustch, 1981.

Guhin, Michael A. *John Foster Dulles, a Statesman and His Times.* New York: Columbia University Press, 1972.

Gupta, A.K. *North West Frontier Province Legislature and Freedom Struggle, 1932–47.* New Delhi: Indian Council of Historical Research, 1976.

Gupta, R.C. *U.S. Policy towards India and Pakistan.* Delhi: B.R. Publishing, 1977.

Gupta, R.L. *Conflict and Harmony: Indo-British Relations*. New Delhi: Trimurti, 1971.

Habberton, William. *Anglo-Russian Relations concerning Afghanistan, 1837–1907*. Urbana: University of Illinois Press, 1937.

Haddad, George M. *Revolutions and Military Rule in the Middle East: Vol. I, the Northern Tier*. New York: R. Speller, 1965.

Hammond, Thomas T. *Red Flag over Afghanistan: The Communist Coup, the Soviet Invasion, and the Consequences*. Boulder, CO: Westview Press, 1984.

Harrison, Selig S. *The Widening Gulf: Asian Nationalism and American Policy*. New York: Free Press, 1978.

Hauner, Milan. *India in Axis Strategy: Germany, Japan, and Indian Nationalists in the Second World War*. Stuttgart: Klett-Cotta, 1981.

———., and Canfield, Robert L., eds. *Afghanistan and the Soviet Union: Collision and Transformation*. Boulder, CO: Westview Press, 1989.

Hayes, Louis D. *The Impact of US Policy on the Kashmir Conflict*. Tucson: University of Arizona Press, 1971.

———. *Politics in Pakistan*. Boulder, CO: Westview Press, 1984.

Haynes, Richard F. *The Awesome Power: Harry S. Truman as Commander-in-Chief*. Baton Rouge: Louisiana State University Press, 1973.

Heathcote, T.A. *The Afghan Wars, 1839–1919*. London: Osprey, 1980.

Hodson, H.V. *The Great Divide: Britain-India-Pakistan*. London: Hutchinson, 1969.

Hoopes, Townsend. *The Devil and John Foster Dulles*. Boston: Little, Brown and Co, 1973.

Hovey, Harold A. *United States Military Assistance: A Study of Policies and Practices*. New York: Praeger, 1965.

Howell, Sir Evelyn. *Story of the North-West Frontier Province*. Peshawar: Government Print and Stationery Office, 1930.

Huntington, Samuel P. *Political Order in Changing Societies*. New Haven, CT: Yale University Press, 1968.

Hurewitz, J.C. *Middle East Politics: The Military Dimension*. New York: Praeger (for the Council of Foreign Relations), 1969.

Hyman, Anthony. *Afghanistan under Soviet Domination, 1964–83*. London: Macmillan, 1984.

Indian Council of World Affairs. *Defense and Security in the Indian Ocean Area*. Bombay: Asia Publishing House, 1958.

Ismay, Lord Hastings Lionel. *The Memoirs of Lord Ismay*. New York: Viking, 1960.

Jafri, H.A.S. *Indo-Afghan Relations, 1947–67*. New Delhi: Sterling, 1976.

Jain, Rashmi. *US-Pak Relations, 1947–1983*. New Delhi: Radiant, 1983.

Jeffries, Sir Charles. *Transfer of Power*. London: Pall Mall Press, 1960.

Jordan, Amos A. *Foreign Aid and the Defense of Southeast Asia*. New York: Praeger, 1962.

Kakar, Hasan K. *Afghanistan: A Study in International and Political Developments*. Lahore: Punjab Educational Press, 1971.

———. *Government and Society in Afghanistan*. Austin: University of Texas Press, 1979.

Kamal, Nazir A. *American Foreign Policy towards Pakistan*. Islamabad, Pakistan: Institute of Strategic Studies, 1977.

Kamrany, Nake. *Peaceful Competition in Afghanistan: American & Soviet Models for Economic Aid*. Washington, D.C.: Communication Service Corporation, 1968.
————. *Six Stages in the Sovietization of Afghanistan*. Boulder, CO: Institute for Research and Education, 1983.

Kaul, K.K. *U.S.A and the Hindustan Peninsula, 1952–1966*. Lucknow, India: Pustak Kendra, 1977.

Kaur, Kulwant. *Pak-Afghanistan Relations*. New Delhi, Deep and Deep, 1985.

Kavic, Lorne J. *India's Quest for Security: Defense Politics, 1947–65*. Berkeley: University of California Press, 1967.

Kaye, Sir John William. *History of the War in Afghanistan*. London: R. Bentley 1851.

Kennedy, D.E. *The Security of Southern Asia*. New York: Praeger, 1965.

Kessel, Joseph. *Afghanistan*. London: Thames and Hudson, 1959.

Kerr, Graham B. *Population and Family Planning in Afghanistan: Social Implications of the Data from Afghan Demographic Studies*. Amherst: SUNY Buffalo, 1978.

Khalizad, Zalmay. *The Security of Southwest Asia*. Aldershot, U.K.: Gower, 1984.

Khan, Ayub. *Friends Not Masters: A Political Autobiography*. New York: Oxford, 1967.

Khan, Ghaffar Khan, Abdul. *My Life and Struggle: Autobiography of Badshah Khan*. Delhi: Hind Pocket Books, 1969.

Khan, Major-General Akbar. *Raiders in Kashmir*. Karachi: Pak, 1970.

Khan, Major-General Fazal Muqueem. *The Story of Pakistan Army*. Karachi: Oxford University Press, 1963.

Khan, Rais Ahmad, ed. *Pakistan-United States Relations*. Islamabad: Area Study Center for Africa, North & South America, Quaid-i-Azam University, 1983. Bombay: 1947.

King, Peter. *Afghanistan: Cockpit in High Asia*. London: Geofrey Bles, 1966.

Kingsbury, Patricia, and Kingsbury, Robert. *Afghanistan and the Himalayan States*. Garden City, NY: : Doubleday, 1960.

Kinnard, Douglas. *President Eisenhower and Strategy Management*. Lexington: University Press of Kentucky, 1977.

Klass, Rosanne, ed. *Afghanistan: The Great Game Revisited*. New York: Freedom House, 1987.

Kolodziej, Edward. *The Uncommon Defense and Congress, 1945–1963*. Columbus, OH: Ohio State University Press, 1966.

Kraus, Willy. *Afghanistan*. Hamburg: Erdmann, 1975.

Kuniholm, Bruce. *The Origins of the Cold War in the Near East: Great Power Conflict and Diplomacy in Iran, Turkey and Greece*. Princeton, NJ: Princeton University Press, 1980.

Laber, Jeri, and Rubin, Barnett R., eds. *A Nation is Dying: Afghanistan under the Soviets*. Evanston, IL: Northwestern University Press, 1987.

Lacquer, Walter. *The Second World War: Essays in Military and Political History*. London: Sage, 1982.

Lohbeck, Kurt. *Holy War, Unholy Victory: Eyewitness to the CIA's Secret War in Afghanistan*. Washington, D.C.: Regnery Gateway, 1995.

Ma'aroof, Mohammed Khalid. *Afghanistan in World Politics: A Study of Afghan-US Relations*. Delhi: Gian Publishing House, 1987.
————. *Afghanistan and Super Powers*. Delhi: Commonwealth, 1990.

Malleson, George Bruce. *History of Afghanistan from the Earliest Period to the Outbreak of War in 1878*. London: W.H. Allen, 1879.

Martin, Frank. *Under the Absolute Amir.* New York: Harper, 1907.

Martin, L.W. *British Defense Policy: The Long Recessional.* London: Institute for Strategic Studies, 1969.

Marwat, Fazal-ur-Rahim Khan. *The Basmachi Movement in Soviet Central Asia: A Study in Political Development.* Peshawar: Emjay Books International, 1985.

Masson, Charles. *Narrative of Various Journeys in Balochistan, Afghanistan, the Panjab and Kalat.* London: Richard Bentley, 1844.

Masters, John. *Bugles and a Tiger.* London: Michael Joseph, 1956.

Maxwell, Leigh. *My God—Maiwand! Operations of the South Afghanistan Field Force.* London: Cooper, 1979.

Mayne, Peter. *The Narrow Smile: A Journey Back to the Northwest Frontier.* London: Murray, 1955.

Menon, V.P. *The Transfer of Power in India.* Princeton, NJ: Princeton University Press, 1957.

Mihaly, Eugene B. *Foreign Aid and Politics in Nepal.* Oxford: Oxford University Press, 1957.

Miller, Charles. *Khyber: British India's Northwest Frontier, a Story of an Imperial Migrane.* London: MacDonald and Janes, 1977.

Mitchell, Norval. *Sir George Cunningham: A Memoir.* London: William Blackwood, 1968.

Mohana Lala, Munshi. *Life of the Amir Dost Mohammed Khan of Kabul.* Karachi: Oxford, 1978.

Molesworth, Leiutenant-General G.N. *Afghanistan, 1919: An Account of Operations in the Third Afghan War.* New York: Asia Publishing House, 1962.

Moon, Penderai. *Divide and Quit.* Berkeley: University of California Press, 1962.

Moore, R.J. *Escape from Empire: The Attlee Government and the Indian Problem.* Oxford, U.K.: Clarendon Press, 1983.

Mosley, Leonard. *The Last Days of the British Raj.* London: Weidenfeld and Nicholson, 1961.

Mountbatten, Lord Louis. *Time Only to Look Forward.* London: Nicholas Kaye, 1949.

Muttam, John. *U.S., Pakistan and India.* New Delhi: Sindhu, 1974.

Newell, Nancy Peobody, and Newell, Richard S. *The Struggle for Afghanistan.* Ithaca, NY: Cornell University Press, 1981.

Newell, Richard. *The Politics of Afghanistan.* Ithaca, NY: Cornell University Press, 1972.

Nollau, Gunter, and Wiehe, H.J. *Russia's South Flank: Soviet Operations in Iran, Turkey and Afghanistan.* New York: Praeger, 1963.

Norris, J.A. *The First Afghan War: 1838–1842.* Cambridge: Cambridge University Press, 1967.

Northedge, F.S. *British Foreign Policy: The Process of Readjustment, 1945–1961.* London: Allen & Unwin, 1962.

Nyrop, Richard F., and Seekins, Donald M. *Afghanistan, a Country Study.* 5th ed. Washington, D.C.: Headquarters, Department of the Army, 1986.

Palmer, Norman Dunbar. *South Asia and United States Policy.* Boston: Houghton Mifflin, 1966.

Panikkar, K.M. *Problems of Indian Defense.* London: Asia Publishing House, 1960.

Phillips, C.H., and Phillips, Mary Doreen. *The Partition of India: Policies and Perspectives.* London: Allen & Unwin, 1975.

Pillai, K. Raman. *The Political Triangle: Pakistan, India and Britain*. New Delhi: Young India, 1970.

Potter, E.B. *Nimitz*. Annapolis, MD: Naval Institute Press, 1976.

Poullada, Leon B. *Reform and Rebellion in Afghanistan, 1919–1929*. Ithaca, NY: Cornell University Press, 1973.

Poullada, Leon B., and Leila D.J. Poullada. *The Kingdom of Afghanistan and the United States: 1828–1973*. Omaha, NE: Dageforde, 1995.

Prasad, Bisheshwar. *India and the War: Official History of the Indian Armed Forces in the Second World War*. New Delhi: Government of India, 1966.

Prasad, Sri Navdan. *Expansion of the Armed Forces and Defence Organization, 1939–1945. Official History of the Indian Armed Forces in the Second World War*. New Delhi: Government of India, 1956.

Princeton University Conference: Current Problems in Afghanistan. Princeton, NJ: Princeton University Press, 1961.

Pyarelal. *A Pilgrimage for Peace: Ghandi and Frontier Ghandi among N.W.F. Pathans*. Ahmedabad: Navajivan, 1950.

Quddus, Syed Abdul. *Afghanistan and Pakistan: A Geopolitical Study*. Lahore: Ferozsons, 1982.

Qureshi, M. Aslam. *Anglo-Pakistan Relations, 1947–1976*. Lahore: Research Society of Pakistan, 1976.

Qutubuddin, Aziz. *Mission to Washington*. Karachi: United Press of Pakistan, 1973.

Rahman, Abdur, Amir of Afghanistan. *The Life of Abdur Rahman, Vols I & II*. London: Murray, 1900.

Rall, Ted. *To Afghanistan & Back*. New York: Nantier, Beall, Minoustchine, 2002.

Ram, Raghunath. *Super Powers and the Indo-Pakistani Sub-Continent*. New Delhi: Raaj Prakashan, 1985.

Ramazani, Rouhollah K. *The Northern Tier: Afghanistan, Iran, and Turkey*. Princeton, NJ: D. Van Nostrand, 1966.

Rao, Kilaru Ram Chandra. *India, United States, and Pakistan*. Bombay: Himalya, 1985.

Rashid, Ahmed. *Taliban: Militant Islam, Oil, & Fundamentalism in Central Asia*. New Haven: Yale, 2001.

Razvi, Mutjaba. *The Frontiers of Pakistan: A Study of Frontier Problems in Pakistan's Foreign Policy*. Karachi: National Publishing House, 1971.

Reeve, Simon. *The New Jackals*. Boston: Northeastern University Press, 1999.

Rittenberg, Stephen Alan. *Ethnicity, Nationalism and the Pakhtuns: The Independence Movement in India's North-West Frontier Province*. Durham, NC: Carolina Academic Press, 1988.

Rizva, H.A. *The Military and Politics in Pakistan*. Lahore: Progressive, 1974.

Robson, Brian. *The Road to Kabul: The Second Afghan War, 1878–1881*. London: Arms and Armour Press, 1986.

Rogers, Tom. *The Soviet Withdrawal from Afghanistan: Analysis and Chronology*. Westport, CT: Greenwood, 1992.

Roy, Olivier. *Islam and Resistance in Afghanistan*. Cambridge: Cambridge University Press, 1986.

Royal Institute of International Affairs. *Defence in the Cold War: The Task of the Free World*. London: Royal Institute of International Affairs, 1950.

Rubenstein, Alvin. *Soviet Policy toward Turkey, Iran and Afghanistan: The Dynamics of Influence*. New York: Praeger, 1982.

———, ed. *The Great Game: Rivalry in the Persian Gulf and South Asia*. New York: Praeger, 1983.

Rubin, Barnett R. *The Search for Peace in Afghanistan: From Buffer State to Failed State*. New Haven: Yale University Press, 1995.

Rudolph, Lloyd I. *The Regional Imperative: The Administration of US Foreign Policy toward South Asian States under Presidents Johnson and Nixon*. Atlantic Highlands, NJ: Humanities Press, 1981.

Saikal, Amin, and Maley, William, eds. *The Soviet Withdrawal from Afghanistan*. Cambridge: Cambridge University Press, 1989.

Sale, Lady Florentia. *A Journal of the Disasters in Affghanistan, 1841–2*. London: J Murray, 1843.

Sareen, Anuradha. *India and Afghanistan: British Imperialism versus Afghan Nationalism, 1907–1921*. New Delhi: Light and Life, 1981.

Sarin, Oleg, and Lev Dvorestky. *The Afghan Syndrome: The Soviet Union's Vietnam*. Novato, CA: Presidio, 1993.

Sayeed, Khalid B. *Pakistan, the Formative Phase, 1857–1948*. London: Oxford University Press, 1968.

Schofield, Victoria. *Every Rock, Every Hill: The Plain Tale of the North-West Frontier and Afghanistan*. London: Buchan & Enright, 1984.

Sen Gupta, Bhabani. *Afghanistan: Politics, Economics, and Society*. Boulder, CO: Lynne Reinner, 1985.

Shapiro, Leonard. *Soviet Treaty Series 1921–1928, Vol. I*. Washington, D.C.: Georgetown University Press, 1950.

Sherwani, Latif Ahmed. *The Partition of India and Mountbatten*. Karachi: Council for Pakistan Studies, 1986.

Sherry, Michael S. *Preparing for the Next War: American Plans for Postwar Defense, 1941–1945*. New Haven, CT: Yale, 1977.

Siddiqui, Marghub. *Background of Pakistan-United States Relations*. Lahore: University of the Punjab, 1971.

Singh, Ganda. *Ahmed Shah Durrani, Father of Modern Afghanistan*. London: Asia Publishing House, 1959.

Singh, Rajvir. *U.S.-Pakistan and India, Strategic Relations*. Allahabad, India: Chugh, 1985.

Singh, Sangat. *Pakistan's Foreign Policy: An Appraisal*. Lahore: Farhan, 1977.

Sinha, Janki. *Pakistan and the Indo-US Relations, 1947–1958*. Patna: Associated Book Agency, 1978.

Singhal, Damodar P. *India and Afghanistan, 1876–1907: A Study in Diplomatic Relations*. New Delhi: South Asian, 1982.

Smith, Harvey H. *Area Handbook for Afghanistan*. Washington, D.C.: U.S. Government Printing Office, 1969.

Snyder, William P. *The Politics of British Defense Policy, 1945–1962*. Columbus: Ohio State University Press, 1964.

Spain, James W. *The Pathan Borderland*. The Hague: Mouton, 1963.

Spear, Sir Percival. *India, Pakistan, and the West*. London: Oxford University Press, 1967.

Stephens, Ian. *Horned Moon*. London: Chatto and Windus, 1953.

————. *Pakistan*. New York: Praeger, 1967.

Suleri, Ziauddin Ahmad. *Pakistan's Lost Years: Being a Survey of a Decade of Politics, 1948–58*. Lahore: Progressive, 1962.

Sullivan, William H. *Mission to Iran*. New York: W.W. Norton, 1981.

Sulzberger, C. L. *A Long Row of Candles: Memoirs and Diaries, 1934–1954*. New York: Macmillan, 1969.

Sutton, John L., and Kemp, Geoffrey. *Arms to Developing Countries, 1945–1965*. London: Institute for Strategic Studies, 1966.

Swinson, Arthur. *North-West Frontier, 1939–1947*. London: Hutchinson, 1967.

Sykes, Sir Percy. *A History of Afghanistan*. London: Macmillan, 1940.

Symonds, Richard. *The Making of Pakistan*. London: Faber and Faber, 1949.

Tabibi, Abdul Hakim. "Aftermath Created by British Policy in Respect to Afghan-Pak Relations." Unpublished PhD dissertation, American University, 1953.

————. *Reminisces of my Four Decades of Diplomatic Life, at the Services of Afghanistan and the World at Large*. Nicosia, Cyprus: Proodos, 1995.

Tahir-Kheli, Shirin. *The United States and Pakistan: The Evolution of an Influence Relationship*. New York: Praeger, 1982.

Tamarov, Vlasislav. *Afghanistan: Soviet Vietnam*. San Francisco: Mercury House, 1992.

Tendulkar, D.G. *Abdul Ghaffar Khan: Faith Is a Battle*. Bombay: Popular Prakashan, 1967.

Terraine, John. *The Life and Times of Lord Mountbatten*. London: Hutchinson, 1968.

Tewari, S.C. *Indo-US Relations, 1947–1976*. New Delhi: Radiant, 1977.

Toynbee, Arnold. *Between Oxus and Jumna*. New York: Oxford University Press, 1961.

Tripathi, Ganga Prasad. *Indo-Afghan Relations, 1882–1907*. Delhi: Rajesh, 1973.

Trousdale, William, ed. *War in Afghanistan, 1879–80: The Personal Diary of Major General Sir Charles Metcalfe MacGregor*. Detroit: Wayne State University Press, 1985.

Truman, Harry S. *Memoirs, Vol. II: Years of Trial and Hope*. New York, Doubleday, 1956.

Ulam, Adam. *Expansion and Coexistance, Soviet Foreign Policy, 1917–1973*. New York: Praeger, 1974.

Upton, Joseph M. *The History of Modern Iran*. Cambridge, MA: Harvard, 1960.

Urban, Mark. *War in Afghanistan*. London: Macmillan, 1988.

Varma, Birenda. *From Delhi to Teheran—A Study of British Diplomatic Moves in Northwestern India, Afghanistan and Persia, 1772–1803*. Patna: Janaki Prakashan, 1980.

Venkataramani, R.M. *The American Role in Pakistan, 1947–1958*. New Delhi: Radiant, 1982.

Vogel, Renate. *Die Persien und Afghanistanexpedition Oskar Ritter von Niedermayers, 1915–16*. Onasbruck: Biblio-Verlag, 1976.

Vorys, Karl von. *Political Development in Pakistan*. Princeton, NJ: Princeton University Press, 1965.

Wakman, Mohammed Amin. *Afghanistan, Non-Alignment and the Super Powers*. New Delhi: Radiant, 1985.

Watkins, Mary Bradley. *Afghanistan, A Land in Transition*. Princeton, NJ: D. Van Nostrand, 1963.

Weston, Christine. *Afghanistan*. New York: Scribner, 1962.

Wheeler-Bennett, John W. *King George VI, His Life and Reign*. New York: St. Martin's, 1958.

Wilber, Donald N. *Afghanistan*. New Haven, CT: HRAF Press, 1962.

Wilcox, Wayne A. *Pakistan: The Consolidation of a Nation*. New York: Columbia University Press, 1963.

Wolf, Charles. *Foreign Aid: Theory and Practice in Southern Asia*. Princeton, NJ: Princeton University Press, 1960.

Wolpert, Stanley. *Roots of Confrontation in South Asia: Afghanistan, Pakistan, India and the Superpowers*. New York: Oxford University Press, 1982.

Woods, Frederick, ed. *Young Winston's Wars: The Original Despatches of W.S. Churchill, War Correspondent*. London: L. Cooper, 1972.

Yusuf, Kaniz F. "Potential Cooperation between Iran, Pakistan and Afghanistan." Unpublished PhD dissertation, Clark University, 1959.

Zeigler, Philip. *Mountbatten: The Official Biography*. London: William Collins, 1985.

Ziring, Lawrence. *Iran, Turkey and Afghanistan: A Political Chronology*. New York: Praeger, 1981.

Articles

"A Real Ally in South Asia." *US News & World Report*, 35 (1953): 44–46.

Abdullah, Sheik Mohammed. "Kashmir, India and Pakistan." *Foreign Affairs* 43 (1965): 528–535.

Abidi, A.H.H. "Irano-Afghan Dispute over the Helmand Waters." *International Studies* 16 (1977): 357–378.

Acheson, Dean. "Building Collective Strength Through the Mutual Security Program." *Department of State Bulletin* 26 (24 March 1952): 463–467.

Akrahamovich, R.T. "Afghan Foreign Policy since the Second World War: The Soviet View." *Central Asian Review* 11 (1963): 403–413.

Alder, Garry J. "The Dropped Stitch." *Afghanistan Journal* 1(1974): 105–113; 2 (1975): 20–27.

Ali, Mohammed. "The Durand Line." *Afghanistan* 10 (1955): 5–12.

———. "A Short History of the Helmand Valley." *Afghanistan* 10 (1955): 3543.

Allen, R.A., and Ramazani, R.K. "Afghanistan: Wooed but Not Won." *Swiss Review of World Affairs* 7 (1957): 16–19.

Armstrong, Hamilton Fish. "North of the Khyber." *Foreign Affairs* 34 (1956): 603–619.

Barnes, Major B.H.P. "Future Strategic Importance of the Middle East to the British Commonwealth of Nations." *Army Quarterly* 57 (1948): 161–177.

Barton, Sir William. "The Afghans and Middle East Defense." *Eastern World* 7 (1953): 15–16.

———. "India's North-West Frontier and the War." *United Empire* 30 (1939), 1101–1103.

———. "Pakistan's Claim to Kashmir." *Foreign Affairs* 28 (1950): 279–308.

Benningsen, Alexandre. "The Soviet Union and Muslim Guerilla Wars, 1920–1981: Lessons for Afghanistan." *Conflict* 4 (1983): 301–324.

Bodansky, Yossef. "Soviet Net Closes in on Afghan Resistance." *Jane's Defence Weekly* 6 (1986) 173–176.

Bowles, Chester. "A Fresh Look at Free Asia." *Foreign Affairs* 33 (1954): 54–71.

Brereton, J.M. "The Panjdeh Crisis, 1885." *History Today* 29 (1979): 46–52.

Byroade, Henry A. "The Position of Afghanistan in Asia." *Princeton University Conference* (1961): 59–76.

Campbell-Johnson, Alan. "Reflections on the Transfer of Power." *Asiatic Review* 48 (1952): 163–182.

Canfield, Robert L. "Western Stakes in the Afghanistan War." *Central Asian Survey* 4 (1985): 121–135.

Caroe, Sir Olaf. "Afghanistan: The Strategic After-Effects of India's Partition." *Round Table* 278 (1980): 129–131.

———. "The North-West Frontier: Old and New." *Royal Central Asian Society Journal* 48 (1961): 289–298.

———. "The Northwest Frontier Revisited." *Asian Review* 57 (1961): 3–20.

———. "The Pathans." *Asian Review* 54 (1958): 1–17.

———. "The Persian Gulf—A Romance." *Round Table,* 39 (1949): 131–137.

Collins, Joseph J. "The Soviet Afghan War: The First Four Years." *Parameters* 14 (1984): 49–62.

Crocker, H.E. "Russia and Afghanistan." *Army Quarterly* 72 (1956): 30–32.

———. "Tibet and Afghanistan." *Army Quarterly* 79 (1960): 93–103.

Cunningham, Sir George. "Reforms in the North West Frontier Province of India." *Journal of the Royal Central Asian Society* 24 (1937): 90–101.

———. "The Frontier Discord: Afghanistan and Pakistan." *Manchester Guardian Weekly* 64 (1951): 5.

Daud, Mohammed. "Statement by Sardar Mohammed Daud: Prime Minister of Afghanistan." *Eastern World* 9 (1955): 26.

DelCroze, Joel. "Afghanistan Today." *Journal of the Indian Institute of International Affairs* 3 (19xx): 29–49.

Dickson, Keith D. "The *Basmachi* and the *Mujahidin:* Soviet Responses to Insurgency Movements." *Military Review* 65 (1985): 29–44.

Dulles, John Foster. "The Cost of Peace." *Department of State Bulletin* 34 (18 June 1956): 999–1004.

———. "Report on the Near East." *Department of State Bulletin* 28 (15 June 1953): 831–835.

Dupree, Louis. "Afghanistan, the Canny Neutral." *Nation* 199 (1964): 134–137.

———. "Afghanistan in the Twentieth Century." *Royal Central Asian Society Journal* 52 (1965): 20–30.

———. "The Durand Line of 1893: A Case Study in Artificial Political Boundaries and Culture Areas" *Princeton University Conference* (1961): 77–94.

———. "Afghanistan: Problems of a Peasant-Tribal Society." *In Dupree and* Albert (1974): 1–12.

———. "Afghanistan under the Khalq." *Problems of Communism* 28 (1979): 34–50.

Fletcher, Arnold. "Afghans and the Frontier" *Economist* 157 (1951): 306–307.

Fleury, Antoine. "La Constitution d'un bloc oriental: Le Pacte de Saadabad comme contribution la secuite collective dans les annees trente" *Review d'histoire de la deuxieme guerre mondiale* 27 (1977): 1–18.

Franck, Dorothea Seeyle. "Pakhtunistan—Disputed Position of a Tribal Land." *Middle East Journal* 6 (1952): 49–68.

Ghosh, K.P. "Afghanistan in World Affairs." *Contemporary Review* 1073 (1955): 325–327.

Gillett, Sir Michael. "Afghanistan." *Royal Central Asian Journal* 53 (1966): 238–244.

Grinter, Lawrence E. "The Soviet Invasion of Afghanistan: Its Inevitability and Consequences." *Parameters* 12 (1982): 53–61.

Guha, Amalenu. "Economic Development of Afghanistan, 1929–61." *International Studies* 5 (1966): 421–439.

Hahn, Peter L. "Containment and Egyptian Nationalism: The Unsuccessful Attempt to Establish a Middle East Command." *Diplomatic History* 11 (1987): 23–40.

Hangen, Welles. "Afghanistan." *Yale Review* 56(1966): 60–75.

Hasan, Zubeida. "The Foreign Policy of Afghanistan." *Pakistan Horizon* 17 (1964): 48–57.

Hauner, Milan. "Significance of Afghanistan." *Round Table* 278 (1980): 240–4.

———. "One Man Against the Empire: The Faqir of Ipi and the British in Central Asia on the Eve of and during the Second World War." In Lacquer, *The Second World War,* London: Sage, 1982: 374–403.

Heyns, Terry L. "Will Afghanistan Become the Soviet Union's Vietnam?" *Military Review* 61(1981): 50–59.

Hutcheson, John M. "Scorched-Earth Policy: The Soviets in Afghanistan." *Military Review* 62 (1982): 29–37.

Ispahani, F.A.H. "The Foreign Policy of Pakistan, 1947–1964." *Pakistan Horizon* 17 (1964): 231–252.

Jalal, Ayesha. "India's Partition and the Defense of Pakistan: An Historical Perspective." *Journal of Imperial and Commonwealth History* 15 (1987): 303–317.

Jernegan, John D. "The Middle East and South Asia—The Problem of Security." *Department of State Bulletin* 30 (22 March 1954): 444–448.

Kakar, Hasan. "The Fall of the Afghan Monarchy in 1973," *International Journal of Middle East Studies* 9 (1977): 195–214.

———. "Trends in Modern Afghan History." In Dupree and Albert, *Afghanistan in the 1970's,* 13–33 (1974).

Karp, Craig M. "The War in Afghanistan." *Foreign Affairs* 64 (1986): 1026–1047.

Keegan, John. "The Ordeal of Afghanistan." *Atlantic Monthly* 256 (1985): 94–105.

Kohzad, Ahmad Ali. "Frontier Discord between Afghanistan and Pakistan." *Afghanistan* 6 (1951): 54–67.

Lerski, George J. "The Pakistan-American Alliance: A Reevaluation of the Past Decade." *Asian Survey* 8 (1968): 400–415.

Liddell Hart, Sir Basil. "Can We Defend the Middle East?" *Military Review* 31 (1951): 30–36.

MacMunn, Sir George. "The Real British Attitude Toward Afghanistan." *Journal of the Royal Artillery* 56 (1929): 469–477.

Maillart, Ella. "Afghanistan's Rebirth: An Interview with H.R.H. Hashim Khan in 1937. *Journal of the Royal Central Asian Society* 27 (1940): 224–228.

Malhuret, Claude. "Report from Afghanistan." *Foreign Affairs* 62 (1984): 426–435.

Mayers, David. "Eisenhower's Containment Policy and the Major Communist Powers." *International Historical Review* (5 February 1983): 59–83.

Mayhew, Christopher. "British Foreign Policy since 1945." *International Affairs* 26 (1950): 477–486.

McGhee, George. "Tasks Confronting the Indian Government." *Department of State Bulletin* 24 (4 June 1951): 892–894.

McMahon, Robert J. "United States Cold War Strategy in South Asia: The Making of a Military Commitment to Pakistan, 1947–1954." *Journal of American History* 75 (1988): 812–840.

Merrill, Dennis. "Indo-American Relations, 1947–1950: A Missed Opportunity in Asia." *Diplomatic History* 11 (1988): 203–226.

Molesworth, Lieutenant General G.N. "Some Problems of Future Security in the Indian Ocean Area." *Asiatic Review* 42 (1946): 26–34.

Mowrer, Edgar Ansel. "New Frontiers for Freedom." *Colliers* 133 (25 June 1954): 34–40.

Mustafa, Zubeida. "Afghanistan and the Asian Power Balance." *Pacific Community* 6 (1975): 283–299.

O'Ballance, E. "Afghanistan." *Army Quarterly* 81 (1961): 224–231.

Odell, Ernest. "Afghanistan and the North West Frontier." *Contemporary Review* 988 (1948): 240–244.

Panikkar, K.M. "The Defense of India and Indo-British Obligations." *International Affairs* 22 (1946): 85–90.

Payind, Alam. "Soviet-Afghan Relations." *International Journal of Middle East Studies* 21 (1989): 107–128.

Poullada, Leon. "Afghanistan and the United States: The Crucial Years." *Middle East Journal* 35 (1981): 178–190.

———. "The Search for National Unity." In Dupree and Albert, *Afghanistan in the 1970's* (1974): 34–49.

Rand, Christopher. "Crisis in Afghanistan." *Commonweal* 63 (1955): 7–10.

Ratcliffe, A.L. "The Strategic Situation in the Middle East." *Military Review* 34 (1954): 95–100.

Reardon, Patrick. "Modernization and Reform: The Contemporary Endeavor." In Grassmuck, Adamec and Irwin, *Afghanistan: Some New Approaches,* (1969): 149–203.

Reincourt, Amaury de. "India and Pakistan in the Shadow of Afghanistan." *Foreign Affairs* 61 (1983): 416–437.

Rubenstein, Alvin Z. "Afghanistan and the Great Powers." *Naval Institute Proceedings* 83 (1957): 52–68.

Schwarzenhach, Annemarie Clark. "Military Importance of Afghanistan." *Living Age* 358 (1940): 577–581.

Slessor, Sir John. "Air Power and World Strategy." *Foreign Affairs* 33 (1954): 43–53

Smith, Brigadier General J.G. "British Troops Leave India." *Asiatic Review* 44 (1948): 69–72.

Spain, James W. "Military Assistance for Pakistan." *American Political Science Review* 48 (1948): 738–751.

———. "Middle East Defense: A New Approach." *Middle East Journal* 8 (1954): 251–266.

Squire, Sir Giles. "Recent Progress in Afghanistan." *Journal of the Royal Central Asian Society* 37 (1950): 6–18.

———. "Afghanistan and Her Neighbors." *Journal of the Royal Central Asian Society* 36 (1949): 68–72.

Sykes, Sir Percy M. "Afghanistan: The Present Position." *Journal of the Royal Central Asian Society* 27 (1940): 141–171.

————. "Afghanistan: Its History and Position in Asia." *Journal of the Royal Central Asian Society* 42 (1955): 11–24.

Tissot, Louis. "Un Grain de ble entre deux meules, l'Afghanistan." *Revue de defense nationale* 6 (1951): 597–606.

Toynbee, Arnold. "Impressions of Afghanistan and Pakistan's Northwest Frontier: In Relation to the Communist World." *International Affairs* 37 (1961): 161–169.

Trager, Frank N. "The United States and Pakistan: A Failure of Diplomacy." *Orbis* 9 (1965): 613–629.

Tulenko, Thomas. "Two Invasions of Afghanistan." *History Today* 30 (1980): 7–12.

Vertzberger, Yaacov. "Afghanistan in China's Policy." *Problems of Communism* 31 (1982): 1–23.

Warren, Avra M. "Pakistan in the World Today." *Department of State Bulletin* 26 (30 June 1952): 1011–1014.

Watt, D.C. "The Sa'adabad Pact of July 8, 1937." *Journal of the Royal Central Asian Society* 49 (1962): 296–306.

Wilber, D.N. "Prospects for Federation in the Northern Tier." *Middle East Journal* 12 (1958): 385–394.

Wright, Esmond. "Defense and the Baghdad Pact." *Political Quarterly* 28 (1957): 158–167.

Wyndham, Colonel E.H. "The Near and Middle East in Relation to Western Defense." *Brassey's Annual* 63 (1952): 40–46.

Yapp, M.E. "A Little Game: Afghanistan since 1918." *South Asian Review* 8 (1975): 401–406.

Yusufzai, Saidai. "Regarding the Views of Sir George Cunningham." *Afghanistan* 6 (1951): 68–74.

INDEX